A HISTORY OF EUROPEAN DIPLOMACY, 1815-1914

Published @ 2017 Trieste Publishing Pty Ltd

ISBN 9780649604623

A History of European Diplomacy, 1815-1914 by R. B. Mowat

Edited by Trieste Publishing Pty Ltd.
Cover @ 2017

www.triestepublishing.com

R. B. MOWAT

A HISTORY OF EUROPEAN DIPLOMACY, 1815-1914

Trieste

A HISTORY OF EUROPEAN DIPLOMACY 1815-1914

A HISTORY OF EUROPEAN DIPLOMACY

1815-1914

BY

R. B. MOWAT, M.A.

FELLOW OF CORPUS CHRISTI COLLEGE, OXFORD

LONDON

EDWARD ARNOLD & CO.

1922

PREFACE

Now that foreign affairs are, as Disraeli said, merely Britain's domestic affairs in foreign parts, it is the duty of every citizen to know about them and to reflect upon them. Things apparently remote from foreign policy must be regarded in the light of our external relations as well as of our internal situation. And it is not merely the relations of Britain to other countries that the British citizen must know about; he must understand the dealings of the other states of Europe and of the world with each other; for the affairs of all the nations are so interwoven that no nation, and no part of any nation, can for a moment live unto itself.

It is with the modest aim of contributing something towards political education that this book has been written. I have tried to continue in a more accessible form the admirable work accomplished by the Strasbourg Professor Koch, author of the *Histoire abrégé des traités de paix*, for the seventeenth and eighteenth centuries. In England we have for the nineteenth century the grand collection of Hertslet—treaties and maps, with neither comment nor narrative: a great repository of truth, but of use mainly for scholars. In France M. Bourgeois, in his *Manuel historique de politique étrangère*, and M. Debidour, in his *Histoire diplomatique*, have placed before their public the results of long study and wide observation. I have aimed at doing something like this for the British citizen: to place before him a hundred years of the diplomatic relations of the chief Powers of Europe, including Great Britain, and so to give him the means of following the stream of history that flows before his own eyes from day to day, and of forming sound judgments about it.

In the quiet of an Oxford College a historian can reasonably profess to write "without hatred and partisanship," *sine ira et studio.* If he still believes in the honour and dignity of his country, it is because study and observation confirm him in this view. The aim of diplomacy is peace and good-fellowship: the normal diplomatist has always been an honourable man; and this is true, on the whole, both of Continental and of British diplomacy. Practical experience of British diplomacy at a significant period of this country's history has confirmed the conclusion formed from study, namely that British men of affairs, the statesmen, diplomatists, and administrators, have the same standard of conduct in managing international affairs as they have in their private dealings. But they cannot go on with their work and maintain its honourable standard unless the people behind them know that they are honest and will honestly support them. Such is the idea which, I trust, will be gleaned from this book.

R. B. MOWAT.

CORPUS CHRISTI COLLEGE,
OXFORD.

September, 1922.

CONTENTS

Part I.—FROM THE CONGRESS OF VIENNA TO THE CONGRESS OF PARIS

CHAP.		PAGE
I	The Diplomatic Profession	1
II	The Congress of Vienna	4
III	The Concert of Europe	20
	§ 1. The Second Peace of Paris	20
	§ 2. The Holy and Quadruple Alliances . .	20
IV	Aix-la-Chapelle	28
V	The Old World and the New	32
VI	The Independence of Greece	46
VII	East and West	54
VIII	Belgium and Spain	70
	§ 1. Belgium	70
	§ 2. The Iberian Peninsula	75
	§ 3. The Spanish Marriages	78
IX	The Dividing Years: Germany and Austria .	85
	§ 1. The Revolutions	85
	§ 2. The Imperial Crown	88
	§ 3. Olmütz	90
	§ 4. Dresden	92
X	The Crimean War	94
	§ 1. The Holy Places	95
	§ 2. The Protectorate of the Greek Church .	96
	§ 3. The First Conference of Vienna . . .	99
	§ 4. The Franco-British Alliance	101
	§ 5. The Seymour Conversations	102
	§ 6. The Second Conference of Vienna . .	105
	§ 7. The Congress of Paris	108

Part II.—THE UNION OF ITALY

XI	Italy from the Congress of Vienna to the Failure of the Revolutionary Movement of 1848	115
XII	The Liquidation of the Revolutionary Movement of 1848	120
XIII	The Italian Question before Europe . . .	125

CHAP.		PAGE
XIV	The Second War of Italian Liberation	131
XV	Villafranca	138
XVI	The Union of the Duchies and the Romagna	143
XVII	The Kingdom of Italy	148
XVIII	Venice	154
XIX	Mentana	159
XX	The Last Days of the Temporal Power	164

Part III.—THE UNION OF GERMANY

XXI	The Rise of Prussia	167
	§ 1. The Zollverein	167
	§ 2. Schleswig-Holstein	171
XXII	The Foundation of the German Empire	184
	§ 1. Gastein and Biarritz	184
	§ 2. The Peace of Prague	192
XXIII	The Franco-Prussian War	196
	§ 1. The Movements of M. Benedetti	196
	§ 2. Luxemburg	199
	§ 3. The War	203
	§ 4. The Treaty of Frankfort	213
XXIV	The Congress of Berlin	219
	§ 1. Three Chancellors	219
	§ 2. The Insurrection in Herzegovina and its Consequences	221
XXV	The Triple Alliance	237
XXVI	The Revival of France	250
XXVII	The Entente Cordiale	255
	§ 1. Egypt	255
	§ 2. Africa	258
	§ 3. The Far East	262
	§ 4. The *Rapprochement*	268
XXVIII	The Eastern Question Again	274
XXIX	Ten Years of Crises	282
Index		299

A HISTORY OF EUROPEAN DIPLOMACY, 1815–1914

PART I

From the Congress of Vienna to the Congress of Paris

CHAPTER I

THE DIPLOMATIC PROFESSION

"There is a European atmosphere. The same ideas are spread everywhere: they are all French, and find naturally in France their most perfect expression."[1] This European atmosphere is the greatest achievement of civilisation; and in spite of wars and furious national rivalries it has existed since the eleventh century. It is evinced in the common observances of religious worship, in community of scholarship and learning, and in a definite standard of conduct and manners. It is this European atmosphere that has led the Powers of Europe to regard themselves as a society of States, who in normal times conduct themselves towards one another with the same courtesy and morality as individuals within a State observe in their mutual transactions. The manners of this society of States is what we mean by Diplomacy.

The French have always been the greatest exponents of the diplomatic art; and among the many gifts which that grand nation has conferred upon Europe there is none more fruitful than this. They have not shone with the same luminousness in the domain of International Law, which differs from, and stands in relation to, Diplomacy, in the same way as ordinary municipal law differs from,

[1] Sorel: *L'Europe et la Révolution Française* (1912), I, 147.

B

and is related to, private manners. But if the Dutch must be allowed to be supreme in the study of International Law, the French must be conceded the same prestige in the diplomatic art. If Diplomacy has any one language, it is French ; and this not merely because it is (or was) the most widespread ; but because of all modern tongues French is the most accurate instrument for putting ideas into words. In the conduct of international relations too much is at stake, to admit of any looseness of meaning ; and so French, in the evolution of the society of European States, has become the language of Diplomacy because it reduces to a minimum the friction, the estrangements, the wars even, that may ensue from misunderstandings of words.

It is unwise to despise the diplomatic art, or to think that, any more than other vocations, it can be followed without careful training and continuous experience. In the Middle Ages there were no diplomats by profession, yet the same people were usually employed in inter-state business—generally clerics, who possessed a common standard of education, manners, and moral outlook. Early in the seventeenth century a diplomatic profession appears almost as an established thing ; and this occurred practically contemporaneously in France and in England—for England, after France, has always in modern times been most distinguished in Diplomacy. Just as, in the reign of King James I, we find the modern Foreign Office beginning, in the Northern and Southern Departments of the Secretary of State, so in the same reign we recognise the regular Diplomatic Corps in Sir Henry Wotton,[1] Sir Thomas Roe,[2] and the other ambassadors, through whose commercial and political treaties England definitely took her place in the society of European States.

Every private person has a sensitive place in his nature, and a wrong word or an injudicious act may make a lifetime of misunderstanding. Governments and nations are sensitive too ; nations indeed are particularly and often unexpectedly so ; and any man who, in conducting the affairs of one State with another, goes the wrong way about the business, will make a lamentable failure of it. There is a right and a wrong way of doing everything ; and apart from the qualities of reasonableness, firmness, and tact, which all professions besides that of the diplomatist require, much actual knowledge is necessary—knowledge of history, of foreign Constitutions, of International Law, of languages, and also of a large

[1] 1568–1639. [2] 1581–1644.

body of *technique*, that is, of the forms of diplomatic documents and the customs and regulations of court and official society.

The first formal treatise on Diplomacy is *L'Ambassadeur et Ses Fonctions* by Abraham Wicquefort,[1] Councillor of State of the Duke of Brunswick. This—published at the Hague in 1681—is a humane work, containing the fruits of a ripe experience. Wicquefort is quite decided about the value of a historical training for a diplomatist: good ambassadors have been good historians, for instance Macchiavelli and Philip de Commines. The ambassador should be college-trained, but not a pedant; he must know the common languages well—Latin and French. He must always be well-dressed, and never allow himself to be surprised in untidiness. The Comte d'Avaux [2] was so scrupulous that he was never seen, even by his servants, in clothes different from what he wore on the most solemn occasions: "he never left his bedroom without his mantle on his shoulders, and never put it off till he returned there to sleep." Yet the ambassador need not strive to be magnificent, for every one knows that this is no index of the real power of his State: no one thought the better of Spain because the Spanish ambassador at Rome, in accompanying the Pope on a country expedition, took six litters, six carriages (each with six horses), two hundred valets, and sixty baggage-carts.

Outward manners are merely the expression of one's inward state. The ambassador must have moral qualities. Servien,[3] the French ambassador at the Congress of Westphalia, had great gifts, but by his hot temper he risked spoiling every negotiation. On the other hand, the President Jeannin [4] (an earlier ambassador) not merely had moderation, he was moderation itself: it was *difficult* to withstand his reasoning, but to withstand the sweetness of his nature was not merely difficult, it was perfectly impossible. Such is Wicquefort's picture of the best type of ambassador: he is a benefactor to his State and to mankind. England has had men like this, at all times in the last hundred years. Lord Clarendon [5] was such a man. And those who saw in practice the conduct of affairs by the British Foreign Secretary in the year 1919 could appreciate the worth of a diplomatist who possessed knowledge, intellect, integrity, and charm.

[1] 1598–1682. [2] 1595–1650. [3] 1595–1669.
[4] 1540–1622. [5] 1800–1870.

CHAPTER II

THE CONGRESS OF VIENNA

The year 1814 brought practically to an end the era of wars which the French Revolution had inaugurated and which Napoleon I had carried on. After the battles at Leipsic in 1813, and the invasion of France in the early months of 1814, the Bourbons were restored, and peace between the Allies and the French was made at Paris on May 30.[1] France was treated very generously; she was left with better frontiers (the frontiers of 1792), and larger territories, than those with which she had started the wars; and no indemnity was taken.

But the French Revolutionary and Napoleonic wars had been something more than a struggle of the Allies (Great Britain, Russia, Prussia, Austria, Sweden, Spain and Portugal) against France; they had been a European convulsion, which had obliterated old landmarks, and had left no state, no people, no family even, untouched by its effects. And so when the war had been fought to a finish, a Congress was gathered together to resettle the public affairs of Europe. Vienna was naturally chosen as the meeting-place, being a grand European city, the capital of one of the successful belligerents, and the seat of a Government which in a special sense represented tradition, law, order, and established institutions.

There are two outstanding points of the Congress of Vienna. In the first place, it was not a "Peace Congress," because peace had already been made at Paris, and all the questions at issue between France and the Allies had been definitely settled. The state of war had ceased both in fact and in law, and France, when the Congress of Vienna met, could claim to associate with the other Powers as a regular member of the European States-system.

The second outstanding point is that the Congress of Vienna did

[1] The "First Peace of Paris," so called to distinguish it from the "Second Peace of Paris," which was made after the Hundred Days, on November 20, 1815 (*see* below, pp. 20–22).

not meet to make a new world out of the old; if anyone had said that in twenty years of warfare the old European system had collapsed beyond repair, the Congress Powers would have denied it; they believed that the old European system had been a stable thing which on the whole had satisfied the needs of mankind, both for law and for liberty; and so they meant not to reconstruct a new system, but to restore the old. This is why the period of the Congress of Vienna, and of the years which immediately follow it, is often called the *Restoration*; but it was not mere mechanical restoration: this was impossible; the European statesmen were by no means fools; it was restoration with a good deal of improvement. It may be that more improvement could have been introduced; certainly the statesmen of 1814–15 were modest in their efforts towards a millennium. Yet, though chipped and changed here and there in the next forty years, the Vienna settlement remained substantially intact till 1860, and gave Europe nearly half a century of comparative quiet.

Article 32 of the First Peace of Paris said, "All the Powers engaged on either side in the present war shall, within the space of two months, send plenipotentiaries to Vienna for the purpose of regulating in General Congress the arrangements which are to complete the provisions of the present treaty." But the Allies, though they had made peace with France, and promised to associate her in the Congress, could not bring themselves to consider her as a normal member. So a secret Article (to which France herself had to assent) stipulated that the settlement to be made at the Congress would be regulated by "the principles determined upon by the Allied Powers among themselves." This meant that the Congress of Vienna was to be effectively composed of, at most, the seven Powers (Great Britain, Russia, Austria, Prussia, Sweden, Spain and Portugal) who had signed the treaty with France. Yet even this number was considered too large, and a subsequent agreement among the big Powers limited the really effective part of the Congress to the "four Courts" [1]—that is to say, to Great Britain, Russia, Austria and Prussia. Actually, when the Congress met, the French representative M. de Talleyrand, by his skilful diplomacy, gained admittance to the conferences of the Four, which thus became a Committee of Five—Great Britain, Russia, Austria, Prussia and France.

[1] Webster, *The Congress of Vienna* (1919), p. 48, n. 4, quoting from F. O. Archives, Continent, S,

This Committee of Five was *the* Congress of Vienna. The hundred or so plenipotentiaries of other Powers who, in addition to the original Eight, came to Vienna, did nothing, except those who were put into certain technical committees. The Congress as a whole never met. The Five deliberated together by themselves, and settled everything by their own decisions. There was not even a formal session of all the Congress, either at the beginning or the end, although at the conclusion the Eight (that is Sweden, Spain and Portugal, in addition to Great Britain, Russia, Austria, Prussia and France) signed the Final Act.

* * * * *

Although Article 32 of the First Peace of Paris had stipulated that the Congress should meet within two months, the Four did not all assemble at Vienna till September 13, 1814. They were, firstly, M. de Metternich, the most experienced and in some ways the most sagacious of European statesmen and diplomatists, although still a comparatively young man, aged forty-one. Next may be mentioned the Tsar Alexander I, personally representing his own Empire, a man of ideas and impulses; Napoleon called him the "shifty Byzantine." Next comes Frederick William III of Prussia, well intentioned but weak. Finally to complete the Four was Lord Castlereagh, the British Foreign Secretary.[1] This hard-working and experienced statesman may have lacked imagination, but his good sense and honesty made him a worthy representative of Great Britain. And now to convert the Four into the Five, mention must be made of Charles Maurice de Talleyrand-Périgord, the most *rusé* of men. He was at this time at the climax of his extraordinary career. The other chief plenipotentiaries were still in the forties: Alexander I was only thirty-seven; Metternich was forty-one; Frederick William was forty-four (though Hardenberg, the effective Prussian delegate was sixty-four); and Castlereagh was forty-five. Talleyrand was already in his sixty-first year. He had begun his working life as a priest, rose early and easily, like any other clerical nobleman of the Ancien Régime, to be a bishop, and sat as such in the fateful States-General of 1789. In the Revolution he had given up his clerical profession, and obtained employment as a diplomatist.

[1] For Casthreagh's correspondence *see* Webster, *British Diplomacy, 1813–1815* (London, 1921), p. 189 ff. The volume consists of a splendid collection of Documents, from the Foreign Office archives, with a short but useful Introduction.

A mission to London in 1791 made him an admirer of England for life. He learned something too when an *emigré* for two and a half years in the United States (1793–5). He was Minister for Foreign Affairs under the Directory, and after their fall, served Napoleon faithfully till 1814; in that fateful year the great Emperor took leave of his supple friend with the words: "you would betray your own father." Talleyrand easily adapted himself to the Restoration, and saved his country from the vengeance of the Allies by drawing a distinction between Napoleonic France which had passed away, and Bourbon France which was not responsible for the late wars. The Congress of Vienna provided him with his most difficult task and gave scope for his greatest successes. He was undoubtedly a real patriot, and continued to serve his country with equal ease under the Bourbon, and later under the Orleans Monarchy. He had, *par excellence*, the manner of the typical French diplomatist—an easy bearing, and a great fund of ironical humour. He died in 1838 at the age of eighty-four.[1]

When the representatives of the Four Powers had assembled at Vienna (September 13, 1814), they began settling the difficult European questions, quite informally, among themselves. The actual treaties, when drafted, were merely to register the decisions previously reached by the Four Allies. The larger Committee, the Eight (Great Britain, Russia, Austria, Prussia, Sweden, Spain, Portugal and France), did meet occasionally; but it had little to do. This did not satisfy Talleyrand, who had arrived on September 23, only to find France excluded from the inner councils of the Four. But he bided his time; he was always something of a friend to England; and now England, in the person of Castlereagh, showed herself a great friend to France. On December 24 the first formal meeting of the Congress (there had of course been many informal meetings)

[1] The representatives of the Great Powers were not limited to these mentioned above. Each State had a Delegation consisting of three or four envoys. The Duke of Wellington was associated with Castlereagh, till Napoleon's return from Elba sent him hurriedly off to command the Army. Nor must Frederick von Gentz (1764–1832) be forgotten. He was the most effective (and probably the most voluminous) writer of propaganda against Napoleon. Originally in the Prussian service he had transferred himself in 1802 to Austria, and from 1812 he was the "*âme damnée* of Metternich." Politically the two were inseparable. Gentz was Secretary to the Congress of Vienna, and to all subsequent Congresses till 1822. The Second Secretary of the Congress was G. F. von Martens, the eminent editor of the *Recueil de Traités*, the invaluable series which still goes on annually.

took place ; and at this, to the consternation of Russia and Prussia, Castlereagh and Metternich proposed and insisted that France should be admitted. The truth is that the Four Powers had nearly come to blows over the questions of Poland and Saxony ; and Great Britain and Austria, in quest of a peaceful solution, saw no other way than to associate France on their side, so as to outweigh the influence of Russia and Prussia, who were working together on the other side. When France's admittance was proposed by England and Austria, she could not decently be refused ; for after all, France was not now an enemy (the First Peace of Paris having been made months before), and moreover Talleyrand was threatening to rouse the Minor Powers to a sense of their due place at the Congress, if France was not treated as one of the Great Powers. So Russia and Austria yielded, and the Committee of Four was transformed into a Committee of Five, which made all the decisions of the Congress.

Meanwhile the concluding months of the year 1814 had slipped away,[1] and nothing substantial had been accomplished towards making a lasting settlement of Europe. *Le Congrès ne marche pas, il danse,* wrote the Prince de Ligne [2] to his friend La Garde.

> You have come at the right moment. If you like fêtes and balls you will have enough of them ; the Congress does not *go*, it dances. There is, literally, a royal mob here. Everybody is crying out : peace ! justice ! balance of power ! indemnity ! As for me, I am a looker on. All the indemnity I shall ask for is a new hat ; I have worn mine out in taking it off to sovereigns whom I meet at the corner of every street.[3]

The distinguished old warrior and courtier had reason to be amused at the mass of royalties and their envoys who flocked to Vienna, hoping to be heard at the conferences of the mighty Four, or at least to see somehow that their interests were not entirely overlooked. Among many entertainments a *Ridotto* was given at the Burg by the Emperor in October :

> Take notice of that graceful, martial figure walking with Eugène de Beauharnais ; that is the Emperor Alexander. And that tall, dignified man, with the lively Neapolitan on his arm, is the King of Prussia. . . . And there in that Venetian suit, the stiffness of which scarcely conceals

---

[1] One good piece of work was accomplished elsewhere than at the Congress. This was the Treaty of Peace between England and the United States of America, signed at Ghent on December 24, 1814.

[2] 1735–1814. Ligne was an Austrian Field-Marshal.

[3] *The Prince de Ligne : His Memoirs, etc.* Selected and edited by K. P. Wormely (1899), II, 263.

his affability, is our own emperor,[1] the representative of the most paternal despotism that ever existed. Here is Maximilian, King of Bavaria, in whose frank countenance you can read the expression of his good heart. . . . Do you see that pale little man, with an aquiline nose, near to the King of Bavaria? That is the King of Denmark, whose cheerful humour and lively repartees enliven the royal parties —they call him the *lustig* of the sovereign brigade. Judging by his simple manners and the perfect happiness of his little kingdom, you would never suppose him to be the greatest autocrat in Europe. But he is, for all that. In Copenhagen the royal carriage is preceded by an equerry armed with a carbine, and the king as he drives along can, if he pleases, order any of his subjects to be shot. That colossal figure, leaning against the column, whose bulk is not lessened by the folds of his ample domino, is the King of Wurtemburg, and next to him is his son the prince-royal, whose affection for the Grand Duchess of Oldenburg has brought him to the Congress, rather than the settlement of public business that will soon be his own. All this crowd of personages who are buzzing round us, are either reigning princes, archdukes or great dignitaries from various countries. With the exception of a few Englishmen (easily distinguished by the richness of their clothes), I do not see anyone without a title to his name.[2] . . .

There was not merely a good deal of social life at the Congress, there was a lot of spying and informing as well. In this respect the Austrians had the greatest advantage, for they were in their own capital, and could employ all the resources of the Vienna police. The waste-paper baskets of all delegates were carefully searched each day, and full reports of everything that had been gleaned were sent regularly to the Emperor Francis.

When the Congress, or rather the Five, at last settled itself to transact the business for which it had met, it accomplished the work rapidly, and, on the whole, well. There were many problems to be settled, but in particular there were nine that were outstanding. These were the Saxo-Polish Question, the Question of the Rhine frontier, the Belgo-Dutch Question, the Dano-Swedish Question, the Questions of Switzerland, Italy, the Germanic Confederation, International Rivers and the Slave Trade.

The Saxo-Polish problem was far the worst. By the Treaty of Kalisch, February 28, 1813 (one of the many conventions made among the Allies during the war in order to satisfy each other), the extension of Prussian territory in North Germany had been promised, while Russia was, by implication, accorded a free hand in the dis-

[1] Francis I, Emperor of Austria, reigned from 1792 to 1835.

[2] Ligne to La Garde, vide Wormely, *loc. cit.*

position of Poland. This Convention was made the basis of a claim on the part of Russia to annex the whole of Poland, while Prussia was to be satisfied with the whole of Saxony—a country which was considered to be forfeit by reason of its king's fidelity to Napoleon. Metternich, however, was by no means anxious that Russia should absorb Galicia and hold Cracow and the line of the Vistula; while Castlereagh too was against this enormous increase of the Tsar's dominion, and was in sympathy with the claims of the Poles to be reconstituted as a State once more. Thus the Four Powers of the Congress were divided into two camps: on the one hand Russia and Prussia, on the other Austria and Great Britain. The unhappy King of Saxony, excluded from all participation in the debates that would settle the fate of his kingdom, could only stay at Pressburg,[1] anxiously waiting for news from day to day. Indeed it looked as though a fearful fratricidal war would start among the Allies, over the carcase of Saxony. The Russian autocrat was used not to be thwarted: "I have 200,000 soldiers in the Duchy of Warsaw; let them try and drive me from it. I have given Saxony to Prussia." So spoke the Tsar to Talleyrand on October 23 (1814). It was not difficult for the acute Frenchman to see that in this division among the Four, France would hold the balance. It was because of this that he confidently demanded admission to the Committee of Four; and it was because of this that Castlereagh and Metternich supported his demand. Admitted on December 24, Talleyrand threw his weight on the side of England and Austria.

In thus definitely choosing the Anglo-Austrian side, Talleyrand rejected the greatest opportunity ever offered to a French statesman. Russia and Prussia would have given almost anything for his support. On December 29, 1814, Hardenberg, acting in conjunction with the Tsar, proposed that if Prussia annexed the whole of Saxony the King of Saxony should, in compensation, be established in a new kingdom on the left bank of the Rhine.[2] This new State was to include the territory of the Duchy of Luxemburg, a portion of the Archbishopric of Trèves, the city of Bonn, and the Abbeys of Prüm, Stavelot, and Malmédy. It would have a population of 700,000.

Castlereagh and Metternich were both absolutely against this proposal—Metternich, because he did not wish Prussia to become too great by absorbing Saxony; Castlereagh, because he did not

[1] It is now called Bratislava.

[2] D'Angeberg: *Le Congrès de Vienne et les Traités de* 1815, pp. 1863, 1869.

wish to see a pro-French State established on the left bank of the Rhine, so near to Belgium. But it is difficult to see why Talleyrand was against the proposal too. The Elector of Saxony was a firm friend to France; the new State would have a Catholic and, in many respects, a Gallic population; its dynasty, remembering the loss of Saxony, would have been certain to be anti-Prussian for many years to come. The new State in fact would have been an admirable buffer between France and Germany, and might have prevented the terrible collisions of later years. If Talleyrand had supported the Prussian proposal of December 29, 1814, Great Britain and France would certainly have fought to prevent it. He preferred not to face this risk, and to accept instead the offer of an Anglo-Austrian Alliance, though this seemed equally likely to involve a war with Prussia and Austria.

On January 3, 1815, Castlereagh copied out with his own hand (so as to ensure secrecy) and signed a defensive treaty of alliance, to which Metternich and Talleyrand put their signatures. Each Power agreed to provide 150,000 men. The former bitter enemy of England and Austria was now their military ally![1] Talleyrand had destroyed the coalition of Europe against France, and rescued her from her isolation. "Now, Sire, the coalition is dissolved, and for ever," he wrote to Louis XVIII (January 4, 1815).[2] In reality "France had only been admitted to the honour of fighting for the security of Austria, and for the triumph of English policy."[3]

Although the treaty of January 3 remained secret at the time, Alexander and Hardenberg could not help noticing the solidarity of England, Austria, and France. They preferred not to have another European war; they decided to compromise. So for the rest of the month of January (1815) the negotiations went better; and at last all parties were, more or less, satisfied.[4] Saxony was not given to the Prussians; it was left as an independent kingdom, but it lost two-fifths of its territory—all the northern portion, with 800,000

[1] The treaty remained secret till Napoleon found the copy of Louis XVIII in the archives at Paris, during the Hundred Days, and published it. Talleyrand does not deal with the affair in his *Mémoires*, except to plume himself on the treaty of January 3, 1815. The *Correspondance inédite du Prince de Talleyrand et du roi Louis XVIII* (ed. Pallain) gives more details.

[2] Talleyrand, *Mémoires*, II, 556.

[3] Houssaye, *1815*: *La Première Restauration*, Livre I, chap. III, § II.

[4] On January 5, Castlereagh was able to write to Lord Liverpool, "I have every reason to hope that the alarm of war is over." (Doc. in Webster, *British Diplomacy, 1813–1815*, p. 282.)

"souls"[1]—which was annexed to Prussia; and the frontier was drawn so as to leave Leipsic on the Saxon side. This by no means assuaged Prussia's land-hunger, but she was promised compensation in Westphalia and on the Rhine.

Russia received the lion's share, for there was no Polish royal family to advance the claims of legitimacy. So Alexander acquired all that we now know as Poland except Posen and "West Prussia" (including Danzig and Thorn), which Prussia retained, and Galicia (including Tarnopol), retained by Austria.

The second problem—what was to be done with the Rhineland—was more easily settled. Peace having already been made with France, there was no question of re-allotting Alsace and Lorraine, There were, however, the territories of the old ecclesiastical principalities—Mayence, Trèves, and Cologne, with other prince-bishoprics—which Napoleon had "secularized" and absorbed into his empire or into his client States. There were also a number of former small lay principalities and Free Imperial cities, which had also fallen victims to the Napoleonic taste for unity and symmetry. These (with the exception of Mayence)[2] were now given to Prussia, and became the province of Nieder-Rhein; along with this, Prussia acquired another province, Westphalia, consisting chiefly of the old prince-bishopric of Munster.

The third question—the Belgo-Dutch—was soon dealt with, because it had already been the subject of engagements entered into at the First Peace of Paris. Belgium, previous to the French Revolutionary Wars, had been known as the Austrian Netherlands. Austria had now no wish to undertake again the responsibility for a distant and dangerously situated province. Yet something had to be done with Belgium; it raised no claim to stand alone; and it must at all costs be kept out of the hands of France (for a revival of French military domination was in 1814 one of the dread phantoms of Europe). Pitt had once thought of annexing it to Prussia, as the best means of defending it against France. The Congress of

[1] Wittenburg, Torgau, and Zeitz were the chief places in the annexed portion of Saxony.

[2] Mayence was not attributed to any State by the Congress of Vienna. It had been annexed by Napoleon and included in the Imperial department of Mont Tonnerre. By a treaty of June 3, 1814, concluded at Paris between Austria and Bavaria, Mayence was obtained by Bavaria. But by one of the treaties consequential to the Vienna Congress, Bavaria ceded Mayence to Hesse-Darmstadt. The fortress of Mayence, however, was at the same time made a fortress of the Germanic Confederation.

Vienna, however, took a better decision, and Belgium was joined to the Dutch State; at the same time the ancient noble and semi-royal family of Orange was recognized as holding the sovereignty of the new State, which thus became the Kingdom of Holland and Belgium. Union is strength: it was hoped that the combined forces of the Dutch and Belgians would ensure that this danger-spot of Europe between the mouths of the Rhine and the Scheldt would remain in safe hands.

The fourth problem concerned Denmark and Sweden. The King of Denmark was also King of Norway, and this ancient union, which is more suitable from the point of view of geography than appears at first sight, satisfied both parties. Denmark, however, had been somewhat roughly handled by the Allies during the wars, and in the last years had thrown in her lot completely with the fortunes of Napoleon. So in 1814 she had to suffer in the downfall of the French Empire: she had to cede Norway to Sweden, receiving in return a certain satisfaction in money and also the former Swedish Pomerania (Stralsund, Rugen, and so forth).[1] Norway and Sweden, which, although situated side by side in the same Peninsula, are physically separated from each other by a very broad and difficult region of mountains, were thus politically united. Denmark's compensation—Swedish Pomerania—was rather far away, so she gave it to Prussia in exchange for the Duchy of Lauenburg on the Elbe. Meanwhile Great Britain had given back to the unfortunate Dane all his lost colonies and islands—except Heligoland, which the British Government retained in full sovereignty.

The State that did best for itself by these Scandinavian arrangements was, in the long run, Prussia. For she had received Swedish Pomerania from Denmark, and had given Lauenburg in exchange; but fifty years later she took back Lauenburg by force of arms. And also, whereas the Dane had lost Heligoland to the British, Prussia eventually got that too, by a peaceful treaty made in 1890. So the spoils practically all fell to Prussia, and she has them still.

The fifth question was concerned with Switzerland, and its solution proved to be the most durable thing achieved by the Congress. There was a strong "Swiss Committee" set up by the Five at Vienna to study this problem; among the members of this Committee were Stratford Canning, already a distinguished diplomatist, although aged only twenty-eight; Count Capo d'Istria, the Tsar's Corfiote

[1] Treaty of Kiel between Denmark and Sweden, January 14, 1814.

diplomatist; and Frederic César La Harpe, a Genevese scholar and publicist, who had once been tutor to Alexander. The task of reconciling the many and often conflicting interests of the Swiss cantons, and of drawing up a fair Federal Act, was extremely difficult, but it was accomplished quite successfully. The Committee took as a basis on which to work the Act of Mediation (although it had been annulled), a very statesmanlike constitution which Napoleon had imposed upon the Swiss in 1803. The result was that the Congress of Vienna recognized the integrity of the nineteen ancient cantons, and added three new cantons—Valais, Neuchatel, and Geneva. Geneva had been an ancient independent city-state, till suppressed in the French Revolutionary Wars. Neuchatel was a principality of the King of Prussia (and remained so till 1857), but was included within the Swiss Confederation, a somewhat curious instance of a monarchical State in a republican federal body. The perpetual neutrality of Switzerland in her new frontiers was guaranteed by the Eight Powers of the Congress of Vienna. This neutrality, in order to protect the southern frontier of Switzerland on the Lake of Geneva, was extended to include the Sardinian territory of Faucigny and Chablais. During time of war, Sardinian troops were bound to retire from these provinces and to give place to Swiss garrisons.[1]

The sixth problem was provided by Italy. During the period of Napoleonic ascendancy, Italian political geography had been greatly simplified by the annexation of the Papal States, Genoa, Piedmont, Venice, and other places, to the French Empire. Restoration, however, was now the order of the day; indeed no other course appears then to have been open to the Powers. So the old dynasties were restored. Pius VII had suffered much at the hands of Napoleon, and his support of the Allies (in spite of his submission to Napoleon by the Treaty of Fontainebleau of 1812) had had considerable influence on the resistance of Spain and Austria—the two most Catholic countries—against France. Accordingly Pius was restored and the States of the Church were reconstituted. Austria, likewise, was restored to dominion in the Milanese, which it had held since the Treaties of Utrecht of 1713. The Republic of Venice, however,

[1] Faucigny and Chablais with the rest of Savoy were ceded by Sardinia to France in 1860; during time of war the French, undertaking the obligations formerly belonging to Sardinia, are bound to retire and to give place to Swiss troops. This actually happened in the war of 1914–18. The neutralisation of Upper Savoy was abrogated by Act 435 of the Treaty of Versailles, June 28, 1919.

which had existed free and independent till 1797, was not restored to itself. In that year, Bonaparte, by the Treaty of Campo Formio, had given it to Austria, though after the battle of Austerlitz and the Treaty of Pressburg in 1805, he had taken it back and absorbed it in the French Empire. At the Congress of Vienna, Metternich took his stand on the Treaty of Campo Formio, and insisted upon getting back Venice, with all the continental and insular dominion which it possessed in 1797. Thus in addition to the Milanese, Austria acquired Venetia, to the east of the Mincio, and also Dalmatia, with the Bocche di Cattaro; and moreover, as the time was not propitious for small States, she likewise acquired the territory of the former Republic of Ragusa, which had retained its independence till absorbed in the Napoleonic Empire in the year 1805. With Dalmatia Austria also got the islands which Venetia had held in 1797, all except Corfu, Zante, Santa Maura, Cephalonia, Cerigo, Ithaca, and Paxo, which by a treaty (November 5, 1815) consequential to the Vienna Congress Act, were constituted as "a single Free and Independent State," under "the immediate and exclusive protection" of Great Britain.

In the Italian settlement, the King of Sardinia, besides being restored to his former dominion, received only a comparatively small accession of territory,—small, but highly valuable—the former Republic of Genoa with its beautiful Riviera, from San Remo to Sarzano. The other exiled Italian dynasties were restored—the Este to Modena, the house of Lorraine-Habsburg to Tuscany. An exception, however, was made with regard to the house of Bourbon-Parma. This family, represented at this time by the Infanta Maria Louisa and her son Don Carlos, was put off with the possession of Lucca (another ancient republic suppressed in the French Revolutionary Wars); while Napoleon's wife the Empress Maria Louisa, in consideration of her being the daughter of the Emperor of Austria, was given the Duchy of Parma for her lifetime. She lived till 1847, when, in accordance with Articles 99 and 102 of the Vienna Congress Act,[1] Parma reverted to the house of Bourbon, while Lucca reverted to the Grand Duchy of Tuscany.

Naples presented a difficulty in the Italian settlement. This

[1] Article 99 of the Vienna Congress Act did not specify to whom in particular Parma was to revert. This was done by a treaty between Great Britain, Austria, Spain, France, Prussia, and Russia, concluded at Paris on June 10, 1817, and included as an annexe in the General Treaty of Frankfort of July 20, 1819.

kingdom had formed one of the client States of the Napoleonic Empire, with Joachim Murat as King. Murat was a good administrator, and southern Italy was much better off under him than it had ever been under its legitimate Bourbon rulers. Nevertheless the principle of legitimacy would have been applied by the Congress Powers, in Naples, as in the rest of Italy, more especially as the British Government felt bound to support the legitimate king, Ferdinand I, who had throughout the War been maintained in Sicily by British sea-power. Metternich, however, in order to detach Murat from Napoleon, had on January 11, 1814, concluded through Count Neipperg a treaty [1] by which Austria guaranteed the crown of Naples to "S.M. le Roi Joachim Napoleon" (Murat had married Napoleon's sister Caroline).

The Neapolitan knot was loosed by Murat's own blindness. Having made his peace with the Allies, he could not keep it. On the night of March 6, 1815, the Powers of the Congress of Vienna were startled by the news that Napoleon had come back from Elba (March 1). Castlereagh had by this time definitely returned to London, leaving Lord Clancarty to take his place at Vienna. When further news came that Murat had broken his treaty with Austria, and had called upon the whole of Italy to rise, Castlereagh knew that the Neapolitan question had solved itself. On April 5 the Allied Governments declared war upon Murat; on May 2, at Tolentino, against an Austrian army, he lost both the battle and his throne.[2] The *beau sabreur*, escaping to France to offer his sword to Napoleon, was contemptuously rejected; he returned to try his fortune again in Italy, was captured, tried under one of his own laws, and shot. Ferdinand I of Bourbon was reigning again at Naples.

The last of the territorial problems to be mentioned is that of Germany. Although legitimacy was the order of the day at Vienna, there was no question of restoring the princes and princelings, lay and ecclesiastical, and the Free Imperial Cities which had been suppressed by the Recess of the Imperial Diet at Ratisbon in 1803, and after the dissolution of the Holy Roman Empire in 1806. The Congress of Vienna even extended the principle of "mediatisation," for instance, by annexing to Prussia the territories of the

[1] Martens, *Traités* (Supplément, 1824) t. IX; *State Papers*, vol. II, p. 228; Sorel, *L'Europe et la Révolution*, VIII, 237. The treaty was concluded at Naples: the Neapolitan representative was the Duc de Gallo.

[2] Sorel, *op. cit.*, VIII, 436.

Princes of Salm-Salm and Salm-Kyrburg. Thus what Napoleon had accomplished towards bringing comparative simplicity and uniformity out of the maze of feudalism which had constituted the political map of Germany before his time, was retained. Yet Germany was not a unity, for the Holy Roman Empire had been dissolved; and now a new system must be created. This was the work of the German Committee of the Congress, and the results of its labour were a "Federative Constitution" published as Annexe IX of the Final Act of Vienna, and with eleven of its most important clauses included as an integral part of the Final Act itself (Arts 53–63). The Germanic Confederation was to include thirty-four sovereigns [1] and four Free Cities, with a Federal Diet or Legislature presided over by Austria. This Constitution for Germany lasted, with considerable vicissitudes, till 1866.

There were two other very important pieces of business accomplished by the Congress of Vienna. One was to enact a general "open" system for international rivers, that is to say, for rivers which separate or cross various States (Arts. 108–117). From the point at which each such river becomes navigable to its mouth the navigation was to be entirely free to all people, subject only to police regulations and necessary tolls which were in no case to exceed those already in existence. Thus the Powers of Europe said good-bye for ever to the policy which, for instance, had kept the river Scheldt closed to navigation from the sea since the Treaty of Munster ("Westphalia") in 1648.

The Slave-Trade was less easily regulated. Great Britain had abolished for herself the traffic in slaves in 1807, and the British Government was anxious to induce the Congress of Vienna to follow her lead. Already an agreement, included in the First Peace of Paris, had been made between England and France, to the effect that at the Congress of Vienna they would use all their efforts to induce the Powers to decree the abolition of the Slave Trade.[2] Actually, however, at Vienna, the most that could be obtained was a pronouncement by the Eight Powers that the universal abolition of the Slave Trade was "a measure particularly worthy of their

[1] There were really thirty-five; the Landgrave Hesse-Homburg, although restored to his possessions of which he had been deprived by the Confederation of the Rhine (Art. 48 of the Final Act of Vienna), was not given a vote in the Federal Diet till 1816 (Treaty of June 30. Hertslet, No. 58).

[2] Treaty between Great Britain and France, Paris, May 30, 1814. Hertslet I, No. 1, p. 20.

attention"; and they added the reservation that "this general Declaration cannot prejudge the period that each particular Power may consider as most advisable for the definitive abolition of the Slave Trade."[1] This document formed Annexe XV to the Final Act of Vienna.

The Final Act which sums up all the work accomplished by the Congress was drafted in a great hurry and signed on June 9, 1815, at a moment when all the delegates were excited and eager to depart, because Napoleon was marching for Belgium, and the great battle, which actually took place nine days later and which settled the destinies of Europe for exactly a hundred years, was imminent to all observers. The Treaty, regarded merely as a text, had many blemishes and not a few obscurities. We must remember, however, that there did not exist in those days the wealth of statistics to which all statesmen of to-day, with their large secretariat and staff of trained men, have access. The "Vienna settlement," it must be borne in mind, is to be looked for in more documents than the Final Act: it was gradually completed by various consequential treaties, of which the last was the great Treaty of Frankfort of July 20, 1819.

No exaggerated claim can be advanced in favour of the Vienna Settlement; in the following hundred years it was whittled piecemeal away. Though very markedly cut into, in 1831 (when Belgium was separated from Holland), and in 1859-60 (when the union of Italy was substantially accomplished), nevertheless its primary object, as stated in the secret Articles of the First Peace of Paris—"a system of real and permanent Balance of Power in Europe"—was attained for over fifty years, till the annexation of Alsace-Lorraine by Germany in 1871 destroyed that Balance.

The Vienna Settlement has been called a work of Restoration and Legitimacy, but it is something more besides. The monarchies, which France had overthrown, were restored, but their old feudal regimes were not restored with them. The new Europe which was born in the Revolutionary wars remained; and so, in concluding this survey of the Vienna Congress we may, as Sorel does at the end of his grand study of the Revolutionary period, render homage to the Frenchman—the ordinary French soldier of the Revolutionary and Napoleonic armies—"*pauvre diable glorieux*, generous of his soul and his person, bruised in his body, infirm, maimed, scattering on

[1] Declaration of February 8, 1815 (Hertslet I, No. 7).

roads the fragments of his broken limbs . . . exposing himself, spending himself, sacrificing his blood and his strength to pursue the ancestral chimera, the human idol of spirit and flesh, liberty the enchantress, the peace which heals the sores of wounds, quenches the thirst of the feverish, consoles the sick, makes to blossom around them children and flowers, ripens the harvest and the generations, and consecrates by its beneficence the anonymous heroes who have won it."[1] With the humble French soldier we must remember his combatants among the Allies, the men who fought in the long campaigns in the Peninsula, who suffered on the terrible fields of Austerlitz or Friedland, or in the glorious triumphs of the War of Liberation and the Hundred Days. It is on the work of these anonymous heroes that diplomacy builds, and it is on them, in the long run, that the diplomatists rely. Moreover, no ideals, if they be honestly held and striven for, are without effect; and out of the conflicting ideals which the French and the Allied Armies represented in the Revolutionary wars, the statesmen of 1814–15 framed an honourable peace which proved that neither side had fought in vain.

Great Britain had no special interests at stake in the Congress of Vienna, and readers will seek in vain though the Final Act for any mention of a cession to this country. The reason for such austerity was that we had already settled all our claims with France, at the First Peace of Paris. As M. Debidour caustically remarks in a note to his chapter on the Congress of Vienna: the wars of the Revolution had been worth to us the occupation of Heligoland, Malta and the Ionian Isles, in Europe; of the colony of the Cape of Good Hope in Africa; of the Isle de France and the Seychelles in the Indian Ocean; of the Isle of Ceylon near India, and of considerable territories on the mainland; of Tasmania in Oceania; of St. Lucia, Tobago and other places in the West Indies. It is the fate of a maritime Power that she can only fight effectively by sinking enemy fleets and capturing enemy islands, and at the final settlements diplomacy gathers in the harvest without effort.[2]

[1] Sorel, *op. cit.*, VIII, *ad fin.*

[2] For the British attitude throughout the Congress of Vienna cp. *The Cambridge History of British Foreign Policy*, vol. I, chap. IV.

CHAPTER III

THE CONCERT OF EUROPE

§ 1. The Second Peace of Paris

The seven or eight years following the Congress of Vienna is a period when the affairs of Europe and America come very close together. The French Revolution had lit a lamp that would *not* be extinguished either in the Old World or the New, and the statesmen of Europe had an anxious time nervously watching to prevent catastrophe to the public system of Europe of which they were the guardians.

During this time the so-called Holy Alliance occupies the stage, and has received from historians much more attention than it probably deserves. On the other hand, the Quadruple Alliance, which is the origin of the Concert of Europe, attracted much less notice at the time, and until recent years was almost passed over in silence by history.

The Quadruple Alliance arose out of the Second Peace of Paris. It will be remembered that the defeats of Napoleon in the War of Liberation in 1813 had led to the invasion of France by the Allies in 1814 and to the conclusion of the First Peace of Paris on May 20 of that year. The Bourbons were restored, and France received at the hands of the Allies the frontier of 1792, with important additions; [1] and no indemnity was taken. Then followed the Congress of Vienna, to settle European affairs other than French. But the work of the Congress, ere it was completed, was suddenly disturbed and threatened with annihilation by the return of Napoleon from Elba and his re-elevation by the French to the Imperial throne. Next comes the battle of Waterloo; and finally the Second Peace of

[1] The most important additions—all on the eastern frontier—were Saarbruck, Landau, Annecy, and Chambéry.

Paris between the re-restored Bourbon Government of France and the Allies (November 20, 1815).

France, by her adhesion to Napoleon in the Hundred Days,[1] lost a great part of the advantages which she had gained at the First Peace of Paris. The Second Treaty of Paris gave her the frontier of 1790 (not, as at the First Peace, the frontier of 1792). She thus lost Philippeville (between Maubeuge and Dinant), and Sarrlouis and Saarbruck; she also lost the important fortress of Landau; south of the Lake of Geneva she lost Annecy ad Chambéry. She was, however, allowed to retain Avignon and the Venaissin. Next she had to undertake payment of an indemnity of 700,000,000 francs, partly to be spent in strengthening fortresses belonging to Powers on the French frontier, and partly to be distributed among the Allied Governments and other States which had suffered at the hands of the French.[2] The total of 700,000,000 francs was to be discharged in the form of bearer bonds, payable in five years, without interest, in fifteen equal sums. Until the indemnity should be paid off, an Allied army of 150,000 men, maintained at the expense of the French, should occupy the north-eastern fortresses. Finally France had to restore the objects of art gained during the Napoleonic Wars from conquered States; these treasures had not been required by the Allies at the First Peace of Paris; and the French felt the necessity of giving them up now as the "most unkindest cut of all."

Such was the Second Peace of Paris, a series of pacts considered, drafted, and signed in about eight weeks.[3] The French have always considered it rather vindictive, but it might have been a great deal worse. It is well known that Blucher wished to blow up the Pont d'Iéna. Two mines were actually laid and exploded under it, ineffectually. Talleyrand's remonstrances to von Goltz, the Prussian minister at Paris, did no good. An appeal to Wellington, however,

[1] It is to be noted that the French people gave their adhesion somewhat tardily to Napoleon on his return from Elba. France wanted peace, and Napoleon, having gradually re-established his authority, would have been content to be left in peaceful possession of France within the limits of the First Peace of Paris—for a time at least. This explains why he was for two months in France after the return from Elba, before he began the Waterloo campaign, when the Allies persisted in their determination to make no peace with him.

[2] Protocol No. 9 of the Second Peace of Paris: *State Papers*, vol. III, p. 242.

[3] The demands of the Allies were presented in outline to Louis XVIII on September 20, 1815. The Main Treaty was signed on November 20.

proved more successful.[1] On one point the Allies were in perfect accord: no terms were to be made with Napoleon. On July 15 he had surrendered himself as a prisoner of war at Rochefort. On August 2,[2] a treaty was concluded between Great Britain, Austria, Russia, and Prussia, to the effect that the care of the ex-emperor should be confided to Great Britain, but that each of the Four Powers and also France should have a commissioner at the place of his internment. So he went to St. Helena, where representatives of the Three Powers (for Prussia did not trouble to spend money on a commissioner), and also a representative of the French Government, watched him for the rest of his life.[3] He died on May 5, 1821, at the age of fifty-one years nine months.

The settlement made at the Second Peace of Paris must be acknowledged to be satisfactory. The Prussian delegates Hardenberg and Humboldt put in a claim for Alsace, but it was disallowed; and subsequent history has proved that the possession of Alsace by France is necessary for the political equilibrium of Europe. Napoleon thought that Great Britain might decently have claimed an island or two from France: "It is ridiculous," he said, "for them to leave Batavia to the Dutch and L'Ile de Bourbon to the French."[4]

The Allies had insisted on the disbandment of the French Army before the Second Peace of Paris was made; the Government of Louis XVIII agreed, and with great difficulty (and not without some deception of the soldiers who, with arms in their hands, by no means wished to be disbanded) carried out the work in six weeks. Louis XVIII in 1814 had also promised not to re-establish conscription, but in 1817 the Army Law of Marshal Gouvion St. Cyr restored the conscription in the form that it retained till 1871.

Metternich left Paris on November 26, less than a week after the signing of the main treaty. He was going to take a holiday, in

[1] *See* Hall: *The Bourbon Restoration* (1909), chap. V.

[2] The treaty is in *State Papers*, vol. III, p. 200. There is no doubt that Napoleon surrendered himself unconditionally. Debidour admits this (*Hist. Dip.* I, 72); *see also* Rose, *Napoleonic Studies*, No. XII. Great Britain appears to have met all the expenses of Napoleon's confinement, about £12,000 per annum.

[3] "Watching is perhaps not the right word, for Sir Hudson Lowe, the British Governor at St. Helena, would never let the Commissioners actually *see* the ex-Emperor" (*see* Rosebery, *Napoleon: the Last Phase*, chap. XI).

[4] *See* Rose's *Napoleon*, chap. XLI *ad fin.* By a treaty signed at London by Castlereagh and Fagel on August 13, 1814, Great Britain restored to the Netherlands all the colonies held by her on January 1, 1803, except the Cape of Good Hope, Demerara, Essequibo, and Berbice. (Hertslet, No. 5.)

Italy, along with his family. He appears to have been pleased with his sojourn and work in Paris, where he had occupied a flat in the house of M. Decrès, in the Faubourg St. Honoré, overlooking the Champs-Elysées.

On seeing from the balcony this immense city, still brilliant with all its towers and spires in the setting sun, I said to myself: "This city and this sun will still greet one another where there are no longer any traditions of Napoleon and Blucher, and least of all, of myself." These are the immutable laws of nature—this specific weight of the masses will always be the same, while we poor creatures, who think ourselves so important, live only to make a little show by our perpetual motion, by our dabbling in the mud or the shifting sand! Let us at least carry away the remembrance of having done some good—and in this respect I would not change with Napoleon.[1]

There is the reflective creed of a high diplomatist!

§ 2. The Holy and Quadruple Alliances

After the great series of Acts settling the affairs of Europe at the end of the long wars, statesmen naturally considered how to make the settlement durable. Already the Tsar had his project complete: it was nothing more or less than to get his brother sovereigns to promise to act towards each other in the spirit of Christian charity.

Alexander's project has been traced back to the year 1804. There is no doubt that he was sincere.[2] He was an egoist, a sentimentalist, sympathetic, and subject to the most generous impulses; and the Holy Alliance was the outcome of his not very clear intellect and soul. He was sustained in his project by the rhapsodies of the Baroness de Krudener, the widow of a Russian diplomatist, a writer of novels, and in her more mature age a pietist. The text of the Holy Alliance, contained in the Declaration of September 26, 1815, was revised by her at Paris before being put before the Allies.

The Declaration consists of a preamble and three articles. The preamble states that the Emperors of Russia and Austria and the King of Prussia have, in consequence of the events of the last three years, acquired the intimate conviction of the necessity of conduct-

[1] Metternich, *Memories* (Eng. trans. 1880), II, 612.

[2] Bourgeois, *Manuel Historique de Politique étrangère*, II, chap. XX, writes most skilfully to convince his readers that Alexander only wanted to gain the support of France and to recover the prestige which he had lost during the conflict over the Saxo-Polish Question at Vienna.

ing their mutual relations according to the sublime truths of the Christian religion; and they solemnly declare that the present Act has no other object than to publish this fixed resolution in the face of the whole world. In article I the three sovereigns promise to consider each other as fellow-countrymen and to lend each other aid on all occasions; article II contains an earnest recommendation to their peoples to strengthen themselves daily in the principles and exercise of the duties which the Divine Saviour has taught to mankind; article III contains a general invitation to all the Powers to accede to the Declaration. France and most of the States of Europe gave their accession. The Prince Regent of Great Britain answered the invitation with cordial sympathy, but declined to accede on the ground that the British Constitution rendered him unable to do so. This was perfectly true; the Holy Alliance was a declaration of the nominal sovereigns of States and not of Governments. Had the invitation to sign been directed to the British Government, Lord Liverpool, the Prime Minister, might have had difficulty in refusing. Anyhow, Great Britain never did sign the Holy Alliance. It was engaged on something more definite.

This something definite was simply an Act of Alliance, for the mutual guaranteeing of the Settlement of 1815. The genesis of this famous treaty must be sought in an instrument negotiated just over a year previously. In the spring of 1814 Napoleon was making a wonderful defence against the Allied invaders; in February it looked as if the Austrian and Prussian armies would be separately defeated and thrown back across the Rhine. With the military failures, rifts began to appear in the political front of the Allies; and Metternich actually made overtures to Napoleon for a separate peace.[1] Lord Aberdeen, the British delegate at Châtillon (where conferences were going on with Caulaincourt, Napoleon's Foreign Minister), wrote to Lord Castlereagh at Chaumont (where the general military headquarters of the Allies were) on February 28 (1814):

> I cannot too often represent to you the real state of the minds of *those weak men* by whom Europe is governed. The seeming agreement at Langres [2] covered distrust and hate. A little success will cement them again; but, if they are to be severely tried in adversity, their dis-

---

[1] Sorel, *op. cit.* VIII, 289. The bearer of this secret mission from Metternich was Baron Esterhazy.

[2] Protocol of the Four Powers, signed at Langres, January 29, 1814.

solution is certain. *Your presence has done much, and I have no doubt would continue to support them in misfortune, but without it they could not exist.*[1]

Lord Castlereagh knew the danger. There was no general treaty of Alliance among the Powers, only a number of particular conventions between separate States, for instance the Treaty of Kalisch (February 28, 1813), between Russia and Prussia, the Treaty of Ried (October 8, 1813), between Austria and Bavaria, and various subsidy treaties between Great Britain and her co-belligerents. Castlereagh laboured incessantly to arrange a general treaty over and above these separate Acts; and on March 1, 1814, he was successful in concluding the Treaties of Chaumont. These consisted of three identical treaties, one concluded between Great Britain and Austria, the second between Great Britain and Prussia, the third between Great Britain and Russia. In each treaty the Contracting Parties agreed (1) to apply all their means to a vigorous prosecution of the war against Napoleon; (2) not to negotiate separately with the common enemy; (3) after the conclusion of peace, if France should begin war again and attack one of the Contracting Parties, to come to the assistance of the Party attacked, with 60,000 men. Moreover in the Treaties of Chaumont the Contracting Parties reserved to themselves "to concert together, on the conclusion of a peace with France, as to the means best adapted to guarantee to Europe, and to themselves reciprocally, the continuance of the peace"—that is to say, the agreement to supply 60,000 men in the case of a renewal of war by France was not to prejudice any wider system of guarantee which might be arranged at the final peace-conference.

When the wars were finally over, and the Second Peace of Paris had been made on November 20, 1815, the principles laid down in the Treaties of Chaumont were solemnly re-asserted by a Quadruple Alliance (also dated at Paris on November 20) between Great Britain, Russia, Austria, and Prussia. By this Act the Contracting Parties promised (1) to maintain the treaty signed that day with France; (2) to support any Party which should in the future be attacked by France, with 60,000 men; (3) "to renew their meetings at fixed periods, either under the immediate auspices of the sovereigns themselves, or by their respective ministers, for the purpose of con-

[1] *Castlereagh Correspondence* (1853), Third Series, I. 298.

sulting upon their common interests, and for the consideration of those measures which at each of those periods shall be considered the most salutary for the repose and prosperity of Nations, and for the maintenance of the Peace of Europe."

Notice how much more definite and business-like this document is than the Holy Alliance. The Holy Alliance was an expression of Christian sentiment, coupled with a vague promise on the part of the monarchs that "they will on all occasions and in all places lend each other aid and assistance." This declaration really committed the signing Parties to nothing at all, for there was no *casus fœderis*, there was no specific condition laid down, under which the assistance mentioned in article II could be claimed. At best the Holy Alliance was what is now called an Entente, an "understanding," not a contract under which one Party could exact the fulfilment of a definite pledge.

The Quadruple Alliance of November 20, 1815, was quite different from this. It was a definite contract with a specific condition, a *casus fœderis* according to which, if a certain eventuality occurred, any of the Contracting Parties could claim the support of 60,000 troops from each of the others. Secondly it contained a guarantee, not, be it noted, of all the multifarious provisions of the Congress of Vienna, but of one particular and limited Act, namely the Treaty of Peace with France signed at Paris on November 20, 1815. The Powers certainly thought it desirable that the execution of the Treaty of Vienna should be guaranteed too, but that would have been an endless task ; so this project was given up. But the treaty with France was the basic rule of the European system and must at all costs be maintained ; so to this limited and practicable extent, the Settlement of 1815 was guaranteed by treaty.[1] Thirdly, the Quadruple Alliance pledged the Contracting Parties to meet together, from time to time, and so began the salutary system known as the Concert of Europe.

It may, then, be claimed for Castlereagh's work on the conclusion of the Great War of 1792–1815 : (1) that it secured the execution of the settlement imposed by the victors in that war ; (2) that by its provision for a Concert it enabled a number of crises, which occurred afterwards, to be settled without fighting. In these two respects

[1] The Quadruple Alliance also contained a specific guarantee of the treaty of April 11, 1814, by which Napoleon and his family were for ever excluded from the throne of France.

Castlereagh's method compares quite favourably with that adopted by the Allied Powers at the end of the Great War of 1914–18, namely the Franco-British-American Treaty of Defensive Alliance of June 28, 1919, which never came into effect, and the Covenant of the League of Nations, which indeed provided for the emergency of a new war, but which, when a new war started in the summer of 1920, was unfortunately not invoked by the Powers. If, once more, the Settlement of 1815 be compared with that of 1919 in its effect upon the vanquished, the comparison is still more favourable; for in France in 1815 the Treaty of Peace was carried out to the letter, and within three years the conquered State had been rehabilitated and accepted as a regular working member of the European States-system.

CHAPTER IV

AIX-LA-CHAPELLE

France, in spite of the Allied Army of Occupation and in spite of indemnities, made a good recovery after 1815 ; so that Castlereagh was probably not surprised to receive news from Lord Clancarty (British Minister at The Hague) that the Austrian Government was suggesting a meeting of the Allies to take into consideration the state of France, and particularly to consider whether the Army of Occupation needed to be kept there any longer (June 5, 1818). About three weeks later his lordship received another dispatch, this time from Mr. Bagot, British Minister at Washington, referring to a conversation with the Secretary of State, Mr. Adams, who desired to know what attitude His Majesty's Government meant to adopt towards the question at issue between Spain and her revolting South American Colonies. In this question, in which, of course, the United States was profoundly interested, Mr. Adams wished to proceed *pari passu* with Great Britain (June 29). Castlereagh was sympathetic, though not enthusiastic. The ideas which Edward Cooke, Under-Secretary of State, put forward in a letter to his chief, may be taken as representing pretty accurately Castlereagh's views. Cooke writes that he would like to see " the admission of France to the Confederacy " (such are his actual words), and he would like also " equality of commercial privileges " with the South American countries. If this last condition were attained, he wrote, " something might follow "—meaning that somehow Spain and her colonies would come to an understanding (August 28, 1818).[1]

Metternich evidently hoped much from the meeting. He acknowledges the Tsar Alexander's fundamental principle of the maintenance of peace, but he greatly disliked his addiction to " moral and political proselytising . . . hence the deluge of emissaries and

[1] See *Castlereagh Correspondence*, Third Series, III, pp. 442, 445, 458, 472.

apostles."[1] At Paris the Russian ambassador Pozzo di Borgo seemed to have all the ear of the French Cabinet. In other countries, Austrian Italy for instance and Spain, there were Russian agents of the underground type, fishing in troubled waters. All this made the high Continental diplomats rather nervous—a condition against which Castlereagh once warned his brother Lord Stewart, and also Clancarty: "I wish that both you and he could borrow a dose of my indifference."[2]

Before the Congress of the Five Powers (the Four Powers of the Quadruple Alliance *and* France) met at Aix-la-Chapelle (which was the agreed place), the Four had arranged that all public questions except those directly relating to France should be excluded; the Congress was merely to liquidate the settlement of the Second Peace of Paris. By September 20 (1818) all the members had assembled at Aix: for Great Britain, Castlereagh (Secretary of State), Wellington (Commander-in-chief of the Allied Army of Occupation), and George Canning (whose official position was President of the Board of Control of India); for Russia, the Emperor Alexander, Capo d'Istria, and Nesselrode (a young but very experienced diplomatist, who had taken part in affairs of highest policy since the interviews at Tilsit and who had signed the Vienna Congress Act); for Austria, the Emperor Francis I and Metternich (with Gentz, as General Secretary of the Congress); for Prussia, King Frederick William, Hardenberg, and Bernstorff; for France, the Duc de Richelieu, with Rayneval the *directeur des chancelleries* at the French Foreign Office, and Mounier, the official in charge of the French indemnity questions.

The really important work that the Congress of Aix had before it was to arrange the evacuation of French territory by Allied troops. Under the terms of the Second Peace of Paris (November 20, 1815), France had to pay an indemnity of 700,000,000 francs, in fifteen equal instalments of 46,000,000 francs and two-thirds of a franc each. The first instalment was due on March 31, 1816, and so on, every four months for five years. When the Congress of Aix met, the French Government had discharged its obligations punctually up to date. The Duc de Richelieu now offered to clear off the rest of the indemnity, by paying a sum of 265,000,000 francs. Of this sum, 100,000,000 francs were to be in the form of French Rentes (Govern-

[1] Metternich: *Memoirs*, III, 163.
[2] *Castlereagh Correspondence*, III, 330.

ment Stock) inscribed in the Great Book of the Public Debt of France and bearing interest from September 22, 1818; the remaining 165,000,000 francs were to be paid in nine (subsequently changed to twelve) instalments through the agency of two English financial houses, Messrs. Hope and Messrs. Baring. The Allied Army of Occupation was to be withdrawn from French territory by November 30, the French Government continuing to provide for the pay, equipment, and clothing of the troops down to that date.

The financial result of the new indemnity-arrangement was as follows: till the meeting of the Congress France had paid off eight instalments of the indemnity, with a total of 368,000,000 francs. She was due still to pay 332,000,000 francs, so as to wipe off the complete indemnity of 700,000,000; but she had till November 30, 1820, to do so, without paying interest. Instead of this she offered immediately 100,000,000 francs of interest-bearing Rentes, and 165,000,000 francs in cash, payable within a year—a total of 265,000,000 (instead of the balance of 332,000,000 francs due under the Treaty of Paris). Moreover she secured the immediate evacuation of French territory, a concession which the Allies appear to have been glad to concede, as their troops were exposed to infection by Revolutionary principles.

This arrangement (financial and military) was embodied in a treaty signed at Aix-la-Chapelle, on October 9, 1818, between Great Britain, Austria, Russia, and Prussia on the one part, and France on the other. The treaty was followed by a Collective Note (November 4) addressed by the Four Powers to France, stating that "they regard this solemn act as the final completion of the General Peace"; and they ended by inviting His Most Christian Majesty "to unite henceforth his councils and his efforts" to those of the Four Allies in the interests of mankind and of France. This invitation was to take effect immediately, for the Allies, in the Note, specifically mentioned the Duc de Richelieu and invited him to take part in the deliberations of the present Congress. The terms of the Note were readily acceded to by the French.

Thus, before separating in November, the Four Powers in Congress had accomplished something very substantial: they had definitely liquidated the great wars of 1792–1815; had brought to an end all claims against France; and had admitted that country as an equal and full member of the Concert of Europe, which was now to consist not of the Four but of the Five Powers. It is true that (still distrusting France in their hearts) they had on November 1 secretly renewed among themselves the Quadruple Alliance of the Four Powers of Great Britain, Austria, Russia, and Prussia.[1] But this renewed Quadruple Alliance never was of any consequence; for France, formally and publicly admitted to the Concert, soon asserted her influence equally with the other Powers; while the Four drifted apart further and further every year, over the question of Italy, of South America, and of Greece.

[1] The Treaty of Chaumont of March 1, 1814, and the Treaty of Paris of November 20, 1815.

CHAPTER V

THE OLD WORLD AND THE NEW

Between 1818 and 1823 attempts seem seriously to have been made by Metternich to make the Holy Alliance a real thing, to make it a regular European Directory for keeping the States of Europe in a fixed political system. It is true there was no formal treaty to this effect: the Quadruple Alliance of November 20, 1815, only guaranteed the treaties of that year, but said nothing about the domestic Constitutions of the European States; and the British Government had always declared that it would have no part in interferences with the domestic affairs of any sovereign body. So Metternich had to trust to sentiment: "this great and noble brotherhood," he wrote to Nesselrode on August 20, 1817, "is of far more value than all the treaties, and will ensure for a considerable time what the good abbé de St. Pierre wished to establish for ever." [1] The plan of the Abbé de St. Pierre, a disciple of Descartes, for maintaining perpetual peace attracted attention when it was produced (1713), but it is more like the Covenant of the League of Nations than the text of the Holy Alliance.

Metternich's policy was frankly repressive. "I am inaccessible to fear," he writes in 1821; "I know no other than the fear lest I should mistake what is good and right. . . . For the first time for thirty years an evil will be publicly combatted which has been represented to weak humanity as the highest good. . . . History has perhaps never displayed such a pitiable crowd of small personages, who only busy themselves with follies. Heavens! how we shall all be abused when the day of reckoning comes—and that day will come. Then some worthy man, who among the hundred thousand pamphlets and in the grocers' shops discovers my name, will find perhaps in the year 2440 that in this far-distant time one being existed who was less wrong-headed than his contemporaries

[1] Metternich, *Memoirs*, III, 69–70.

who carried self-estimation so far as to believe themselves arrived at the culminating point of civilization." [1]

Metternich's complacency was ill-founded, for he failed to impose peace on the constitutionalists of Spain, France, or South America; he was scarcely successful among the German States, and even in Italy and Austria he saw his edifice crumbling at the end of his life. When, fleeing from the Revolution, of 1848 he found refuge in Brighton, he may at last have wondered whether a little timely concession to the spirit of the times might not have averted the volcanic outburst which all his life he had been trying, by force, to prevent.

He had got the Tsar on his side. That liberal potentate had maintained his generous sentiments for a time, and in February, 1818, had, in accordance with article 1 of the Treaty of Vienna, given Poland a constitution.[2] At the Congress of Aix-la-Chapelle, however, he had been anxious to engage the Powers to impose peace on the revolted Spanish-American Colonies; and at the same time had been impressed by a pamphlet on the condition of Germany written by Alexander Stourdza—a Roumanian whose memoir on the Greek Question had impressed the Tsar at the Congress of Vienna in 1815. Stourdza now represented Germany as hovering on the brink of revolution. There were other events which about the same time affected the Tsar's outlook. Just before the Congress of Aix there had been a meeting of German students at the Wartburg to celebrate the third centenary of the Reformation and the fourth anniversary of the battle of Leipsic. The meeting was rather inflammatory, and resulted in a bonfire being made of some of the text-books of absolutism (October, 1817). Next, on March 23, 1819, the eminent dramatist August Kotzebue was assassinated by Karl Sand at Mannheim. Kotzebue had been a kind of political literary agent of Alexander I; his business was to report to the Tsar on the condition of politics and public opinion in Germany. The sentimental autocrat began seriously to question the wisdom of his liberalism; and Metternich, with the subtle pen of Gentz to help him, was ever ready to aid the Tsar's conversion.

There was no doubt that Alexander was coming round to absolutism, but Prussia was causing the Austrian Chancellor some

[1] Metternich, *Memoirs*, II, 483, 485.

[2] Austria and Prussia had undertaken the same obligation with regard to their Polish subjects, but they did not fulfil it.

difficulty. Austria was the pre-eminent Power in Germany, but Prussia was a persistent, though passive, rival that could not be overlooked. Metternich acted boldly: he arranged a meeting with Frederick William at Teplitz (July 30, 1819), and threatened to withdraw Austria altogether from the Germanic Confederation; the king, faced with this prospect, agreed to fall into line: this was an anticipation of the submission at Olmütz, thirty-one years later.[1]

With the preliminaries thus settled, Metternich was able to get his policy put legally in force throughout most of the States of Germany. At Carlsbad in Bohemia, on August 7, 1819, there was opened a German Conference, including representatives of Austria, Prussia, Bavaria, Baden, Nassau, Wurtemburg, Mecklenburg, Hesse (Electoral), and Saxe-Weimar. The only opposition was from Winzigerode, the minister of Wurtemburg, whose sovereign had granted a constitution to his subjects. In spite of this, the Conference passed a series of decrees which became famous; one decree enacted that every university should have a Curator (to supervise the political aspect of its teaching), to be appointed by the sovereign in whose State the university was. All unauthorized student societies were to be dissolved. For the public Press a censorship was established. Most drastic of all, a Commission was set up at Mayence to inquire into the origin of revolutionary movements; its labours were to be retrospective, and the local States were to arrest, even on mere suspicion, all individuals designated by the Commission. The Decrees of Carlsbad were converted into Federal Laws by the Diet of Frankfort. The preposterous Commission of Mayence does not seem to have been particularly severe to individuals, nor to have discovered any dangerous conspiracies, although with true German thoroughness it had produced thirty-four volumes of reports by the end of the year 1822.

Having thus consolidated Germany behind him, on the side of repression, Metternich was ready for the next European Congress, which was to take place at Troppau, in Austrian Silesia, in the year 1820. This year was to be one of revolutions, which seemed to justify the complacent self-congratulations of the Chancellor on his pessimistic outlook. In Spain, an army had been for a year on the Isle of Leon at Cadiz, waiting for transport to take it to South America. On January 1, 1820, it mutinied, and demanded the "Constitution of the year 1812." On July 2 there were similar

[1] *See* below, pp. 90–92.

mutinies, in favour of a constitution, in the Kingdom of Naples, at Nola and Avellino. This was the most telling blow of all: "since I have known Prince Metternich, I have never seen him struck by any event as much as he was yesterday," writes Gentz. It was with political upheaval threatening the whole of Italy that the Congress of Troppau met on October 25, 1820.[1]

M. Bourgeois, the eminent author of the *Manuel historique de politique étrangère*, holds that the project of a European Congress was put forward at this time most insistently by the Tsar Alexander with the deliberate object of embroiling the European Powers with each other, and of making a general war by which Russia and France, acting together as allies, would effect the ruin of Austria: "it was less, particularly, against the Revolution, than against the peace, that the Powers at Troppau were going to conspire, on the interested demand of the Tsar Alexander."[2] No one can say that such a design was not possible to be conceived in the mind of that bizarre sentimentalist, Napoleon's "shifty Byzantine," the conspirator of Tilsit. Yet it is scarcely credible; a more likely scheme was to induce the Powers publicly to proclaim a police-system for Europe, under the direction of the Holy Alliance.[3] In any case, Metternich was clever enough to steer the Congress through the worst difficulties. Alexander was present with Capo d'Istria and Nesselrode; Francis I with Metternich, Gentz, Lebeltzern, and Mercy; Frederick William with Hardenberg and Bernstorff. The British Government sent no special delegate, but was represented by Lord Stewart (Castlereagh's brother), who was Ambassador at Vienna. France likewise (to the disgust of Alexander) sent only her ambassadors from Petersburg and Vienna—the Comte de la Ferronays (who was a friend of the Tsar) and the Marquis de Caraman, who had been an important diplomatist as far back as the reign of Louis XVI and was a great admirer of Metternich. The result of the Congress was that the Concert of Europe, as far as it included the Five Powers, was broken up; the English and French representatives would not join in any vote deciding the fate of an independent State. So Metternich, having Prussia firmly on his side, easily got his way against Alexander; he obtained a vote of

[1] It had been decided at Aix-la-Chapelle, in 1818, to hold another Congress for consideration of the affairs of Europe.
[2] Bourgeois, *Manuel*, II, 636.
[3] Debidour takes this view, *Hist. Dip.*, I, 148.

the Three Courts (the original signatories of the Holy Alliance) in favour of an Austrian intervention in Naples. In conclusion (on November 13, 1820) they drew up resolutions against any State which should permit innovations in its constitution dangerous to the tranquillity of its neighbours. The resolutions were circulated by Russia on December 8. Any State which, in consequence of a revolt, suffered any alteration in its interior régime, was to cease to be part of the *alliance européenne*; and if such constitutional alteration should prove dangerous to the State's neighbours, the Powers could take steps to set it right, first by friendly negotiations, and, failing in this, by force—*elles emploieront pour les ramener au sein de l'alliance, premièrement les démarches amicales, en second lieu, une force coercitive, si l'emploi de cette force devenait indispensable.* While giving due credit to the sincere desire of the monarchs of the Holy Alliance to prevent an outbreak of anarchy, of which there is always a real danger, one must admit that their system would have prevented any political progress at all, and would probably have in the long run provoked an appalling outbreak of this very anarchy. Castlereagh, in reply to the Tsar's circular, vigorously repudiated the principle of intervention.

The Congress at Troppau was followed by a short-lived but important Congress at Laibach, in the valley of the Save (January 8 to March 12, 1821). The Emperor of Austria was present with his Chancellor; the Tsar came too.[1] The centre of the stage was held by the old King Ferdinand I of Naples, who, having sworn to his subjects to be faithful to the new constitution, came nominally to mediate between them and the Powers, but really to invoke their aid in his breaking his word. The results were the annulling of the Neapolitan Constitution by the Congress (that is to say, by the Holy Alliance Powers—Austria, Prussia, and Russia), and a mandate given to Austria to "execute" this annulment with a military force. General Frémont's brief campaign was the result. Ferdinand I followed in the wake of the Austrian army, and so was restored to his absolute power, his spies and his proscriptions. Facts always seemed to be proving Metternich to be right. Before

[1] The Tsar was now practically completely absolutist, swayed by Metternich's arguments. Capo d'Istria, who was still one of his advisers, fought in vain against this tendency: "Capo d'Istria twists about like a devil in holy water; but he is in holy water, and can do nothing." Metternich, *Memoirs*, III, 480.

the Congress closed came an appeal from the King of Sardinia, to be saved from *his* revolutionary subjects. The Austrian troops had for long been massed in Lombardy for such eventualities. An expedition crossed the Ticino, scattered the revolutionaries in a brief fight at Novara (April 8), and occupied Turin. The Ancien Régime was restored in Piedmont. The Congress ended in May, after drafting a document for circulation among the Governments of Europe. This circular stated the objects of the European Alliance to be the maintenance of treaties, the general peace, and the happiness of nations; useful and necessary changes in the legislation and administration of States were to proceed only "from the free will, the reflective and enlightened impulsion of those whom God has rendered responsible for the power." France and England had no part in all this: "Austria," wrote Rayneval, "takes a large payment for the aid which she gives to the royal cause." Lord Stewart, the British delegate, wrote: "The first acts of Troppau framed an alliance between the Three Courts which placed them entirely in a new attitude from us, and they have now, I consider, hermetically sealed their treaty before Europe."[1]

Yet the Holy Alliance did not prosper. It might, even in the volcanic soil of Italy, suppress the forces of nature for a time, but the flames were bursting forth in a dozen other quarters of the world. While the Congress of Laibach was still in session, news came that General Alexander Ypsilanti (formerly in the Russian service) had crossed the Pruth into Moldavia and had started an insurrection against Turkey in favour of the independence of Greece. Spain was not exactly in revolution, but the mutineers had been successful, and had obtained from Ferdinand VII the concession of constitutional government; under this he now reigned at Madrid, with the help of the energetic Evaristo San Miguel,[2] one of the earliest of the "political generals" who were so prominent a feature in the history of Spain in the nineteenth century.

[1] Quoted by A. Phillips, *The Confederacy of Europe*, p. 232. Metternich's immediate object was to suppress "particularism" (the rights of small States) in Italy, as he had already done in Germany. "What we began together in July, 1819 [at Teplitz and Carlsbad] can be finished . . . in 1821." Metternich, *Memoirs*, III, 527.

[2] San Miguel was born in 1785 at Gijon on the coast of Northern Spain. He fought for his country against Napoleon; against the Duc d'Angoulême's army in 1823 (when he was wounded); against the Carlists; and died as a Marshal of Spain in 1862.

In the New World, South America was aflame with revolution against the mother-country, Spain. On July 9, 1816, the provinces of the Argentine, by the Convention of Tucuman, had established themselves as an independent Confederation. Dr. Joseph Francia had been Dictator of Paraguay since 1817—a position which he was to hold for the next twenty-three years. In Venezuela, Simon Bolivar, the "Liberator," had established a dictatorship in 1813; and by the victory of Boyaca (August 17, 1819) he had freed Colombia. Juan José San Martin, a Spanish regular officer born in La Plata, after contributing to free the Argentine, was now (1821) performing the same service for Peru. In Mexico General Augustin Yturbide first wrung from the Viceroy Juan O'Donogu the grant of autonomy (by the Treaty of Cordova, August, 1821), and then made himself Emperor (May, 1822).[1] In Brazil a similar change was taking place, although on rather more regular lines; John VI, the head of the House of Braganza, who had been in refuge at Rio since the conquest of Portugal by Napoleon, returned to Lisbon in 1821, leaving his son Pedro as regent in Brazil. Pedro became independent and made himself Emperor in May, 1822.

The Holy Alliance (or rather the Tsar, for neither Austria nor Prussia took much account of the New World) directed its eyes to Spain and her colonies. Curiously, while exercising an influence in favour of constitutionalism in Paris (through Pozzo di Borgo his ambassador), in Madrid (through his minister Boulgary) Alexander was in favour of reaction. He would have liked, indeed, to send a Russian army to Spain, to restore Ferdinand VII to absolutism, but Villèle would not hear of a suggestion for letting the Tsar's troops march through France.

The Comte de Villèle had become Premier of France on December 22, 1821, on the fall of the Duc de Richelieu. Villèle, like Richelieu, was a faithful servant of the Bourbon Monarchy, but rather less liberal. Under him France became more highly centralised: "the Restoration was the golden age of officials, who took possession of France on behalf of the Royalist party, and held it for long."[2] The elections to the Chamber were carefully controlled, and the Royalists, whom Villèle was politic enough to keep within certain bounds, were steadily extending their power. But France was

[1] Yturbide was the first Emperor of Mexico, and, like the second (the Archduke Maximilian forty years later) he was shot after a very precarious reign.

[2] Bourgeois, *Modern France*, I, 41.

beginning to erupt: first there was a meeting among the cadets at the military school of Saumur, in favour of Napoleon II, the Duke of Reichstadt, who was living in Austria. There were, about the same time, a number of other little "affairs" among the officers at Belfort, Neu Breisach, Strasbourg, and La Rochelle. The French Royalists became very afraid of the infection of Spain; and on the ground of protecting southern France from the yellow fever (though it was probably political contagion that was feared), the Government formed a "sanitary cordon" of troops along the departments near the Pyrenees. Soon military intervention in Spain began to be talked of. It was under these circumstances—revolutions in the Old World and the New, and the question of military intervention in both worlds being raised—that the third [1] of the great series of Congresses met at Verona, in the middle of October, 1822.

To this momentous assembly came the Emperor of Austria, the Tsar of Russia, the Kings of Prussia, Sardinia, and Naples, along with the Grand Duke of Tuscany, the Duchess of Parma, and the Duke of Modena. There was a numerous body of high diplomatists, of whom Metternich was the chief. The head of the French delegation was the Duc de Montmorency (Minister for Foreign Affairs), whose active life went back to the American War of Independence, in which he had taken part, and to the States General of 1789, of which he had been a member. With Montmorency was associated the Vicomte de Chateaubriand, the eloquent author of the *Génie du Christianisme*, and now French ambassador at London. The chief English delegates were the Duke of Wellington and the Marquis of Londonderry, better known as Lord Stewart, the younger brother of Castlereagh. Castlereagh, who himself had only lately succeeded to the Marquisate, had been appointed the first British delegate, but when almost on the eve of starting for Verona, had committed suicide (August 12, 1822). His successor at the Foreign Office, George Canning, stayed at home. He had no liking for the policy of Metternich.

The Congress took into consideration two grand problems of the European situation—the problems of Spain and Italy. Montmorency threw caution to the winds; declared that France could not endure the anarchy of Spain; and proclaimed that France

[1] Aix-la-Chapelle, September, 1818; Troppau, October, 1820. The meeting at Laibach in January, 1821, may be counted as the completion of the Congress of Troppau.

would take military action beyond the Pyrenees. Chateaubriand vied with the Duc in bellicose propositions; his poetic imagination had conceived the plan not merely of "pacifying" Spain in the Royalist interest, but of pacifying the revolted Spanish colonies, and making them into a confederation of States ruled over by Bourbon princes. Austria, Russia, and Prussia supported the French proposals, and on November 19 sent an ultimatum to the Spanish Cortes, which led to the withdrawal of the Powers' ambassadors from Madrid. Alone England stood aside, and through Wellington declared that the British Government would not countenance intervention.

In the excitement caused by the debates on Spain, the affairs of Italy fared lightly. It was indeed proposed by Metternich to establish a Commission at Piacenza, like the famous Commission of Mayence, to bring revolutionary plots to light. The design was defeated by the opposition of the Papal delegate, Cardinal Spina, who in memorable words drew the attention of the Congress to "the number of those who hate Austria, and groan at the slavery in which she holds Italy." So much for the Italian question: the Greek problem was mentioned, but scarcely discussed: in truth the Holy Alliance dared not touch it, for to Metternich the Greeks were rebels against legitimate authority, while to Alexander they were co-religionists struggling for their lives. So the Greek mission never got nearer to the Congress than Ancona.[1] The Congress came to an end on December 14 (1822).

And now we come to the crucial year 1823, when a great drama was played on both sides of the Atlantic, which put an end to the Directory of Europe. M. de Villèle, the prudent French premier, had his hand forced by Chateaubriand, who had succeeded Montmorency as Minister for Foreign Affairs at the beginning of the year. On January 28, Louis XVIII declared war on the Spanish Cortes. Chateaubriand was filled with joy. "We are now," he wrote to the French Ambassador in London, "liberated from the tutelage of misfortune, and have regained our military rank in Europe."[2] In March a French army invaded Spain under the supreme command of the Duc d'Angoulême, nephew of Louis XVIII. On May 24, they occupied Madrid, and on August 31 the

[1] Its leader was Andrew Metaxas, who was one of the most prominent Greek statesmen (somewhat in the Russian interest) till his death in 1860.

[2] Quoted in Bourgeois, *Modern France*, I, 56.

Duc dictated terms to the Cortes (which had retired to Cadiz, taking the King with them) by the Treaty of the Trocadero (August 31, 1823). The Cortes surrendered the King unconditionally, and he returned to his capital where, with the support of French bayonets, he re-established his absolute power.

When the victorious French generals returned with their troops to Paris, the Bourbons experienced some brief moments of glorious popularity. But both France and Spain ultimately paid dearly for the war and for the Treaty of the Trocadero. Had Ferdinand VII remained faithful to the Constitution of 1812, it is unlikely that Spain would have gone through those forty years of Carlist Wars and *pronunciamentos* which compose her unhappy history between 1830 and 1870; nor would France, possibly, have been troubled by the "Hohenzollern Candidature," which, at the end of this disturbed period in Spain, was the proximate cause of the Franco-Prussian War.

France had invaded Spain on her own authority, and was proud of it. Metternich was indifferent: "the war and the victories of the French in Spain," he wrote to Gentz, "do not cause me much uneasiness. They will not bring on the general war."[1] The invasion of Spain, in fact, was useful to the Austrian Chancellor, in diverting French sympathy and French support from the Greek insurgents. But some one in France was looking further afield than Spain. Chateaubriand was dreaming of extending his system to South America; and perhaps the Tsar Alexander, who had for years himself contemplated enforcing peace there, would have helped him. There was one man, however, determined to keep the New World free and independent, open to European commerce, but not to European armed intervention. This man was George Canning. He had played a grand part in the middle period of the Napoleonic Wars, but after fighting a duel with Castlereagh in 1809, had been lost to the Foreign Office until his great rival's death in 1822. Now, in the last stage of his brilliant career, Canning was to display his greatest talent.

Foreseeing French designs in South America, Canning held out his hand to the young but powerful North American Republic. The memory of the war of 1812–14 still rankled in the United States, and some difficult questions involved in that war were even yet unsettled. The relations between England and the United

[1] Quoted in Bourgeois, *Manuel*, II, 694.

States were nevertheless improving. The English minister at Washington, Stratford Canning, was one of the finest diplomatists of the nineteenth century, and of all times; and between him and Mr. Adams, the American Secretary of State, difficulties began to melt. In London the American minister, Mr. Rush, proved equally earnest in efforts to bring the two Anglo-Saxon nations together.

On August 3, 1823, while the French army was still in Spain, Canning in a dispatch to the American Secretary of State suggested that the United States might act in concert with Great Britain in checking the designs of France in the New World. The answer of the United States Government was the sending of a Message by President Monroe to Congress, on December 2, 1823. This Message —which is the text of the famous "Monroe Doctrine—" ran as follows:

It was stated at the commencement of the last Session, that a great effort was then making in Spain and Portugal to improve the condition of the people of those countries; and that it appeared to be conducted with extraordinary moderation. It need scarcely be remarked, that the result has been, so far, very different from what was then anticipated. Of events in that quarter of the globe with which we have so much intercourse, and from which we derive our origin, we have always been anxious and interested spectators. The Citizens of the United States cherish sentiments the most friendly, in favour of the liberty and happiness of their fellow-men on that side of the Atlantic. In the Wars of the European Powers, in matters relating to themselves, we have never taken any part, nor does it comport with our policy so to do. It is only when our rights are invaded, or seriously menaced, that we resent injuries, or make preparation for our defence. With the movements in this Hemisphere, we are of necessity more immediately connected, and by causes which must be obvious to all enlightened and impartial observers. The Political System of the Allied Powers is essentially different in this respect from that of America. The difference proceeds from that which exists in their respective Governments. And to the defence of our own, which has been achieved by the loss of so much blood and treasure, and matured by the wisdom of their (sic) most enlightened citizens and under which we have enjoyed unexampled felicity, this whole nation is devoted. We owe it therefore to candour, and to the amicable relations existing between the United States and those Powers, to declare, that we should consider any attempt, on their part, to extend their system to any portion of this Hemisphere, as dangerous to our peace and safety. With the existing Colonies or Dependencies of any European Power, we have not interfered, and shall not interfere. But with the Governments who have declared their Independence, and maintained it, and whose Independence we have, on great consideration, and on just principles, acknowledged, we could not view any interposition, for the purpose of oppressing them, or controlling, in any manner, their destiny, by any European Power, in any other light than as the manifestation of an unfriendly disposition towards the United States. In the War between those new Governments and Spain, we declared our neutrality at the time of their recognition, and to this we have adhered, and shall continue to adhere, provided no change shall occur, which in the judgment of the competent Authorities of this Government shall make a corresponding change on the part of the United States indispensable to their security. . . .

In regard to these Continents, circumstances are eminently and conspicuously different [from Europe]. It is impossible that the Allied Powers should extend their political system, to any portion of either Continent, without endangering our peace and happiness.[1]

In effect, the Message declared: (1) that the United States had no interest in, and would not interfere with, the politics of Europe; (2) that it demanded a similar detachment, on the part of the States of Europe, from the politics of the New World—in fact that the United States would fight any Power which tried to impose or extend its political control in America; (3) that the United States would not interfere with the existing colonies or dependencies of European Powers. This latter part of the Message was not inconsistent with the recognition which the Washington Government had extended to the Spanish colonies. These, having detached themselves from the mother-country, and having made themselves into Republics, had been recognised as sovereign States by President Monroe's Government in April, 1822.

The Monroe Doctrine is one of the controlling facts of the modern world's history. What is not generally known is that it was issued with the approval of the British Government, and indeed was perhaps first suggested by Great Britain. It is almost certain that if France had accepted the challenge and had sent her navy to take troops to aid the Spanish forces in America, the British fleet would have supported the United States in repelling them. In fact, Great Britain, as a wide-spread empire, depending on sea-communications, is just as interested as is the United States in keeping America clear of foreign dominion. For these reasons an American writer has declared that the Monroe doctrine has always rested "upon the broad back of the British Navy." [2]

[1] *State Papers*, 1824 (vol. XI), p. 4.

[2] Owen Wister: *A Straight Deal, or the Ancient Grudge* (London, 1920), p. 115.

Canning obtained what he wanted. The Constitutional cause had been lost in Spain, but it was gained in South America. On October 17 (about six weeks before the delivery of the Monroe Message) the British Government had sent consuls to the chief cities of Latin America. The dwindling Spanish forces steadily lost what little grip they possessed in South America; on December 8, 1824, they fought their last battle, and lost it, at Ayacucho in Peru. On February 2, 1825, Great Britain made a regular treaty of amity, commerce, and navigation, with the Argentine Confederation, thus recognising its complete independence.[1] Simultaneously Canning was setting the seal to the independence of Brazil. Queen Carlota, the strong-minded and somewhat intriguing wife of John VI of Portugal, would not acquiesce in the separation of Brazil under her eldest son, the Emperor Pedro.[2] Along with her second son Don Miguel—whose influence later in Portugal was almost fatal to that country—she tried to get the old and easy-going John VI to abdicate, so that she would have a free hand. The enterprising French minister at Lisbon, Baron Hyde de Neuville, seized the occasion to establish the influence of France in place of that of Portugal's ancient ally, England. He worked hard to get the dispute referred to the French Government for settlement, and he even offered to John VI to bring French troops from Spain (where there were still some French garrisons) into Portugal. Canning heard of this and at once took action. He was well versed in Portuguese affairs, having once himself been British envoy at Lisbon (1814–1816). Now he threatened to withdraw British support from Portugal; and he put forward the principle of non-intervention to Villèle, who was trying to moderate the energy of his romantic Foreign Minister Chateaubriand. Villèle recalled Hyde de Neuville (December, 1824); so no French troops went to Lisbon and consequently none (as Chateaubriand had really intended they should do) to Brazil.

The interventionist policy of the Holy Alliance, just when it seemed to be establishing itself as a hard fact in Europe, broke down over the Spanish-American and Brazilian questions. With pardonable pride Canning could declare in the House of Commons:

> If France occupied Spain, was it necessary, in order to avoid the consequences of that occupation, that we should blockade Cadiz? No, I

---

[1] Treaty of Rio de la Plata, February 2, 1825 (Foreign Office 93, No. 3–1). It is printed in Hertslet, *Commercial Treaties*, III, 44.

[2] *See* above, p. 38.

looked another way; I sought materials of compensation in another hemisphere. Contemplating Spain, such as our ancestors had known her, I resolved that if France had Spain, it should not be Spain "*with the Indies.*" I called the new world into existence to redress the balance of the old.[1]

---

[1] Canning, *Speeches* (ed. Therry), vol. VI, p. 111. *Address on the King's Message*, December 12, 1826.

CHAPTER VI

THE INDEPENDENCE OF GREECE

The area situated between the Danube and the Ægean, and generally known as the Balkans, became an important factor in diplomatic affairs quite early in the nineteenth century. The Serbians under Milosh Obrenovitch gained autonomy in 1815; Greece had a similar aspiration, and her cause was mentioned at the Congress of Vienna by the Tsar Alexander and Capo d'Istria; but the question was put aside, for the Powers were divided, Austria wishing to guarantee Turkish integrity, and Alexander, naturally, opposing this policy.

Six years later the storm broke. On March 6, 1821, Prince Alexander Ypsilanti, a Greek in Russian service, crossed the Pruth and tried to raise a rebellion against the Turk in Moldavia and Wallachia. He met with some success, but was ultimately forced to flee across the Transylvanian frontier. Metternich (who in any case had no love for the Greek cause) maintained strict neutrality, and kept Ypsilanti interned at Munkacz till 1827: he died at Vienna in 1828.

The raid into Roumania aroused the ardour of the Greeks nearer home; and insurrections broke forth in the Peloponnese and in the Islands. The Turkish Government was in difficulties at this time owing to a war with Persia, and owing to the rebellion of Ali Pasha of Joánnina.[1] The Tsar Alexander of Russia was for many reasons in favour of the Greeks, but on the other hand he was involved in the toils of the Holy Alliance which he had himself created. So the Congresses of Troppau and Verona took no action in the affairs of Greece. Many volunteers gave their services—Santa Rosa and Collegno, the authors of the Revolution of 1821 in

[1] The Persian War was not concluded till July 28, 1823, by the Treaty of Erzerum (Martens, *Nouveau Recueil*, t. VI, partie I, p. 282). Ali was killed on February 5, 1822.

Piedmont, Colonel Fabvier, an exiled opponent of the Restoration Monarchy in France, Lord Byron, Lord Cochrane, Sir Richard Church from England, and many others; but the European Governments would take no part.

From 1821 to 1825 the Greeks, acting by themselves, were fairly successful. In 1822 they drafted a constitution with a President (Alexander Mavrokordátos) and a Legislative Assembly. Greek Committees were formed in Geneva, Paris, and London; and public opinion, which, largely owing to the influence of scholars, was already in favour of Greece, was encouraged in every way. The highly educated people of Paris, especially the growing, though repressed, Liberal party, were strongly Hellenic in sentiment; the Marquis de Noailles actually pressed for a "Crusade" against Mussulmans. In England, all the statesmen, both Tory and Whig, had been educated in the classical tradition at Eton, Harrow, or Westminster, and at the two ancient Universities. Foreign policy, like everything else in government, is keenly susceptible to the influence of public opinion; and it gradually became obvious that public opinion would force France and England to take action in the Greek question, even if the Russian Government, which had for a century been always either at war, or on the point of war, with Turkey, did not do so. Public opinion in Western Europe became more aroused than ever when the Sultan Mahmoud II summoned the troops of his powerful Egyptian Pasha, Mehemet Ali, to help him. In February, 1825, the Egyptian troops under Mehemet's son Ibrahim landed in the Morea, and the war became more terrible than ever, and the Greek cause grew desperate. George Canning, however, maintained the neutrality of England, though by diplomatic action he hoped to accomplish something substantial for Greece. The situation about the same time became a little clearer owing to the death of the vacillating Tsar Alexander I on December 1, 1825. He was succeeded by his younger brother, Nicholas I.

Nicholas was young and martial. Moreover, all the traditions of Russian foreign policy prompted him to support the Greeks. In addition, there was a standing cause of friction between Russia and Turkey, inasmuch as the Porte had not executed article 5 of the Treaty of Bucharest (May 28, 1812), which stipulated that all Turkish troops should evacuate Moldavia.

Now George Canning was a firm upholder of the "Pitt tradition," which included the maintenance of the integrity of Turkey. At the same time he strongly sympathised with the Greeks in their struggle for freedom. So he had to do two things, each very difficult to accomplish, because they were almost incompatible with each other. He had to engage Russia to join with England in promoting Greek freedom; at the same time he had to prevent her from doing so by the obvious method of war.

The agent whom he chose to carry out the negotiations for putting this very difficult policy into effect was the Duke of Wellington. The Duke was a strong Tory, and had no particular sympathy with rebels, even when those rebels were the descendants of the heroes of Thermopylæ and Salamis. But he had one object in life, to do his duty; and so when Canning asked him to accept the Petersburg Mission, he did so and carried it out to the best of his ability.

Canning could not have made a better choice. The Duke—a great nobleman, a disciplinarian, the most famous living soldier—naturally appealed to the autocratic martinet of Russia. He arrived at Petersburg on February 26, 1826. Relations between Russia and Turkey were extremely strained, and the Tsar's ambassador had been withdrawn from Constantinople. An ultimatum was on the point of being sent to the Porte; in fact, Count Nesselrode, the Russian Chancellor, tried to get rid of the unwelcome visitor by saying that the ultimatum had already gone.[1] The Duke, however, maintained his point; and when he met the Tsar pointed out to him the disadvantage of war—for instance, that the Porte might stir up trouble among the Tsar's Mohammedan subjects. Nicholas seemed to agree. At the next interview he told Wellington that he was ready to act with England in order to prevent a Russo-Turkish War. Accordingly a protocol was drafted and signed at the Russian capital by Count Nesselrode, Prince Lieven (Russian ambassador to London), and Wellington (April 4, 1826). This document stated that mediation should be offered to the Porte [the Greeks on their part had already asked for mediation]; and if the Porte accepted this, the two Powers—Great Britain and Russia—should bring about some arrangement on the lines of Greece becoming autonomous but paying tribute to the Sultan (article 1). Even if the Porte did not accept the mediation, the system of autonomy *plus* tribute was to remain the basis of any future arrangement which the two Powers might make on the

[1] The ultimatum was sent on March 17, 1826, but it allowed six weeks for the Turks to consider it.

Greek question (article 3). The protocol was to be communicated to the Courts of Paris, Vienna, and Berlin ; and they were to be invited to guarantee along with Russia the treaty which should reconcile the Greeks and Turks (article 6).[1]

When the Protocol of Petersburg was signed, Wellington and Nicholas parted good friends. The document was duly sent to the Courts of the Great Powers, but gained no support except in Paris ; and on July 6, 1827, it was converted into a formal treaty, at London, between Great Britain, France, and Russia. It was further agreed in the treaty that if the Porte refused the mediation, the Powers would accredit consular agents to Greece—and would also, as far as possible, prevent collisions between the two belligerents, "without, however, taking any part in the hostilities." Instructions in conformity with these arrangements were to be sent to the Admirals commanding the squadrons of the High Contracting Parties in the Levant (additional article 2).

The Treaty of London was Canning's last important work. He had become Prime Minister in April, 1827, on Lord Liverpool's illness and resignation. He died on August 8, 1827. Lord Goderich became Prime Minister and Lord Dudley Foreign Secretary.

Events now began to move fast ; and indeed something had to happen if Greece was to survive. On April 22, 1826, Missolonghi had been taken by Ibrahim, after the garrison had made a heroic attempt to cut its way through the Turkish lines. On June 5, 1827, the Akropolis of Athens, defended by Colonel Fabvier, had to capitulate. Stratford Canning was now at Constantinople as British ambassador, labouring to induce the Porte to accept the Three Powers' offer of mediation. On his way out he had discussed the question with Mavrokordátos at Hydra. With the Turks, however, his task was more difficult, as their arms were now victorious. During the siege of the Akropolis, Stratford Canning gained from the Sultan Mahmoud II a decree forbidding bombardment of the ancient monuments ; but he could not get the Porte to accept mediation. With the surrender of the Akropolis, practically the whole of continental Greece was subdued. It was just a month after this that the treaty of July 6 was signed by the Three Powers.

[1] England was not to be asked, "as His Britannic Majesty cannot guarantee such a Treaty." I cannot understand why Wellington inserted this in the Protocol, except that if "guarantees" were not mentioned in his instructions, he would have nothing to do with them.

The united squadrons of Great Britain, France, and Russia, acting under the command of Admiral Sir Edward Codrington, blockaded Navarino Bay, where the Turkish Fleet was. The effect of the Allied blockade was that the Greek cause, which was quite lost on the Continent, survived in the islands. Continental Greece suffered in the usual way: more particularly the villages around Navarino Bay were being devastated under the very eyes of the Allied Squadrons. On October 20, Codrington gave orders for the ships to sail into the bay. His object was to parley with the Turkish command, in order to induce it to put an end to the ravaging; but both sides really expected that the result would be a fight. The first shot came from the Turkish side, and a regular battle ensued, in which twenty-nine Turkish ships were sunk. "Never since Lepanto had the Turkish empire experienced such a naval disaster." [1]

In spite of the battle of Navarino, Great Britain adhered to her "neutrality." The King's Speech (which was given by commission, January 29, 1828), contained the following curious passage (no doubt, the composition of Wellington):

> Notwithstanding the valour displayed by the Combined Fleet, His Majesty deeply laments that this conflict should have occurred with the Naval Force of an Ancient Ally; but he still entertains a confident hope that this untoward event will not be followed by further hostilities, and will not impede an amicable adjustment of the existing differences between the Porte and the Greeks.[2]

Lord Goderich's Ministry had fallen with the news of Navarino, and Wellington was now Prime Minister. The only use he would make of the battle was to induce Mehemet Ali to sign a Convention at Alexandria for withdrawing the Egyptian army from the Morea—a convention which was not actually made till August 6, 1829. Before this arrangement could be carried into effect the French Government sent General Maison with 14,000 men to the Morea, and the Turkish and Egyptian forces evacuated it almost without a blow.

It was the Russians, however, who were to bring the Greek War of Independence to a close. For years there had been friction between them and the Porte over the execution of the Treaty of Bucharest. It was in consequence of this that war had nearly broken out in

[1] Miller, *The Ottoman Empire* (1913), p. 98.
[2] Hansard: XVIII, p. 3.

1826. George Canning and the Duke of Wellington, to avoid a single-handed war of Russia with Turkey, had made the Protocol of Petersburg (see above); and following upon this, Russia made the Treaty of Akerman (October 7, 1826) with Turkey. This confirmed the Treaty of Bucharest, and more specifically secured the privileges of the Danubian Principalities and of Serbia.

So, if Mahmoud II had only behaved with restraint after the Battle of Navarino (which, it must be allowed, *was* rather provoking) he would have avoided further war with Russia, and would have received from the Three Powers (Great Britain, France, and Russia) the "London Terms"—that is, Greece, autonomous, but tributary. Instead of behaving in this way, he thought to take advantage of a war which then broke out (1826) between Russia and Persia, to refuse to accede to the London terms. There is no doubt that Mahmoud was inspired, not merely by a natural, if unstatesmanlike, indignation at the armed action of the Powers, but also by the veiled, though quite perceptible, opposition of Metternich to them. The Russo-Persian war, however, terminated in the usual way, and by the Treaty of Tourkmanchai (February 22, 1828) Persia ceded the provinces of Erivan and Nakhitchevan. Mahmoud became more furious than ever. He had already repudiated the Treaty of Akerman. But Nicholas was now ready to act. On April 26, 1828, he declared war upon Turkey.

The campaign of 1828 was not a great success for the Russians. That of 1829 went better, and on August 20 General Diebitsch led his army into Adrianople. The road to Constantinople was thus opened; Diebitsch advanced and occupied a line, which nearly a century later was to come into great prominence in diplomacy, the line Enos-Midia.[1] The Turks gave themselves up for lost: even Stratford Canning does not seem to have suspected that Diebitsch was really at the end of his resources, and that the Russians would have had to retreat in face of a firm resistance. General von Müffling, Prussian representative at Constantinople—noted as a soldier, and later as a statesman and historian—threw his influence on the side of peace; and on September 14, 1829, the Treaty of Adrianople was signed—one of the most costly pacts in the long-drawn-out tale of losses of Turkey in the nineteenth century.[2]

[1] *See* Moltke: *Der russisch-türkische Feldzug.*

[2] It gave Russia all the Delta of the Danube; Poti on the Black Sea; and Akhaltsykh in the Caucasus, through which runs an important road.

The Danubian principalities—Wallachia and Moldavia—were made practically independent of Turkey. They were to elect their own Hospodars (or Princes), who were to hold office for life. Tribute was to be paid on the death of a Hospodar. Article 10 of the treaty freed Greece likewise; the Sublime Porte declared its adhesion to the London Treaty (July 6, 1827)—making Greece autonomous but tributary—and also to a consequential Protocol of the Three Powers (March 22, 1829) defining the boundaries of Greece. Besides losing Greece, the Turks lost the Delta of the Danube, ceded to Russia (article III).

The Greeks were now quite safe. The Egyptian army had left the Morea; Turkish military power had suffered in the Russian war; and Turkish prestige had been ruined by the Treaty of Adrianople. So, although that treaty had only secured for the Greeks the "London Terms"—autonomy *plus* tribute—they now refused to accept these. The Conference, which had been meeting for months intermittently at London, resumed its sittings. Lord Aberdeen, the Foreign Secretary, Prince Lieven, the Russian ambassador, and M. Montmorency-Laval, the French ambassador, were the members of this Conference. The English view was now in favour of going beyond the London terms; for Turkey was believed to be without any power of resistance, so that a vassal-state of Greece would merely provide opportunities for Russia to interfere, as she did in the vassal-states of Wallachia and Moldavia. On February 3, 1830, the three statesmen "at the close of a long and difficult negotiation," as they stated in the document, signed a protocol securing independence to Greece. Her territory was to consist of Eubœa, the Devil's Islands, Skyros, and the Cyclades. On the Continent the new State was to include the Morea, and to the north of the Gulf of Corinth all land from the mouth of the Spercheios to the mouth of the Aspropotamos. The sovereignty was to be confided to a prince who should not be a member of the reigning families of the Three Powers. No troops of any one of the Three Powers were to enter the new State without the consent of the other two Powers [1] (article 8).

[1] This is the *legal* justification of the occupation of Salonica by Great Britain, France, and Russia in 1915. The essential terms of the Protocol are mainly omitted in the brief extract given in Hertslet, vol. II, No. 149. The full text must be found in *State Papers*, XVII, p. 191, and Oakes and Mowat, *Great Treaties*, p. 120.

On February 11, 1830, the newly created throne was offered to Prince Leopold of Saxe-Coburg, who accepted it, but renounced it a few weeks later. Capo d'Istria, who had been President of Greece since 1827, is said to have influenced him to change his mind. On October 9, 1831, Capo d'Istria was assassinated outside the Church of St. Spirídon at Nauplia by Constantine and George Mavromichális. Civil war ensued. In February, 1832, the Three Powers offered the crown to Prince Otto, the second son of the Phil-Hellene King of Bavaria. On May 7, 1832, a treaty was signed at London between the Three Powers and Bavaria, regulating the Bavarian succession, giving Greece the islands specified in the Protocol of February 3, 1830, but a more extended land frontier, namely from the Gulf of Volo on the east to the Gulf of Arta on the west. This extension gave Akarnania, with the exception of Fort Punta, which Turkey retained till 1912, to the new State.[1]

[1] These arrangements were accepted by Turkey, by a convention signed at Constantinople on July 21, 1832. *See* Hertslet, No. 161.

CHAPTER VII

EAST AND WEST

There was no definite Eastern Question facing Europe before the year 1830, although it had been partially raised in the time of Pitt and Napoleon, and also during the Greek War of Independence. Broadly defined, the Eastern Question is: What to do with Turkey? Guizot, in a speech in the Chambre de Députés on July 2, 1839, answered the Question as follows: The proper policy is "to maintain the Ottoman Empire in order to maintain the European equilibrium; and when, by the force of circumstances, by the natural course of events, some dismemberment takes place, when some province detaches itself from that decadent Empire, the right policy is to favour the transformation of that province into a new and independent sovereignty, to take a place in the family of States, and to serve one day in the new European equilibrium, the equilibrium destined to replace that of the ancient elements when they are no longer in existence."[1] This is the best explanation of the Eastern Question; and tested by it, the policy of British and French statesmen in the last hundred years becomes intelligible and sound.

From the French point of view, the Eastern Question had both a general and a particular aspect. The general aspect of the Question was that given above, in the words of Guizot, and was currently described as the Question of Constantinople. The particular aspect was concerned with the portion of the Ottoman Empire which was known as Egypt (for the Mediterranean and the coast of Northern Africa were felt to be vital French interests). This was called the Question of Alexandria. Between the years 1830 and 1840 the complete Eastern Question (Constantinople and Alexandria) became sharply defined, and vitally influenced the mutual relations of the Five Great Powers. It produced too the memorable crisis of

[1] Guizot: *Mémoires pour servir à l'histoire de mon temps* (1861), IV, pp. 330–1.

1839–40, when a European War, with France on one side and England on the other, was avoided by a hair's breadth.

The contemporary ruler of Turkey was Mahmoud II (1808–1839), who was, in his own way, a reformer and a strong-willed man. But he had a stronger man among his subjects, Mehemet Ali, a former Albanian tobacco-dealer, and Colonel in the Turkish Army, who had risen to be Pasha (or Governor) of Egypt. During the Greek War of Independence, the Sultan had had to appeal to his vassal for help; Mehemet's forces had nearly reconquered the rebel Greeks, and, indeed, but for the intervention of the Powers, would have done so. After the Greek War was over Mehemet, although he had been given Crete to rule, thought he had been rather badly paid for his efforts by the Sultan. He meant at least to become independent.

> Mehemet Ali could contemplate with self-complacency the condition of Egypt as compared with that of the Turkish empire. A French officer had organized his army; a French constructor had rebuilt his fleet; a French doctor had taught his physicians; he was the sole landowner, the sole manufacturer, the sole contractor in the country, where human lives were reckoned of as little account as in the time of the Pharaohs.[1]

Mehemet easily found a cause for war with the Porte, and in 1832 his son Ibrahim invaded Syria, and advanced right into Asia Minor. On December 21, the Turkish army was defeated and its leader taken prisoner at Konieh. The way to Constantinople itself was now open.

Mahmoud II had a passionate hatred of his over-mighty subject, and once said he would give Constantinople and the Empire if some one would bring him Mehemet Ali's head. After vainly appealing to England,[2] he resolved on a momentous step—almost equivalent to losing Constantinople and the Empire—rather than make terms with Mehemet. He invited the armed support of Russia. Nicholas I accepted with alacrity. In February, 1833, a Russian squadron entered the Bosphorus; a Russian army encamped on the Asiatic shore; and shortly afterwards 5,000 Russian troops were landed at Buyukdere, on the European side, close to Constantinople.

[1] Miller: *The Ottoman Empire*, p. 145.

[2] Mahmoud personally asked Stratford Canning to arrange an alliance with England. "Direct proposals to form an alliance have recently been made to me, first by the Reis Effendi, and, subsequently, by the Sultan himself. . . . Their immediate object is the submission of the Pasha of Egypt." F.O., Turkey, August 9, 1832.

Then ensued, in and around the oft-contested arena of the Sublime Porte, a diplomatic struggle in which the Russian Embassy easily won. For a time, indeed, things appeared to go sufficiently well with all the Powers. The show of Russian force, and the representatives of the European Chancelleries and of the Foreign Office, induced Mehemet Ali to be reasonable; and in the spring of 1833, he made peace with the Sultan, on condition of receiving the Governorship of Syria and Adana, as well as being "restored" to the hereditary Governorship of Egypt.[1]

Still, the Russian troops and ships did not depart; and the splendour of their leader, Prince Orloff, who conducted himself almost with something of the style of a grand viceroy, disquieted the Western ambassadors a little. At last the Russians departed early in July, but almost immediately it began to be suspected that they had not left empty-handed.

These suspicions were justified. On July 8, 1833, just before his departure, Orloff had signed with the Reis Effendi and the Seraskier Pasha a treaty of alliance, at the palace of Unkiar Skelessi, on the Asiatic side of the Bosphorus.

The treaty had both a patent text and a secret article, although neither the patent nor the secret articles were officially communicated to the British Foreign Office till over seven months had passed.[2] The patent treaty was bad enough, from the point of view of the Western Powers; it contained a mutually defensive alliance between Russia and Turkey, to endure for eight years. But the secret article was far worse: it ran:

> H.M. the Emperor of All the Russias, wishing to spare the Sublime Ottoman Porte the expense and inconvenience which might be occasioned to it by affording substantial aid, will not ask for that aid if circumstances should place the Sublime Porte under the obligation of furnishing it; the Sublime Ottoman Porte, in place of the aid which it is bound to furnish in case of need, according to the principle of reciprocity of the patent treaty, shall confine its action in favour of the Imperial Court of Russia to closing the Strait of the Dardanelles, that is to say, to not allowing any Foreign Vessels of War to enter therein under any pretext whatsoever.[3]

[1] The Settlement is sometimes referred to as the Convention of Kutayeh. I cannot, however, find any specific Convention. The Sultan by *firman* conceded to Mehemet Ali the Governorship of Syria with Damascus and Aleppo, and to Ibrahim the collectorship of Adana (Concessions of March-April, 1833). *See* Martens, *Nouveau Recueil*, tome XVI, Part I, pp. 17–18.

[2] Palmerston to Ponsonby, February 15, 1834. F.O., Turkey, No. 234.

[3] Text in Hertslet, II, No. 168.

The effect of this secret article was to convert the Dardanelles into a Russian fortress.[1] If Russia went to war with any Power whatsoever, and called upon Turkey to close the Straits, the Turks were bound to do so. Thus no Power could attack Russia through the Straits; but Russian warships could issue through them into the Mediterranean and make an attack where they pleased.

Although the Russian Government did not communicate the terms of the treaty till the spring of 1834, Western Europe was not long left in the dark. On July 25, 1833, the well-informed Constantinople correspondent of the *Morning Herald* sent to London a fairly accurate summary of the patent treaty, which the newspaper published on August 21. On October 16, the *Morning Herald* was able to publish a summary of the secret article. Naturally, feeling in Parliament, and in London and Paris generally, was strongly aroused. As a matter of fact, the Reis Effendi (a new Reis, not the one who had signed the fatal treaty) patriotically gave to Lord Ponsonby, the British ambassador, a copy of the treaty and secret article, in September, 1833.[2] Palmerston did not get excited, but he instructed Ponsonby to let it be known to the Porte that they could have the support of the English Mediterranean Squadron in time of need, if they preferred that to a Russian force under the terms of Unkiar Skelessi.[3] The French Government was equally resolute. In October, 1833, the Duc de Broglie, Minister of Foreign Affairs, had written to the French ambassador to the Court of the Tsar: The Court of St. Petersburg "has determined, in the face of Europe, to proclaim openly, to erect into a principle of international law, its exclusive, exceptional preponderance, in the affairs of the Ottoman Empire." [4]

Certainly France and England could not tolerate this. Unfortunately, the Tsar had got a kind of sanction from the other two Powers —Austria and Prussia. This had been obtained in one of those monarchical promenades which took place from time to time in Central Europe, "in some little town, whose half-barbarous name

[1] Col. Yeames to Palmerston: Reports from Odessa that Count de Witte had said, *nous devons aujourdhui considérer les Dardanelles comme nos frontières.* (F.O., Turkey, January 14, 1834.)

[2] Ponsonby to Palmerston, September 15, 1833, F.O., Turkey, No. 224. Actually, Pisani, the Dragoman of the Embassy, had got wind of the treaty on July 10 (Pisani's Report in F.O., Turkey, July 10, 1833).

[3] Palmerston to Ponsonby, March 10, 1834, F.O., Turkey.

[4] Text in Guizot, *Mémoires*, IV, 384 (Pièces historiques).

resounded for the first time in the ears of the news-mongers."[1] The particular place with which we are concerned at the moment was Münchengrätz, in Bohemia, where the Tsar, with Count Nesselrode, the Emperor Francis II, with Metternich, and the Crown Prince of Prussia met from September 10 to 20. This conference affirmed the right of any sovereign to appeal for assistance to any other sovereign, and added : " it shall not henceforth be permissible to any Power, not so appealed to, to intervene for the purpose of hindering such assistance." It is true that Nicholas at the same time assured Metternich, who did not like the Treaty of Unkiar Skelessi, that he would not invoke the treaty without accepting the mediation of Austria first. Even with this qualification, Unkiar Skelessi remained a danger to Europe : " in reality, the situations and the intentions remained the same."[2]

France and England were quite agreed in opposing the Russian claim ; but they were not agreed on other points of the Eastern Question. It was this divergence between France and England that made the ultimate settlement in 1839–40 so difficult.

For years, however, the divergence did not appear. Then, in 1839, clouds began to loom on the horizon. Mahmoud II was known to be on the point of attacking Mehemet Ali, whom he could never forgive for the campaign of Konieh. Palmerston, then English Foreign Secretary, was anxious to restrict Mehemet Ali's power and at the same time to challenge the Russian claims under the Treaty of Unkiar Skelessi. When he saw that the quarrel between the Sultan and the Pasha of Egypt was renewed, he felt that he would now either get rid of the Treaty of Unkiar Skelessi, or the Russians would finally enforce it.[3] Out of hatred of Mehemet, who had extended his power into Arabia, Mahmoud seems to have himself suggested to the British Government that it should occupy Aden—which it promptly did.[4]

The French Government, of which Marshal Soult was then Prime

[1] Haussonville : *Histoire de la Politique Extérieure du Gouvernement Français*, 1830–1848 [1850], I, p. 41.

[2] Guizot, *op. cit.*, IV, 53.

[3] It is quite untrue, as the French asserted, that Palmerston incited Mahmoud to attack Mehemet Ali. See F.O., Turkey, August 23, 1834, Palmerston to Ponsonby : Ponsonby to warn the Porte that France and Britain could not help him if he provoked a war.

[4] Early in 1839 the Board of Control sent orders to the Governor-General of India to occupy Aden, in terms of a treaty concluded with the Sultan of Aden. (F.O., Turkey, No. 384.)

Minister, was of opinion that Lord Ponsonby at Constantinople was urging the Sultan to war. M. de Bourqueney, who was in charge of the London Embassy in the absence of his chief General Sebastiani, called on Lord Palmerston at the Foreign Office, to complain of this attitude. Lord Palmerston assured Bourqueney that the instructions sent to Ponsonby were for him to use all his influence in favour of peace. M. Bourqueney suggested that perhaps Lord Ponsonby did not carry out these instructions as he ought. At this, Lord Palmerston touched a bell, and ordered to be brought to him Ponsonby's correspondence for the last four months, and the correspondence of Colonel Campbell (Consul at Cairo) for the last two years. These documents all gave evidence of peaceful influence.[1] The incident also throws a light on Palmerston's method of work. He seems to have mastered thoroughly all the business of the Foreign Office, and to have kept abreast of all the correspondence that came in.

If war did break out between the Sultan and Mehemet Ali, Soult and Palmerston were agreed on one point—namely, that if, in the course of the struggle, the Russians should sail to Constantinople under the terms of Unkiar Skelessi, France and England would make war upon them.[2] The Russian Government knew this, and preferred the way of peace. On June 17 (1839) Nesselrode wrote to Pozzo di Borgo (who had been transferred from the Parisian to the London Embassy) that he wished to avoid any crisis which would bring in the Treaty of Unkiar Skelessi. Lord Clanricarde sent the same information from St. Petersburg. The crisis came on quickly enough: on June 21, 1839, near the village of Neseb, west of the Euphrates, the Turkish forces were signally defeated (and 9,000 taken prisoner) by the ever-victorious Ibrahim. Before the news of this disaster arrived at Constantinople, Mahmoud II died (July 1). At the same time the Turkish Admiral handed over his fleet to Mehemet Ali at Alexandria. "In three weeks, Turkey had lost her Sultan, her army and her fleet."[3]

The situation in the Near East at this moment was undoubtedly very acute, and there was serious danger that the equilibrium of

[1] Bourqueney to Soult, July 9, 1839, in Guizot, IV, 333–5. Guizot himself believed that Palmerston did not want war, and living at the same time, and knowing Palmerston and the other English leaders personally, he makes out our Government to have been not at all Macchiavellian. Contrast Bourgeois (*Modern France*, chap. VII).

[2] Guizot, IV, 338.

[3] *Ibid.*, 342.

Europe would be upset. The Five Powers were all agreed that they must settle the difficulty by concerted action, and not leave the new, inexperienced Sultan Abdul Mejid and Mehemet Ali to patch it up between them. Russia made no attempt to claim her rights under the Treaty of Unkiar Skelessi. A joint note was drafted to this effect:

> The undersigned have received this morning from their respective governments instructions in virtue of which they have the honour to inform the Sublime Porte that accord on the Eastern Question is assured among the Five Great Powers; and they have to engage it to suspend all definite determination without their concurrence, and to await the result of the interest which the Powers are taking in it.[1]

On July 27 (1839), the ambassadors of the Five Powers, headed by Admiral de Roussin, presented this note to the Porte. Thus common action in the interest of the whole of Europe had been attained; and in this common action France seemed to stand at the head of the European Concert.

It was just here, however, that divergence between France and England became obvious. In fact the "accord" mentioned in the famous note of July 27 was by no means assured. In London, before the note was delivered, Lord Palmerston and M. Bourqueney had a conversation at the Foreign Office (June 17); the English Minister talked about opening negotiations on the double basis of securing Egypt for Mehemet Ali in heredity, and, at the same time, bringing about the evacuation of Syria by him. This was precisely what the French Government did not want. They wished Mehemet Ali to keep Syria. Russia was now on the British side, having no desire to see Mehemet Ali's power (under French protection) extending up to the Taurus—perhaps glad, too, to drive a wedge into the Franco-British Alliance, which had existed practically since 1830. When General Sebastiani returned to the London Embassy in the autumn of 1839, a regular diplomatic contest took place between him and Baron Brunnow, the Russian envoy, sent specially by Nesselrode to deal with the crisis. Sebastiani was firm, calm, sagacious, but a little slow, and rather sparing of speech or writing; imperturbable, however, and far-seeing. Brunnow, nourished in the traditions and designs of the Russian Chancellery, was well-instructed, adroit, persevering without obstinacy—never exacting or impatient—an abundant and spirited talker—a well-trained and

[1] Guizot, IV, 348.

prompt writer of dispatches—clever at seeing the aims of other people, while enveloping his own under a dense mantle of concessions, reserves, and comments. Here is a picture of two of the most expert diplomatists of the nineteenth century.[1]

Sebastiani saw well enough the way the wind was blowing; and he warned Soult, who was still Prime Minister, that France would be left out in the cold if she persisted in supporting Mehemet Ali's pretensions to Syria. But Soult was prepared to take the risk, and deliberately said that if the Four Powers cared to make a coalition among themselves, France would let them go their own way—such a coalition was against Nature and would not hold long together.[2]

Soult was gambling on the chance that Great Britain and Russia (and consequently Austria and Prussia, who always went with Russia then) would not agree. But they did! The Foreign Offices of London and Petersburg, Palmerston and Nesselrode, put their heads together. Palmerston, who did not wish to cold-shoulder France,[3] confidentially told Sebastiani that Russia and England understood each other, and Sebastiani forwarded the news to Paris. It must have come like a thunder-clap to Soult. He must now either give up his protection of Mehemet Ali and waive the Syrian claim; or else see France shut out from the European Concert. But he made one more effort to get what he wanted—to win over the British Government to the French point of view. He recalled Sebastiani and sent Guizot to the London Embassy.

Guizot belongs to the type of the best French public men—a scholar, a statesman, a man of affairs. His lectures delivered at the Sorbonne on *The History of Civilization in Europe* were, in their published form, already becoming a classic. His profound studies in English history, especially on the Great Rebellion and the Revolution, had given him a real appreciation of the English character and of English public life. He was already an experienced statesman, although his sphere had hitherto been confined to that of Ministry of Public Instruction. And yet, while he may be said to have been the one Frenchman best acquainted with England, he had never been in that country. *Je n'avais jamais été en Angleterre,*

[1] Guizot, IV, 359.
[2] *Ibid.*, IV, 366.
[3] Guizot, who had no reason to put the English case in a favourable light, is quite clear about this: *Mémoires*, IV, chap. 26 *passim*.

et je n'avais jamais fait de diplomatie. Such was his condition when he landed at Dover, on February 27, 1840, *en route* for the London Embassy, which at that time was established at Hertford House, in Manchester Square.

Guizot's task was terribly difficult. He was to maintain the accord with England, to retain France's membership of the Concert of Five Powers; and yet to insist upon getting Syria for Mehemet Ali as an indispensable condition. Such were Soult's instructions.[1]

The new ambassador soon got into touch with the leading men in English government and society. He found Lord Palmerston perfectly frank and friendly. Guizot was careful to point out that Mehemet Ali deserved consideration at the hands of the Powers, because, in the conflict with Turkey, he had not been the aggressor. A most interesting scene took place at the Foreign Office: Ain-Tab, said Guizot, where the first collision took place, is within Egyptian territory. "I believe not," said Lord Palmerston, and he went to look for a map. Guizot had brought his own map with him—one lately published at Gotha (Gotha is still famous for its maps); and it showed Ain-Tab plainly on the Egyptian side of the Sed-Jour river. How often have the destinies of nations been jeopardized by the obscurities or omissions of maps! In this case, however, the maps agreed, and spoke with no uncertain voice. Palmerston abandoned this argument, but stuck to his ground that the power of Mehemet Ali must be restricted. Thiers (who had succeeded Soult as Premier on March 1) would not concede this point.

Guizot already began to feel the coming isolation of France. Little could be gathered from the attitude of the diplomatic corps in London. The Baron von Bülow, Prussian ambassador, was friendly, and often met Guizot to talk about philosophy and literature as well as politics; but he was too nervous about his health to be depended on: the wind, the fog, the heat, the cold, company, solitude—all agitated him and made him ill. From Baron Neumann, the Austrian ambassador, nothing could be gathered: he was trained entirely in the Metternich school, and was that great diplomatist's confidential servant; he was intelligent, prudent, and solemnly discreet, avoiding above everything else to compromise his Government. Brunnow, the Russian ambassador, kept out of Guizot's way altogether for six weeks.

[1] Guizot, V, 27.

On March 12 (1840), Guizot wrote to Thiers telling him of his conversations with Palmerston, and stating that, if France persisted in supporting Mehemet Ali, she might have to retire from the Concert. Thiers, like Soult, was prepared to do this: "the situation has been created neither by you nor by me; we cannot have anything to do with it."[1] Like Soult Thiers was gambling—gambling on two chances: (1) "that Mehemet Ali would resist energetically any combination to take Syria from him," and (2) "all the means of compulsion that might be attempted against him would be vain."[2] The future was to show speedily that Thiers was gravely miscalculating.

In April the Turkish Ambassador at Paris, Nouri Effendi, came over to London and presented a note to the Foreign Office and the ambassadors of the rest of the Five Powers, adverting to the hereditary pasha-ship of Egypt (without Syria) as the sole condition on which the Porte would make peace with Mehemet Ali. Two days later Guizot, at a reception at Holland House, was told privately that the English, Russian, Austrian, and Prussian plenipotentiaries were agreed on the reply each would make to this note. On the next day (April 13) he received a note from Lord Palmerston:

MY DEAR AMBASSADOR,—

Here is a copy of the reply which I have sent to the note of Nouri-Effendi. Won't you reply somewhat in the same sense?

The English reply said nothing about limiting Mehemet Ali to Egypt. But Thiers instructed Guizot to make no reply at all to the Turkish Note: "it would be superfluous," wrote the French Premier to his ambassador, "to prolong such a debate indefinitely." So Palmerston's friendly invitation was declined. The Prussian and Austrian ambassadors, and also the Duke of Wellington, had also written, to support the invitation.

For the next two months the Eastern Question ceased to bulk as it had done in Guizot's diplomatic business. He was occupied with a commercial dispute between England and the Kingdom of Naples, and he was able, by his friendly offices, to help to smooth over the friction between those two countries. Then Thiers wrote to Guizot (May 4) ordering him to ask permission from the British Government to transport the ashes of Napoleon from St. Helena to

[1] Thiers to Soult, March 21, 1840 (Guizot, IV, 63).
[2] Guizot, V, 65.

France. Guizot was a little surprised at this decision, in view of the strength of the Napoleonic Legend and the insecurity of Louis Philippe's throne. He went at once to Lord Palmerston, who also, when the matter was explained, seemed a little surprised: in fact, a slight smile, quickly repressed, passed across his lips. But he received the request courteously, and promised to bring it before the Cabinet. Two days afterwards the consent of the Cabinet was conveyed to Hertford House.

Meanwhile nothing happened between the French Embassy and the Foreign Office with regard to the Eastern Question; and Guizot had time to extend his relations in English society, especially with Lord and Lady Holland, whose home, Holland House, was the social centre of the Whig Party; with Lord Clarendon, just returned from the Madrid Embassy; with Lord Lansdowne, than whom Guizot had never met a *grand seigneur* more enlightened, more generously and judiciously liberal; with Lord Grey, *ce grand chef Whig*; with Peel; with Lord Aberdeen, whose high-mindedness, sense of responsibility, and public spirit he admired above all; with Hallam, Macaulay, Sidney Smith and other eminent writers "on the borders of political life." He had leisure too to visit Eton (where he met Hawtrey), Rugby (where he met and was greatly impressed by Arnold), and a large school for poor children at Norwood. As a sincere French Protestant, too, the religious condition of England greatly interested him.

Towards the end of May a new Turkish ambassador came to London, Chekib Effendi. Thiers told Guizot not to talk with him. "He will repeat to you the follies of the Seraglio without approving of them. For the question will not be settled at London with the Turkish Plenipotentiary."

Thiers was mistaken. On July 17 Palmerston invited Guizot to come to the Foreign Office and there read to him a careful note stating that the Four Powers—Great Britain, Austria, Russia, and Prussia—in view of the refusal of France to join with them, had by themselves concluded a treaty for the definite settlement of the dispute between the Sultan and Mehemet Ali. The momentous Four Power Treaty of July 15 was an accomplished fact, and France was not in it!

This treaty of July 15, 1840 (including a Separate Act annexed to it), was signed at London between Great Britain, Russia, Austria, and Prussia on the one hand, and Turkey on the other. It enacted that the war between the Sultan and Mehemet Ali should be ended, on condition of Mehemet getting the hereditary pashalic of Egypt and also, for life only, Acre and Southern Syria. The offer of Egypt and Southern Syria was to hold good for ten days, the offer of Egypt alone for twenty days. The Four Powers were to put pressure upon Mehemet by blockading him. If the Egyptian army advanced to Constantinople, the Four Powers, on the invitation of the Sultan, were to co-operate for the defence of it (this part of the agreement, it will be noticed, practically amounted to a renunciation by Russia of her exclusive right to defend Constantinople under the terms of Unkiar Skelessi). Article 4 maintained "the ancient rule of the Ottoman Empire" to keep the Dardanelles closed to foreign ships of war when the Porte is at peace.[1]

The news of the treaty was a great shock to the pride of France. The treaty had been courteously communicated, but the French Government felt that they ought to have been invited to sign it before it was completed, although (as Thiers admitted) [2] it was perfectly well known that they would not sign it. Why had Palmerston acted so quickly and so secretly? It was because Thiers himself, through M. Pontois, ambassador at Constantinople, was carrying on a separate negotiation, with a view to concluding peace between the Sultan and Mehemet on the French terms. It was because of this that Thiers had told Guizot to make no concession to Palmerston on the question of Syria; he was expecting from moment to moment to hear that Pontois had made peace at Constantinople, and that Mehemet consequently had got Syria. With this treaty signed and sealed, he would then face Palmerston with a *fait accompli*. But Ponsonby got wind of the negotiation at Constantinople (where any secret can be bought), and sent word of it to London.[3] So Palmerston hastily made his treaty of July 15, and faced Thiers with the *fait accompli*. The French Premier had meant to steal a march upon Palmerston; instead of this, Palmer-

[1] The Four Power Treaty of July 15, 1840, contained in the Preamble a statement that the Powers were "animated by the desire of maintaining the Integrity and Independence of the Ottoman Empire as a security for the Peace of Europe." This statement did not provide a guarantee of the integrity of the Ottoman Empire, but it expressed an intention on the part of the Powers, and it did constitute, in a limited sense, an obligation on their part.

[2] Circular Note to the French Diplomatic Agents, August 6, 1840. Text in Haussonville, I, 167.

[3] "L'arrangement direct entre le Sultan et le pacha lui paraissait imminent" (Guizot, V, 229).

ston, seeing through the game,[1] had stolen a march upon him. It was for this reason that Thiers exploded in anger; and for this reason the armed forces were mobilized and the war cloud hung over the Channel and the Rhine.

For months war was very seriously threatened between France and the rest of Europe. The French Chamber had for two years been in a somewhat chauvinistic frame of mind, and had been steadily imbibing the Napoleonic legend, and renewing its appetite for glory. In vain Molé and Soult had tried to satisfy this appetite with expeditions to Algiers. But "the nation cared nothing for colonies. . . . Louis Philippe tried in vain to stay by a homœopathic treatment this fever of martial memories with which the bourgeoisie had infected the nation."[2] The uninformed nation was eager enough for war, and none of the responsible statesmen (except Louis Philippe himself) was doing anything to restrain it. The only hesitation in Thiers' mind seems to have been whether he should direct the attack particularly against England or Prussia. Two additional classes of conscripts were called to the colours, and the threat to Prussia was sufficiently definite to arouse the composition of the *Wacht am Rhein.*[3]

Meanwhile events had begun to move quickly again in Syria. Mehemet Ali had refused the terms conveyed in the treaty of July 15. The English ambassador at Constantinople, for some time, had been stirring up revolt against Mehemet in the Lebanon.[4] On September 11, Admiral Sir Charles Napier bombarded Beyrout, and captured it. Shortly afterwards he won a complete victory on land in command of the Turks against the Egyptian forces at Nahr-el-Kelb. On September 14, the Sultan pronounced the deposition of the Viceroy of Egypt. France must fight now or never.

Perhaps Thiers never seriously meant to fight. Louis Philippe certainly did not, if he could help it. The Comte de St. Aulaire, minister at Vienna—a courageous, highly-educated man of the

[1] In May and June, 1840, a French Agent, M. Costé, was writing to Prince Achmet Tethi, urging him to get the Porte to make a separate arrangement with Mehemet Ali. Ponsonby, with Achmet's knowledge, got copies of the letters, and they are now in F.O., Turkey, No. 394.

[2] Bourgeois, *Modern France*, I, 202–3.

[3] By Max Schneckenburger.

[4] "If Ibrahim advances, it will be easy to raise all the Syrians against his government. I can answer for the inhabitants of the Lebanon. . . ." Ponsonby to Palmerston, April 23, 1840. Text in Haussonville, I, 295. *See also* Ponsonby to Palmerston, June 23, 1840, in F.O., Turkey, No. 394.

world—was a moderating influence: and Thiers confessed to him: "to involve France in a struggle in which she would stand alone against the whole of Europe, would be to incur a terrible responsibility."[1] The Four Powers were standing together in the Eastern Question; their co-operation was like a renewing of the Treaty of Chaumont of 1814 against France. Yet the news of the deposition of Mehemet Ali seemed to break all the dams of prudence in France: the recruiting offices became crowded, and war was eagerly expected any moment. In Germany similar scenes took place; and once more, as in 1813, a unified, conscious nation seemed to be coming into existence there against the French peril. Palmerston, however, thought war would not take place: he counted upon the wealthy manufacturers and proprietors in France to turn the scale gradually in favour of peace.[2]

For this to take place, however, a little care must be shown for the reasonable susceptibilities of the French. They had stood out for securing Syria to Mehemet Ali; and now they found him legally deposed even from Egypt. This was, indeed, a slap in the face for France; but Palmerston[3] softened the effects by assuming, in his conversations with Guizot, that the Sultan's deposition of Mehemet Ali was only held over him *in terrorem*, to show what would happen to him if he persisted in his obstinacy. So Walewski at Alexandria received orders to bring Mehemet Ali to reason—to point out that the Pasha of Egypt could not in any case hold out against the forces of the Four Powers.[4]

[1] Bourgeois, *Modern France*, I, 218.

[2] "I think that peace will be preserved, as Louis Philippe is very much against any wars."—Malmesbury, *Memoirs of an ex-Minister* (1884), I, 122, dated September 11, 1841.

[3] He was, however, quite ready to fight. To Bulwer at Paris he wrote on September 22, 1840, "with that skill of language which I know you to be master of, convey to Thiers in the most friendly and inoffensive manner possible, that if France throws down the gauntlet we shall not refuse to pick it up" (Ashley: *Life and Correspondence of Palmerston*, I, 379). Bulwer was *chargé d'affaires* at Paris. Later (October 8, 1840), Palmerston wrote to Granville, ambassador at Paris, in a more conciliatory strain: "Then as to a declaration: *If France makes a friendly communication tending to lead to an amicable discussion of the present state of affairs, we shall receive it and deal with it in the spirit in which it is made*" (*ibid.*, I, 385).

[4] As a matter of fact, it was doubtful whether Mehemet Ali could hold out much longer even against the Sultan alone. Mehemet had 196,000 men under arms, who had to be supported out of a population of only three millions —a population already much wasted by exactions. (Ponsonby to Palmerston, June 5, 1840, in F.O., Turkey, No. 394.)

So, on October 8 (1840), France made her peace-offer to England. In effect it came to this, that if England and the rest of the Four Powers would secure Egypt in heredity to Mehemet Ali, France would withdraw her demand that he should be maintained also in the possession of Syria. The Note of October 8 did not state this plainly: it was couched rather in the form of an ultimatum, that France insisted upon Mehemet Ali having the possession of Egypt, and would make no concessions on this point. If the Powers cared to make a settlement on the principles of the treaty of July 15 (i.e. Egypt for Mehemet Ali) France was willing to join.[1]

This probably was all that the Powers wanted—the pronouncement of Mehemet Ali's deposition was probably only made in order to bring him to reason. This seems to have been Admiral Napier's view, for after his victories at Beyrout and the capture of Acre [2] on November 3, he brought the Fleet down to Alexandria, and on November 27 dictated to Boghas Bay, Mehemet Ali's representative, "one of those brusque Conventions so common with English agents."[3] This Act engaged Mehemet Ali to evacuate Syria, on condition of his retaining Egypt in heredity. This was practically equivalent to the terms demanded by France in the note of October 8. The Powers agreed to uphold Napier's Convention, and in the early months of 1841 the negotiations, in which France, in the person of Baron Bourqueney,[4] took part, were brought to a successful issue. On February 12 (1841), the Sultan was induced to issue a Firman, recognizing Mehemet Ali as hereditary Viceroy of Egypt, but without either Syria or Crete. The final act of the European settlement was made by a Conference at London and issued on July 13 (1841). This treaty, signed by Great Britain, France, Austria, Prussia, Russia, and Turkey, re-enacted the "ancient rule of the Ottoman Empire," that foreign ships of war should be

[1] Text of Note in Guizot, V, 505. (*Pièces historiques.*)

[2] Acre was believed in France to be impregnable. Its capture created a profound sensation.

[3] Haussonville, I, 196. The text of the Napier Convention is in Martens, *Nouveau Recueil Général*, t. XV, p. 489.

[4] The Thiers Cabinet had fallen on October 20, 1840. Thiers wished to make the speech from the throne firm and haughty. The King wished it to be conciliatory. As Thiers persisted in his view, Louis Philippe dismissed him, and called Soult to form a Ministry. Guizot gave up the London Embassy and returned to Paris as Minister for Foreign Affairs.

prohibited from entering the Dardanelles or Bosphorus, so long as the Porte is at peace. Thus Russia's special position under the Treaty of Unkiar Skelessi was done away with, the Four Power Treaty of July 15, 1840, was superseded (though not annulled), and France became again a member of the European Concert.[1]

[1] *The Cambridge History of British Foreign Policy*, vol. II, chap. IV. § 1.

CHAPTER VIII

BELGIUM AND SPAIN

§ 1. Belgium

Between 1830 and 1840 the European family of States was much troubled by the affairs of Belgium and of Spain, as well as by those of the East. A general war, however, was never really threatened by the affairs of Belgium and Spain, and a settlement for each country was gradually arrived at, which has worked sufficiently well, and has stood the test of time.

The union between Belgium and Holland, arranged by the Congress of Vienna, came to a practical, though not to a legal end, on August 25, 1830. On this day, a movement for autonomy, intensified by the example of the Paris Revolution of July, came to a head. From a demand for autonomy, the Belgians, reacting against the strong resistance of the Dutch, proceeded to a demand for independence, and established a Provisional Government (October 4, 1830). This act was contrary to the treaties of 1815, and required international sanction. It was, moreover, peculiarly dangerous to Europe, as it seemed to give the French an opportunity of breaking down the barrier which the Powers had set up on their north-eastern frontier in 1815.

The Belgian affair was indeed difficult, and in dealing with it the new monarchy of Louis Philippe gained its greatest success, and established its prestige in Europe.

> The new French Government, in presence of these great difficulties, put to its first test, did not hesitate to lay down one of those principles which decide the future and prescribe the fate of a nation. M. Molé, Minister of Foreign Affairs at this time, at which were laid out all the land-marks of the new French diplomacy, proclaimed in public and in his official correspondence the system which has since been called *non-intervention.*[1]

[1] Haussonville, I, 18.

This famous principle, liberally interpreted after the manner of Canning, led M. Molé, who had been trained by Napoleon, to warn the Baron Werther [1] that if Prussia (anxious to intervene on the Dutch side) sent troops into Belgium, a French army would be immediately dispatched there also. The threat was apparently effectual. About the same time Talleyrand, French ambassador at London, whose diplomacy at this time was responsible for the European recognition of Louis Philippe, signed a protocol with Lord Aberdeen, British Foreign Secretary, on October 15, 1830. By this Act the two Powers most directly interested in the Belgian question agreed that it should be settled by the Five Powers.

Under the presidency of Lord Aberdeen a Conference of the Five Powers was assembled at London. The Northern Courts (as the Austrian, Prussian, and Russian Governments were then called) were against the "dislocation" of the Kingdom of Holland. France of course was in favour of it, partly because of her sympathy with a suppressed nation, partly because the enlarged Kingdom of Holland had been created as a military barrier against her. The British Government was, from the point of view of its own interests, in favour of maintaining this barrier; but it sympathized with the national and constitutional aspirations of the Belgians. The upshot was that two agents, M. de Bresson (afterwards a distinguished ambassador at Berlin) on behalf of France, and Mr. Cartwright, on behalf of England, were sent to Belgium, thus practically recognising the Provisional Government as independent (November, 1830). In the same month the English Tory Government fell and was succeeded by a Whig Ministry under Earl Grey, with Lord Palmerston as Foreign Secretary. The handling of the Belgian affair was thenceforth in Palmerston's hands; but it must not be forgotten that the lines of the settlement were laid down by Lord Aberdeen.

It is doubtful, however, if even the Anglo-French *entente* would have so soon secured Belgian independence, in the face of the opposition of the Three Northern Courts, had not a terrible insurrection broken out in Russian Poland (November, 1830). This resulted in a regular war in Eastern Europe, heroically contested by the Poles, till the last great battle that laid them low, at Ostrolenka (May, 1831). The Polish Insurrection distracted the

[1] Prussian ambassador at Paris. He was father to the more famous diplomatist who was Prussian ambassador at Paris, 1869–70.

attention of the Three Courts, and gave the Anglo-French *bloc* a clear field.

The Conference which Lord Aberdeen had convened in London, continuing its labours under Palmerston, recognised in principle the independence of Belgium on December 20, 1830; and, amplifying its work with the opening of the New Year, it agreed that the new State should be neutral (January 20), after the manner of Switzerland. The settlement of the whole affair was being left more and more in the hands of Great Britain and France, for beside the rising in Poland, there were revolutions which broke out—unsuccessfully—in the Papal States and Italian Duchies; so that the attention of Austria, generally regarded as the protector of the treaties of 1815 in Italy, was fully occupied there.

The chief resistance to a European settlement of Belgium came, not unnaturally, from King William I of Holland, who did not like losing half of the dominion secured to him by the Congress of Vienna. The King of Prussia, who was his kinsman, supported him. On the other hand, France strongly supported the Belgian claims; but Europe was naturally a little suspicious of France's interest in that country, considering the years of war required aforetime to expel the French from Antwerp. Fortunately for Belgium, for France, and for Europe, a very strong man succeeded the rather dubious ministry that had held office in the first year of Louis Philippe's reign. This man was Casimir Périer, the President of the Chamber of Deputies.

Casimir Périer, though he had served in the French Revolutionary armies, was really a man of business, and had made a fortune in banking. When called to the premiership on March 13, 1831, he was sixty-four years of age. Tall in stature, with a commanding presence and a rather passionate manner, he impressed his personality on all his colleagues, and even on Louis Philippe himself. His policy was order at home and peace abroad; and it may fairly be said that in the thirteen months that were left to him to live, he accomplished these aims.[1]

At the suggestion of Great Britain Prince Leopold of Saxe-Coburg (who had accepted and then refused the nomination to the Greek

[1] Heroic intrepidity is the chief quality attributed to him. In a country where ministers are particularly susceptible to the force of public opinion, he was inflexible. "The mere idea of yielding before a popular caprice made the blood mount to his face." *See* Thureau-Dangin, *Histoire de la Monarchie de Juillet*, t. I, p. 406.

throne) was elected King by the Belgian National Congress on June 4, 1831; and a basis for the settlement of the new State was laid down in an agreement known as the Treaty of Eighteen Articles, signed at London on June 26, 1831, by the representatives of Great Britain, France, Austria, Russia, and Prussia. This treaty provided for the neutrality of Belgium (Article 9), for her commercial freedom (rivers and canals), and to some extent for her frontiers. The treaty (including the neutrality) was accepted by the Belgian National Congress on July 9. "This neutrality was in the real interest of this country, but our good Congress here did *not* wish it, and even opposed it; it was *imposé* upon them." [1]

King William of Holland, however, was still hostile as ever to the partition of his dominion. On August 1 (1831), he denounced the armistice which he had been induced to make with the Belgians, and thrusting back the inferior forces of King Leopold he advanced almost to Brussels. Casimir Périer was quick to act. Fifty thousand French troops marched across the frontier under Marshal Gérard, and occupied Brussels. The Dutch had to retire.

This lightning-stroke (which was quite bloodless) of French military diplomacy somewhat startled the London Conference, but the agitation subsided when the French troops, having freed Brussels from the Dutch peril, were speedily withdrawn (August 20). The way being thus clear, the Conference quickly dispatched its work, with a protocol of twenty-four articles (October 24), incorporated next month in the well-known treaty of November 15, 1831, concluded between Great Britain, France, Austria, Prussia, and Russia on the one part, and Belgium on the other.

This treaty defined the territory of Belgium. Holland was left with the seven historic provinces of the United Netherlands and the fortress of Maastricht. Limburg and Luxemburg were both divided between the two States; the portion (eastern) of Luxemburg left to Holland contained the City of Luxemburg itself; it was not incorporated with Holland but continued as a separate Grand Duchy with the Dutch King as Grand Duke. The left bank of the estuary of the Scheldt (as well as the right bank) also remained with Holland.

The treaty of November 15, 1831, was not accepted by the Dutch Government, which still held military possession of Antwerp.

[1] King Leopold to Queen Victoria, February 15, 1856 (*The Letters of Queen Victoria*, ed. 1908), III, 172.

Although Casimir Périer was now no more,[1] his system of government was carried on by the next premier, Marshal Soult; and again Marshal Gérard (this time with the approval of England and the co-operation of an Anglo-French squadron) crossed the frontier. The citadel of Antwerp was besieged and the Dutch garrison, which made a good fight, compelled to surrender on December 20 (1832). Thus the independence of Belgium, and the frontiers as defined by the Treaty of London (November 15, 1831), were in effect established.[2]

Yet although *in effect* established, Belgium was still not clear of international difficulties, because Holland would not come to terms, in spite of an Anglo-French blockade of her coast. It took rather more than five years to put the relations of Holland and Belgium on a regular footing. In the meantime a curious condition of affairs prevailed between the two countries—a condition that was not entirely *de jure*, nor yet merely *de facto*. For the Dutch Government, without specifically recognizing the rights of the Belgian State, was induced by Palmerston and Talleyrand (who was still ambassador at London) to sign a treaty on May 21, 1833, agreeing not to recommence hostilities against Belgium, and to leave the navigation of the Scheldt entirely free. This solution of the trouble, while not entirely satisfactory, is creditable to the spirit of forbearance of all the parties concerned—and especially on the part of the Dutch, whose minister at London, the Sieur Solomon Dedel, was a man of very pleasant and conciliatory temper; and on the part of the Belgians, whose minister at London, Sylvain van de Weyer, gained golden opinions among all who came into contact with him. The final settlement did not take place till the Dutch Government at last made the Treaty of London with the Five Powers, on April 19, 1839. This took the place of the London Treaty of November 15, 1831 (the provisions of which were incorporated in it) and remained the international instrument which regulated the position of Belgium till it was abrogated by article 31 of the Treaty of Versailles, June 28, 1919.[3]

[1] He died on May 16, 1832.

[2] One curious way in which the British Government tried to obtain international recognition of the new kingdom of Belgium, was by asking the Sultan of Turkey to receive a Belgian envoy at his Court. *See* Palmerston to Lord Ponsonby, F.O., Turkey, July 11, 1834.

[3] "Germany, recognizing that the Treaties of April 19, 1839, which established the status of Belgium before the war, no longer conform to the require-

Altogether there were three treaties concluded concerning the Belgian Question, on April 19, 1839. The first was between the Five Powers (Great Britain, Austria, Prussia, France, and Russia) on the one part, and the Netherlands on the other. The Netherlands recognised the dissolution (already eight years old) of the union with Belgium (article III). An annex of twenty-four articles provided for the frontiers, the division of the Public Debt,[1] the navigation of the Scheldt and Meuse, and other matters, among which was Belgian neutrality. Article VII of the Annex ran: "Belgium, within the limits specified in articles I, II, and IV, shall form an independent and perpetually Neutral State. It shall be bound to observe such neutrality towards all other States." At the same time article II of the main treaty declared that the Annexed Articles were all "placed under the guarantee of their said Majesties" (i.e., of the sovereigns of the Five Powers).

The second treaty was purely consequential—it was made between the Netherlands and Belgium, and enacted peace and friendship between them. The third treaty was made among the Five Powers only, and again it placed the Annexed Articles under the Guarantee of the signing Powers. The neutrality of Belgium (article VII of the Annex) was thus doubly assured by Five Power treaties.

§ 2. The Iberian Peninsula

The years 1830–40 were certainly a troubled time for Europe, for in addition to the Eastern Question and the Belgian Question, there were revolutions in Italy, Spain, and Portugal, not to mention disputes between France and the Argentine owing to the high-handed proceedings of the Dictator Rosas (whose power lasted from 1833 to 1852).

The Iberian trouble arose out of disputes that were really dynastic, although they had a certain constitutional flavour. The Portuguese trouble was the easier to bring to a settlement. When Napoleon I sent General Junot with an army into Portugal in 1807, the Royal

ments of the situation, consents to the abrogation of the said Treaties and undertakes immediately to recognise and to observe whatever conventions may be entered into by the Principal Allied and Associated Powers, or by any of them, in concert with the Governments of Belgium and of the Netherlands, to replace the said Treaties of 1839."

[1] Belgium undertook a charge of five million Netherlands florins of annual interest (article XIII).

family was conveyed for safety across the Atlantic to Rio de Janeiro, and did not return till the year 1821. Even then the heir to the Portuguese throne, Dom Pedro, was left behind in Brazil; and when his father, King John VI, died at Lisbon in 1826, Dom Pedro preferred to stay on in Brazil, of which he was the Emperor. His daughter Maria became Queen in Portugal, but her uncle Miguel contested her right, and began a civil war.

The Spanish trouble arose in a somewhat similar way. On September 29, 1833, King Ferdinand of Spain died. His successor under a recent law was his daughter Isabel, aged three years, and represented by her mother Christina as regent. Don Carlos, Ferdinand's brother, claimed to be King instead of Isabel, under the "Salic Law"; and like Miguel in Portugal, he started a sanguinary civil war in Spain.

Only two countries (besides Spain and Portugal themselves) were vitally interested in the affairs of the Iberian Peninsula. These two countries were Great Britain and France—France as being a near neighbour, and Great Britain as being an ancient friend, who had come closer still in the Peninsular War. Both France and Great Britain supported the woman's side in Spain; in Portugal Great Britain was practically left with a free hand, and she gave her support to Doña Maria. The Governments of Isabel and Maria were on the whole the more constitutional and progressive, as contrasted with the absolutist (and clerical) Carlists and Miguelites.

The Peninsula, however, was too big to have its affairs settled by merely diplomatic means: the Civil Wars had to burn themselves out. But the process of extinction could be aided by diplomacy; and with this object in view Palmerston offered the alliance of Great Britain to the Governments of Queen Isabel and Queen Maria. The offer was accepted and a Triple Alliance treaty was concluded in January, 1834. Talleyrand (who for this once was taken absolutely unawares) heard of it only after it was concluded. The old diplomatist was considerably mortified, for the truth is the French Government had been contemplating single-handed intervention (it was to prevent this that Palmerston had concluded the Triple Alliance). Making the best of it, however, Talleyrand demanded that France should be included in the association. This was done, and the Triple now became the Quadruple Alliance (April 22, 1834).

The importance of the Quadruple Alliance appears to have been exaggerated by subsequent historians. It was not so much a sign of Anglo-French unity as of Anglo-French divergence: it was a useful but quite artificial link between two countries who were competing rather dangerously in the Peninsula. The practical effect was certainly not very great. In Portugal, the cause of Maria was really won by the victory of Vice-Admiral Charles Napier (in the Portuguese service) off Cape St. Vincent, and the campaign of Villa Flor (Duke of Terceira) in the lower Tagus Valley, in 1833. The Quadruple Alliance showed Dom Miguel that his failing cause was hopeless, and under the terms of the Convention of Evora (May 24, 1834) he retired from the Peninsula for life. The Convention secured a pension to the royal exile, which, however, though a poor man, he never drew.

The Spanish Civil War lasted longer. The treaty of Quadruple Alliance only engaged the Spanish and Portuguese Governments to co-operate with their forces (article 1); Great Britain was bound only to co-operate with a naval force (which had nothing to do but to use the weapon of blockade); while Louis Philippe was only to do "whatever might be settled by common consent between himself and his three August Allies." Louis Philippe was scarcely faithful to the spirit of this not very generous engagement. When Great Britain invited him to intervene in Spain (March 18, 1836), he was angling (unsuccessfully) for a marriage between one of his sons and an Austrian Archduchess. Metternich was naturally "Carlist" in sympathy; so Louis Philippe refused the English invitation; and when Thiers, who was then Premier, increased the recruiting of the Foreign Legion (for service in Spain), the King dismissed him, and packed off the Legion to the war in Algeria (September, 1836). In the year 1835 an English Legion had, with the permission of the British Government, been recruited by the Spanish Government, and taken to Spain under command of Colonel de Lacy Evans. It fought well, but returned in 1838 without the war being finished. But by the year 1840 Isabel's cause was gradually brought to complete success by General Espartero.[1] The efforts of British

[1] The struggle was practically ended by one of Don Carlos' generals, Maroto, taking matters into his own hand, and concluding with Espartero (who acted on behalf of Christina's Government) the Convention of Vergara, August 31, 1839. By this Convention Maroto's men laid down their arms, and were permitted to enter the Christinist service. English diplomacy, working behind the scenes, helped to bring about this Convention; accordingly the

diplomacy (represented by Lord Clarendon, Minister at Madrid from 1833 to 1839) were chiefly directed to attempting to assuage the horrors of the civil war, and especially to stop the butchering of prisoners on each side.[1]

§ 3. The Spanish Marriages

The *entente* which had superficially existed since 1830 (with some interruptions) between Great Britain and France, but which had never been very secure, came to an inglorious end in 1846 over the Spanish marriages. Even before this there was friction, at the time of the French punitive expedition against Morocco in 1844, and (in the same year) over the arrest by the French of Mr. Pritchard, an English missionary and consul in Tahiti whom the French had seized for inciting the natives against their power. With regard to the Moroccan war, in which the bombardment of Tangier by the French seemed to threaten our influence in Gibraltar, the British Government showed itself especially sensitive; but Louis Philippe was careful to use his victory with moderation, and to conclude peace (by the Treaty of Tangier, September 10, 1844), assuring to the Sultan easy terms. *L'Affaire Pritchard* was also discreetly managed; acting on the remonstrances of Great Britain, the French Government agreed to pay him an indemnity—an act which the French public stigmatized as a base surrender. So inflamed was French opinion on the subject, that King Louis Philippe paid the indemnity out of his own pocket.[2] Nevertheless the French were not pleased with Louis Philippe's even lukewarm complaisance towards the British Government, and his position in France was weakened. On the other hand, the Spanish Marriage Question, in which he showed himself not at all complaisant towards the British Government, broke up the Anglo-French *entente*, and so indirectly helped to weaken his power of resistance at home.

To understand the Spanish Marriage Question, it must be borne in

Marquess of Londonderry and Lord Aberdeen spoke against Lord Clarendon later, in the House of Lords, accusing him of having suborned the Carlist General to an act of treachery. Lord Clarendon, however, made a good defence both of himself and of Maroto. *See* Hansard (1840), vol. LII, pp. 544–579.

[1] Besides using the regular minister at Madrid, Great Britain also sent a special envoy, Lord Eliot, who in 1835 (April 27) brought about the Convention of Logroño between the belligerents, for fair treatment and exchange of prisoners: *see* Hertslet, II, No. 176.

[2] Guizot, VII, 107.

mind that a Bourbon dynasty had been ruling at Madrid since the year 1700. The French were naturally proud of this fact, although they recognised that a union of the Spanish and French Crowns was barred by the public law of Europe (Treaty of Utrecht, March 15, 1713, Article VI). Since the accession of the Bourbon Philip V in 1700, the succession to the Spanish throne had been from male to male until 1833, when Isabel became Queen. She had survived the Carlist War of Succession, and was now (1845) approaching marriageable age.[1] The question of the day, both personally for the Queen herself and publicly for Europe, was, Whom should she marry? It was the public aspect of the question, naturally, which exercised the diplomatists. The French wished to see the Bourbon line continued by the marriage of Isabel to another member of the house of Bourbon, which had several branches with many male scions; the British Government rather favoured the idea of marrying the Spanish Queen to a prince of the house of Coburg—a plan which, it was expected, would promote constitutional government at Madrid, just as Coburg princes were promoting constitutional government at London and Brussels. The whole question, however, was further complicated by the fact that Queen Isabel had a sister (the Infanta Louise), concerning whose future husband great care must be taken, for supposing Isabel's marriage did not produce any children, then Louise's line would succeed to the throne.

It is considered that if only the Tory Government of Sir Robert Peel had remained in power in England, the whole affair could have been easily settled. Lord Aberdeen was Foreign Secretary, and Guizot, the French Minister for Foreign Affairs, had made friends with him at London in 1840, and completely trusted him. Aberdeen was so sincerely devoted to the cause of peace, and so transparently honest, that the French Government, for once, was prepared to treat us without that background of reserve which is nearly always present in their relations with us. The prevailing habit in France is to regard our statesmen as much more subtle and clever than they really are, and seldom to take what they say at its face value. Between Guizot and Lord Aberdeen, however, no such difficulty existed.

In September, 1843, Queen Victoria had paid a visit to Louis Philippe at the Château d'Eu—the first time an English sovereign had been to France since the reign of Henry VIII. The cordial

[1] Isabel was born on October 10, 1830.

visit was returned by the French King in 1844; and again in 1845 (September) Queen Victoria went to the Château d'Eu. She was accompanied by the Foreign Secretary, Lord Aberdeen; and Louis Philippe, in receiving her, was accompanied by Guizot. The question of the future Spanish Marriages (i.e., Isabel's and Louise's) was discussed; for Isabel's hand there were several candidates, princes of the house of Bourbon, but in the discussion at Eu they were reduced to two, namely the cousins of Isabel, Francisco Duke of Cadiz [1] and his brother Henriques Duke of Seville. Don Francisco was considered to be a political reactionary, and also rumoured to be physically incapable of having children.[2] Don Henriques, on the other hand, was a Progressist (or Liberal) in politics, and had no physical disqualification, so Great Britain favoured the pretensions of the Duke of Seville.

> Both the King and Guizot said they had no objection to the Duke of Seville. . . . With respect to the Infanta, they both declared in the most positive and explicit manner, that *until the Queen* [Isabel] *was married and had children,* they should consider the Infanta precisely as her sister, and that any marriage with a French Prince would be entirely out of the question.[3]

It is quite clear, and denied by nobody, that the French Government undertook that the marriages of the Queen and of the Infanta should not be simultaneous. On the other hand, Guizot at Eu made it clear that France was absolutely against the idea of a Coburg-Spanish marriage. And Lord Aberdeen had assured him that the British Government would not support the candidature of the prince of Coburg. "As for the Coburg candidature, you can be tranquil on this point; I answer that it will be neither avowed nor supported by England." [4]

[1] Francisco de Asiz (Assisi), son of Francisco de Paula, who was second son of King Charles IV.

[2] This view was expressed freely at Madrid. *See* Bulwer to Palmerston, September 2, 1846 (F.O., Spain, No. 699), after the marriage of Isabel to the Duke of Seville, "by whom, it was said but a month ago, that she was not likely to have children." On the other hand Palmerston, even in the most secret correspondence, never mentions the report. Bulwer himself after a later interview with the Duke of Cadiz writes, "I am inclined to form a more favourable opinion of him in some respects than is generally entertained" (September 22, 1846, in F.O., Spain, No. 699).

[3] The Earl of Aberdeen to Sir Robert Peel, September 8, 1845 (*Letters of Queen Victoria,* chap. XIV.)

[4] *Revue Retrospective,* p. 19. The conversation is here reproduced by Louis Philippe in a letter to the Queen of the Belgians, dated September 14, 1846.

There is no doubt at all about the French promise that the Infanta would not marry a French prince simultaneously with the Queen. Guizot, in the laboured defence of his policy which he makes in his Memoirs, does not deny it.[1] But after making the promise at Eu, he seems to have reflected that it did not sufficiently safeguard France's interests: so he resolved to define and indeed to amplify the condition made at the interview at Eu, concerning the Coburg candidature. On February 27, 1846, he indited a Memorandum which contained the statement that:

> if the marriage of the Queen [Isabel] with Prince Leopold [of Coburg] or with any prince other than a descendant of Philip V, became probable or imminent, the French Government would consider itself quit of all engagement, and would regard itself free to demand the hand of the Queen or of the Infanta for the Duc de Montpensier.[2]

The Memorandum was sent to M. de St. Aulaire, French Ambassador at London, who forthwith went to the Foreign Office and read it to Lord Aberdeen (March 6, 1846). Lord Aberdeen, no doubt, listened with his habitual courtesy and patience, but he could not agree to the view that the compact concerning the Queen's marriage issuing in children *before* the Infanta should marry could be made to depend on the complete banning of the Coburg candidature. All that he had agreed to was that the British Government would not support the prince of Coburg. But they could not interfere with the Queen Isabel's freedom of choice.

Then, in June, 1846, came the fall of the Tory Government, after the repeal of the Corn Laws. The Whigs came into office, with Lord John Russell as Prime Minister and Lord Palmerston as Secretary of State for Foreign Affairs. Louis Philippe and Guizot, and the French generally, had no love and no trust for Palmerston, especially since the Eastern affair of 1839–1840. They thought he was sure to be working to outwit France, and to get a prince of the house of Coburg for Queen Isabel.

In these suspicions the French had some justification. A perusal of Palmerston's correspondence shows that he was not greatly interested in the personality of any of the candidates for Isabel's hand, but that he considered a prince of Coburg to be quite a possible candidate. But he thought that Don Henriques, the brother

[1] Guizot, *Mémoires*, t. VIII, p. 226: "quand la reine Isabelle sera mariée et aura des enfants. . . ."
[2] *Ibid.*, p. 254.

of the Duke of Cadiz, was the most suitable person for Isabel's hand.[1] His chief preoccupation, however, was, at all costs, to maintain the separation of the French and Spanish thrones, according to the rule established by the Treaty of Utrecht. He would have acquiesced in the marriage of Isabel to a Bourbon prince (of one of the cadet branches), and in the marriage of the Infanta to a son of Louis Philippe, but only after Queen Isabel's marriage should have issued in children. This was strictly according to the Eu Compact. It had been agreed, however, that England would not support the candidature of the prince of Coburg. Therefore when he *did* ultimately bring forward the name of Leopold of Coburg, he acted in a highly impolitic manner, although there was nothing exactly dishonourable in this, as he did it with full knowledge of the French Government.

Although, however, Palmerston acted quite openly, the same course was not so easy for the English minister at Madrid, Henry Bulwer. He knew that a Coburg marriage would be unobjectionable to England, and so he did not discourage the Queen Regent when she approached the Coburg family with a view to her daughter's marriage with a prince of this House.

> I did not think myself called on to express an opinion on the course she had adopted. I did, however, fully explain that a Coburg marriage would not be considered in England as an English one; that no support could be expected from us on that ground; but I allow that I also stated, it appeared to me that a marriage so reasonable and unobjectionable could not be persistently opposed by the King of the French.[2]

This occurred while Lord Aberdeen was still Foreign Secretary, shortly before Palmerston came into office. Aberdeen, when he learned what Bulwer had done, sent him a severe reprimand, and also informed Guizot. But the suspicions of the French had, not unnaturally, been aroused; and when Palmerston became Foreign Secretary, they felt that he could not be trusted to treat them as frankly as Lord Aberdeen had done. The best thing which Aberdeen or Palmerston could have done then would have been to recall Henry Bulwer, and to put in his place some one, perhaps Lord Clarendon, in whom the French had confidence. As Bulwer was left at Madrid, the very enterprising French minister there, M. Bresson, felt that the English Government was really working for

[1] Palmerston to Bulwer, July 24, 1846. (F.O., Spain, No. 694.)
[2] Bulwer, *The Life of Viscount Palmerston*, III, pp. 223–4.

its own ends, and therefore that he was justified in over-reaching it if possible. In fact Bulwer and Bresson were pitting themselves against each other. In this struggle M. Bresson scored the most brilliant success of his diplomatic career (although the ultimate results were disappointing).

M. Bresson was certainly watching affairs very closely.[1] The Queen Mother, who was at first inclined to Bulwer's side, came round to Bresson's point of view. She had no love for the proposed marriage of her daughter with the Duke of Cadiz, as she doubted *qu'il ne fut homme*; but if the marriage was to take place, she was not prepared to make the Infanta Louise's marriage with Montpensier depend on the uncertain prospect of Isabel having children. So Bresson made a bold move, which, if successful, was calculated to secure eventually the throne of Spain for the Duke of Montpensier's [2] descendants. On July 12 (1846), he took upon himself to declare to the Regent that if Queen Isabel married the Duke of Cadiz, the French Government would consent to a *simultaneous* union of the Infanta Louise with the Duc de Montpensier.

Louis Philippe's first instinct, when he heard of Bresson's *coup*, was to act according to his promise (as given to Lord Aberdeen at Eu), and to disavow his zealous ambassador; and indeed he wrote to Guizot to this effect on July 20, 1846: "a formal disavowal is indispensable . . . give it promptly and clearly on the point of simultaneity. . . ." [3] But on the very day when Louis Philippe was taking steps to keep to his engagement, Lord Palmerston communicated to Jarnac, French *chargé d'affaires* at London, a copy of instructions which had been sent on the previous day to Bulwer at Madrid. These instructions mentioned three possible candidates for the hand of Queen Isabel: the prince of Coburg, the Duke of Cadiz, the Duke of Seville.[4] The mere mention of a prince

[1] On April 3, 1846, Bresson had learned that Queen Isabel had just become marriageable. He sent a telegram to Paris: *La Reine est nubile depuis deux heures.* Lord Cowley, British ambassador at Paris, somehow got a copy of the telegram and dispatched it to the Foreign Office. (*See* F.O., Spain, April 8, 1846.)

[2] The youngest of Louis Philippe's five sons. He died in 1890 and left issue.

[3] Louis Philippe to Guizot, July 20, 1846; *see also* letter of July 24, 1846. Haussonville, *Pièces*, II, 157, 159.

[4] Dispatch of July 19, 1846. The dispatch included some very disparaging references to the lack of constitutionalism of the Spanish Ministers (*Parliamentary Papers*, 1847, No. LXIX, p. 280). But this passage was noted in the document not to be for communication to the Spanish Government. The full dispatch is in F.O., Spain, No. 694.

of Coburg made Louis Philippe (acting on Guizot's advice) believe that he was being tricked by Palmerston, and that he was now free from the engagement made at Eu: "We have to prepare," he wrote to Guizot, "a riposte to that astonishing and detestable dispatch."[1]

It was not merely Louis Philippe who was incensed by Palmerston's now famous dispatch of July 19. The Spanish Ministers were, it seems, equally angered, not by the suggestion of a Coburg marriage, but by the denunciation of Spanish arbitrary government which the dispatch also contained, although Bulwer had been instructed not to communicate this part of it to them. So Louis Philippe was persuaded (by Guizot) not to send his disavowal to Bresson; and the Spanish Government was persuaded (by Bresson) to consent to a double and simultaneous marriage with the French royal house. On September 14 the Cortez gave its approval,[2] and, in spite of Palmerston's loud protests, the two marriages were celebrated—that of Queen Isabel to the Duke of Cadiz, and of the Infanta Louise to the Duc de Montpensier, both on October 8.

The result of the Spanish Marriages was such as few people could have expected. Queen Isabel and Don Francisco of Cadiz had issue, and their line reigns at Madrid to-day; the Infanta and the Duc de Montpensier had issue too, but it is no nearer to the Spanish succession than ever; while Louis Philippe's line within two years ceased to rule in France, so that the union of the French and Spanish dynasties became in any case impossible. The grand result of the whole affair was that by breaking the Anglo-French *entente* it rendered quite ineffective the protests of Palmerston and Louis Philippe against the destruction of the Polish Republic of Cracow. This unfortunate little State was, contrary to article VI of the Treaty of Vienna, suppressed by the Courts of Austria, Russia, and Prussia on November 6, 1846.

[1] July 25, 1846, Haussonville, *Pièces*, II, 165.

[2] Bulwer to Palmerston, September 18, 1846 (F.O., Spain, 699). Bulwer did not think the approval of the Cortez signified much. He told Palmerston that the deputies were mere adventurers and place-hunters.

CHAPTER IX

THE DIVIDING YEARS: GERMANY AND AUSTRIA

§ 1. The Revolutions

It has been remarked that diplomacy played only a secondary rôle in Europe during the years 1848 and 1849.[1] This was because every State was either in revolution or threatened with revolution; and consequently each Government was too much occupied with its own affairs to have leisure for transacting business with another. In France, a socialist movement was being tried, and was failing; in the rest of Europe Liberal, national movements were struggling for recognition, and for this time at least, were failing too. In those circumstances the diplomatists could only fold their hands and do nothing, for these were internal questions; and even the dull, long drawn-out duel between Austria and Prussia in the years 1850–51, was more a domestic German question than one directly involving international relations.

The Revolution started in France with a riot on February 22, 1848. On the 24th, the aged king Louis Philippe abdicated in favour of his grandson, the Comte de Paris, but this act was unavailing. On the same day he had to fly to Honfleur, *en route* for England. A republic was proclaimed in Paris, and a new government established with Lamartine as its provisional head. This great poet held the portfolio of Foreign Affairs.

The Revolution of 1848 was partly the work of the bourgeoisie, partly that of the artisans. It was animated by the ideals of 1792, and aspired, though less violently, to help other nations to their freedom. No sooner was the republic established than Lamartine issued a manifesto to Europe (March 5). In this, while protesting that the republic was in no sense aggressive, he declared that France would accept war, though she did not threaten it; and he added

[1] Debidour, II, p. 1.

that " the treaties of 1815 no longer exist in law in the eyes of the French Republic ; however, the territorial circonscriptions of these treaties are a fact which it admits as basis and point of departure in its relations with the other nations." [1]

The treaties of 1815 were certainly again upon trial. The system of territories which they had established was shaken to its foundations, tottered, seemed on the point of collapsing, and then marvellously recovered. The recovery must be largely ascribed to the Austrian statesman, Prince Schwartzenberg.

The revolution in Paris seemed to be the signal for similar movements, which had for years been germinating, to break out elsewhere. One of the first places to move was Munich, but this attempt came to nothing, for it was only occasioned by the king's infatuation for Lola Montes, and died down when she was expelled. More serious were the risings in Poland, but Austria, Russia and Prussia each moved masses of troops into their respective portions of that land, and quelled the insurrection (March-April, 1848). In Germany itself, however, things were not so easily settled. Insistent demands for constitutions were put forward everywhere ; and all the little Courts, who were much more at the mercy of public opinion than those of the large States, made concessions to the times. But the real blow to legitimacy came when Vienna rose, on March 13 (1848). Metternich fled to Holland ; and with the fall of this Nestor of statesmen, the Habsburg dominion disintegrated. Venice, under Daniele Manin, expelled the Austrian garrison, and re-established the republic ; Milan, the capital of Lombardy, also expelled its Austrian garrison, in spite of the valiant efforts of Marshal Radetzky. On March 24, Charles Albert, King of Sardinia, issued an appeal to the Italian nation, and joined in the war for freedom. Nearer home the Habsburgs were no less troubled. Vienna was twice pacified and twice again it revolted (the last revolt began on October 6, 1848). Bohemia was also in revolution, but the worst blow came from Hungary, where in the same month Austrian authority almost wholly disappeared, and a national government under Kossuth, and powerful armies under able generals—Bem and Görgei—came into existence.

The Austrian empire was always shaky, and depended for its existence upon a nicely adjusted ponderation of forces. That

[1] The full text is given in Lamartine, *Histoire de la Révolution de* 1848 (Paris, 1849), II, pp. 34–41.

ponderation was now destroyed. It was expected, too, that the French would intervene on the side of the Italians: the discreet Austrian ambassador in London, Dietrichstein, himself gave this impression to Lord Malmesbury.[1]

The way in which the Austrian monarchy, with all its dominions in eruption, fought its way back to stability, must be recognised as one of the heroic tales of history, in spite of the sympathy which the cause of the vanquished naturally evokes. On June 17, 1848, Field-Marshal Windischgrätz entered Prague after bombarding it; on October 31, he re-captured Vienna. In November the Emperor Ferdinand I performed almost his last public act, and perhaps his most important: he summoned Prince Schwartzenberg, aged forty-eight, from the Legation at Naples, and made him Chancellor (November 21).

The new Chancellor at once made his influence felt. He was no sooner installed than he induced the colourless Emperor to resign, in favour of his nephew, the eighteen-year old Francis Joseph. Meanwhile success had attended the Austrian arms in Italy; Radetzky had re-taken Milan; the insurgents in Venice were closely besieged. The racial antagonisms in the Austrian Empire proved, at the moment, convenient. Jellachich, the Ban (or Governor) of Croatia, led his men against Hungary.

The *coup de grace*, however, was not given by Jellachich, nor by Windischgrätz, but by a Russian army. In the summer of 1848 Russian forces had occupied Moldavia and Wallachia, on the occasion of revolutionary movements which were going on there, as in most of the rest of Europe. The Hungarian national insurrection, if it had been successful, would certainly have caused the revival of the Roumanian national movement, and would have made the Russian hold upon the Principalities impossible to maintain; and this, in turn, would have been fatal to all Russian aims in the Balkans. It may be that some such reasoning influenced the Tsar Nicholas I; doubtless, too, he had a more generous motive, and wished to help a youthful brother monarch in distress. In May, 1849, the Russian columns passed the frontier into Hungary. Assailed by Austrian, Croatian and Russian arms, the Magyars were forced to submit. On August 13, General Görgei and his men laid down their arms before the Tsar's Commander-in-chief, Prince Paskievich, at Vilagos in Transylvania.

[1] *Memoirs*, I, 229 (March 8, 1848).

§ 2. The Imperial Crown

The Austrian dominions thus were at peace again, and the unwieldy Habsburg empire was functioning, not altogether inefficiently, under the vigorous and adroit leadership of Schwartzenberg. And now the duel between Austria and Prussia was to begin.

The Austro-Prussian trouble became serious over the question of Federal Reform. The old Holy Roman Empire had been dissolved in 1806. In place of this, the Congress of Vienna had established a loose Federal Government, consisting of a Diet, in which all the Sovereign German States should be represented—Austria and the larger States by one vote each, the smaller States by halves, fourths or sixths. The total number of votes in the Diet was seventeen; Austria, according to article LVII of the Vienna Congress Act, was to be perpetual president.

This Federal Constitution had during the next forty years been not altogether a dead letter; so long as Austria and Prussia saw eye to eye with each other, its decrees, such as those enforcing censorship of the press, had proved fairly effective. There was, however, a strong body of Liberal opinion growing up in Germany, which desired a more representative system. This opinion was fostered chiefly by university professors and men of letters; they were numerous and earnest; and in the middle of the century it seemed certain that Liberal opinions would triumph.

The movement for Federal reform was quite unofficial, but it was none the less potent for that; and after the February Revolution in France it was carried forward very methodically. First a powerful, self-appointed committee of publicists met at Heidelberg (March 5, 1848); then a Vor-Parliament of about 500 members drawn from the various State Legislatures came together at Frankfort (March 31); and this in turn arranged for elections to be held throughout Germany for a National Assembly. These elections took place, and the National Assembly met at Frankfort on May 18, 1848. The next step was to frame a Constitution (to supersede that established by the Vienna Congress Act), and to find an effective head for it. The obvious head was now Prussia—a powerful state with a large Liberal party—instead of Austria, which since 1815 had been steadily in favour of the *status quo*.

The German movement was not merely Liberal. It was also

strongly national; a very eminent school of historians, led by Leopold von Ranke, were by their wide and thorough researches bringing home to every German the knowledge of the past greatness and extensiveness of the German people. It was remembered that Alsace and Lorraine had formerly been within the Empire. And when King Christian VIII of Denmark died on January 20, 1848, and his successor Frederick VII declared his intention of incorporating Schleswig and Holstein with his other hereditary dominions (instead of keeping them separate under his Crown), Prussian troops, with the approval of the German nationalists, invaded these duchies, and even Jutland itself (April, 1848). It was not till four months later that the Powers of Europe were able to arrange a long armistice (Malmoë, August 26, 1848).

Meanwhile the Austrian dominions were still in revolution, and the Frankfort National Parliament was able to carry on its work unimpeded. The choice of an emperor had not yet been made, but an *imperial vicar* had been found—the Archduke John, the soldier-son of the Emperor Leopold II, and a man of Liberal outlook. The appointment of a Habsburg as Vicar did not deceive Schwartzenberg into thinking that Austria was to be given the headship of the new Confederation. So he began sending very firm notes to the Frankfort Diet, and to insist that Austria should be in the Confederation, not merely as regards her German territories, but as regards her non-German territories—Hungary, Croatia, even Lombardy and the rest. The Frankfort Assembly, however, under the Presidency of Freiherr Heinrich von Gagern, a life-long Liberal and a firm supporter of Prussia, insisted (January 14, 1849) that Austria could only be admitted for her German territories—a condition which was needed to satisfy the national aspect of the German movement, and also to prevent Austria from preponderating by the sheer weight of her miscellaneous dominions.

After this affairs began to move more quickly, and on March 12, 1849, the Frankfort Assembly definitely offered to Frederick William IV of Prussia the position of Emperor. And now Prussia stood at the parting of the ways, and looked for a moment down the long vistas of time; and then she turned her head aside. King Frederick William would not take up the gage of battle against Austria, even with an Austria still struggling against powerful rebel armies in Hungary; still less, at this moment, would he accept an imperial crown offered to him by the Liberal constitutional politicians of

Germany. An empire created in this way would necessarily have been strictly parliamentary, and would have functioned through a Ministry responsible not to the Emperor, but to the Imperial Assembly. He was fortified in this view by the Junker politicians —the Kreuzpartei or Party of the Cross—General Leopold von Gerlach, the jurist Heinrich von Gerlach, General von Manteuffel, and, less prominently, Otto von Bismarck. The upshot was that Frederick William, after many hesitations, refused the Imperial Crown (April 28, 1849).

We are not done with this somewhat vague prince. We shall meet him again at Olmütz. But at this moment he comes forward with the greatest precision of which he is capable, before he retires again to that shadow-land of religious-historical mysticism to which he naturally belongs.

> vidi e conobbi l'ombra di colui
> che fece per viltate il gran rifiuto.[1]

The great German Liberal experiment was at an end. On June 18, the rump of the Frankfort Assembly, which had removed itself to Stuttgart, was dissolved by the Wurtemburger soldiery.

§ 3. Olmütz

After the rejection of the Imperial Crown, Prussia makes an independent bid for a limited headship of Germany, or rather for the headship of a limited part of Germany; but she is brought smartly to heel by Schwartzenberg, just before he closes his brief but remarkable career.

At the beginning of summer, 1849, an insurrection, coupled with a demand for a constitutional government, occurred in Saxony (May, 1849). It was quelled by the Royal Saxon Government, with the help of two battalions of Prussian troops. A similar insurrection quelled with similar means occurred in Hanover. Frederick William IV felt himself to be on the crest of a wave, and impelled by his confidant, the fiery anti-constitutionalist Joseph Maria von Radowitz, he took a decisive step towards forming a limited German union under Prussia. On May 26, 1849, he concluded at Berlin a League of the Three Kings—Dreikönigsbundniss—with Saxony and Hanover. On this league was to be based a "Union," to

[1] "I saw and recognised the shade of him who through cowardice made the great refusal." Dante, *Inferno*, III, 59.

include all the North and Central German States, under the headship, of course, of Prussia. The plan met with a fair measure of success, and a Union Parliament, elected from Prussia and her satellites, met at Erfurt (March 20, 1850).

The Erfurt Parliament, however, under the ægis of Prussia, was to have no more success than had the Frankfort National Assembly. Schwartzenberg, now by the help of Russia quit of the Hungarian insurrection, was in his inscrutable way, engaged in sapping the Union's foundations; and he had useful, though not exactly intentional, allies in the medium-sized German States—Saxony, Hanover, Bavaria, Wurtemburg—which had no desire to be enfeoffed to Prussia. In particular he was helped by the expert Saxon Foreign Minister, Count Beust. Beust's plan was to keep his State clear both of Prussia and of Austria: and to establish between these two powerful competitors a Middle German Union. This he actually accomplished with the aid of the Bavarian Minister Freiherr von der Pfordten, when a League of Baden, Bavaria and Saxony was concluded on February 27, 1850. Thus the Erfurt Parliament when it met a month later was already doomed.

On April 26, 1850, Schwartzenberg launched his grand attack on the whole Prusso-Union policy by inviting all the German sovereigns to send delegates to a General Assembly at Frankfort, a Diet of the old Confederation—still legally in force—as established by article LVI of the Treaty of Vienna. This Assembly actually met, and Prussia, although protesting, felt bound to have representatives there. The Presidency of the Assembly was, of course, with Austria.

Then occurred a rising in Hesse-Cassel, and the Elector had to flee. He naturally betook himself for sympathy and support to Austria, the great upholder of legitimacy. Acting under Austrian influence, the Diet at Frankfort decreed that the Elector must be restored by Federal troops. But before they could get to Hesse, Prussia had already sent troops into the electorate, claiming, as head of the Erfurt union, to have the right of restoring order there. For a few days Prussian and Federal (Bavarian-Austrian) troops faced each other in the neighbourhood of Fulda, and a collision took place at Bronzell. Fortunately no loss of life resulted, although some Austrians were wounded, as was also a Prussian horse, which thereupon became famous in history (November 8, 1850). Actually the King of Prussia had already decided to retire, and not to submit his claim for the hegemony of Germany to the ordeal of battle.

On November 1, a momentous Crown Council had been held at Berlin, and Count Brandenburg (a son of Frederick William II) gave his earnest advice in favour of negotiation with Austria. Five days later he was dead, but he had done his work. Frederick William IV had decided on peace, and the Prussian troops in Hesse were given the order to retire.

Schwartzenberg was all for boldness, and he seized the opportunity to press his attack home. On November 25 he presented an ultimatum, demanding Prussia's consent within forty-eight hours to the occupation of Cassel by the Federal (that is the Bavarian-Austrian) troops. The *attaque brusqué* succeeded marvellously: Frederick William offered immediately to send a representative to discuss matters in person with Schwartzenberg. The firm and clear-sighted Austrian had in effect gained his point. On November 29 he and Manteuffel met at Olmütz and signed a "punctuation" according to which Prussia and Austria both agreed to demobilise, but Prussia was to begin demobilising first. Frederick William IV was to abandon his Union-project; and the Germanic Confederation was to go on with Austria as President. Thus Prussia, having first refused the headship of Germany when it was offered by the Liberals at Frankfort, had now failed to win it off her own bat. Olmütz was the day of her greatest humiliation until the fatal year 1919.

§ 4. Dresden

The end of the troubled period 1848–50 came with a Conference of the German States, held at Dresden in December (1850). The Prussian Government was still drinking small beer. Bismarck, then a man of considerable though not commanding influence, mentions in his Memoirs the contrast at Dresden between "Prince Schwartzenberg on the first-floor with his liveries, silver-plate and champagne," and "the Prussian minister with his clerks and his water-bottles one pair higher." [1] Yet Austria did not get everything that she wanted at Dresden: and when the final liquidation was reached she was left as head of the old Confederation, but without the inclusion of her non-German provinces.

So the arrangements of the Congress of Vienna, so far as concerned Germany, were left intact. Yet the matter had been treated

[1] Bismarck: *Reflections and Reminiscences*, Chap. III. *ad fin.*

throughout as a purely German affair, with which the rest of Europe was not concerned. This was, however, not the view of Louis Napoleon, who on March 5, 1851, issued through the *Ministère des Affaires Étrangères* a note to the Powers signatory of the Treaty of Vienna. This note stated the really obvious truth that the federal organisation of Germany could not be changed without the assent of the eight Powers who had established it. It is a pity that this elementary truth was lost sight of in the next twenty years.

One result at any rate stands out clear from the history of the years 1848–50. The Habsburg Empire had gained another lease of life. But the man who gave it this lease was not himself to share in it. On April 5, 1852, Prince Schwartzenberg, the second founder of the Germanic Confederation, the last great Austrian, died, in the fifty-second year of his age.

CHAPTER X

THE CRIMEAN WAR

Various opinions have been expressed about the Crimean War; and current opinion concerning it has been frequently revised. In the light of the Great War of 1914, the view may be taken that France and England made a mistake in fighting Russia in 1854—that it would have been better to let Turkey be partitioned and her people thrust out of Europe. Yet the grand fact remains outstanding that even after the Great War, and the complete defeat of a perfidious Turkey by the same Allies, it has still been found necessary to leave the Turk in Constantinople.

A second outstanding fact is that—whatever other motives went to produce the war—the Crimean War was, as far as England was concerned, fought in defence of a treaty—the Treaty of London, July 15, 1840, between the Four Powers, in the preamble of which the Powers stated their intention of maintaining the integrity of the Ottoman Empire.

In purely British history the Crimean is prominent as being the only big war of the Victorian Age, and yet a war which scarcely interrupted the solid comfort of that period. Politically it was important as confirming the strong tradition of the Foreign Office in favour of Turkey. On the French side it is always remembered as the glorious period of the otherwise rather inglorious Second Empire—the last time under Napoleon III that "French diplomacy spoke a language worthy of herself,"[1] when the Emperor's policy was clear-sighted and firm, and his arms strong and successful.

The periods into which the diplomatic preliminaries of the war are naturally divided are (1) the Affair of the Holy Places; (2) the Question of Protectorate of the Greek Church; (3) the Vienna Conference.

[1] P. de la Gorce, *Histoire du Second Empire*, I, 216.

§ 1. The Holy Places

The first definite cloud to come upon the Eastern horizon since the crisis of 1841 was when the disputes between Latin and Greek monks in Palestine attracted the attention of the Governments of Europe.

Since the time of the Crusades, France had stood in the position of protector of pilgrims in Syria and Palestine. In modern times this claim was recognised by Turkey in a Capitulation, negotiated by France and the Porte, in 1740.[1] With the development of Russian power, however, in the eighteenth century, the members of the Orthodox Church in the East began to raise their heads, and to look to the Tsar as to a protector; and the Greek monks took heart of grace to dispute the pre-eminence of the Latins.

It was not till the year 1850, however, that the dispute seriously attracted the attention of the Governments. On May 28, 1850, General Aupick, French Ambassador at Constantinople, addressed to the Turkish Minister for Foreign Affairs a note demanding restitution to the care of the Latin monks of various sanctuaries seized by the Greek monks. The chief grievance, perhaps, was that the Greeks excluded the Latins from the Church of the Nativity at Bethlehem, and had removed from the Grotto of the Sacred Manger a silver star which had been there for years, and which pilgrims greatly venerated.

After General Aupick had left Constantinople, the negotiations were carried on by the Marquis de la Valette, a diplomatist of long experience whom we shall meet again in the fatal year 1866. On the Russian side, M. de Titoff, the Tsar's ambassador, was very insistent at the Sublime Porte. The matter is said to have caused a good deal of mystification and some ironical amusement to the Turks; while to the Tsar Nicholas, and to the Russian upper classes in general, who always took a great interest in foreign affairs, it caused considerable irritation.

In 1852 M. de la Valette was replaced at the French Embassy

[1] Capitulation May 25, 1740; France had no right of protectorate over the native Christians; but foreign Christian subjects were allowed to travel in the Turkish dominions, *Sous la bannière de l'Empereur de France* (the Kings of France always styled themselves Emperor in dealing with the Sultan). The essential parts of the Capitulation are given in Albin: *Les Grands Traités* (1912), p. 128.

by M. de Lacour, the dispute being still unsettled. The Porte cannot be said to have acted quite straightly, for it had a *firman* of the Sultan issued publicly in favour of the French monks, and a secret *firman* communicated to the Tsar's Government, in favour of the Orthodox monks. But soon the Question of the Holy Places was overshadowed by another matter—the Question of a Protectorate over all Greek Christian subjects of the Porte. So urgent was this affair that Stratford Canning, the English ambassador at Constantinople, went straight to M. de Lacour and urged him to finish the question of the Holy Places without losing an hour. On this point, which, after all, was secondary, France should be conciliatory.[1] Thus adjured, M. de Lacour, with the help of Sir Stratford, induced the Porte, who were now getting rather alarmed, to issue a *firman* (May 4, 1853), re-establishing the *status quo ante*, as between the Latin and Greek monks: the Latins were to have their keys to the Church at Bethlehem, and the star was to be replaced in the Grotto of the Sacred Manger.

The Question of the Holy Places was now closed. It is worth remembering for three reasons: it focussed the public attention of Europe, relaxed since 1841, once more on Constantinople; it showed that city to be, as it will remain till the end of Western Civilisation, the nerve-centre of Europe; it ended with a slight, yet obvious, rebuff to the proud autocrat Nicholas I, and so put the Russian Government into a condition of suppressed irritation that was very unfavourable for the settling of the next question.

§ 2. The Protectorate of the Greek Church

The next question was certainly more serious. "Regarded as a whole," says the historian of the Second Empire, "the Question of the Holy Places has a certain grandeur; reduced to its details, it takes on the aspect of a discussion, not religious, but simply liturgical, and lending itself, in some respects, to raillery."[2] The French people were too sensible to fight over that; and the correspondence of Stratford Canning with Lord Clarendon, the Secretary of State for Foreign Affairs, shows that the English people, on their side, took little real interest in it. In fact, *The Times*, a faithful mirror

[1] *See* Lord Stratford de Redcliffe to the Earl of Clarendon, April 4 and April 20, 1853, in *Parliamentary Papers*, 1854, No. LXXI, pp. 154, 155.

[2] De la Gorce, I, 141.

of public opinion in the nineteenth century, was during the dispute for the Holy Places, distinctly anti-French.

But the Question of the Greek Protectorate was a different thing. As the premier Orthodox Power, the Russian Government had, quite reasonably, come to consider herself as in a sense the protector of the interests of all members of the Greek Church, of whom in 1853 there were about eleven million under the sovereignty of Turkey. Russia, however, had no right, under international law, to intervene in the internal affairs of Turkey. The most she had ever gained was by article 14 of the Treaty of Kutchuk Kainarji, July 21, 1774, according to which there was to be a Greek Church in Galata under the protection of the Russian Government.[1]

On February 23, 1853, the diplomatic corps at Constantinople was startled by an announcement of their Russian *confrère*, M. Ozerof, that an Envoy Extraordinary was shortly to be expected from St. Petersburg. This was no less a person than Prince Mentchikoff, who belonged to the inner ring of the inner ring of the governing class of Russia, and who had held the highest posts in administration (as Governor of Finland), in the Army (in the Persian and Turkish Wars), and in the Navy (as Admiral of the Black Sea Fleet, and Minister of Marine).

The arrival of such a high personage portended something tremendous. When he came, expectations were not disappointed, for he had an *entourage* worthy of a monarch, a staff as brilliant as could be produced by the magnificent Imperial Russian Court. The attitude of Prince Mentchikoff was as haughty as his mundane splendour could justify or excuse. He deigned to make a formal call upon the Grand Vizier, but he passed by deliberately the open doors of the *bureau* of the Minister for Foreign Affairs (the Reis Effendi). The Sublime Porte was considerably impressed by this behaviour, and the Minister for Foreign Affairs, as he was apparently not a *persona grata* to the Tsar, was replaced by another.

It so happened that at Mentchikoff's arrival, both the French and British Ambassadors were on leave; meanwhile M. Benedetti (later famous as Ambassador at Berlin in 1870) and Colonel Rose (known better in Anglo-Indian history as Sir Hugh Rose or Lord Strathnairne) were *chargés d'affaires*. Their letters to Paris and London displayed the profoundest disquietude. Drouyn de Lhuys,

[1] Article XIV: printed in Hertslet, III, 2011.

the very sensible and level-headed Minister of Foreign Affairs in France, took a serious view of the news; but Lord Clarendon, the British Secretary of State, was inclined to make little of it, although M. Walewski, the French Ambassador (who knew the East well, having been consul at Cairo during the crisis of 1840–41), was insistent on the danger. The Russian Chancellor, Count Nesselrode, the only Congress of Vienna statesman still in active work, made light of the whole thing. To the British Ambassador, Sir Hamilton Seymour, he confessed that Russia had no complaints against the Porte: Mentchikoff had only to deal with "some outstanding private claims . . . the demands which form the current business of every Chancellery."[1] No one, however, believed that the highest grandee in the Russian Empire had been sent on mission to Constantinople merely to regulate a few details.

The mystery was soon to be solved. In an interview with the Grand Vizier, on March 22, 1853, Mentchikoff demanded that an addition should be granted by the Sultan to the rights secured to the Tsar under the Treaty of Kutchuk Kainarji. The Tsar was to be acknowledged as protector of the Orthodox subjects of the Sultan, and this position was to be secured by a formal treaty between the two Governments. When Stratford Canning came back from his holiday a fortnight later (April 5, 1853), he saw at once that Colonel Rose was right: it was now a question of the independence of the Ottoman Empire.

This was the opinion firmly held by Stratford Canning;[2] and it was at this moment that he went to M. de Lacour and gave him the urgent advice, already noticed, to make all possible concessions over the question of the Holy Places, as being only a secondary matter; but on the question of the treaty, an energetic line must be followed. The upshot of Mentchikoff's mission was that the Sultan offered, by a "spontaneous act" to confirm the immunities and privileges of his Orthodox Christian subjects, but refused to make a bi-lateral treaty to this effect, as such treaty would give

[1] Seymour to Clarendon, March 24, 1853 (*Parl. Papers*, 1854, No. LXXI, p. 118).

[2] Canning (de Redcliffe) was by no means an undiscriminating supporter of Turkey. His policy from 1830 onwards was to get the Foreign Office to follow a definite line—either to let Turkey be disintegrated or to keep it intact. He had clear ideas on the means of carrying out each policy, but he did not wish the policies to be confused. See his long Memorandum on the Eastern Question, in F.O. Turkey, No. 211 (December 19, 1832).

Russia a permanent ground for intervention (May 18, 1853). On the 22nd Mentchikoff took his departure from Constantinople.

§ 3. The First Conference of Vienna

The scene now shifts for a time from Constantinople to Vienna, for Austria, though not yet a Balkan Power, was at any rate a Danubian Power, and highly interested in the Eastern Question. The Austrian Chancellor was Count Buol-Schauenstein, rather a commonplace man, aristocratic, stiff, self-satisfied, but with good intentions. He had been brought up on the pure milk of Metternich, and held the belief (only he lacked Metternich's ability to carry it out), that crises could be tided over, and the affairs of Europe adjusted, by a prudent diplomacy. The aged Metternich was still behind the scenes; his letters to Count Buol [1] fortified the Chancellor in his design to keep the peace of Europe.

In the middle of the summer of 1853 Count Buol assembled the ambassadors of the Great Powers at his palace, and discussed the crisis with them.[2] This meeting, regularly repeated throughout the following months, came to be known as the Conference of Vienna. Buol acted as President of the Conference, and conducted the discussions with dignity and efficiency. The task of the Conference was to find some formula which would satisfy the demands of the Tsar, without compromising the independence of the Turks. The matter was pressing, for on the refusal of the Porte to enter into a treaty, the Tsar Nicholas had given the order to his troops to occupy the Principalities. On June 3, 1853, the first Russian columns actually crossed the Pruth. There was no resistance, because the Turks did not keep garrisons in Moldavia and Wallachia; and, in fact, the Russians, who had occupied certain points in the Principalities in 1848, had never completely evacuated them.[3] The occupation of the Principalities was not precisely an act of war, because under the Treaty of Adrianople, September 14, 1829, Russia had a special position there, although they were under the

[1] *See* Metternich, *Mémoires*, t. VIII, pp. 348, 350.

[2] The Russian Ambassador at Vienna, M. de Meyendorf, did not take part in the meetings; he was the brother-in-law of Count Buol.

[3] By the Treaty of Balta Liman, May 1, 1849, Russia had undertaken to evacuate the Principalities "after the tranquillity of the said frontiers shall be re-established," but the execution of the treaty, which was a complicated arrangement, was put off on various grounds, and Russian troops remained in Moldavia till 1854. Deb. II, p. 38 n.

sovereignty of Turkey. Still Nicholas' action obviously brought war nearer.

The result of the deliberations at Count Buol's palace was the adoption of a Note on July 27, 1853. This Note was actually drafted by the Emperor Napoleon III and communicated through M. Bourqueney at Vienna to Count Buol. The important part of this Note was in the form of an acknowledgment by Turkey of the rights of Russia:

> If at every period the Emperors of Russia have shown their active solicitude for the maintenance of the immunities and privileges of the Orthodox Greek Church in the Ottoman Empire, the Sultans have never refused to consecrate them afresh by solemn acts which testify their ancient and constant benevolence towards their Christian subjects.[1]

The Tsar at once acceded to this Note, and Count Buol congratulated the Conference and himself on having settled the crisis. When the Note reached Constantinople, Stratford Canning (who was in the complete confidence of the Porte) at once advised its acceptance. But the Porte referred it back to the Conference at Vienna, with certain modifications.[2]

At this moment the public opinion of Europe was undoubtedly against Turkey. The Ambassadors at Vienna had made what seemed to them a fair compromise; Russia had accepted it; why would not Turkey do so too? But almost immediately opinion came round decidedly in favour of Turkey, when the Russian Government communicated to M. Drouyn de Lhuys, the French Foreign Minister, a despatch containing *Observations on the Turkish Modifications of the Vienna Note* (September 20, 1853).[3] This commentary, which was the work of Count Nesselrode, showed

[1] French text in Kinglake, I, 501.

[2] The note as amended by the Porte said: "If at every period the Emperors of Russia have shown their active solicitude for the maintenance of the immunities and privileges of the Orthodox Greek cult and Church, the Sultans have never ceased to watch over the maintenance of the immunities and privileges which they have spontaneously accorded on various occasions to this cult and Church in the Ottoman empire and to consecrate them by solemn acts. . . ." The important addition was obviously the word *spontaneously*.

[3] It had been drawn up for the information of the Tsar alone. By some inadvertence it was sent to Vienna, thence to the other Cabinets, and finally by another indiscretion, found its way into a Berlin newspaper (see *Diplomatic Study of the Crimean War*, Russian Official Publication, Trans. 1882, I, 214–7).

that the Russian Government interpreted the Vienna Note in a much more drastic sense that that in which the Ambassadors had meant it. Such was the opinion of Drouyn de Lhuys, and also of Lord Cowley, British Ambassador at Paris.[1]

With the refusal of Russia to acquiesce in Turkey's modifications of the Vienna Note, the war-cloud grew blacker. The Russians were now massing along the Danube; in Constantinople the war-fever appeared. There is absolutely no doubt that Stratford Canning, though he did not think the Turks should give way to the Russians, urgently and honestly advised them not to declare war.[2] But declare war they did, in a grand Council held on September 26, 1853. At the moment, they stood absolutely alone.

§ 4. The Franco-British Alliance

Both the French and British Governments now felt that the integrity of Turkey was at stake; and although they would have been in favour of further negotiation, yet now that Turkey had declared war, they would not allow her to be defeated, and either partitioned or made into a Russian Protectorate. On October 2, 1853, the French and English fleets together anchored in Besika Bay. On the 25th they passed through the Dardanelles, consistently with the Convention of 1841 which only stipulated that the Straits should be closed while the Porte was at peace. On November 27, a Turkish squadron, sailing with troops and provisions to Batoum, was met and annihilated by Admiral Nakhimof's squadron off Sinope. The news caused a perfect storm of indignation in France and Great Britain, not because the battle of Sinope was unjustifiable as an act of war (no one could seriously hold this view), but because it was a direct flouting of the French and British Fleets which had anchored in the Bay of Beikos and thrown their protecting ægis over the Turks. *The Times* led the warlike spirit of the British nation, and proclaimed that the peace which England had enjoyed for forty years seemed now almost certain to be broken. Lord Aberdeen's Cabinet certainly did not desire war, but it is really impossible to see how they could at this juncture have avoided it, unless they definitely adopted the Quaker view of life which John

[1] "Russia put a very different interpretation upon the sense of the Vienna Note from that intended by the Conference." Cowley to Clarendon. September 20, 1853, in *Parl. Papers* (1854), LXXI, p. 545.

[2] Lane-Poole: *Life of Stratford Canning*, II, 291.

Bright was so resolutely maintaining. Palmerston, Home Secretary, was never in favour of turning the other cheek, and undoubtedly he had the opinion of all England with him. There is nothing in the memoirs of the time to indicate that Napoleon III was unreasonably bellicose: the Austrian diplomatist, Baron Hübner, takes the view that he was pacific, but was bound to stand in with England. On January 4, 1854, the French and British Fleets left Beikos Bay and were towed into the Black Sea.[1] It was not, however, till February 4, that M. de Kisselef left the Russian Embassy at Paris, and that his colleague, M. de Brunnow took his passports and departed from London. Even yet all hope was not at an end. Kisselef and Brunnow had orders not to go far away from their former embassies, so they marked time for a period at Brussels and Frankfort. Sir Hamilton Seymour and Castelbayac had not yet quitted the English and French Embassies at St. Petersburg; but on February 20 they, too, left.[2] On February 27, a courier brought to St. Petersburg a final demand from France and Britain that Russia should evacuate the principalities. No answer was returned. The official notification of war was made in Paris on March 27, in London on March 28; the Russian Government alone made no declaration of war. The treaty of alliance between Great Britain, France and Turkey was made on March 12.

§ 5. The Seymour Conversations

The question is often asked: was the Crimean War a mistake? This can only be answered by another question: was it worth while to defend Turkey? On this point opinions differ; but if it be granted that Russia should not be allowed to partition Turkey, then it must be acknowledged at the same time that there was no way to prevent this except by war. When, before hostilities actually began, the Russian Government took exception to a speech made by Lord John Russell in the House of Commons (February 17, 1854), the British Government replied by publishing as a Parliamentary Paper, all the documents relative to the Eastern Question.[3] These

[1] *Parl. Papers*, 1854, No. LXXI, p. 808 (Stratford de Redcliffe to Clarendon, January 5, 1853).

[2] Nesselrode offered Seymour his passports on February 13. Seymour accepted, but remained at the Embassy for another week, *ibid.*, pp. 933, 944.

[3] *Parliamentary Papers*, 1854, No. LXXI, p. 835 ff. The whole volume contains perhaps more diplomatic documents of the highest historical interest than any other volume of the great series of command papers.

contained, among other things, a record of the now celebrated conversations between the Emperor Nicholas and Sir Hamilton Seymour, the British Ambassador at St. Petersburg. The first conversation took place at an Assembly on the evening of January 9, 1853, in the palace of the Grand Duchess Helena. The Emperor, in private conversation, referred to his excellent relations with the British Government and to his long acquaintance of forty years' standing with the universally respected Lord Aberdeen. After further conversation, being pressed by Seymour to "add a few words which may tend to calm the anxiety with regard to the affairs of Turkey," the Emperor said, "in an open and unhesitating manner":

> The affairs of Turkey are in a very disorganized condition; the country itself seems to be falling to pieces; the fall will be a great misfortune, and it is very important that England and Russia should come to a perfectly good understanding upon these affairs, and that neither should take any decisive step of which the other is not apprised.[1]

The words were striking and hinted a great deal. Seymour, who throughout the whole affair acted with the highest skill and prudence, pressed gently for enlightenment: then came the famous remark:

> Tenez; nous avons sur les bras un homme malade—gravement malade.

The next interview took place on January 14, when Seymour was summoned to a private audience: the Emperor, after observing that Russia was already quite big enough, if not too big, continued (in reference to the "sick man"):

> eager as we all are for the prolonged existence of the man (and that I am as desirous as you can be for the continuance of his life, I beg you to believe), he may suddenly die upon our hands. . . . I put it to you, therefore, whether it is not better to be provided beforehand for a contingency than to incur the chaos, confusion and the certainty of an European war. . . .
>
> Now I desire to speak to you as a friend and as a *gentleman*; if England and I arrive at an understanding of this matter, as regards the rest, it matters little to me. . . . Frankly, then, I tell you plainly, that if England thinks of establishing herself one of these days at

[1] Sir G. H. Seymour to Lord John Russell, January 11, 1853 (*Parl. Papers*, 1854, vol. LXXI, pp. 835–6). The conversation was in French. Seymour reported the above passage in English.

Constantinople, I will not allow it. I do not attribute this intention to you, but it is better on these occasions to speak plainly; for my part I am equally disposed to take the engagement not to establish myself there, as proprietor that is to say, for as occupier I do not say; it might happen that circumstances, if no previous prevision were made, if everything should be left to chance, might place me in the position of occupying Constantinople.[1]

The Tsar could scarcely have spoken more explicitly. He simply proposed to occupy Constantinople and to partition Turkey, by arrangement with England. He dismissed the ambassador with a charge to convey the Tsar's views to the Queen's Government. On February 20, Nicholas again returned to the subject. On learning from the Ambassador that Great Britain refused to discount the Ottoman Succession before the end was even in sight, the Tsar expressed his regret at the decision, and persisted in declaring that Turkey was utterly collapsing:

I report to you that the sick man is dying; and we can never allow such an event to take us by surprise. We must come to some understanding; and this we should do, I am convinced, if I could hold but ten minutes' conversation with your Ministers—with Lord Aberdeen, for instance, who knows me so well. . . .

At the fourth interview (February 21), the Tsar asserted that the catastrophe was imminent, and proceeded to sketch out a rough plan of partition: Serbia and Bulgaria were to be independent, under Russian protection. "As to Egypt," said the Tsar, "I quite understand the importance to England of that territory. I can only say, that if, in the event of a distribution of the Ottoman Succession upon the fall of the Empire, you should take possession of Egypt, I shall have no objections to offer." The brilliant prize was thus held out, but Seymour brushed it aside. England only desired, he said, "a safe and ready communication between British India and the mother country." A fifth interview on April 19 carried the negotiations no further.

There were no more of these conversations. They show perfectly clearly that Nicholas deliberately designed to partition Turkey when the Sultan should die, or when any suitable crisis should occur in the Ottoman Empire; he recognised that he could only do this by arrangement with England; and accordingly he pro-

[1] All this paragraph was reproduced in the French original in Seymour's report.

posed to share the spoils with England but *to exclude France* as Seymour remarks in his dispatch to Lord John Russell on February 21. When England refused to make a partition arrangement, Nicholas, proud and powerful despot as he was, resolved to go his own way. The reply of England to this was the Crimean War.

There is a curious resemblance between the negotiations of February, 1853, and those between Germany and England in July, 1914. Just as Nicholas I offered through Seymour a gigantic bribe for England, to the detriment of France ; so in 1914 did the German Chancellor offer, through Sir Edward Goschen, the ambassador in Berlin, the prospect of great gain, to the detriment of France. On both occasions Great Britain followed the straight course, and refused to enter into any plot to overset that balance of power, of which France is an essential part.

§ 6. Second Conference of Vienna

The Crimean War, fought with equal heroism on both sides, and with an evident determination to conduct it according to the dictates both of honour and humanity, came practically to an end with the capture of Sebastopol on September 8, 1855. The military objective of the Allies was attained. The enemy, on their part, had held the fortress to the last, and, on its becoming untenable, had evacuated it, and marched away in strength. Circumstances clearly pointed to the proposal by the Allies, and the acceptance by the Russians, of an honourable peace.

As a matter of fact, however, formal peace-negotiations did not begin, and even an armistice was not arranged, till nearly six months after the capture of Sebastopol. On the other hand, long before the fall of that fortress, the diplomatists, both neutral and belligerent, had been busy discussing peace-terms, and had at any rate arrived at a basis on which peace might be concluded.

The first difficulty to be got out of the way was the Russian occupation of the Principalities of Wallachia and Moldavia. It was this occupation that really created a state of war between Russia and Turkey. The unsuccessful siege of Silistria, heroically defended by Turks under the command of two English volunteers,[1] resulted in the fortune of war on the Danube turning in favour of Turkey. Meanwhile Austria had mobilised her army. She had

[1] Lieutenants Ballard and Naysmith.

no intention of letting Russia hold possession of provinces on her Danubian and Transylvanian frontier. At this period Prussia was following steadily in the wake of Austria. On April 20, 1854, the two Powers signed a Convention by which they guaranteed the security of each other's territories, and agreed jointly to recommend Russia to evacuate the Danubian provinces. But Prussia, although she consented to enter into this treaty, was not very enthusiastic about it. The Russian orientation, which only a few years later Bismarck was to champion so ardently, was already becoming evident, and the relations between Berlin and London were growing cool. The Chevalier de Bunsen—a popular figure in English society—was recalled from the Prussian Embassy, and replaced by General von Groeben, a pro-Russian Junker. It appears that the Prussian Government delayed the dispatch of the demand for evacuation of the Principalities, in the hopes that meanwhile the Russian army on the Danube would capture Silistria.[1] But the siege dragged on, and the Turkish flag still waved over Silistria when the courier left Vienna on June 3, bearing the Austro-Prussian Note. Then followed the usual period of prevarication, an art in which Nesselrode the Chancellor and Gorchakoff his most prominent pupil were particularly skilled; at last, on August 7, 1854, the Tsar formally declared that the Principalities had been evacuated. The truth is that for military reasons the Tsar had, since the defeat of his forces at Giurgevo on July 7, been steadily withdrawing his forces.

Thus by August 7 the Principalities were evacuated,[2] but Russia had not abandoned any of her claims. Meanwhile the Allies were no nearer to forcing her to conform to their demands; not a single soldier had landed in the Crimea. But Russia seemed in a fair way to having the greater part of Europe against her, for Austria was taking steps to join the Allies. On August 8, 1854, the ambassadors of England and France at Vienna exchanged with Count Buol notes which contained stipulations which became subsequently famous as the *Four Points of Vienna* (of December 28, 1854). These points were: (1) the Russian protectorate of the

[1] Deb. II, 117.

[2] By a treaty concluded between Austria and Turkey on June 14, 1854, Austria was authorised to occupy the Principalities, and she actually did send forces into them. By the Treaty of Paris, March 30, 1856, article 21, all occupied territories were evacuated. Mention is especially made of the Austrian treaty in this article.

Danubian provinces was to be replaced by a collective protectorate of the Powers; (2) the navigation of the Danube was to be free; (3) the treaty of July 13, 1841, was to be revised in such a way as "to connect the existence of the Ottoman Empire more completely with the European equilibrium, and to put an end to the preponderance of Russia in the Black Sea"; (4) Russia was to renounce her claim to any exclusive patronage of the Christian subjects of the Porte. Then came the landing of the English, French, and Turkish forces in the Crimea (September 14, 1854), and the victories of the Alma (September 20), Balaclava (October 25), and Inkerman (November 5). These events stimulated the somewhat sluggish chivalry of Austria, and on December 2, Count Buol signed an actual Treaty of Alliance with France and England. By this treaty Austria engaged, if peace was not made on the basis of the Four Points within a year, that she would deliberate with France and England "upon effectual means for obtaining the object of their alliance."[1] This was as far as Austria went on the way towards war. It cannot be said that her diplomatic support in the slightest degree helped France and Great Britain, or shortened the war by a single moment. The Anglo-French armies had to fight the war to the bitter end, till they took Sebastopol ten months later. All that the Court of Vienna had really done was to fulfil the prophecy made by Prince Schwartzenberg, after the Tsar had helped to quell the Hungarian revolt: that Austria would some day astonish the world by her ingratitude.

Yet for a time it was to appear as if peace would really be made in Vienna, for on January 7, 1855, Russia accepted the Four Points as a basis for negotiation. So nothing apparently remained to be done except to open the Peace Conference—a ceremony which Count Buol actually performed on March 15.

The Conference of Vienna, which was absolutely ineffective, lasted two and a half months, and was attended not merely by the Allied ambassadors—Lord Westmorland and M. de Bourqueney—but also by the English Secretary of State for the Colonies, Lord John Russell, and the French Minister for Foreign Affairs, M. Drouyn de Lhuys. And although Russia and the Allies were still at war, and although not even an armistice had been concluded, the Russian ambassador Prince Gorchakoff took part in the negotiations as a regular member of the Conference.

[1] The treaty is in Hertslet, II, No. 252.

The first two points, concerning the protectorate of the Danubian provinces and the navigation of the Danube, were conceded by Russia. On the third point—the security of the Ottoman Empire, involving the *limitation of Russian forces in the Black Sea*—Prince Gorchakoff, after many and long delays, finally gave a refusal, because, as he not unreasonably said, a Great Power only consents to the limitation of its forces after a great reverse, "and we have not come to that." He was a very skilful and courteous man. Another remark of his (made before the Conference met) was: "We are not at the *Caudine Forks*, and I still presume to speak in the name of a great State." All this was true enough, and as Russia refused to neutralise the Black Sea, the Allies went on fighting till she changed her mind, which proves that they won the war. But Austria was not in it: where Count Buol, with all his grandeur, all his great words, feared to tread, the black-coated, bespectacled Cavour rushed in: on January 26, 1855, he had signed a treaty of adhesion to the Anglo-French alliance, and 15,000 Sardinian troops left Genoa for the Crimea.

§ 7. The Congress of Paris

Sebastopol was evacuated by General Gorchakoff (the brother of the diplomatist) on September 8, 1855. On all sides it was felt that peace was imminent; and Count Buol thought to resume his commanding diplomatic rôle. "Austria is now the possessor of the Danubian Principalities," he remarked to Count Beust, whom he met on a summer holiday at Golling near Gastein.[1] France was weary of war and ready for peace; but Lord Palmerston was by no means willing to sacrifice the fruits of the Allies' victory to the egoism of Austria. He had foreseen that Austria would try to bring about an unsatisfactory peace.[2]

As happens in every war, there were plenty of neutral parties ready to offer their good offices. Among these were two ministers of the minor States of Germany. In those days the minor States still had a policy and a spirit of their own, and aspired to keep outside the orbit of either Prussia or Austria. It so happened,

[1] Beust, *Memoirs* (Eng. Trans. H. de Worms, 1887), I, 141.

[2] Ashley's *Palmerston*, II, 106 [ed. 1876] (a characteristic letter of January 24, 1856, to Hamilton Seymour, who was now ambassador at Vienna).

too, that the House of Romanoff had for years formed its marriage alliances chiefly with the dynasties of the minor German States. For these reasons the enterprising ministers of Bavaria and Saxony (Freiherr von der Pfordten and Count von Beust) were able to act as very influential intermediaries between the Courts of Paris and St. Petersburg. The result of their labours was that Russia offered to make peace without paying indemnity or ceding territory; while France would make peace if the Black Sea were neutralised. Great Britain was not quite so accommodating; and Lord Palmerston roundly told the French Government that England would continue the war by herself along with Turkey; and this was no empty threat, for the English forces were at their very best, especially in respect of equipment and provisioning, when Sebastopol was taken. At last it was agreed that all the belligerents should come together at Paris to make peace on the basis of the Four Points of Vienna, *plus* a provision for rectifying the frontier of Moldavia. Austria was to be a member of the Congress, as she was vitally interested in the Eastern Question, and also because she was the author of the project of peace.

The Congress of Paris sat from February 25 to April 18, 1856. The delegates were, for France, M. Walewski, Minister for Foreign Affairs, and M. de Bourqueney, Ambassador to the Court of Vienna; for Great Britain, Lord Clarendon, Secretary of State for Foreign Affairs, and Lord Cowley, Ambassador at Paris; for Austria, Count Buol, Chancellor, and Count Hübner, Ambassador at Paris; for Sardinia, Cavour, and Villamarina (Minister at Paris); for Turkey, Ali Pasha, the Grand Vizier; for Russia, Counts Orloff and Brunnow. The Prussians had had no concern in the Crimean War, but as signatories of the Convention of the Straits, 1841, they were admitted to the Congress on March 16, when the question of the neutralization of the Black Sea was broached. They participated in the rest of the sessions, and signed the treaties. M. Walewski was elected President of the Congress, and M. Benedetti, who at this time held the post of Director of Political Affairs at the Ministère des Affaires Etrangères, was appointed General Secretary.

As there was very little technical work to be got through, no statistics to be compiled, no elaborate researches into history, finance, and ethnology to be made, the Congress accomplished its task without overworking. Its first act was to conclude an armistice, to last till March 31. It usually sat every other day; from the 14th to the 18th of March there were no sessions at all, because on the 14th the Empress began to labour in child-birth, and the event was important enough to overshadow everything else. On the 16th the Prince Imperial was born, and on the 18th all the plenipotentiaries went to the Tuileries to see the baby. The treaty was signed at the Ministry of Foreign Affairs on Sunday, March 30, at half-past one o'clock.

Peace was concluded without indemnities, on the basis of the territorial *status quo ante bellum*, with one exception. This exception was contained in article 20, by which a strip of Bessarabia, along the lower Pruth and along the most northern mouth of the Danube, was detached from Russia and added to Moldavia. Thus Russia lost the Danube Delta (which she had gained by the Treaty of Adrianople, 1829 [1]), and also the north bank of the Kilia mouth and the east bank of the lower Pruth. Although this was a cession of territory by Russia, there was nothing in the treaty to suggest compulsion: article 20 merely stated that the rectification of the Emperor's frontier in Bessarabia was in exchange for the towns in the Crimea which the Allies undertook to restore to him.[2] As M. de Bourqueney remarked later to Count Beust: "When one reads the treaty of March 30, no apparent sign reveals who is victor and who is vanquished." [3]

Article 11 establishes the neutralisation of the Black Sea, opening it to the Mercantile Marine of every nation, and interdicting it to the Flag of War of every Power. Consequentially to this, article 13 engages the Tsar and the Sultan not to establish or maintain on the coast of the Black Sea any military-maritime arsenal.

This prohibition was a terrible check to a great nation. One wonders whether the Russian Chancellery acceded to it all the more easily because, as the shrewd Count Beust wrote to Nesselrode, "it was against the nature of things to forbid an empire of eighty million inhabitants to have ships of war in its own

[1] See above, p. 51.

[2] "In exchange for the Towns, Ports and Territories enumerated in Article IV of the Present Treaty, and in order more fully to secure the freedom of the Navigation of the Danube, His Majesty the Emperor of All the Russias consents to the rectification of his Frontier in Bessarabia. The new Frontier shall begin from the Black Sea, etc., etc."

[3] Beust, I, 144.

waters."[1] As a matter of fact the prohibition remained in force for only fifteen years.[2]

The neutralisation of the Black Sea was the special provision for securing the safety of the Ottoman Empire from Russia. A more general provision was contained in article 7, which declared the Sublime Porte admitted to the Public Law and Concert of Europe, and at the same time guaranteed the independence and territorial integrity of the Ottoman Empire.

By article 9, all the Signing Powers explicitly disclaimed any pretension to interfere, either collectively or separately, in the relations between the Sultan and his subjects. Thus the question of the Russian Protectorate was solved. In the same article, the Powers took note of the Firman which the Sultan, "in his constant solicitude for the welfare of his subjects," had issued on February 18, "emanating spontaneously from his sovereign will." This Firman (the Hatti-Hamouin), like all its brethren, contained an admirable list of reforms—freedom of conscience, equal taxation, and so forth—but being carefully made to depend simply on the will of the Sultan, and not on any guarantee of the Powers, it was not worth the paper it was written on.

Article 15 extended the force of the Vienna Congress Act, relative to the freedom of navigation of international rivers, to the Danube. To facilitate the navigation, a Commission of all the Signing Powers (Great Britain, Austria, France, Russia, Prussia, Sardinia, and Turkey) was established to clear the mouths and to carry out all the necessary technical works below Isatcha.

Article 22 guaranteed the privileges of Wallachia and Moldavia under the suzerainty of the Porte. No right of exclusive protection might be exercised by any of the guaranteeing Powers. The Principality of Serbia also had its privileges confirmed and placed under the collective guarantee of the Contracting Powers.

Finally, in accordance with a stipulation which had been incorporated with the Four Points in the preliminaries of peace, the Powers dealt with certain matters pertaining to the affairs of Europe in general. One of those matters was annexed to the Main Treaty, and was declared to have the same force and validity as if it formed a part thereof. This was a convention by which

[1] Boust, I, 142.
[2] *See* below, pp. 215–6.

Russia undertook not to fortify the Åland Islands, so that the Swedes could feel safe in Stockholm.

A second matter was mediation to prevent war. Statesmen believed that if two Powers, on the point of war with each other, would submit their dispute for consideration to a third party, this consideration, even if it did not solve the difficulty, would, merely by reason of its delay, so allow passions to cool that war might not ensue. It was in this hope that the Powers, in the 23rd Protocol of the Congress of Paris, signed on April 14, expressed "the wish that States between which a serious difference may arise should, before taking up arms, so far as circumstances may allow, have recourse to the good offices of a friendly Power." This Protocol was appealed to by the British Government, in 1866, and again in 1870, but with no result.[1]

A more effective step was taken by the Congress in drafting a Declaration on Maritime Law. The Powers took the opportunity to settle the old question of neutral trade in time of war. As usual, Great Britain was the target at which they aimed, and as usual the British Government was hard put to it to avoid the loss of the right it has always claimed and exercised, to stop the sea-borne trade of neutrals with its enemies. The ghosts of the Armed Neutralities of 1780 and 1800 were hovering over Paris. In the end, if Great Britain lost some of her power to stop neutral trade, she gained something in the matter of blockade and privateering. For the British Navy is big enough to make its blockades effective, and not to require the help of privateers. The Declaration of Paris was signed on April 16, 1856. It is: (1) Privateering is, and remains, abolished; (2) the Neutral Flag covers Enemy's Goods, with the exception of Contraband of War; (3) Neutral Goods, with the exception of Contraband of War, are not liable to capture under Enemy's Flag; (4) Blockades, in order to be binding, must be effective, that is to say, maintained by a force sufficient really to prevent access to the coast of the enemy.

One more thing must be noted. On April 8, the Congress,

[1] The *voeu* (wish) of the Protocol was introduced in the Congress by Lord Clarendon. By article 8 of the Treaty of Paris the *voeu* was made compulsory for disputes between Turkey and any one of the Signing Powers. If such a crisis were to arise, the disputants were bound, before having recourse to arms, to submit the question at issue to the consideration of the other Contracting Parties.

having finished the Russo-Turkish Question, was exercising its roving commission over the affairs of Europe. It was then that Lord Clarendon made his dramatic attack on the political condition of Italy. No resolution was taken, but Lord Clarendon's remarks, with Walewski's more moderate comments, were engrossed in the Protocol. The Italian Question had been placed before Europe.[1]

[1] *See* below, p. 129.

115

PART II

The Union of Italy

CHAPTER XI

ITALY FROM THE CONGRESS OF VIENNA TO THE FAILURE OF THE REVOLUTIONARY MOVEMENT OF 1848

During the Napoleonic Wars, part of Italy had been annexed to France, part was erected into a "Kingdom of Rome" directly under French control, while the Kingdom of Naples and Sicily, under Joachim Murat, was definitely within the French system. Italy, in fact, for the first time in modern history, had become not indeed politically a unity, but at any rate, to some considerable extent, politically homogeneous. Administration, throughout the length and breadth of the Peninsula, conformed to the enlightened French type. Soldiers, raised from every part of the country, fought together in the Grande Armée of Napoleon; and the national consciousness, which had never been extinguished even amid the multitudinous territorial divisions of the mediæval period, became manifest and distinct.

The Powers at the Congress of Vienna naturally swept away all French domination from Italy, but only to instal another alien Power instead. This was Austria, who acquired Lombardy (she had held this province previously from 1715 to 1797), and also the great territory of Venice on the Italian mainland—the Powers thus restoring the vast bribe that Bonaparte had given her by the Treaty of Campo Formio, 1797.

In most other respects, Italy was restored to her eighteenth-century condition. Pope Pius VII returned to the States of the Church; the old Bourbon dynasty, in the person of Ferdinand I, was restored to the Kingdom of Naples and Sicily; a cadet branch of the Habsburgs again ruled in Tuscany; the Este family came back to Modena; Parma was left to the Empress Maria Louisa (wife of Napoleon)[1]; the Kingdom of Sardinia-Savoy got back Piedmont, to which the ancient republic of Genoa (with Spezzia) was now added, so that San Marino alone was left of the Mediæval City States of Italy.

The Kingdom of the Two Sicilies (or Naples) included the island of Sicily and the southern mainland of the Peninsula; its northern frontier was within fifty to sixty miles of Rome. The States of the Church extended over the greater part of Central Italy, northwards to the River Po: their chief divisions were (1) the Patrimony of St. Peter (with Rome in the centre); (2) Umbria; (3) the Marches of Ancona (on the Adriatic side of the Apennines); (4) the Legations of Bologna, Ravenna, Forli, and Ferrara. The total extent of the States of the Church was between 15,000 and 16,000 square miles, and the population was something over three millions. The administration was paternal and unprogressive; there was no constitution; and as the years went on, the existence of the Temporal Power became more and more of an anachronism.

Tuscany, the other large state of Central Italy, had great traditions coming down from Medicean Florence, and from the Habsburg princes, who were types of the "enlightened despots" of the eighteenth century. Modena and Parma were insignificant bodies, and by virtue of certain treaties were practically client-states of the Austrian Government. North of the Po, the only independent power was the Kingdom of Sardinia. This State included Savoy and Nice (which are now part of France), and in Italy it had Piedmont, stretching as far east as the Ticino, and containing also the Genoese territory south of the Po, between the Apennines and the Gulf of Genoa. To the east of the Ticino was the rich land of Lombardy (or "the Milanese"), populous and fertile, and strengthened by the famous Quadrilateral of fortresses—Mantua, Peschiera, Verona, Legnago. The boundary between Lombardy and Venetia was the Mincio.

The idea of extending Austrian territory to the south of the Alps was strategically quite sound if the ambitions of a military France advancing through North Italy were still to be feared. The experience of the nineteenth century, however, was to show

[1] On her death in 1847, the Duchy lapsed to the Bourbon Duke Charles II.

that Europe was in no danger from France. The result of the rigid partitions within which the Congress of Vienna confined Italy was that the country seethed with political agitation for the next fifty years. All the States were despotically ruled; in none was there a constitution.[1]

The national spirit in Italy was kept alive and fostered in the period between 1815 and 1848 by scholars and men of letters. The poetry of Leopardi (a genius afflicted by constant ill-health) with its beauty and its terrible sadness, made Italians more than ever conscious of their unsatisfactory condition. He died, still a young man, at Naples in 1837, before any sign of political dawn had come. The Count Manzoni, in his great historical novel, *I Promessi Sposi* (published 1825), brought the Italy of the seventeenth century to the knowledge of every household. Vincenzo Gioberti—priest, philosopher, politician—wrote of *The Civil and Moral Primacy of the Italians* (1843)—Italians who in this work recognised themselves as a great nation, though divided and held down. By the year 1843, Italian audiences in the opera-houses, from Milan to Naples, were able to acclaim in Verdi the great composer common to all the race, and when they shouted *Viva Verdi*, it was known to mean *Viva Vittorio Emanuele, Re d'Italia.* But more than all, Giuseppe Mazzini of Genoa fanned the flame of patriotism. In 1831 he founded (at Marseilles, for Metternich had got him interdicted from his native country) the society of Young Italy—an improvement on the old secret society of the Carbonari. From this time he was the indefatigable organiser and propagandist of the movement towards Italian unity—a strenuous, self-denying man, willing to give up everything, even his dear republicanism, to unite and free his country.

Such was Italy before the year of Revolutions, a country of little States more or less comfortably governed under despots, but with the ideas of Dante and Macchiavelli, for the union of the whole, agitating the people throughout the length and breadth of the country. It was at this time that a new Pope was elected, a man whose work, it seemed, was to forestall the revolution which threatened his State.

Giovanni Maria Mastai Ferretti was fifty-four years old when he was elected Pope in 1846. His education, his experience (he

[1] In 1847–48 all the Italian States, except the Austrian provinces and Naples, received constitutions from their sovereigns.

was an archbishop at the age of thirty-five), his travels (he had been on a mission for the Papal Government to Chile in 1824), fitted him to be a statesman; his natural tendency was towards liberalism. So much were his advanced views feared by the Austrians, that the Vienna Government had actually put a veto on his election as Pope, but the Archbishop of Milan, who brought the Austrian instructions to Rome, arrived twelve hours too late.

Pius soon showed that he was a reformer in earnest. In March, 1848, he issued a *Statuto Fondamentale*, which established a regular constitution for the Papal State, with a legislative assembly of two chambers, one nominated, the other being elective. The Pope became the idol of his country, and was hailed enthusiastically by Mazzini and the other reformers. And indeed if only he could have thrown himself whole-heartedly into the Revolutionary movement that was then breaking out, he would certainly have become the head of a democratic Confederation of Italian States. But for this end he would have had to join in the national war against Austria, and this step he would not take.

The first step towards the union of Italy had been taken by the King of Sardinia, Charles Albert. In February, 1848, the Revolution had broken out in France and Louis Philippe had abdicated; this was followed immediately by a revolution in Vienna and by the flight of Metternich, the most determined upholder of Conservatism. The time was ripe for a revolution in Italy, and in March, 1848, Charles Albert called upon all Italian patriots to join his forces, and declared war on Austria. Milan and Venice had already risen in revolt and driven out their Austrian garrisons; and when Charles Albert crossed the Ticino, Marshal Radetzky, an octogenarian hero of the Napoleonic wars, could scarcely hold his own.

Radetzky was defeated at Goito on the River Mincio, had to abandon the strong fortress of Peschiera, and retired to Verona; but in July, having received considerable reinforcements from Austria, he came forth and routed the Sardinian army at Custozza, 10 miles south-west of Verona (July 25, 1848). Ten days later he re-entered Milan.

In the first part of the war, while Charles Albert's enthusiastic army was steadily driving back the Austrians, the Pope seemed likely to be carried away by the impulse towards national freedom. General Durando, commanding the Papal army in the Legations, was a patriot, who, like so many other soldiers of the Liberation period, had fought in the constitutionalist armies of Spain and Portugal. After Radetzky's defeat at Goito, Durando had on his own initiative crossed the Po, and marched towards Venice to cut the Austrian army's communications. It was then that Count Mamiani, one of the enlightened statesmen of Pius IX, pressed the Pope to throw in his lot completely with the national movement, by joining in the war against Austria. But Pius would not do so. Turning his back on the future, he took his stand by the *ancien régime*. Durando was recalled, but preferred to transfer his sword to the Sardinian service. The cause of Italian unity seemed lost, and on August 9, 1848, Charles Albert was only too glad to accept an armistice through the mediation of the French and English Governments.[1]

The refusal of Pius IX to declare war on Austria brought matters to a head in Rome. In November, 1848, a revolution broke out; Pius had to flee to Gaeta in the Kingdom of Naples, and a Republic was established. In March, 1849, Charles Albert was stimulated by the success of the Roman Revolution once more to take up arms; but a campaign of only four days resulted in his complete defeat by the skilful Radetzky at Novara (March 23, 1849).

The battle of Novara ended the First War of Italian Independence, but it left many things to be settled. The Roman Republic still defied the Pope under Mazzini and Garibaldi, while Venice, under the heroic Daniele Manin, held out against its Austrian besiegers. The Revolution in Italy had yet to be liquidated, and it is with the liquidation that diplomatic history is primarily concerned: *cedant arma togæ*; it is when fighting is over that the men of the gown begin really to count.

[1] Bianchi: *Storia della Diplomazia Europea in Italia* (1869), V, 317–20.

CHAPTER XII

THE LIQUIDATION OF THE REVOLUTIONARY MOVEMENT OF 1848

When the Sardinian Army suffered defeat at Novara on March 23, 1849, the Roman Republic was still in full vigour, and Manin was unconquered in Venice. Moreover Sardinia and Austria were at war, although it was obvious to every one that the struggle could not continue longer. Austria was triumphing over the rebels in Vienna and in Hungary, while in Italy Radetzky wielded overwhelming power. The Revolution was failing in Italy; the only question was whether the failure would be fatal to the cause of Italian liberty, or whether something would be saved from the shipwreck.

The first thing necessary was for Sardinia to get free from the Austrian War, without having to accept disastrous terms. The decisive step towards this end was taken by Charles Albert himself, who, on the evening of the day on which he had been defeated at Novara, abdicated the throne. He had fought to free Italy from the Austrians, and now he accepted martyrdom for the cause. He retired to Portugal, and died at Oporto a few months later (July 28).

Charles Albert had shown himself an inveterate enemy to the Austrians; but the son who succeeded him was not prejudiced in the same way. Victor Emmanuel, at this time twenty-nine years old, was a prince of a retiring and hardy disposition. Hating the etiquette and formalism of the court of Turin, he spent his time chiefly in hunting in his native Alps. As a soldier he had shown ardour and bravery in the campaigns of 1848 and 1849, but he had not engaged in politics. His family connections were with the Courts of Vienna and Florence; he was nephew to the Grand Duke of Tuscany, and had married the Austrian Archduchess Adelaide. With all this in his favour, and with the diplomatic support of France and England, he was able to get peace without irreparable sacrifices.

The first thing necessary was for Victor Emmanuel to obtain an armistice, and for this he had to pay sufficiently dearly. By a convention signed on March 26 (1849), the Austrians were to occupy the Sardinian territory between the Ticino and the Sesia, and to place a garrison in the fortress of Alessandria. This made any resumption of hostilities impossible, and showed the completeness of the Sardinian collapse.

Nevertheless, the government of Victor Emmanuel continued to hold its head high, and in spite of its defeat in the field, possessed considerable prestige. "Do the Piedmontese fancy that it is they who won the battle of Novara?" remarked Thiers. Indeed it almost seemed as if they thought so, and Massimo d'Azeglio, the new President of the Royal Sardinian Council, showed no inclination to play the part of the vanquished.

The Cavaliere d'Azeglio was exactly the man to get his country out of its troubles. Born in 1798 at Turin, a member of an old noble family, he had early identified himself with the national movement in Italy. At Rome, where his father was ambassador, he had attained some distinction as a landscape-painter; later, by his historical novels, he encouraged the national spirit. In the War of 1848 he received a wound at the battle of Vicenza from which he was still suffering when called by Victor Emmanuel to be President of the Council. Acceptable to all Italians as an ardent patriot and enthusiast for the liberty of the nation, he was, on the other hand, not unpleasing to the Austrian Government, being an aristocrat, and a man of moderate views, who had never joined any of the secret political societies or been mixed up in any conspiracy. Frank and generous, brave, firm-minded, and cultivated, no better man could have been found to guide Sardinia out of its troubles.

A satisfactory peace, in fact, was more easily agreed to by the Austrians than by the Sardinian people themselves. Austria had won the war, but her position was not too secure. The Revolution of the Magyars was not yet quelled; Venice held out, the Roman Republic still defied the anathemas of Pius IX; Revolutionary France showed cordial sympathy with the Italians, and by the famous Manifesto of the previous year (March 5, 1848) had declared that the Treaties of Vienna did not exist and that the territorial circumscriptions which they had made must be completely modified.[1] Piedmont was always regarded by French statesmen and soldiers as a buffer State between them and Austria, and throughout the Austro-Sardinian War a French army was kept massed along the frontier of the Alps. Finally Austria always had to reckon with the British Foreign Office, at this time under Lord Palmerston, who openly testified the warmest sympathy with the Italians and Magyars, and whose vigorous speeches and dispatches always sounded as if they might be followed at any moment by a demonstration in force.

It is not surprising, therefore, that Prince Schwartzenberg, the Austrian Chancellor who succeeded to Metternich's place, should, after duly weighing all considerations, decide that he would be well quit of the Sardinian War, on the basis of the *status quo ante bellum*. The Austrian armies could then return from Italy to finish off the Hungarian War, and time would be gained to deal with the Italian question later.[2]

Accordingly, after negotiations conducted through the mediation of France and England, Victor Emmanuel obtained peace without loss of territory, on condition of paying an indemnity of 75 million francs (Treaty of Milan, August 6, 1849). The Austrian Government would have liked to see the Sardinian Constitution revoked (granted by Charles Albert in the previous year), and in return for this they would have reduced the indemnity. But Victor Emmanuel refused such a bargain. Even so, the Sardinian Assembly thought the peace too dearly bought, and refused to ratify it till the Chamber had been twice dissolved and a more moderate body of representatives obtained. The treaty was finally accepted by the Assembly on December 20 (1849).

If the First War of Liberation had been a military failure, it yet resulted in great political gain. The Papacy had been practically ruled out of the contest; there was now only one possible head for United Italy, and that was the Sardinian State and the Sardinian Dynasty, which had risked all for the cause. Moreover, by his firmness in refusing to abolish the free constitution of the country, Victor Emmanuel had gained the respect and confidence

[1] See above, p. 84.

[2] M. de la Gorce is of opinion that had Schwartzenberg not been cut off by an untimely death "he would without doubt have contained or reduced his feeble adversary [Sardinia]." (*Hist. du Second Empire*, II, 267.)

even of the republican patriots. Henceforth Sardinia, the only liberal and really independent state of Italy, became the refuge and rallying-point of all patriots. Before the Treaty of Milan had even been signed we find Azeglio looking forward to a speedy extension of his State, to annexing Parma and Piacenza, and forming a customs-union with Tuscany.[1] Such was the spirit which, through many vicissitudes, finally brought the Italians to the goal of their unity in Rome.

The two great events in Italy in 1849 were the battle of Novara and the defence of the Roman Republic. It is with this second event that we have now to deal, for out of it came the French occupation of Rome, which retarded the union of Italy and ruined the diplomacy of Napoleon III.

Lamartine's Manifesto of March 5, 1848,[2] had shown the sympathy and good intentions of Revolutionary France towards the Italian patriots. But such attention as the French Government had to spare for foreign affairs was naturally directed towards Piedmont and Lombardy. The battle of Novara made the French tremble for the safety of Piedmont, which they regarded as a bastion against Lombardy. It must be borne in mind that the Congress of Vienna had deliberately placed the Austrians in Lombardy in order that they might check any recrudescence of French ambition in North Italy, and the French, naturally, did not wish them to come any closer. Accordingly, after Novara the Legislative Assembly at Paris voted that in order to guarantee the integrity of Piedmont it might be necessary to occupy some portion of Italy.[3] The authority thus obtained was used by Louis Napoleon to carry through one of the most astounding acts of his astounding career. He had been elected President of the French Republic in the previous December, largely owing to the Catholic vote, and to the influence of the clergy. He could not afford to estrange the sympathy of the ultramontane party in France; nor, moreover, would it suit him to allow the Austrians to get the credit of restoring Pius IX to Rome, and, in fact, to occupy the greater part of Italy. Accordingly an expeditionary force was assembled under General Oudinot, the son of Napoleon's Marshal,

[1] Dispatch of July 16, 1849, in Gorco, II, 268. Cp. Bianchi: *Storia della Diplomazia*, V, 589 (Emanuel d'Azeglio to Palmerston, July 6, 1850).

[2] *See* above, pp. 85, 121.

[3] March 30, 1849.

and dispatched to Civita Vecchia. Oudinot, having disembarked at Civita Vecchia on April 25, straightway advanced upon Rome, and delivered an assault which was repulsed with great bloodshed (April 30). The General then settled down to await reinforcements, while three other competitors for the honour of restoring the Pope—an Austrian, a Neapolitan, and a Spanish force—advanced from different directions towards the city.

At the same time, faithful to his tortuous method of always having at least two policies, Napoleon sent Ferdinand de Lesseps, a member of the French diplomatic service of long experience, to conduct negotiations with the Republican Government of Rome. Lesseps carried out this, his last, diplomatic mission with great ability and succeeded in concluding with Mazzini a convention by which Rome was to be placed under the protection of the French troops, who, however, were not to occupy it (May 31). Thus the city would be saved from the Austrians and Neapolitans.

This arrangement, however, was only made to be broken. In the middle of the same month of May (1849), fresh elections to the French Assembly had resulted in the return of members generally favourable to reaction in Church and State. Louis Napoleon saw his way to becoming Emperor. Throwing over Lesseps (who never obtained diplomatic employment again) and disavowing the Convention with Mazzini, he ordered Oudinot to attack Rome. After a brilliant defence, conducted throughout the month of June, the city fell, and Mazzini and Garibaldi had to betake themselves to the Apennines. The Pontifical Government was re-established by the French bayonets, and the occupation of Rome, to endure for many years, had begun.

After the fall of Rome came that of Venice. For five months Daniele Manin had held the city. It capitulated on August 24 (1849), and Manin left the scene of his greatness to live and die as a teacher of Italian in Paris.

CHAPTER XIII

THE ITALIAN QUESTION BEFORE EUROPE

Italia fara da se is what King Charles Albert had proudly declared in his proclamation of 1848; but the result of this policy had been simply defeat. The next step in the movement for Italian unity was the War of 1859; and in this case the way was very carefully prepared by diplomacy. To expel the Austrians, to conciliate the Republicans, the Federalists, the local interests of the various Italian States, and to deal with the most formidable obstacle of all, the Temporal Power, required the assistance of some strong ally and the support of public opinion in Europe; these requisites were secured by the patient efforts of Cavour. Even so the difficulties in the way of Sardinia, a State of only secondary strength, seemed insuperable; but to the weapons of diplomacy and war were added the powerful agency of luck. "One does not know which to admire most," says M. de la Gorce,[1] "the refinement of cleverness which presided over the enterprise, or the incredible strokes of fortune which allowed it to be crowned."

Camillo Benso, Count Cavour was the man of destiny for Italy. Few people, however, would have recognised the master-diplomatist of the age in the little, stout, short-sighted, black-coated delegate of the Piedmontese Parliament. Yet this little man, with all his quiet manners, and constant amiability, was one of the most ambitious of his kind, and one of the deepest. Born at Turin in 1810, he had followed the usual course of a young Piedmontese nobleman, concluding his education with a commission in the army. He left the army, however, in 1831, and never bore arms again. Although somewhat lacking in physical vigour, he was filled with a perfect intensity of intellectual activity: by reading, conversing and travelling he acquired an encyclopædic knowledge of things

[1] Gorce, II, 260.

and of men, a knowledge which was always available in his methodical, orderly brain. Geneva, Paris, and London were the places where he seemed most at home, yet he despised the position of the many Italians who lived abroad, a sort of *intellectual condottieri* as he called them. Returning to Piedmont, he bought land (chiefly by borrowing) and farmed it for profit, taking the same energetic care of his investments as he did of everything that he touched. Equally at home in railway enterprises, in irrigation schemes, or in banking developments, he soon turned to journalism and founded a paper at Turin—*Il Risorgimento* (1847)—which, supported constitutional liberty of the English pattern, and which in fact, largely helped to gain the *Statuto Fondamentale* from Charles Albert. In the First War of Italian Liberation Cavour had no chance to show his political ability; but in 1850 he entered the Azeglio cabinet as Minister for Agriculture. Two years later he became President of the Royal Council. Long before this he had fixed his aim to be minister of a United Italy.[1]

M. de la Gorce has neatly distinguished the three steps which Cavour planned and successfully made, in the long effort to convert Sardinia into United Italy.[2] The first was to create an "Italian Question"; the second was to proclaim this Question solemnly in the face of Europe; the third was to solve it by a swift attack on Austria, accompanied by a powerful ally. Each step involved the utmost difficulties; yet each was made with complete success.

The first was perhaps the easiest, and yet it required an immense labour. There was no Italian Question when Cavour became President of the Royal Council: the wrongs of Italy make little appearance in the English press before 1850, and it is difficult to say whether the British public sympathised more with Austria or with Sardinia in the War of 1848–49. George Meredith's novel, *Vittoria*, which, though written later, represents the views of an ardent friend of liberty who had lived through the time of the War, gives an attractive picture of the Austrian army as well as of the Italian patriots. But after 1850 the Italian Question comes distinctly into existence, and begins to cry for solution in Europe; and this was largely the work of diplomacy and of the encouragement and direction given by statesmen to journalists. It was the Marquis d'Azeglio who began the policy; and Cavour, when he

[1] *Lettre édite et inédite*, tome I, p. 287, in Gorce, II, 278.

[2] *Ib.*, 285.

succeeded to his position as First Minister, continued it with admirable skill. Turin had become the refuge for Italian patriots who could not live in their own States—Neapolitans, Romans, Florentines, Lombards, Venetians, all inflamed with the grievances, real and imaginary, of their people, and all burning to place their wrongs before the judgment-bar of Europe. All Italians speak and write fluently; and the exiles of Turin, many of them highly educated men, furnished splendid foreign correspondents for the *Times*, the *Matin* and for a newspaper which had great influence among Continental liberals, the *Indépendance Belge*, as well as for others. There was no need for Cavour to buy their pens, but he gave such encouragement and help as a tactful and powerful minister can easily supply.

In such a contest Austria had no chance: it is certainly easier to attack than to defend in literature; and, besides, Austria had only the cause of Absolutism, bureaucracy and religious intolerance to defend, and for this she had no army of brilliant scribes like the leisured exiles of Turin; and no one in France or England wished to hear what she had to say. It is easily understood, therefore, how the wrongs of Italy became a commonplace to all who read the newspapers in the Victorian Age. And the Italian correspondence of the *Times* or the *Matin* was judiciously extracted and reproduced in Cavour's inspired journals in Turin, thus strengthening his hands for the work in which he wished to engage his own not too ardent countrymen.

The work of the journalists engaged the sympathy of peoples. It was even easier to gain the sympathy of Governments. The Whig ministers of Great Britain were nearly always cultivated, travelled gentlemen, who knew Rome, Naples and Venice, and who naturally disliked the unprogressive Papal rule and the bureaucratic, militaristic regime of the Austrians. It so happened also that Sir James Hudson, British Minister at Turin from 1852 till 1863, was in the strongest sympathy with the views of Cavour, and gave all the help he could in the relations between the Cabinets of Turin and London. In France some difficulty lay in the strong clerical party, and in the fact that French troops now garrisoned Rome; but the personal sympathies of the Emperor had always been with Young Italy, and although his public official policy was not favourable to Cavour, his secret policy (and he always had a secret policy) was at this time all on the side of Sardinia. The dispatches of the Marquis Villamarina, Sardinian Minister to the Court of the Tuileries, made this clear to Cavour.

After creating the Italian Question in Press and Diplomatic circles, Cavour had next to place it specifically before the tribunal of European statesmen. The Crimean War gave him his chance. What interest had Sardinia in the War in the Crimea ? Well—none : except that if the Eastern Question was a subject which every European Power was bound in duty and honour to deal with, Sardinia would show that she was a European Power ; and having thus demonstrated the solidarity of the enlightened European States, she would expect them to take similar disinterested action with regard to the Italian Question.

France and Great Britain had bound themselves by a Treaty of Alliance (March 12, 1854) to make war upon Russia. The war ensued, but did not go particularly well for the Allies. By the autumn of 1854 the British army was short of men, and recruiting in England was slow. An auxiliary was needed, and as Cavour had let it be known both in London and Paris that he might join in the war, the British Government thought of getting the services of the hardy Piedmontese soldiers, well fitted to stand the rigours of the Crimean climate. But Cavour would not hear of becoming an auxiliary : Sardinia must be an Ally, equal with France and England, and able to appear at the final Peace Congress as a full member. At last, on December 13 (1854), the glad message came to Turin, when Sir James Hudson handed to Cavour a dispatch from Lord Clarendon, containing a request for Piedmontese adherence to the Franco-British Alliance. Cavour wished to make conditions, particularly that at the end of the War the Allies would take into account the condition of Italy. But, as it was still possible that Austria too might join in the war against Russia, France and Britain refused. So Cavour and his master, Victor Emmanuel, took the responsibility of joining in the war without reserve and without conditions : they would not even accept a subsidy, but only a loan of two million pounds sterling from England. On January 26, 1855, the Treaty of Alliance was signed, and in due course 15,000 picked troops, under General La Marmora, embarked at Genoa for the Crimea. They saw little fighting for a considerable period, but at the battle of the Traktir Bridge, on August 16 (1855), they covered themselves with glory.

The Congress met at Paris in February and April, 1856, to conclude the Crimean War. Here Sardinia was admitted as a full representative, although Count Walewski, the French Foreign Minister, rather pointedly said to Cavour: "You have too much tact to take part in affairs which do not concern you." The Sardinian delegates at the Congress were Cavour himself and Villamarina. The English delegates were Lord Clarendon (Secretary of State for Foreign Affairs) and Lord Cowley, the Ambassador to the Court of the Tuileries. Clarendon was extremely sympathetic with the Italian designs. The French delegates, Walewski and Baron Bourqueney (Minister to the Court of Vienna) had no liking whatever for Cavour's policy. The general secretary of the Congress was a member of the French Diplomatic Service, Count Benedetti, who was a firm supporter of Italian liberation; but his influence at this time was not great. Only the Emperor gave any encouragement, and in conversations with Cavour (in which, of course, the Sardinian minister did most of the talking), held out hopes for the future. Napoleon promised that the Italian Question would be broached after the final treaty had been signed.

The main Treaty of Paris was signed on March 30 (1856), and on April 8 Walewski, who was President of the Congress, delivered a discourse on the affairs of Europe, in which he made a number of colourless references to the condition of Italy. At the end of the discourse, Lord Clarendon, one of the most dignified and moderate of Whig aristocrats, commenced speaking. To the surprise of every one, his words were a long and passionate indictment of the Italian Governments other than Sardinia. About Austria, whose delegates Buol and Hübner were present at the session, naturally nothing could be directly said; but the views of the Papal, Neapolitan and Ducal Governments were laid bare before the assembly of horrified diplomatists. Cavour, for the only time in his life, was carried away by excitement, and at the end of the session impulsively pressed Lord Clarendon to join in a future war against Austria. But nothing more happened. Lord Clarendon was once again the suave and correct diplomatist. He made no engagements. Nor did Napoleon III make any; only on taking final leave of the Sardinian minister the taciturn Emperor allowed himself to make the following remark: "I have a presentiment that the actual peace will not last long." And this was all that Cavour had to take back from the Congress of Paris, in recompense for the efforts of La Marmora's hardy soldiers who were still encamped around

Sebastopol. But perhaps it was gain enough: the Italian Question had been dramatically placed before Europe: England's sympathy had been definitely won—and this meant that the Austrian Government had incurred the moral judgment of English public opinion, which every European Chancellor in the nineteenth century has feared and striven to avoid. Finally Cavour had begun to get Napoleon III in train for an attack upon Austria.

131

CHAPTER XIV

THE SECOND WAR OF ITALIAN LIBERATION

Napoleon III has always been something of a mystery. Few people ever thought him to be a really great man; on the other hand, it is a mistake to call him shallow. He was a silent man who mingled in great affairs, and in all showed a certain amount of competence. And, besides, he had imagination, and till his last few years had the necessary boldness and decision to try and carry out some of the things he dreamed of. "To do the things that one dreams of doing is success in life." Of this success Napoleon III had a good share. He had dreamed of becoming Emperor of the French, and he had dreamed of helping to make Italy a united nation; and both these dreams came true. In the *Idées Napoléoniennes,* written by Louis Napoleon when he was thirty years old, he explains that one of the objects which the first Napoleon set before himself and succeeded in accomplishing (till the reactionary Powers of Europe undid the work) was to re-create a free and independent Italian nation.[1] As a young man of twenty-three, Louis Napoleon had fought in the rebellion of 1831 in the Romagna—a campaign in which his elder and only surviving brother succumbed to sickness. Later the prince became a citizen of the free Confederation of Switzerland, and held a captain's commission in the artillery of Berne. There is indeed no reason to doubt that he had a sincere interest in the freedom of nations, although, for his own purposes, he was not above fettering the liberty of the French. Doubtless, too, he did not engage in the Italian War of 1859 without seeing the advantage it would be to his throne if the attention of the French people was absorbed in glorious battlefields abroad; and finally with his romanticism he mixed a little business, and expected to get something tangible out of the deal, as in fact he did get for his country the solid gain

[1] *Idées Napoléoniennes,* chap. IV.

of Nice and Savoy. Napoleon's taciturnity did not hide his motives from Cavour, who played upon each motive in turn to bring the Emperor to the battlefield.

The attempt of Felice Orsini upon the Emperor's life took place on January 14, 1858. This was the fourth time that Napoleon narrowly escaped assassination at the hands of Italian patriots. A few weeks later the *Moniteur de l'Empire* published a letter written by Orsini in prison, saying: "So long as Italy is not independent, the tranquillity of Europe, no less than that of your Majesty, is a mere chimera." And he concluded the letter: "May your Majesty not reject the last wish of a patriot on the steps of the scaffold: deliver my country, and the blessings of twenty-five million citizens will follow you in posterity." This letter had been read in full by Orsini's advocate, Jules Favre, at the trial. Before he was executed Orsini wrote a second appeal for Italy to the Emperor, and was publicly executed with the cry *Vive l'Italie!* on his lips. There is no question in this affair with regard to Napoleon's personal courage: while Orsini's bomb was still fresh in people's minds, the Emperor ostentatiously drove or rode about Paris without an escort. The excitement caused by the attempted assassination and the dying appeals of the criminal were used to work up public feeling for a policy of intervention which may already have been decided on.

It must be noticed in passing that the Orsini affair reverberated elsewhere than in Italy. It produced intense irritation between France and England, for the conspiracy had been hatched in London. To meet the remonstrances of the Imperial Government (in a famous dispatch from Count Walewski, written on January 20, 1858), Lord Palmerston introduced into Parliament a bill to deal with "Conspiracy to Murder"; the opposition provoked by this apparent surrender of Britain's position as a refuge for foreign patriots brought about the fall of the Palmerston Government, and the accession, for a brief period, of Lord Derby and Mr. Disraeli. The French Government behaved with praiseworthy restraint, and went out of its way to placate English feeling by sending Marshal Pelissier, Duc de Malakoff, of glorious Crimean memory, as ambassador to London in place of M. de Persigny. The excitement passed away, and no more was heard of the Conspiracy to Murder Bill.

By this time the feelings existing between Austria and Piedmont had become tense. It must be allowed by every one that the Austrian Government showed itself singularly patient against the constant irritation which Cavour inflicted upon it. At the end of 1856 and in the beginning of 1857 the Emperor Francis Joseph made a tour of his Italian provinces, was particularly mild and gracious towards his subjects, and appointed his own brother, the Archduke Maximilian, as viceroy. All this of course was gall and wormwood to Cavour; the Piedmontese Press was allowed to be more venomous than ever against the Austrians, to such a degree that, after a little diplomatic fencing between the two Governments, Count Buol recalled the ambassador from Turin (February, 1857); Cavour withdrew the Sardinian representative from Vienna, and for the next two years the two Governments had no diplomatic relations.

Still Sardinia was without an ally for her great enterprise; the English Government was no help, for while friendly to Piedmont, it was equally friendly towards Austria, continually giving counsels of moderation and suggestions for reform to Count Buol—advice to which the Austrian Chancellor listened with courtesy and attention. In May, 1858, however, there arrived in Turin the Doctor Conneau, whose acquaintance Cavour had made during the time of the Congress of Paris. Conneau was a very old friend of Napoleon III, and had helped him to escape from the military prison of Ham in 1846. He was an unofficial diplomatist, used by the Emperor as an agent of his secret policy. Arriving at Turin, he visited Cavour and remarked that the Emperor was going to spend a month at Plombières, quite close, said the Doctor, to the Sardinian frontier. Plombières is a pleasant little spa in the Vosges, fourteen miles south of Epinal, and was not at all near the Sardinian State. But the diplomacy of the Second Empire—not the diplomacy of the Quai d'Orsay but that of Napoleon III himself—worked by hints and *double entendres.* Cavour was all alive to the suggestion, and although no further word of invitation came to him, he set out in July to go to Plombières. The Sardinian Minister was an agreeable middle-aged bachelor with many friends, and his journey had all the appearance of a short holiday tour, such as this incredibly hard-working statesman took and enjoyed every year. On this occasion he went into Switzerland, travelling by easy stages, and staying on the way with some friends, enjoying the air and the scenery of the Alps, and diverting himself with light reading.

He had said that he was going to breathe the fresh air of the mountains away from politicians, and he carried out this part of his plan exactly, and thoroughly enjoyed his Swiss tour. Nevertheless, he must have been still more pleased with a letter which was forwarded to him at Geneva, in which one of the Emperor's aides-de-camp said that Napoleon would be charmed to see him. On the evening of July 20, 1858, Cavour arrived by railway at Plombières and drove to his hotel. Next day he met the Emperor by appointment at 11 o'clock, and the two talked together till three in the afternoon. Napoleon, according to Cavour's account, went directly to the matter which was in both their minds, and offered to make war upon Austria, on condition that Sardinia found a good diplomatic pretext. The real object was to extend the Sardinian State "from the Alps to the Adriatic," and to organise the whole Peninsula as a Confederation under the nominal presidency of the Pope. As a reward for help rendered and as a compensation for the increase of the Sardinian State, France was to get Savoy from Victor Emmanuel and also, Napoleon suggested, Nice. Cavour reserved any decision with regard to Nice, but agreed to the rest. Later in the afternoon these two highly placed conspirators went for a drive through the environing woods, and the Emperor, who was driving the phaeton himself, then asked for a marriage contract between the Princess Clothilde (daughter of Victor Emmanuel) and his pro-Italian cousin, Prince Jerome Bonaparte. This was an affair which Cavour could not settle himself, but when he got back to Turin he induced Victor Emmanuel to agree to it. The head of the ancient House of Savoy was by no means attracted by the projected marriage with the *parvenu* Bonapartes, though he had no objection to a military alliance with their *parvenu* Empire. However, he had to agree to both.

The affair of Plombières was not a regular diplomatic negotiation; it really was a conspiracy deliberately to break the peace of Europe. The news was not published to the world, but Austria can have had no doubts on the subject, especially when Napoleon, in his levée of New Year's Day, 1859, made his famous remark to the Austrian ambassador, Baron Hübner: "I regret that our relations with your government are not so good as formerly; but I pray you to tell the Emperor that my personal sentiments have not changed." In any court such a remark would have been something of the nature of a fuse to a powder magazine; much more significant was it under the Second Empire when amid the general repression of all public discussion, every word of the Emperor rang out clearly from the universal silence.[1] Meanwhile Cavour was continuing his work of inspiring complaints against the Austrian and Papal *régimes*, and inflaming public opinion on every side. The intense hatred of Austria that was now burning in Italian breasts is splendidly expressed in Fogazarro's *Piccolo mondo antico.* In January, 1859, King Victor Emmanuel, who mixed as little as he could in political affairs, was inspired to say, in opening the Sardinian Parliament, " our situation is not without dangers, for, if we respect the treaties [of Vienna], on the other hand we are not insensible to the cry of pain which arises to us from so many parts of Italy." This was something like a trumpet-call. When it was followed by a gigantic loan (50 million lire, gigantic at least for those days and for times of peace), issued in Turin, and by a semi-official pamphlet—*L'Empereur Napoléon III et l'Italie*[2]- issued in Paris, war seemed to be inevitable. The only thing that prevented hostilities was that Austria refused to take offence ; Sardinia and France could scarcely attack Austria, when they had no reason to allege before Europe for fighting. In the previous year Cavour had confidently told Lord Odo Russell at Turin that he would force Austria to commence hostilities, and he had actually named the day—the 15th of May—when the event would take place. But could it be conceived that Austria would commit such an incredible blunder ?

All this time the British Foreign Office was working hard to avert war. But if it was difficult for Napoleon to begin the war, because he had no obvious reason for fighting, it was still more difficult for the Foreign Office to avert the war, because there was no obvious difficulty to explain away. Lord Cowley at Paris had many conversations with M. Walewski, who (being really out of sympathy with Napoleon's policy) always showed himself most reasonable. With Napoleon himself, however, the English ambassador could do nothing. No one could have worked more honestly to keep the peace than did Lord Malmesbury, the Secretary of State for Foreign Affairs under Lord Derby. In February, 1859, he proposed that England should mediate between the disputing

[1] See Gorce's remarks, II, 381.

[2] The pamphlet enunciated the theory of nationalities, with special reference to Italy.

parties, and he enunciated four points as a basis for settlement: (1) The cessation of all foreign occupation of the Papal States; (2) the introduction of administrative reforms in the Lombardo-Venetian Kingdom; (3) the revision of the treaties which bound the minor Italian States to the Court of Vienna; (4) the re-opening of better relations between Austria and Piedmont. Lord Cowley went to Vienna and found Count Buol ready to accept the Four Points, and further to give a written engagement that Austria would not attack Sardinia. At this moment the Russian Ambassador at Paris, M. Kisselef, was stepping in to propose at the Quai d'Orsay a settlement of the Italian question by a European Congress. This was not quite so palatable to Austria as the English mediation would have been, because a Congress acts as a kind of tribunal, whereas mediation provides a means of private settlement between two parties. Brought before the bar of Europe, Austria was sure to suffer some considerable loss of power in Italy.

Meanwhile Sardinia had been completing its military preparations, and on March 9, 1859, the decree of mobilisation was actually issued. Yet even with the Sardinian army on a war-footing, the Turin Government could not take the step of making an unprovoked onslaught on Austria; and the Viennese Government continued its somewhat stiff, but undeniably patient attitude. England officially accepted the proposal for a Congress, provided that it did not take into consideration the question of territorial re-adjustments in Italy, and that all the Italian States were excluded (Sardinia being one of them). This last condition was not so strange as it appears; if Sardinia were admitted, then all the other Italian States in fairness would have to be admitted; and if all the Italian States were present at the Congress, Austria would have all of them (except Sardinia) on her side.

For a time it really looked as if the proposed Congress would take place. Austria consented to it, on the same conditions as England, and with the additional proposal that Sardinia should put its army once more on a peace footing. This proviso was not unreasonable, as the Congress was an alternative to war, and so the Sardinian mobilisation would be quite unnecessary. On April 18 Walewski made his supreme effort for peace; he offered by telegram to London to procure that Sardinia would disarm, if Great Britain would agree to admitting the Italian States to the Congress: "If you reply *yes*, my telegram to Turin will leave immediately." The Foreign Office at once telegraphed assent, and the same evening Walewski's message was sent over the wires to Turin. With a sad heart Cavour bowed before reason; and on the 19th telegraphed his Government's assent to the Quai d'Orsay and to London. The conditions of disarmament were to be regulated by the Congress. The War of Liberation, so long prepared, so patiently engineered amid all manner of obstacles, now all but realized, was at last, as it seemed, averted. On that self-same day, the Austrian Government, seized with madness, and before it heard of the Sardinian concession, dispatched an ultimatum.

What induced Count Buol, who had shown exemplary patience for so many years, to take this fatal step, it is difficult to say. It is likely he was acting under orders from the Emperor Francis Joseph, a man who, though he figured little in public politics, had a strong and very sinister will. All that is known is that when Lord Loftus, the British Ambassador at Vienna, went to the Ballplatz on April 20, and conveyed the glad tidings of the Sardinian disarmament to Count Buol, and to congratulate him on the peaceful issue of the affair, the Chancellor gravely informed him that on the previous evening an ultimatum, demanding immediate disarmament, had been sent out by hand on its way to Turin. Still, the bearers of the ultimatum could be stopped before they had traversed Lombardy: but the Austrian governing class has always been the proudest in the world, and would not consent to retract: "You do not understand," said Count Buol to the French Chargé d'Affaires, "if you think that we can *revenir sur nos pas*."

When Cavour received at Turin from the Austrian messengers (Baron de Kellersberg and Count Caschi de Santa Croce) the demand for immediate disarmament, his heart must have bounded with joy. It was one thing to agree to disarm at the request of the Powers of Europe in concert; it was quite another thing to do so at the single-handed demand, at the point of the pistol, so to speak, of Austria. This moment was what he had dreamed of and laboured for for years: the moment, which after all, but an hour ago, he thought would never come. Preserving his countenance, however, and without committing himself by a word, he dismissed the two Austrians, and took the three days allowed by the ultimatum to transact much urgent business connected with the coming war. At the expiration of the time, he met the two Austrians and declared his refusal. It was Austria that offered the wager of battle, and the Government of Vienna stood forth before Europe as the aggressor. The last qualms of the doubting Emperor of France were removed, and France flew to the succour of her assaulted friend.

139

CHAPTER XV

VILLAFRANCA

The rejection of the Austrian ultimatum was reported in Vienna by telegraph on the same day as it was delivered to the Austrian envoys at Turin. This sudden starting of the war by Austria, in the midst of European negotiations which had every appearance of being successful, was really quite inexcusable, and was certain to be a tremendous political blunder unless it resulted in some great military coup. And, indeed, had the Austrian forces which were then concentrated under General Giulay to the number of 100,000 men on the left bank of the Ticino, at once crossed the river, they could in a few days' rapid march have occupied Turin. Actually, they did not cross till April 29 (three days after the expiration of the ultimatum), being delayed, it is said, by orders from the Vienna Government which was at the last moment again hearkening to English proposals for mediation. Once across the Ticino, however, the Austrian commander had no further excuses for delay. Turin was only four days' march distant, and the Sardinian forces only numbered 50,000 men. He failed, however, to get into touch with the enemy till May 7 ; by this time the French troops were being poured into Piedmont by way of Susa and Genoa. All chance of swiftly dictating peace to Victor Emmanuel in his capital had gone for ever.

In the fighting that followed the Franco-Sardinian forces won the brilliant victories of Magenta and Solferino, and the Austrians were driven back into the Quadrilateral of Mantua, Verona, Legnago and Peschiera. Every one was confidently expecting a renewed effort, which would drive the Austrians out of Venetia, as they had already been driven out of Lombardy, when suddenly Napoleon III, who was quartered at Valeggio, sent one of his generals to the headquarters of the Emperor Francis Joseph at Verona and proposed an armistice (July 6). The Austrian ruler concurred, and a truce was concluded, to last till August 15.

Still, however, people believed, or affected to believe, that the war was not at an end. For Napoleon had promised Cavour at Plombières that Italy should be freed *to the Adriatic*. This decision he had solemnly confirmed in two published manifestoes; the first was on May 3, announcing the opening of the war between France and Austria, and declaring that Italy would be *libre jusqu'à l'Adriatique*; the second was after the battle of Solferino, when the Emperor entered Milan amid the joyful shouts of the liberated citizens: there he had confirmed the fondest hopes of Italian patriots: *unissez-vous*, he had proclaimed, "unite, with a single aim, the liberation of your country; my army . . . will not oppose any obstacle to the manifestation of your legitimate desires." It was expected, therefore, by Victor Emmanuel and Cavour, that Napoleon would demand from Austria the cession of at least Venetia as well as of Lombardy, so as to bring the Sardinian kingdom *jusqu'à l'Adriatique*; and as Austria would probably refuse these terms, further fighting would be necessary.

In any case, even if the armistice issued in serious peace negotiations, the Sardinian Government cannot have for a moment dreamed that they would not themselves be included as a party to those negotiations. It is true there seems to have been no written convention between the Allies for concluding peace in concert; but at the worst, it is only a defeated ally that wishes to break away and make a separate peace. That the victorious Napoleon should separately go off and make a single-handed peace with Austria, and then present the Sardinian Government with a *fait accompli*, was surely incredible: all the more so as the *fait accompli* was not what Napoleon had originally promised to do for them, yet this is what actually happened. He may have feared the spreading of revolution throughout the rest of the Italian Peninsula; he had some apprehension of the intervention of the Germanic Confederation, on the Rhine frontier of France; his sensitive nature was appalled by the casualties of his army in the field and by the outbreak of typhus. For one reason or another, he took his sudden resolve.

On July 11 (1859) Napoleon rode out with his staff from Valeggio and met Francis Joseph by appointment at the village of Villafranca. There each monarch, leaving his Staff outside, entered a villa (Guadini Morelli) and held a long conversation. To Francis Joseph the offer of the interview must have seemed like a gift from heaven. Instead of having to defend his cause in front of some mediatory Power (which was the regular way of ending a war), or of negotiating as the vanquished with the Sardinian Government whom he despised and hated, he now had the means of making a quiet and personal arrangement with his brother-monarch. By his conduct, Napoleon had practically committed himself to making peace; his army held Lombardy (except Peschiera and Mantua); so Francis Joseph could not refuse him that; but the Austrian army still held Venetia, so when Napoleon asked for that too, he was refused: and having practically committed himself to peace, what could he say to the refusal? Napoleon demanded that the Duchy of Parma (in the north of the Apennines, a natural prolongation of Piedmont) should be given to Victor Emmanuel. To which, probably, Francis Joseph replied that it was not his to give. Again, Napoleon had no answer.

Thus, in a conversation *à deux*, Napoleon, who liked doing things in a striking and unconventional manner, ended a great European War, and made a settlement of the Italian question: a settlement, however, which was perfectly unstable and did not endure for a year. For though a little conversation saves a lot of hard work, it is no royal road to solving complicated territorial and political affairs, which require careful study and minute precautions. Returning from Villafranca to Valeggio, the Emperor from memory gave to his secretariat the substance of the understanding which he had made by word of mouth with Francis Joseph. On the afternoon of the same day the Prince Napoleon took the notes to Verona, and the text of the so-called Preliminaries of Villafranca was there indited and signed (July 11, 1859). Lombardy (except the fortresses of Mantua and Peschiera) was to be ceded to France; the rights of the sovereigns of Modena and Tuscany (who had had to fly from their domains) were restored; Venetia was to remain under Austria, but as part of an Italian Confederation of which the Pope should be head; about Parma, of which the Regent Duchess was in flight, nothing at all was said.

The action of Napoleon III in thus untimely and on his own sole initiative ending the common War of himself and Sardinia, can bear no palliation. If France and Sardinia had continued the war for a short time more, Venice would almost certainly have been taken instead of requiring another great war in 1866. Even without continuing the war in 1859, Napoleon might still have carried out his promises and got Venice for Sardinia, if he had negotiated in the regular way and in concert with his ally. But his separate and private negotiations really put him at the mercy of his adversary, Francis Joseph, who escaped most of the consequences of his defeats; for he not merely kept Venetia, but by retaining the Lombard fortresses of Mantua and Peschiera, he preserved the Quadrilateral intact—a tremendous bastion of defence for Venetia towards Italy. No wonder that Cavour cast the text of the treaty to the ground and resigned his portfolio. Once again he was cheated out of the reward of his incredible labours by the inscrutable Emperor of the French, who had no real will, but only hasty, incalculable fancies. But if Cavour's conduct was natural, it was not particularly statesmanlike. More surprising was the conduct of King Victor Emmanuel: this reckless, pleasure-loving sovereign, who had always left the conduct of state affairs to Cavour, now stepped forth as a restrained far-seeing statesman. Suppressing all his irritation, he thanked the French Emperor for what he had done, and with dignified gratitude indicated his acceptance of Lombardy which Francis Joseph had ceded to Napoleon. Further, he agreed without difficulty to add his signature to the Preliminaries of Villafranca, stipulating only for the reservation *per quanto mi regardono,* "as far as they concern me": which meant that the Sardinian Government accepted no responsibility for the clauses which recognised the old *régimes* in the Duchies and in Romagna. It was not unreasonable that the King of Sardinia should make a reservation in signing a treaty which he had had no part in making. It was, as a matter of fact, in this reserved area that he was to get some compensation for what he had lost through his ally's action at Villafranca.

143

CHAPTER XVI

THE UNION OF THE DUCHIES AND THE ROMAGNA

As soon as the war between Austria and Sardinia began, in April, 1859, revolutions occurred in Central Italy. These movements had been carefully prepared by the Italian National Society, an organisation which had very numerous members, and which worked in close, though unofficial, association with Cavour. Its leading spirit was Giuseppe La Farina, a Sicilian *émigré* who, in consultation with Cavour, had founded the society in 1857. The revolutions, which were methodically planned, were carried out with the greatest ease and almost without friction. The ducal families left Tuscany, Modena and Parma without any manifestation of violence being shown to them; indeed they were personally not unpopular, and most people regretted the necessity of their disappearance. Provisional Governments were set up at Florence, Modena, Parma, and also at Bologna for the Papal Legations, now bereft both of their Austrian garrisons and of their papal administrations.

The next step was for the Provisional Governments to decide the eventual destiny of the Central Italian States. The old electoral laws which had come into brief existence during the revolutionary movement of 1848 were revived, and general elections were held. The Constitutional Assemblies which resulted from those elections all voted that their country should be annexed to Sardinia; and in the months following the Preliminaries of Villafranca deputations came from Florence and the other Central Italian capitals, informing King Victor Emmanuel of the votes given by the assemblies, and requesting to be annexed to the Sardinian Crown. To these deputations the King, naturally, gave encouraging answers, without actually committing himself to accepting their offers.

For, indeed, he had to proceed very warily. The Preliminaries of Villafranca constituted a binding treaty, which declared that the legitimate sovereigns should be restored to their States and that Italy should be a Confederation under the Pope. During the rest of the summer of 1859 delegates from Paris, Vienna and Turin were in conference at Zürich, busy converting the Preliminaries into definite treaties of peace. It was a little difficult in the meantime for the Government of Sardinia to ask Napoleon III to stand by and see the Treaty of Villafranca being torn to pieces.

That unfortunate monarch was gyrating among the most baffling perplexities. He had promised that Italy should be free to the Adriatic; and he had not carried out the promise. He had agreed at Villafranca that the Central Italian sovereigns should be restored, but he had assured the Sardinian Government that he would never allow any force to be used to compel such restoration. What was to happen, then, if the populations of Central Italy refused (as they positively did) to take back their old ruling families?

Meanwhile the diplomatists at Zürich went steadily on with their labours, and on November 10 (1859) concluded a set of three treaties between Austria and France, France and Sardinia, and between Austria, France and Sardinia. The result of these acts was that the cession of Lombardy to Sardinia was finally arranged; the Lombardo-Venetian frontier was delimited; and Sardinia undertook a proportionate share of the Lombardo-Venetian public debt, agreed to pay the pensions of old Lombardo-Venetian officials, and accepted other equitable arrangements with regard to Austrian property and interests in the ceded province. No mention was made of the Central Italian rulers and of the proposed Italian confederation. The Treaties of Zürich were confined rigidly to affairs over which Austria had had sovereign authority and which Sardinia now claimed to arrange. The affairs of Central Italy were outside the jurisdiction of Austria, and so far as she was interested in them, she had entered into certain engagements with France at Villafranca, and to those she (quite reasonably) still held. This was the substance of the dispatches which came to the Quai d'Orsay from Count Rechberg, the Austrian Chancellor, who had replaced Count Buol. The Provisional Governments of Central Italy, however, paid no attention to the Treaty of Villafranca; and even Sardinia treated it as something of a dead letter, for Victor Emmanuel's troops were now in all the Central Italian capitals, helping the Provisional Governments to keep order. When, in deference to repeated advice —almost appeals—from Napoleon III, the King agreed to withdraw his troops, he could do so with a quiet mind, for by that time the

Provisional Governments had forces of upwards of 30,000 men to depend on, volunteers who enrolled themselves to defend their newly-found liberties. A Sardinian general was allowed by Victor Emmanuel to resign his commission (with the assurance that he could get it back again) and to become commander of the Central Italian forces, which were known as the League. Numerous other Sardinian officers had the same facilities granted to them when they wished to transfer their services to the League.

The affairs of Central Italy obviously cried out for settlement. If the Treaty of Villafranca could not be carried into effect, then a Congress was the recognized method of solving the difficulty. The project of a Congress was discussed in the European Chancelleries, and in none was any objection raised; the only difficulty was that the Congress ran a risk of having nothing to do: Central Italian affairs were rapidly settling themselves, under the energetic measures of the Provisional Governments there—notably under the Marquis Ricasoli, dictator of Tuscany—and helped by the doctrine of non-intervention. This doctrine had been accepted as a maxim of British statesmanship since the days of Canning; and now, more than ever, it was combined with a lively sympathy with the side which required merely *not* to be interfered with, in order to triumph. On June 10, 1859, the Tory Cabinet of Lord Derby, which disliked the abrogation of the Treaties of Vienna as regards Central Italy, fell from power, and a Whig Ministry, with Lord Palmerston as Premier and Lord John Russell as Secretary of State for Foreign Affairs, came into office. Both were sincere friends of Italy and strong upholders of all liberal movements abroad. The speeches of Lord John Russell set the tone of the public opinion which, in England at this time, was beginning to be loudly in favour of Italy. The *Times* and *Morning Post* had many columns every week on the affairs of Central Italy, all in favour of the patriots, and their foreign correspondence was quoted freely in the press of Europe, and appeared even in the *Moniteur de l'Empire* itself. At first sight it always appears as if force alone ruled in international affairs, but it is not so. Public opinion—wherever that mysterious motive power is lodged—has enormous influence, and no Governments, however preponderant in physical force, can afford to disregard it. And that is why England, by her outspoken and fervent opinion in favour of Italy, effectually assisted the Italian cause in the autumn of 1859, just as France by her glorious and costly sacrifices on the battlefield had done in the summer. Further than this, the moral support of the British Government and public not merely fortified the will of the Italians and gave them the confidence which ensures success ; it also had the very solid result of making impossible any outside intervention. Austria could have claimed to restore the Papal Government in Romagna, and the Ducal Governments elsewhere, and in doing so could have pointed to the engagements of Villafranca. But the British Government stood firmly for non-intervention, so that the Italian movement was free to run its course.

Napoleon III had still to be reckoned with, however. He still could not bring himself to countenance the annexation of Central Italy, more especially of Tuscany and of Romagna ; and without the concurrence of France, Victor Emmanuel could not tear up the Treaty of Vienna, in the face of the hostility of Austria and the chilly disapprobation of Prussia and Russia. England's moral support alone was not enough. All through the autumn of 1859 and the spring of 1860 the Emperor was besieged by semi-official Italian envoys, and no man can have been more sick of the name of Italy than this maladroit statesman, struggling in the web which Cavour, even in retirement on his country estate, still spun round him. The web became closer when, on January 20, 1860, Cavour was recalled to power as President of the Council at Turin, in place of his friend the General La Marmora, who had in truth merely continued the old policy. In the previous month, December 22, 1859, a pamphlet had appeared in Paris called *Le Pape et le Congrès.* Like *Napoléon et l'Italie* (see p. 135), this pamphlet was anonymous, but was believed to be composed by M. Arthur de la Gueronnière from the notes of the Emperor. Its object was to show, under the colour of an extreme solicitude for the Pope, that both the Spiritual and the Temporal Power would be much more assured if the Papal State were restricted to Rome and its environs. Thus it became known that the Emperor no longer held by the Treaty of Villafranca, and that he would acquiesce in the expulsion of the Papal administration from Romagna. If this were acquiesced in, the cause of the Ducal Governments must be considered also as lost. On January 4, 1860, M. Walewski, a strong upholder of the treaties of Vienna and attached to the old prudent traditions of diplomacy, received his dismissal, and was replaced at the Quai d'Orsay by M. de Thouvenel, whose accession was considered as a victory for the Italian cause. With the way thus made clear, Cavour was able to finish the affairs of Central Italy with surprising speed. The Cavaliere Nigra, who in later days was to be so influential at the Tuileries, now came into prominence. He had fought as a volunteer in the army of Charles Albert in 1848, had subsequently entered the diplomatic service, and had been taken into the confidence of Cavour, accompanying him to the Congress of Paris. No man knew so accurately the aims and methods of the great Sardinian minister; and as Napoleon refused now to accept a visit from Cavour himself, the Cavaliere Nigra, only thirty-two years old, was sent as an inoffensive person, who could be trusted to do exactly as his master would have done. With him was associated for greater dignity the Marquis d'Arese, a Milanese nobleman, a friend of Louis Napoleon's youth, and a man trusted by the Emperor because he was not a politician and had no ambitions.

The mission of Nigra was a complete success. Napoleon had never forgotten how Cavour and he together had arranged at Plombières that in return for freeing all North Italy, France should have Savoy, and perhaps even Nice; but as he had not carried out the freeing of all North Italy, he had not claimed his compensation. Now, however, he returned to the idea. The acquisition would be a great thing for France and would restore Napoleon's prestige there. Cavour, on his side, was quite eager to satisfy the Emperor, because if France were committed to taking a share of the spoils arising out of the Italian Question, she could not place any obstacles in the way of the Central Italian annexations. It was not all plain sailing for Nigra, however; many difficult points had to be settled; especially the principle of nationalities—so prominent in the *Idées Napoléoniennes*—must be carefully observed. At last all was arranged. Plebiscites by universal suffrage were to be held in all the territories in question—in Nice and Savoy, as in Romagna, Tuscany and the rest. In Central Italy the plebiscites were held in March (1860), and were practically unanimous in favour of annexation to Sardinia. In the same month, on March 24, M. Benedetti, the head of the Political Department at the Quai d'Orsay, sent on special mission to Turin, signed with Cavour the treaty which transferred Savoy and Nice to France. Plebiscites held in April again showed almost unanimous adherence to the transfer. Only Great Britain and Switzerland protested, but without any effect. It was, in fact, not unreasonable, that as Sardinia was growing rapidly to be a kingdom of Italy it should be confined to the Italian side of the Alps.

CHAPTER XVII

THE KINGDOM OF ITALY

In the year 1860, an amazed Europe saw not only Romagna, Tuscany, Modena, and Parma added to Sardinia, but all of a sudden the Kingdom of the Two Sicilies and almost all that remained of the Papal States follow suit. In the last months of his life Cavour was able to make in the South of Italy gains as wonderful as those which had taken him years of intense labour to achieve in the north. The account of these annexations belongs properly to diplomatic history, and yet the diplomatists had little enough to do with either the beginning or the end of the affair. In Italy the public law of Europe scarcely received lip-service ; and diplomacy did not even have the compliment paid her of being asked to draw a decent veil over naked acts of piracy.

There is no doubt, whatever, that Cavour was privy to the plots which the Italian National Society was preparing, in order to upset the existing state of affairs in South Italy. The first man to set affairs in train for a revolution in the Kingdom of the Two Sicilies was Mazzini, who was a republican with no love for the Kingdom of Sardinia. But Francisco Crispi, the Sicilian *émigré* who was actually to raise the rebellion, soon found he must act with the support of Piedmont. This led him to concert matters with Garibaldi, who was able to use the Port of Genoa for his base, and from this moment all went well.

In April, 1860, the expected revolution against King Francis II broke out in Palermo, and Garibaldi only waited to complete his preparations and to gain some definite news (a very difficult matter), about the state of affairs in the island ; and on the night of May 5, 1860, he sailed with 1,085 companions in arms, on the steamships *Lombardo* and *Piemonte* from the Port of Genoa. The members of the expedition were volunteers equipped with rifles sent by the National Society from Milan, and the ships were chartered from the

Rubattino company. The Sardinian authorities had been curiously blind throughout the weeks when the expedition was being arranged, and they remained equally unconscious when on the night of May 5 a sham assault was made on the two ships (to give the Rubattino a pretext of *force majeure*) and the *Lombardo* and *Piemonte* were taken out of the port into the Gulf, en route for Sicily. On their way they could, of course, easily have been stopped by the Sardinian squadron which under Admiral Persano was cruising off the western coast. Persano telegraphed for instructions to Cavour: if the navy was to stop the expedition Cavour was to telegraph *Cagliari*; if to let it go on, *Malte*. The reply came *Cagliari*, so Cavour could say he had behaved with perfect correctness. Nevertheless Persano knew that the Minister meant *Malte*, and he let Garibaldi's ships pass. One wonders why he telegraphed at all, unless it had been arranged that he should give Cavour the chance of *formally* ordering the stopping of the expedition.

On May 11 the *Lombardo* and *Piemonte* appeared off Marsala in Sicily. Two Neapolitan warships began to oppose the disembarkation, but desisted when the chief of the English squadron that was present asked for time to get all his men on board before fighting should begin. The result of this semi-diplomatic intervention of the English officer was to give Garibaldi time to disembark his forces. One thousand men were a small number to oppose to twenty thousand regular Neapolitan troops, but the audacity of the great adventurer was justified by results. The insurrection gained impetus from his arrival—his skill, his ardour, his romantic personal attraction, brought him success everywhere; and on May 30 the Neapolitan general, Lanza, surrendered the capital Palermo. The necessary diplomatic mediation was provided by the British admiral, Mundy, and the interviews between the combatants took place on H.M.S. *Hannibal*.

Cavour was waiting for these successes; but the game he was now playing was something far more subtle than the ancient plan of boldly recognising the agents, whom he would have disavowed and sacrificed had they failed. He had no intention of recognising Garibaldi yet, for that would have identified the Sardinian Government with a filibustering expedition, and would at most have procured the annexation of the Two Sicilies. He was playing for something bigger—for the Papal States as well. His plan was to intervene in the Kingdom of the Two Sicilies, but only, as it were, to preserve order and to prevent the spread of revolution ; and the same necessities (for the excitement caused by the Sicilian affair was bound to spread somewhat) were to take him into the Papal States —not into Rome, for Napoleon's battalions still guarded this ; but into Umbria and the Marches.

The plan was brilliantly attractive, but the hoped for results were almost too brilliant to come to pass. Doubtless Cavour would have thought himself lucky, if he gained only a substantial portion. For the complete success which crowned his efforts he had to thank fortune, his own wonderful skill and patience (the patience that never let him make a false step), and the attitude of England.

In France public opinion was deeply aroused against these violent assaults on the settled condition of South Italy, and against the power of the Pope—for it was clearly seen that Garibaldi's efforts would not stop with the frontiers of Naples. Napoleon, always swaying between love of Italy and respect for the Catholic Church and fear of the Clerical Party, proposed at this time that Garibaldi's effort should be localised in Sicily by the simple method of blockading the Strait of Messina with an Anglo-French squadron. Lord John Russell, however, refused, on the ground that such action would be contrary to the principle of non-intervention ; and in the beginning of August, Garibaldi and his now much enlarged force crossed the Straits.

Still Cavour made no sign of recognising the liberator. At this time envoys from the young King Francis II were at Turin, soliciting an alliance between Sardinia and Naples ; and it was perhaps a little difficult for Cavour to avoid giving this sign of good faith ; however, the envoys remained month after month, and no alliance took place. Meanwhile the Marquis Villamarina, Sardinian minister to Naples, was actively engaging the sympathies of the Neapolitan ministers and officials ; and Admiral Persano, who had arrived in the Bay of Naples with his squadron, was equally successful in winning the private support of the officers of the Neapolitan navy. The daring Persano did more than merely use his inviolable flag-ship as a safe place for furthering the Sardinian conspiracy ; on one occasion he disguised himself, and mixed with the men of the royal dockyard, and so damaged the machinery of some ships that King Francis II, when he came to flee, had to take passage on a Spanish steamer, not on a ship of his own navy.

Before this happened, however, Cavour had begun to make it

clear that in the interests of public order, and of the protection of Italian liberals, he would have to intervene not merely in Naples, but in the Papal States, where, he averred, feelings had become greatly excited. Farini and General Cialdini were despatched on a mission to Napoleon III, who was making a tour of Savoy. It was the great weakness of the Second Empire that the Emperor was continually detaching himself from his ministers, and engaging himself in secret diplomatic affairs of extraordinary gravity. On this occasion the results were almost as momentous as those of the secret meeting at Plombières. Farini and Cialdini met Napoleon at Chambéry on August 26, and, according to Cialdini's account, the Emperor, when they asked what view France would take of an occupation of Umbria and the Marches, replied: *Fate presto*—"do it quickly." This was all Cavour had been waiting for.

On September 6, Francis II, having found the vacuum caused by desertions, both civil and military, ever widening around him, had left his capital, and sailed to the little fortress of Gaeta. No one opposed his exit, which was almost immediately followed by the entrance of Garibaldi, who leaving his army behind, had hastened forward, almost alone, in the railway-train from Salerno. At the same time as Naples was occupied by the Garibaldians, an insurrection was being planned in Umbria and the Marches, and became overt on September 8. Cavour immediately presented an ultimatum to Pius IX, which said that King Victor Emmanuel could not remain indifferent to the bloody repression by which the papal mercenaries suppressed all manifestations of the national sentiment; and in view of this he called on the Papal Government to disarm its foreign soldiers. On receiving the expected refusal, General Cialdini and Fanti were given the order to march over the frontier.

The Papal States, apart from Rome, which was still garrisoned by French Imperial troops, were defended by about 40,000 men, raised from volunteers of many nations, under Lamoricière, a retired French General in the service of Pius IX. These troops were disposed in various garrisons, but a small mobile army of about 14,000 men was kept to oppose the invaders. While attempting to get to the papal fortress of Ancona, Lamoricière came into collision with Cialdini's force at Castelfidardo on September 18, and suffered a bloody reverse. With the remnants of his force he shut himself into Ancona, and defended it till the 28th.

Umbria and the Marches having thus fallen before the Sardinian troops, it only remained to reduce Gaeta, still held by the last Neapolitan Bourbon, who showed a spirit more than worthy of his immediate predecessors. The Sardinian army besieged Gaeta on the land side, but the Sardinian navy was unable to blockade it from the sea because Napoleon III instructed his Mediterranean squadron to keep the port open. For a couple of months this curious system prevailed, the town being relentlessly bombarded from the land, and at the same time provisioned, and even reinforced by volunteers, from the sea. At last, being pressed by the British Foreign Office to abandon the help, which was only prolonging a death agony, Napoleon withdrew his squadron, on January 19, 1861. Francis II held out for nearly another month, and finally capitulated on February 13.

The annexation of the Two Sicilies and of Umbria and the Marches was by this time assured. On October 27, 1860, Lord John Russell had sent to Sir James Hudson, who was still Minister to the Court of Turin a dispatch destined to be famous in the annals of the United Italy movement. This message declared that the Italians had a right to depose their bad Governments and to join themselves in a large State. Cavour wanted nothing better than this moral sanction from the British Government whose opinion commanded universal respect in Europe. Plebiscites held in the occupied territories had already resulted in decisions in favour of Sardinia. On November 7, King Victor Emmanuel arrived at Naples. Even yet the Sardinian Government had no public official relations with Garibaldi who was still in international law only an adventurer, who had seized a friendly and independent Kingdom. The great condottiere, however, crowned his work by a fine act of self-sacrifice. Refusing all reward for himself, he retired from the scene and betook himself to Caprera, his beloved rock in the Strait of Bonifacio. Thus the course was left clear to Victor Emmanuel, who completed the Sardinian mission of keeping order and preventing revolution by issuing decrees of annexation for the Two Sicilies, Umbria and the Marches. Thus the Treaties of Vienna were again torn across, while the European diplomatists looked helplessly on. In March, 1861, Victor Emmanuel assumed the title of King of Italy. Cavour, whose great mind and will had from Turin controlled all these complex forces which thus surprisingly made a Power in Italy where many little States before had been, was not to live much longer to watch the prospering of his work. He was still planning to complete this work by the incorporation of Rome, which he said would take two years, when death cut him off on June 6, 1861. He was fifty-one years of age. His work, though less imposing at the time than that of Bismarck, has proved to be much more wholesome and enduring, and was accomplished with vastly less bloodshed. His methods were to employ diplomacy, and in the last resort only, war to achieve a union which already existed in the hearts of all thinking Italians, so that the new Italian State which was the result of his efforts, was a realm of freedom and enlightenment; it had not required in the making, nor did it require for its continuance, naked methods of blood and iron.[1]

[1] The story of Italian Unity down to the year 1860 has been told by Mr. G. M. Trevelyan in three volumes which already rank almost as classics.

CHAPTER XVIII

VENICE

When the Kingdom of Italy had been made, and Piedmont, Lombardy, Tuscany, Umbria, Naples and Sicily all joined together, people could see plainly that before long Venice, and even Rome itself, must gravitate towards the great Italian State. The question of Rome was complicated by the French military occupation, and by the interest of the Catholic world in the maintenance of the old Papal system. But the question of Venetia had no such complexity; it was an alien and outlying province of Austria, and it was surely not beyond the power of human intelligence to arrange some scheme which would satisfy Italian aspirations, and at the same time save the *amour propre* of the Habsburgs. Any one could see that the days of Austria in Venetia were numbered; it was only a question now of arranging for a peaceful death.

This was the view of French, English and Italian statesmen. The diplomatic relations between these three countries were excellent; and an arrangement between Italy and Napoleon with regard to Rome seemed possible, through the tactful management of M. Nigra, who was now installed as Italian ambassador at Paris, of M. Benedetti, who was for a time French ambassador at Turin, and M. de la Valette, another friend of Italy, who was French minister to the Vatican. But Garibaldi disliked the slow methods of diplomacy: a straight fight was the method he favoured, and he was always threatening a descent upon Venetia or Rome. In 1862 he was able to take a small force through South Italy and to invade the Patrimony of St. Peter; the Italian Government, anxious to divest itself of all suspicion of complicity (for it would be fatal to repeat the machinations of 1860), sent a military force, and at Aspromonte, on August 29, 1862, a collision occurred with the Garibaldians. Some shooting was done (there was no general engagement) and Garibaldi was shot in the foot. He and his followers surrendered, and were taken to Genoa for trial, but before the trials could be held, King Victor Emmanuel amnestied the prisoners.

The affair of Aspromonte excited the national feeling greatly, more especially as for a time it appeared as if Garibaldi, whose wound had become inflamed, would die, the victim of an Italian bullet, in a fight for the union of all Italy. The Government of Victor Emmanuel were quite alive to the necessity of taking action, both with regard to Rome and Venice, but as Venice presented the easier problem, they directed their attention to it first.

The project favoured by the British Government was the simple one of purchase. Austria was to give up the province (which was useless to her now and was only the source of endless friction) in return for payment of an indemnity by the Kingdom of Italy. The Government of Vienna, however, refused thus to bargain for its territorial integrity.

The next plan was less simple, as might be expected with anything that proceeded from the brain of Napoleon III. This was to allow Austria compensation in the Danubian Principalities of Wallachia and Moldavia, which were dissatisfied with their Prince, Couza (and as a matter of fact deposed him in 1866). This "Roumanian solution," however, never proceeded further than conversations between Napoleon and the Cavaliere Nigra at the Tuileries and St. Cloud.

In 1865, however, the air began to clear a little in Italy, in proportion as the clouds darkened in Germany. Austria and Prussia had, in the previous year, gone into iniquitous partnership against Denmark, and had jointly seized the Duchies of Schleswig and Holstein. In 1865 (as the joint possession only increased their mutual jealousies), they divided the spoil by the Convention of Gastein; but finding no rest here, they proceeded to more bitter disputes, which involved nothing less than the leadership of Germany. Bismarck in fact saw that Prussia would have to fight Austria, which was still considered to be a strong military Power. To make victory secure, he was anxious to engage the Kingdom of Italy, which had a large and enthusiastic army, to attack Venetia, while the Prussian army invaded the Austrian Empire from the north. Early in 1865 Count Usedom, the Prussian minister at Florence (to which the Italian capital had been removed in 1864), broached the subject of an alliance to General La Marmora, who had succeeded Ratazzi as head of the Italian ministry. La Marmora was a good soldier, and a sensible statesman. He saw the advantages of the proposed Prussian alliance, but he did not trust the Prussian Government. Next year, in March. he sent General Govone to Berlin "to study the system of fortifications." The choice was not perhaps the best that could be made. Govone was subtle, too subtle, and thought by diplomatic fencing to over-reach Bismarck, who (he knew) was only bent on over-reaching the Italians. Thus the negotiations, started and carried on in mutual distrust, proceeded slowly and issued finally in a very half-hearted alliance. For each feared that the other would use the alliance merely as a lever at Vienna, to get the Austrian Government to make concessions without fighting. It is indeed very difficult to understand why the Austrians, to whom the Prusso-Italian danger had been long visible, did not at any moment detach Italy by the cession of Venetia. But the unhappy Vienna governing-class has always tended to run to its ruin, not indeed through perfect blindness, but through perfect obstinacy. Thus, on April 8, 1866, Prussia and Italy concluded an alliance to endure for three months, with the objects of gaining Venice for Italy and the supremacy of North Germany for Prussia. The moment of attack on Austria was to be chosen by Prussia. It was not a diplomatic instrument of which either party could be very proud, as its aim was pure aggression and its spirit was that of mutual distrust—hence the three months' limit. But both parties were pleased at the time; Bismarck knew that he was now certain to defeat Austria, which could not fight successfully on two flanks, while La Marmora could feel certain that a war between Prussia and Austria would surely take place. At the last moment peace seemed to raise its head again, when Napoleon (on May 26) proposed a European Congress: the proposal was actually agreed to, not merely by England and Russia but also by Prussia and Italy. But Austria consented only on condition that no modifications of territory should result from the Congress. Thus once more the extraordinary pride of the Habsburgs drove them to the fatal war.

This war was not long in breaking forth. On June 17, the Prussians occupied Hannover; and about the same time La Marmora began an invasion of Venetia. On June 23, he crossed the Mincio, and next day was defeated near the village of Custozza by the Archduke Albert. The Prussian armies, on the other hand, carried everything before them, and on July 3 (1866), broke the forces of Austria at Sadowa in Moravia. The way now lay in front of Bismarck to Vienna, barred only by the lines of Florisdorf, which it was calculated would cost the lives of 2,000 men to storm.

It was then that Austria—too late, as was her habit—resolved on concession. A Council was held at Schoenbrunn, and it was decided to give Venetia to France (for conveyance to the Italian Government) and to invite the Emperor Napoleon's mediation. Next day Napoleon held a council at St. Cloud—a meeting which has been rightly marked as the most momentous in the whole reign. The question discussed was whether France should throw her military forces into the scale to save Austria, or should confine herself to peaceful mediation. Peaceful counsels prevailed, and Benedetti (who was now ambassador at Berlin) was sent to the Prussian Headquarters. All this only decided Bismarck to deal himself directly and quickly with Austria, for he knew that interference from the outside would cost him much of his gains. On July 22, he arranged an armistice with Austria, and on the 26th signed the Preliminary Treaty of Nikolsburg, which gave him all he wanted.

Meanwhile Napoleon had received the investiture of Venetia and had intimated to the Italians that he would hand it over to them. Then took place one of the most extraordinary situations in the world's history. The Italians had made the war, to get Venetia, and this fact was inscribed in their treaty with Prussia. But now that they were offered the glorious prize, they refused to accept it. For one thing the Austrians had defeated the Italian army at Custozza; and two days before the Prusso-Austrian armistice, they had defeated the Italian fleet at Lissa. After these signal disasters, to receive Venetia at the hands of France would, La Marmora said, simply ruin the prestige of the Italian Government in Italy. So the army was once more ordered to advance into Venetia; the rest of the campaign, however, was just a farce, for the Austrians simply retired into the Quadrilateral and refused to defend the country, so that on July 30 the Italian Government felt compelled to suspend arms.

The end of the war, though it gave them what they had begun the war for, was a bitter disappointment to the Italians. For the war, after all, was a common effort, in which Italy and Prussia had pooled their resources; so that the victory in the northern theatre ought to have redounded to the advantage of both allies. The individual defeats of the Italians could not make any difference to the fact that the war was a war shared in common, and the final success must be a success shared in common. Austria had been so badly beaten that she could not have refused to cede the "Italian" Tyrol as well as Venetia. Bismarck, on his part, was able to say that the allies had agreed, by the treaty of April 8, not to make peace separately, until the objects stated in the treaty had been gained. Now, they had gained Venetia—the stated object—so she could not in law or reason object to Prussia seeking peace. Even Napoleon, in his most expansive moments, had never held out the prospect of getting more for Austria than Venetia; when in 1863 the Marquis d'Arese, on a visit at the Tuileries, had said, "and the Italian Tyrol," Napoleon replied: "Ah, I cannot thus put the dots on the i's." Thus Italy had to be content with her bond—with Venetia, and with the old Venetian land frontier, very unfavourable strategically to the Italian State. This was secured by the Treaty of Vienna, October 3, 1866.

159

CHAPTER XIX

MENTANA

After the annexation of Venetia in 1866, the only part of the Italian Peninsula which remained outside the Kingdom of Victor Emmanuel was the shrunken dominions of the Pope. These consisted of the districts of Viterbo, Civita Vecchia, Velletri, and Frosimone, with Rome in the centre of all. The eyes of the people of the Kingdom were directed towards this remnant of the State of the Church, which many Italians then commonly alluded to as "the Pontifical Enclave." All Europe knew that they meant to incorporate it, and yet many influential Catholics hoped that some *modus vivendi* might still be arranged, which would ensure the continuance of the Papal independence. Such was the contention of the veteran statesman, Massimo d'Azeglio, the most honest and conscientious of men, who, in the last months of his life, urged the Italian parliament to leave Rome itself as an autonomous town under the suzerainty of the Pope. "I can scarcely conceive that Catholicism can ever comprehend, by the side of the Pope at the Vatican, the King of Italy at the Capitol." It was some such system as this that seemed to be attained by the Convention of September 15, 1864.

This famous instrument was signed by Drouyn de Lhuys for the Emperor Napoleon, and by Nigra for the King of Italy. It comprehended three points: (1) The Italian Government agreed not to attack the existing territory of the Papal State and to prevent any aggression from the outside; (2) France agreed to evacuate its garrison from Rome within two years; (3) the Italian Government agreed to fix its capital at Florence.

By this arrangement Napoleon III was to get quit of the incubus of the Roman garrison. The Italian Government resigned all prospect of conquering the Papal State, or of annexing it as the result of some raid by Garibaldi; and as an evidence of its *bona fide* renunciation of Rome as a capital it was to take the magnificent city of Florence for the metropolis of the Italian State. The Pope therefore seemed tolerably safe if both sides kept their engagements—if France withdrew her garrison and if the Italian Government prevented any raids, like the Expedition of the Thousand. The only other danger which might bring about the fall of the Papal State would be a revolution from within, but that was not likely to happen. In the City of Rome and its district in the years before 1870 life was very easy, and the condition of affairs was not conducive to political agitation and progress.

Napoleon III at once began to carry out his part of the Convention of September 15, 1864. The French battalions were withdrawn successively, and by December, 1866, the evacuation was complete. At the same time, to enable the Pope to have a reasonably strong military force, French soldiers and officers were allowed to enrol themselves, under an Imperial decree of January 30, 1866, in a Papal legion. This force, which was joined by many ardent young French Catholics, was collected at Antibes, near Cannes, and therefore received the name of the *Légion d'Antibes*. When the Imperial battalions were withdrawn from Rome the Légion d'Antibes took their place.

This was the first blow to the Convention of September 15. The Italians said that the French had not *bona fide* evacuated Rome. On the other hand, the French Government could scarcely have prevented its subjects from enrolling themselves in the Papal Army ; only, it need not officially have encouraged the recruiting as it did in several ways. It ought to have stood by as the impartial onlooker. The conduct of the Imperial Government was injudicious, but it was not in any sense a breach of the Convention of September 15.

The events that happened shortly afterwards, however, resulted in the complete destruction of the Convention, and for this the Italian minister, Ratazzi—a rather supple man who had succeeded to the uncompromising Tuscan noble Ricasoli—cannot be held blameless. In February, 1867, it became known that Garibaldi had left Caprera and had appeared in Venice. At once warlike ardour was rekindled throughout Italy. The great revolutionary soldier was soon at the frontier between the Italian and Papal States, obviously waiting for some insurrectionary call from the Pope's territory. In September, however, he was away at the

Congress of Peace at Geneva; then he came back to Florence, where he had an effusive welcome from the populace; from here he took the train towards Rome. Ratazzi's Government was certainly somewhat too complaisant towards the movements of the patriot, but at last it decided to meet the protests of the French Government by a stern act of good faith. On September 23 it stopped Garibaldi at Asinalunga and had him conveyed as a prisoner to Alessandria; but soon he was released and allowed to retire to Caprera.

The master had gone, but the master's spirit remained behind. His work was still going on; the revolutionaries were completing their preparations; and on September 28, five days after Garibaldi's arrest at Asinalunga, a Garibaldian company invaded the Papal Province of Viterbo. Soon other bands crossed the long, irregular frontier at various points, and the Italian gendarmes at the frontier stations seemed powerless (and quite unwilling) to stop them. The Government, however, kept cruisers guarding Caprera, but Garibaldi evaded the blockade and arrived safely at the mainland. On October 22 he was at Florence, where his presence was advertised by public acclamations; from Florence, where crowds conducted him to the railway station, he left by special train for Terni. Ratazzi, as if unable to contend with the complexities of the situation, resigned from the Government, his place being taken by General Cialdini. By this time, however, Garibaldi had crossed the frontier into the Papal territory.

To judge from the number of decisions and counter-decisions which Napoleon III made at this time, it is clear that he was suffering from cruel agitation. He wished to get quit of his position of protecting power over Rome, and to cut once and for all the meshes in which the diplomacy of the Italian Government entangled him. But he never was able to do so, and to the last the affairs of Italy tied his hands and clogged all his movements. He could not wash his hands entirely of Italy and leave the Pope to his fate: his credit in Europe seemed to depend on his maintaining the protection which had existed now since 1849, and the powerful Catholic party in France—the most conservative element in the Imperial State—would never allow him to give way.

When it became clear that the Italian Government was not preventing attacks on the Papal territory, and thus was not carrying out the Convention of September 15, Napoleon took steps to restore his military protection to the Pope. The Légion d'Antibes was now part of the Papal army, but more was required. Accordingly, a division of the French regular army was concentrated at Lyons, under General Failly, and after many hesitations and changes of mind, Napoleon at last allowed the expedition to sail (October 26, 1867). There was indeed little time to be lost if Rome was to be saved. When the squadron disembarked Failly's division at Civita Vecchia on October 28, Garibaldi was already descending the valley of the Tiber within five miles of Rome. Had he at once pushed on he could have taken Rome, as the Papal General Kanzler had decided to defend only the Vatican and the rest of the Papal city on the right bank of the Tiber. Garibaldi delayed, however, and on October 30 the advance-guard of Failly's force entered Rome. The rest of the French soon followed, and on November 3 the Franco-Papal forces were able to attack the Garibaldian positions at Mentana (in the Sabine country about twelve miles N.E. of Rome). This was not a sanguinary skirmish, like Castelfidardo, nor a slight brush like Aspromonte; it was a regular battle, in which both sides showed great determination and valour. The Garibaldians were routed, with the loss of a thousand killed and wounded, victims to the long shooting and accuracy of the new-pattern French rifle, the *Chassepot*.

The revolutionary invasion was thus quelled, and Pius IX reigned undisputed throughout his little principality. The 6th of November, when the victors of Mentana re-entered Rome, was, wrote the French *chargé d'affaires*, "the last ray of sun of the Pontifical Power." [1] It did indeed add three years to the expiring life of the Papal State. Besides this it had three results: it brought back the French battalions to Rome; secondly, it obviously wiped away the already useless Convention of September 15; thirdly, it removed the last tie that bound the Italian Government to the French Empire. "The Chassepots have done marvels," wrote Generally Failly in his report of the operations, and these words, in spite of the opposition of M. de Moustier, the Minister for Foreign Affairs, were published in the *Moniteur de l'Empire*. As this good shooting was all done at the expense of Italian lives, the Government of Victor Emmanuel naturally felt the remark to be in bad taste. It seems to have been published at the instance of Marshal

[1] In Gorce, V, 307.

Niel, but whether as a warning to Italy or to Prussia is not known. At any rate the Italian Government felt no call to sacrifice its men and treasure for France three years later.

That nothing should be wanting to rivet the chains of the Roman occupation round the Emperor's neck, a notable speech was made by M. Rouher, speaking for the Imperial Government in the Chamber, on November 3. As M. Thiers, one of the party of opposition, had testified sympathy with the Pope, M. Rouher in his reply felt bound to outdo him, and in a long speech, becoming more and more emphatic, ended by proclaiming: "Never will Italy take possession of Rome; never would France support such violence done to her honour, to her Catholicity." Rouher's *jamais* scored a temporary political success in the Chamber, but it ruined the efforts of the Quai d'Orsay to keep France safe.

CHAPTER XX

THE LAST DAYS OF THE TEMPORAL POWER

The Temporal Power was to disappear at the same time as the Pope was to make with success the most tremendous assertion of authority in spiritual affairs. In these last years Pius IX had become more and more resigned to the old ways. He had once been liberal and progressive, but now he no more thought of that. He saw that the trend of the age was against him, and his kindly soul was troubled by the consciousness of this, for he wished to be at peace and in amity with all men. He never doubted, however, that he was right, and he had no intention of resigning one whit of his temporal or spiritual authority. Many people expected that the old man would die and give place to some more adaptable pontiff, with whom the Italian State might make some reasonable compromise. But time dealt kindly with the aged man; his constitution, if not robust, seemed to become more equable as the years rolled on. To the many visitors whom he admitted to audiences, he presented the picture of a healthy, kindly, and rather garrulous old gentleman; he seemed to live among the ideas of the Middle Ages, complaining of the modern tendencies but not agitating himself much about them.

As a matter of fact, the mind of Pius IX was a good deal deeper than people thought, and his determination more inexorable. He was ever ready to assert his authority, and even greatly to increase his prerogatives. In 1861 (March 26) he had excommunicated King Victor Emmanuel, with all the vigour of a Hildebrand or an Innocent III. On December 8, 1864, he issued a document which became very celebrated: it revived the extreme claims of the Mediæval Church to arbitrate between sovereigns and their people; it denied the supreme sovereignty of the secular State, and the liberty of religion and of the Press; and it concluded with the extraordinary warning—"Cursed be he who shall say: the Roman

Pontiff can and ought to reconcile himself and put himself in accord with modern progress, liberalism and civilisation." Finally, on December 8, 1869, a great Œcumenical Council was held at the Vatican—the first General Council of the Church which had been held since the Council of Trent in the sixteenth century. In the last twenty years the Catholic Church had suffered much at the hands of the State; establishments, lands and courts might have disappeared; but on the other hand vast extensions had taken place in Asia and Africa; even nearer home, especially in England, notable accessions had occurred. The time seemed ripe for a great reunion, and the Council of 1869–70 was worthy of the occasion. Seven hundred and fifty fathers attended; but as one-third of these were Italians the Pope had a solid body to vote as he wished.

As if to assert more definitely the Papal independence the Catholic sovereigns were not invited to send their accredited representatives. There was, perhaps, an additional reason for this: Pius IX could scarcely have invited Victor Emmanuel, his spoiler, to take part, so he solved the difficulty by inviting no sovereigns at all. The programme of the Council and the method of discussion and voting having been carefully arranged in the interest of the Pope, the proceedings went as might be expected. By July, 1870, all the important business had been transacted, and on the 13th of that month the dogma of papal infallibility was carried by 513 votes against 88. Thus the absolute authority of the Pope over all Catholics was accepted as an article of faith. The spiritual sovereignty of the Pope became unlimited.

Almost simultaneously the last shreds of the Temporal State disappeared. Just before the opening of the Franco-Prussian War, Count Beust, the Austrian Chancellor, tried to arrange an agreement between Italy, Austria, and France, to enforce mediation upon Prussia; Victor Emmanuel consented on condition that Napoleon III would abandon Rome, which French troops still occupied. The Emperor refused. His constancy cost him his empire but it did not save Rome. On August 19 (1870) he withdrew his troops from the Holy City. The fall of Napoleon's Empire on September 4, after the battle of Sedan, gave the Italian Government the opportunity to repudiate the Convention of September 15, which, in spite of Mentana, was still supposed to be in existence. The Provisional Government of the Third Republic signified their acquiescence in the suppression of the Convention, and on September 12 the Italian ultimatum to Pius IX was launched. The uncompromising Pope would not cede a tittle of his territory, prerogatives, or dignity. On September 20 the Italian army, under General Cadorna, entered Rome, to which the capital of the State was immediately transferred.

After the entrance of the Italians by force into Rome, Pope Pius IX seems for a moment to have thought of accepting the situation, and of making terms with the Italian State. His period of hesitation was, however, short. He issued a formal protest against the Italian annexation, and maintained his seclusion in the Vatican. On May 13, 1871, the Italian Legislature passed the Law of the Guarantees (*La Legge delle Guarantigie*),[1] securing inviolability and sovereign honours to the person of the Pope, and a civil list of 3,225,000 *lire*. It was hoped that the Law would be accepted by the Pope, and that it would thus become, in effect, a bi-lateral treaty. But the Papacy has never given its assent. In September, 1870, just after the Italian occupation of Rome, Cardinal Antonelli cashed at the Italian Treasury papal drafts for 50,000 crowns to meet the current expenses of the Vatican. But the action was never repeated: this was the first and last sum accepted from the Italian Government.

[1] A French translation of this law will be found in Albin, *Les Grands Traités*, p. 99.

PART III

The Union of Germany

CHAPTER XXI

THE RISE OF PRUSSIA

§ 1. The Zollverein

The part taken by Prussia in the Napoleonic War (at least, in the last years of the War) had proved her to be a Great Power. Austria, however, had taken a great part too, and Austria was an older, a more legitimate, an Imperial State. The existence of these two practically co-ordinate Powers seemed to make the prospect of a real union of Germany hopeless.

The German Committee of the Vienna Congress appear to have taken this view, for they drafted a constitution in outline, and left it so, as if they despaired of filling it in. The Confederation established by the Federal Act of 1815 had a President (Austria) and a Parliament or Diet. But the Diet consisted simply of ambassadors from the Sovereign German States, and it had no power to enforce its behests. Yet if the Legislature was futile, the Executive was in a worse case, because, in fact, there was no Executive at all. When the monarchs of Germany were agreed on a common policy, as they were during the period of Metternich's ascendancy from 1819 to 1833, then the Confederation was a real thing, and its rules were enforced. But for the rest of the period of its existence it was little more than an airy nothing: it met and talked and was kept quiet by the diplomacy of the Austrian President.[1]

The early advances of Prussia were made very quietly, and their success was due to the patience, consistency, and moderation

[1] The first President was Count Buol-Schauenstein, father of the later Chancellor of Austria.

of the statesmen who designed the plan and carried it into effect.

The half-century after the Vienna Congress was the era of great publicists in Germany. The practical influence of these men began with the pamphleteers of the Napoleonic period, of whom Gentz was the greatest. After the wars were over, the publicists turned their attention to internal affairs. Some wrote on questions of liberty and constitutionalism; but the Governments frowned on such writings, and the authors were apt to find themselves some day either in prison or in exile. Others studied political economy, others researched into history—Roman history, in Niebuhr's studies; German history, in those of Leopold von Ranke. The influence of these historical researches in fostering a desire for German Imperial unity is seen at its highest in the works of Heinrich von Treitschke, who in 1857 began his remarkable career as a lecturer at Leipsic.

In the first thirty or forty years after 1815, it was the economists, rather than the historians or political philosophers, who dynamically influenced public affairs. The economists, then as now, were divided into two schools, protectionists and free-traders—the chief protectionist being List, whose *System of National Economy* is still worth reading, and the chief free-trader, K. G. Maassen. Free-traders and protectionists were agreed on one principle, that within the same economic area there should be no customs barriers. Out of this belief came the policy of free-trade, first between the different parts of Prussia, and next between the different States of Germany —always excluding Austria, which was never admitted to any customs-union. The union of different States was called a Zollverein. Its object was to include all German States (except Austria) and to bring it about that within this union all commercial intercourse should be free, and that Prussia should be actually, though not formally, head of it. Such was the plan explicitly defined by the Prussian Finance Minister, F. C. A. Motz, in 1829. The diplomatist who negotiated the important early treaties was J. A. F. Eichhorn, a disciple of Stein, and a high official in the Prussian Ministry of Foreign Affairs.

In 1816, by a decree of July 16, the Prussian Government had abolished internal customs, as between its different territories. In 1818 (May 26) another tariff-law went still further, and reduced all duties on imports below the rates of the other German States.

The next step directly impinged upon Prussia's neighbours. All goods imported through Prussian territory into the *enclaves* of other States, had to pay the Prussian import-dues. This rule was accompanied with an invitation to the States which owned the enclaves, to come to an understanding with Prussia for a division of the dues. The effect was immediate: on October 25, 1819, Schwartzburg-Sondershausen concluded a treaty of admission to the Prussian customs-union. In 1823, Schwartzburg-Rudolstadt followed suit, and a number of other minor German States in the following years.

So far, however, no *Zollverein*, no economic federation, existed. The minor States merely agreed that customs-receipts should be divided between Prussia and themselves in proportion to the numbers of their respective populations; but they had no voice in directing commercial policy, which remained entirely under the control of Prussia. The real Zollverein came with the Prussian-Darmstadt Treaty negotiated by Eichhorn and Motz on February 14, 1828. The consent of Darmstadt was made necessary for the validity of all commercial treaties negotiated by Prussia, so long as the Prussian-Darmstadt union was in force. It was to last till 1834, and if not denounced by that date was to run for another six years.

Meanwhile rivals were in the field. In 1826 Bavaria and Würtemburg formed themselves into a Zollverein, and on September 24, 1828, a Mid-German Commercial Union was formed by Saxony, Hannover, Brunswick, Oldenburg, Bremen, Frankfort, and some other States. The Mid-German Union, which owed its existence to the skill and energy of the Saxon minister, von Carlowitz, had considerable sources of strength, controlling, as it did, the North Sea Coast, and many of the internal waterways. But the Prussian Union was much more efficiently managed, and so, as efficiency is the only indispensable thing in commerce, the Bavarian and Würtemburg Governments decided to come in. On May 27, 1829, they made a free-trade treaty with the Prussian-Darmstadt Union, which thus obtained direct communication from the Baltic to the Danube. The Mid-German Union still stood apart; but the struggle really came to be a question of highroads. Whichever union could first make a great trunk-road through Germany would gain the bulk of German trade. To such a question there could only be one answer: of course the Prussian Union built its road first, the highway from Langensalza to Wurzburg, and besides this numerous other roads were made.

Weimar was the first State to break away from the Mid-German Union and to join the Prussian-Darmstadt Zollverein (1831). In 1833 Electoral Hesse joined, and thus established through communication between Brandenburg and Prussia's Rhenish Provinces. At last, on March 22, 1833, Bavaria and Wurtemburg agreed, not merely to have free trade with the Prussian Union, but actually to join it. This is why the year 1833 is usually taken as the date of the full establishment of the Zollverein.

After 1833 the Zollverein did not include all Germany; notably Hannover and Austria still stood outside it, as well as Oldenburg and the Hanse towns. After the duel between Austria and Prussia in 1850, and the humiliation of Prussia at Olmütz, the Minor States raised their heads, and the more powerful of them—Bavaria under von der Pfordten and Saxony under Beust—began to get away from the orbit of Prussia. Austria, having just won at Olmütz, was ready to go further.

The blow came in 1851, when Prince Schwartzenberg, with the warm support of Beust and Pfordten, demanded the inclusion of Austria into the Zollverein. This he might have obtained, in spite of all the cleverness of Bismarck (whose star was now beginning to rise), but for his untimely and lamented death (April 5, 1852).

After the death of the last great Austrian statesman, Prussia made up for her defeat at Olmütz. Already she had got Hannover into the Zollverein, by offering her very favourable terms, and valuable railway facilities. The treaty with Hannover was concluded on September 7, 1851. Then, when the other States pressed for the inclusion of Austria, the Prussian Government denounced the General Zollverein Treaty at the end of 1851.[1] It was just after this that Schwartzenberg died and was succeeded by Buol-Schauenstein. Bismarck, who was Prussian delegate to the Diet of Frankfort, was sent on a mission to Vienna in the summer of 1852. He thought nothing of Buol's ability, and advised the Prussian Government to adopt a firm attitude. The result was that Austria failed to gain admission to the Zollverein, and had to be content with a treaty negotiated by the finance minister

[1] The Zollverein had been renewed for twelve years in 1841, with a provision that it could be denounced at the end of 1851.

Bruck on February 19, 1853. This treaty gave Austria some commercial advantages, but not admission to the Zollverein. The Zollverein was itself reconstituted by a Conference of the former members, held at Berlin in the following month. It was renewed for a period of twelve years from January 1, 1854, and from this time it comprehended all Germany, except the Hanse towns, and, of course, Austria.

The Zollverein was not a State. It had no connection of any sort with the German Confederation, and none of the States who were members of it surrendered any of their rights of sovereignty. It depended upon treaties, which could be denounced at the end of their term by any member. Each State which joined the Zollverein joined on such terms as it was able to negotiate with the rest, and thus different States enjoyed different privileges in the Union. The Union met in Conference from time to time, but no member was bound by the decisions of these Conferences unless it assented. Prussia had no special position in the Zollverein, and her ascendancy in it was merely due to the value of her trade and to the energy and initiative of her officials. That the Zollverein would grow into a political State some day was probable enough, for its members were united by race, language, tradition, and by economic ties which, the longer they existed, were bound to become ever closer.

§ 2. Schleswig-Holstein

Since the year 1459 the King of Denmark had also been Duke of Schleswig and Duke of Holstein. In 1815 Holstein was included in the Germanic Confederation by article 53 of the Vienna Congress Act. Schleswig remained outside the Confederation ; both Duchies still had the King of Denmark as their Duke. Although not the same in race (the Holsteiners being mainly German, and the Schleswickers to a large extent Danish), the population of the two Duchies desired to remain always politically united ; a Charter of the Danish Crown (Charter of Ribe), issued in 1460, had guaranteed their indivisibility. They were equally determined that the Duchies should not be incorporated in a common constitution with Denmark. Finally, they contended that the line of succession in the Duchies was strictly from male to male, and not in heirs general as was the case with the Danish Crown.

Out of these contentious points grew all the Schleswig-Holstein trouble. As the feeling of nationalism grew stronger in Europe, a sharp antagonism arose between the political party (the Eider-Dansk) in Copenhagen on the one hand, who desired to incorporate the Duchies in a common Danish constitution and nation, and on the other hand the German nationalists (strong in Holstein, at any rate) who wished to retain the ancient individualism of the Duchies. In the years following 1830, German national feeling was greatly fostered by the eminent historians of that time. When the Schleswig-Holstein question became acute in 1848, the German nationalists of the Duchies had no more ardent champion than Gustav Droyssen, then a professor at Kiel, famous in later days as the historian of the rise of mediæval Prussia.

In the year 1848 the idea of nationalism was everywhere in the air. In Denmark the Eider-Dansks triumphed, for in February the King, Frederick VII, issued a draft constitution which was to be common to all his dominions. This act would have destroyed the individualism of the two Duchies; it would also have separated Holstein from the Germanic Confederation. The immediate result was to provoke an insurrection in the Duchies in March. This insurrection aroused the warmest sympathy throughout Germany, which was at this time making the great national and liberal experiment inaugurated by the Vorparliament at Frankfort (March 31). In April Prussian troops, and also quotas of other German States which had answered to a call of the Frankfort Diet, invaded Holstein. A considerable amount of fighting ensued, but on July 2 (1848), on the mediation of Sweden, a truce of three months was arranged at Malmoë. The truce was renewed again on August 26, for seven months. But hostilities were actually recommenced in February, 1849; a Danish squadron was defeated at Eckernförde, but the German attack on Fredericia was completely defeated. Great Britain, Russia and Sweden were all working for peace; the negotiations were rendered somewhat difficult by the attitude of Bunsen, the Prussian, ambassador at London, who was warmly in sympathy with the German nationalist view of the Schleswig-Holstein Question. Great Britain accordingly acted through the British ambassador at Berlin not through the Prussian ambassador at London. By this means, peace between Prussia and Denmark (the Frankfort Parliament no longer counted for anything) was signed at Berlin on July 2, 1850. No attempt was made to settle the constitutional issue. The Contracting Parties reserved their rights; and the Danish Crown was authorised to re-establish its authority by force of arms—as it successfully did after the withdrawal of the Prussian troops from the Duchies.

Two years later a Conference of the interested Powers was held in London, and an attempt was made to settle at any rate a part of the Danish Question. The result was that on May 8, 1852, a treaty was signed between Great Britain, Austria, France, Prussia, Russia, and Sweden; by this Act these Powers "engage . . . to acknowledge in His Highness the Prince Christian of Schleswig-Holstein-Sonderburg-Glücksburg" [Frederick VII, the reigning king, being childless] . . . "the Right of Succeeding to the whole of the Dominions now united under the sceptre of His Majesty the King of Denmark" (article 1). The High Contracting Parties also acknowledged as permanent the principle of the Integrity of the Danish Monarchy. This treaty cannot be claimed to contain any *guarantee*: what it did contain was a statement of the principles which these Powers declared would always actuate them with regard to the Danish Monarchy.[1]

As the reign of Frederick VII seemed drawing to a close, the Schleswig-Holstein Question, which continued to agitate Northern Europe, became more acute. It affected not only Schleswig and Holstein, but also Lauenburg, a Duchy on the Lower Elbe, which Denmark had acquired in 1815, "in full sovereignty," but which nevertheless was also a member of the Germanic Confederation.[2]

Just before the Treaty of London was concluded, the Danish Government announced that there was to be a common constitution for the whole monarchy, with, however, provincial estates which should control, under their own ministers, affairs not common to the whole. In the announcement of this constitution, sent by Frederick VII to Vienna, the King undertook that Schleswig should not be incorporated in the monarchy. In 1855 the common constitution was definitely established throughout the Danish dominions; the provision for transaction of purely provincial

[1] The Duke of Augustenburg surrendered all his landed estates in Denmark to the Danish Crown, and received about £350,000 in compensation. At the same time he promised, for himself and for his family, to do nothing against the method of succession to the Danish Dominions, as settled by the Protocol of London.

[2] Lauenburg was ceded by Prussia to Denmark in exchange for Western Pomerania (Treaty of Kiel, June 4, 1815).

business by provincial estates was maintained, but it was left to the Danish Government to decide what business was common to the monarchy. The Schleswickers and Holsteiners, and their numerous sympathisers in Germany, naturally considered themselves aggrieved.

The next step in the Danish Affair is the attempt of Lord John Russell to settle it. In September, 1862, Russell was at Coburg as minister-in-attendance to Queen Victoria. Robert Morier, at this time attaché at Berlin, was also at Coburg, acting as Russell's private secretary. On the advice and information of Morier, Russell, on September 24, drafted a dispatch which attained great celebrity. Briefly it offered to Denmark and to Prussia the mediation of the British Government, on the basis of complete autonomy for Schleswig. The dispatch contained some straight speaking to the Danish king: it stated that "the constitution of 1855 has no force in Holstein, Lauenburg, or Schleswig"; and it refers to the "Royal promise [of 1852] that Schleswig shall not be incorporated with Denmark." Morier wrote to Jowett (the Master of Balliol) at a later date: "I was the moral author, when attending Lord John Russell as private secretary at Coburg, of the celebrated dispatch proposing mediation on terms, which if accepted, would have prevented the international deadlock, which three years later forced on that series of great European wars from the consequences of which we are still suffering."[1]

Most of the States of Europe approved of the dispatch. Bismarck was favourable, or at least expressed himself favourably concerning Russell's proposal; Count Rechberg, the Austrian Chancellor, was for it. Only Denmark and English public opinion were against it: "the Danish Cabinet felt the pulse of Printing House Square."[2] On March 30, 1863, the Danish Crown took a further step, and issued a new constitution for Holstein, thus definitely separating it from Schleswig. Then Lord Palmerston on July 23, 1863, made in the House of Commons a speech which "produced all the effect which the most determined well-wisher to European disquiet could desire."[3] Lord Palmerston said:

> I am satisfied with all reasonable men in Europe, including those in France and Russia, in declaring that the independence, the integrity,

---

[1] *See* Wemyss: *Memoirs and Letters of Sir Robert Morier* [London, 1911], I, pp. 385–8.

[2] Morier, *ibid.*, p. 390.

[3] *Ibid.*, p. 391.

and the rights of Denmark may be maintained. We are convinced —I am convinced at least—that if any violent attempt were made to overthrow those rights and interfere with that independence, those who made the attempt would find in the result that it would not be Denmark alone with which they would have to contend.

No wonder the Danes thought they could safely refuse mediation.

During this time feelings were growing very inflamed in Germany, and for some months an ultimatum (delivered in April, 1863) had been running its course. The ultimatum, giving Denmark six months in which to withdraw the patent of March 30, had been carried through the Germanic Diet on the motion of the Grand Duke of Baden. The Danish Government replied with another constitution—a common constitution for Denmark and Schleswig—on September 28; and this act brought down upon the Danes a vote of "Federal Execution" in the Frankfort Diet on October 1. Shortly after this King Frederick VII of Denmark died (November 15, 1863).

The new king was Christian IX, the Duke of Schleswig-Holstein-Sonderburg-Glücksburg, and descended on his mother's side from the extinct Danish Royal House. The early part of Christian's reign was to be very troubled, and the treaty of 1852, which had been made with a view to his accession, would have to be called into action. Already Napoleon III had tried to act as a "Napoleon of peace," by proposing that a European Congress should meet to settle the Schleswig-Holstein Question (November 5); but as he had included in this proposal an announcement that the treaties of 1815 were no longer in force,[1] the British Government would have nothing to do with it.

Scarcely had the breath left the body of Frederick VII, when Duke Frederick of Augustenburg declared himself Duke of Schleswig-Holstein (November 16). King Christian IX, who inherited a strong Eider-Dansk ministry from his predecessor, continued their policy and on November 18 signed the new Danish Constitution—a common constitution for all the territories of the Monarchy, to take effect from the following January. Indignation blazed high in Germany, and most of the Governments refused to recognise Christian as Duke of Holstein. Austria and Prussia did not commit

[1] "Si l'on considère attentivement la situation des divers pays, il est impossible de ne pas reconnaître que, presque sur tous les points, les Traités de Vienne sont détruits, modifiés, méconnus ou menacés." Napoleon III to Queen Victoria, in *Parliamentary Papers*, 1864, vol. I.

themselves. On December 7 the Diet at Frankfort voted that the "Federal Execution," which had already been decreed, should be proceeded with, and a Federal Army under the Saxon General von Hake was ordered to occupy Holstein. Lord Russell, the British Foreign Secretary, made another attempt at mediation by sending Lord Wodehouse to Copenhagen: but Danish national feeling would allow no compromise on the question of incorporating Schleswig, and so Wodehouse's mission failed, more especially as the Danes fully believed that Great Britain would uphold their integrity. By January 8, 1864, Holstein had been occupied by the Federal troops, chiefly Hannoverian and Saxon—the Danish forces evacuating the land peacefully as the Federalists advanced. The Duke of Augustenburg took up his residence and formed a government at Kiel.

Meanwhile the British Government returned to the charge with a note addressed to the Frankfort Diet, demanding a Conference. But the Diet, which in any case had never acceded to the treaty of 1852, was in no mood to listen to the British Note. Then Bismarck acted, not alone, but in company with Austria, the great upholder of custom and legitimacy. An Austro-Prussian ultimatum was sent to Copenhagen, demanding that the Danes should agree, within forty-eight hours, to withdraw the Constitution (January 16). There was no doubt the demand would be refused, and then Austro-Prussian troops would be dispatched swiftly into Schleswig, before it could be occupied by the Federal troops. Austria and Prussia had signed the treaty of 1852, but their acknowledgement of the integrity of the Danish dominions was contingent (so Bismarck argued) on the simultaneous Danish Royal promise not to incorporate Schleswig. The Duchy was now to be occupied by Austro-Prussian troops, and held as a pledge for the fulfilment of this promise. Nevertheless, as Bismarck confesses in his *Reflections*, "from the very beginning I kept annexation steadily before my eyes."[1]

Nor was Great Britain altogether blind to this. On January 20, the Prussian Field Marshal Wrangel's forces had already crossed the frontier into Holstein, and were advancing towards Schleswig, which the Danish Government showed every intention of defending. On that very day, Lord Russell sent a note to the Powers proposing a European Conference; and when this proposal failed, even stronger measures were contemplated. But neither Russia nor

[1] Bismarck, *Reflections*, vol. II, chap. XIX.

France would consent to take action. The Russian Government was already in debt to Bismarck. During the Polish Revolt of 1863, the Russians were greatly helped by the very benevolent neutrality of Prussia. Bismarck had gone so far as to conclude with Prince Gorchakoff, the Russian Chancellor, a Convention (February 8, 1863), by which he not merely undertook to give no assistance to the Poles, but actually gave permission to Russian troops to enter Prussian territory, in pursuit of rebels. In France considerable sympathy had been shown to the Poles; and M. Drouyn de Lhuys, the Minister for Foreign Affairs, had proposed (February 21) that Great Britain and Austria should jointly protest against the Convention of February 8. Lord Russell, however, had refused to associate Great Britain with this scheme. Needless to say Count Rechberg, the Austrian Chancellor, who believed in friendship with Prussia, gave no concurrence to France.

Thus the complaisance of Bismarck towards Prince Gorchakoff during the Polish Revolt tended to put Russia out of action during the Schleswig-Holstein affair; and possibly the Russian attitude was strengthened by anticipation of further favours to come.[1] On the other hand, France, was disinclined to take strong measures with regard to Schleswig-Holstein in 1864, partly because she was still deeply involved in the Mexican Expedition, and partly because, since Great Britain's refusal to co-operate over the Polish Question in 1863, she had no faith in the British Government's firmness. And so now, when Denmark looked like being conquered, and when the British Cabinet made to France a definite proposal[2] with a view to joint armed intervention, M. Drouyn de Lhuys in a dispatch of June 14, 1864, somewhat tartly refused. This dispatch, a celebrated one in French diplomatic history, was directed to the French ambassador in London, to guide his attitude towards the British Government. It indicated that France could not ally with a power like England which (according to Drouyn) would confine its support to the easy task of gaining command of the Baltic Sea, while the

[1] Six years later, on October 29, 1870, Russia, with the connivance of Bismarck, denounced the Black Sea Convention of the Treaty of Paris of 1856.

[2] Rothan, *La Politique française en* 1866, p. 19, says that Lord Cowley actually offered an offensive and defensive alliance to the French Government, and that Lord Clarendon visited Paris with a definite plan for co-operation to be placed before the French Cabinet.

French would have to wage a continental war against the combined forces of Austria and Germany.[1]

Meanwhile, before it became finally clear that neither France nor Great Britain would interfere, much had happened. The advance of the Austrians and Prussians through Holstein was not delayed, although collisions with the Federal troops already in occupation of the Duchy were only narrowly avoided. In the early days of February the Austrian and Prussian troops crossed the Eider and advanced into Schleswig. The Danes wisely made no attempt to hold the Dannevirke, but retired to Düppel, the lines on the mainland which defended the passage of the strait to Alsen. The Prussians pressed forward to occupy Jutland. The Austrian Government was against such an extension of the war, but the conciliatory Manteuffel, whose moderation and patience had proved so useful at Olmütz, was sent to Vienna, where he managed to patch up an agreement with Count Rechberg (March, 1864). On April 18, Düppel was stormed by the Prussians, who thus gained possession of the bridge-head of Alsen Island. Yet the Danish Government showed no signs of coming to terms; and a Conference [2] was shortly to be opened at London, from which the Danes hoped for great things.

This Conference, which was due to the pacific efforts of Lord Russell, was opened on April 25. Lord Russell presided. Denmark was represented in chief by G. J. Quaade, Prussia by Bernstorff, Austria by Count Apponyi, Sweden by Count Wachtmeister, Russia by Brunnow, France by La Tour d'Auvergne, the Germanic Confederation by Beust. The first thing which the Conference did was (on the proposal of Prussia) to arrange that an armistice should take place from May 12 to June 24. In the discussions for a permanent settlement, Bernstorff clearly stated the Prussian view, that the treaty of 1852 was now dead, and must not be taken into account (May 12). Five days later, he took a further step and announced that the solution of the Schleswig-Holstein Question lay in the political independence of the Duchies and their common union with each other. Independence from what?—that was the question which the rest of the Conference desired to be answered.

[1] "Le gouvernement anglaise se bornerait-elle à l'envoi d'une flotte dans la Baltique, reduisant ainsi sa rôle à une tâche facile, tandis que la France aurait à subir une guerre continentale, à lutter contre les forces combinés de l'Autriche et de l'Allemagne?" (Rothan, *loc. cit.*).

[2] The Protocols of the Conference are in *State Papers*, vol. 54, p. 173 ff.

Bernstorff would not commit his Government further. People hoped that it might mean that Prussia would approve of the Duchies being constitutionally detached from Denmark, while remaining in a personal union under the Danish Crown. This was the plan favoured by Count Rechberg. But Bismarck never meant to have it, and the Danish representatives themselves absolutely refused to consider it. With the treaty of 1852 now out of the way (although the British Government refused to regard it in this light), and with the Danes positively refusing to abate their claim to keep the duchies incorporated in the Danish Constitution, Bernstorff was now able to treat the affair of the Duchies as an open question. The next thing to do was to get rid of the Conference, and to have this open question settled between Prussia and Austria by themselves.

Yet the Duke of Augustenburg was still carrying on his nominal government of the Duchies from Kiel, and the opinion of nearly all the smaller states of Germany, led by Beust, was in favour of him. Count Rechberg, too, now that a personal union of the Duchies with the Danish Crown seemed impossible, was in favour of Augustenburg, although, out of deference to Bismarck, he would not support the motion to this effect which Beust proposed in the Diet at Frankfort. So to get the Augustenburg candidature definitely out of the way, Bernstorff, with almost incredible boldness, proposed on May 28 at the Conference that the Duchies should be made an independent State under the hereditary Prince of Augustenburg. The proposal was rejected by Great Britain, France, Russia, Sweden, and of course by Denmark. A proposal of Lord Russell, that Schleswig should be partitioned, so that the northern part, which was indisputably Danish in race, should remain with Denmark, gained more support, but was hotly resisted in Germany, in the Duchy, even (it is said) in the northern part of it, and by the Prince of Augustenburg, who could not conscientiously consent to receive a divided Schleswig. So the partition-scheme fell to the ground; and with it, the Augustenburg claim, without people being aware of the fact, was buried.

It was still by no means clear that the British Government would not stand by the Danes. On May 1, Lord Palmerston had privately told Count Apponyi that if an Austrian squadron entered the Baltic, a British squadron would go too [1]—that is to say, without committing itself to fight by land, the British Government would

[1] Ashley: *Life of Lord Palmerston*, II, 432–3.

protect the Danish islands with its fleet.[1] The threat was effective, for to have Great Britain in the war was the last thing that Austria or Prussia wanted. Some time in June, Lord Palmerston made overtures to France, with a view to armed intervention: it was then that Drouyn de Lhuys sent his famous refusal (June 14).

By this time, however, even the Danish Government was beginning to reconcile itself to the prospect of a partition of Schleswig. Lord Russell seized the occasion to invoke the 23rd Protocol of the Congress of Paris, concerning recourse to the good offices of a friendly Power before going to war. In this case, the friendly Power (France was meant) would decide on the line of partition. Rechberg (who clearly foresaw, and dreaded the Prussian annexation of the Duchies) was for accepting the British proposal, until Bismarck headed him off by arranging an interview between King William and the Emperor Francis Joseph at Carlsbad. Some sort of agreement was reached, which was luckily confirmed by the Danish Government rejecting mediation. Shortly after this, the armistice expired (June 24). The last—and merely formal—session of the Conference of London was held on June 25. Two days later the Prussians crossed the Alsen sound, and without great loss conquered the whole island.

All hope of intervention was now over, both in Copenhagen and in London. On July 4 a notable debate was opened in the British Parliament, but it was confined on the part of the Government to explanations why Great Britain had not intervened; there was no idea of asking for a mandate from the legislature to fight.

The Danes, realising at last that they stood absolutely alone, bowed to the necessity of facts, and asked for an armistice, which was conceded from July 20. Five days later Quaade, Bismarck, and Rechberg met at Vienna to arrange a peace. The Germanic Confederation (to whom the war really belonged from the preliminary negotiations to the outbreak at the military entry into Holstein) was completely ignored, in spite of the quite justifiable efforts of Beust to get his hand in. Great Britain and France might surely have claimed that the peace and settlement were really a European affair; but they were given no chance by Bis-

[1] This idea of limited belligerence is identical with that explained by Sir Edward Grey in the House of Commons on August 2, 1914: "If the German fleet comes into the Channel or through the North Sea to undertake hostile operations against the French coasts or shipping, the British fleet will give all the protection in its power."

marck, nor could the Danish plenipotentiary afford to prolong the negotiations in face of the imminent prospect of a renewed and intensified campaign by the Prussian forces. So on August 1 the Preliminary Treaty of Peace was signed and Bismarck went back to Berlin.

By the treaty thus so rapidly concluded the King of Denmark renounced his rights over the Duchies of Schleswig, Holstein, and Lauenburg in favour of the Emperor of Austria and the King of Prussia (article 1). Article 2 stated that " the cession of the Duchy of Schleswig comprehends all the isles belonging to this Duchy as well as the territory situated on terra firma." By the same article, Denmark abandoned the Jutlandish *enclaves* in Schleswig and received in return an equivalent portion of the Duchy contiguous to the district of Ribe and of Kolding. The Duchies were to accept responsibility for a portion of the debt of the Danish Monarchy (article 3). The expenses of the war were to be reimbursed to Austria and Prussia by the Duchies (*ibid.*). All these conditions were inserted in the definitive Treaty of Peace concluded at Vienna on October 30, 1864.[1]

Thus the course of events had brought it about that an agitation which had been begun in order to secure the autonomy of the Duchies had ended by putting them under the heel of the Dual Alliance. For this amazing result British critics freely blame the British Government, while French writers blame the French. England certainly had played a very sorry part. No one could have been more precise in his statement concerning the sanctity of treaties than Lord Russell. It is true he recognised that Denmark was wrong in trying to force a common Danish Constitution upon Schleswig. On December 17, 1863, in a dispatch to Lord Wodehouse (then on mission at Copenhagen) he quoted the Danish recognition (made on December 6, 1851), that " the [Danish] King has promised, and again declares that neither any incorporation of the Duchy of Schleswig into the Kingdom shall take place, nor any steps leading thereto shall be taken. . . ." [2] But in another

[1] The Preliminary Treaty of August 1, 1864, was signed by Quaade and Col. Kaufman for Denmark, by Rechberg and Baron Brenner for Austria, and by Bismarck and Werther for Prussia. Text in *N.R.G.*, XVII, ii, p. 470. The Final Treaty of October 30, 1864, was signed by the same, except that Balan took the place of Bismarck, who was not present.

[2] *Parliamentary Papers*, 1864, vol. III (*Correspondence relating to the Affairs of the Duchies of Schleswig, Holstein and Lauenburg*).

dispatch he vigorously denies that a violation of this promise by Denmark could be taken as annulling the obligations entered into by the Powers in the Treaty of May 8, 1852.

> A violation of the engagements taken by Denmark in 1851–2 towards Germany is an offence which may be properly resented, and for which redress may be justly demanded. But such violation cannot cancel a solemn European engagement taken towards other parties. . . . The whole foundation of the Treaty stipulations of Europe would be subverted, if such a reason could be admitted as an excuse for breaking a plain and simple Treaty engagement.[1]

A similar dispatch was sent on the same date to Sir A. Buchanan, ambassador at Berlin, with the additional remark that although Denmark's promises of 1851–2 may have been the prevailing motive with Austria and Prussia for entering into the treaty of May, 1852, yet they formed no part of the treaty, which was an absolutely independent instrument, supported only by its own conditions.[2] This dispatch was not merely for Buchanan's private guidance: he was empowered by the British Foreign Secretary to read it to Bismarck.

Although the treaty of May, 1852, did not contain any specific guarantee of Danish integrity by the signing Powers, it was regarded generally in France and England as imposing a moral obligation in this direction, and all official British statements assume this obligation as fundamental to the whole Danish Question. Moreover Russell had obtained from the Prussian Government an acknowledgment of this obligation. On February 4, 1864, Bernstorff had communicated to the Foreign Office a Note sent by Bismarck:

> The Government of the King, by basing on the stipulations of 1851–52 the rights which, in concert with Austria, it is proceeding to enforce upon Denmark, has by this very act recognized the principle of the integrity of the Danish Monarchy, as established by the transactions of 1851–52. The Government of the King, in proceeding to the occupation of Schleswig, do not intend to depart from this principle.

The Note concluded with a statement that if events made any change necessary in the dispositions of 1852, " no definitive arrange-

[1] Russell to Murray (Minister at Dresden), December 17, 1863 (*Parl. Papers*, 1864, vol. III).

[2] Russell to Buchanan, *ibid.*, p. 382.

ments could be made without the concurrence of the Powers who signed the Treaty of London." [1] It is almost incredible that after obtaining this admission, Russell could allow Prussia and Austria by themselves to settle the conditions of peace with Denmark privately at Vienna.

That Great Britain might reasonably have taken steps to suppress the inconvenient treaty of 1852 was the view of Sir Robert Morier. He confesses that he suggested the offer of British mediation in September, 1862, in the hope that the Prussian Government would accept it, while the Danes would reject it, so that the British Government might then say: We have done all we could, we have made a fair offer, and as the defendant in the suit refuses our arbitration on the basis of autonomy, we wash our hands of the whole business. Morier plainly says he made the suggestion in order

> that Lord John Russell, in the event of one party agreeing to the proposal, and the other not, should declare, that having failed to obtain the constitutional basis presupposed by the Treaty of London, Great Britain withdrew from obligations which would involve the violation of constitutional rights.

Morier then goes on to say:

> Lord John Russell saw this; but the rest of the Cabinet pooh-poohed it, with the result that we returned to the *status quo ante*, and that when the casus fœderis arose we abandoned like curs the country whose resistance to all compromise had been solely and entirely based on the belief that we should keep faith with her, and acknowledge the sacredness of engagements.

The result was fatal to the peace of Europe and nearly fatal altogether to England. "With the abandonment of Denmark began that decadence of our position and *prestige* in Europe which has landed us in the *quantité négligeable* of Bismarck." [2] There were only two statesmen in Europe who saw clearly the issues at stake: one of these was engaged in shaping the issues and the other was powerless to prevent them. These two men were Bismarck and Beust. Lord Russell was, over the Schleswig affair, a mere bungler;

[1] *Parl. Papers*, 1864, vol. III, p. 639.

[2] All the above quotations from Morier come from Wemyss' *Memoirs and Letters of Sir R. Morier*, I, pp. 388–90. M. Rothan (*La politique française en* 1866, p. 17) is equally severe upon France: "Le gouvernement français . . . est celui qui a le plus contribué au démembrement danoise."

Lord Palmerston was apparently too old to face a great war. It has sometimes been suggested that the English Court was against intervention, and there is some evidence to support this view. On the other hand the Prince of Wales, who had married the Princess Alexandra of Denmark, was strongly Danish in sympathy.

CHAPTER XXII

THE FOUNDATION OF THE GERMAN EMPIRE

§ 1. Gastein and Biarritz

Before the Treaty of Vienna of October 30, 1864, was concluded, Count Rechberg, the Austrian Chancellor, had fallen. He was a statesman of some moderate ability and was by no means the dupe of Bismarck. Bismarck indeed had a considerable respect for him, and calls him an "irascible though honourable man." [1] Rechberg's policy was to maintain the alliance with Prussia, and to prevent Austria from being excluded from Germany. With this last object in view, no sooner was the Danish War over than he opened the question of Austria's admission into the Zollverein, according to article 25 of the treaty of 1853.[2] Bismarck was prepared to make some concession to this policy; but the Austrian *Reichsrat* itself threw over Rechberg on account of what they considered his undue deference to Prussia (October 27). In his place, Francis Joseph chose as Chancellor Count Mensdorff-Pouilly, who was a *persona grata* with the King of Prussia, but was really under Anti-Prussian influence. The Austrians would have done better if they had held by Rechberg. Rechberg saw clearly enough that Prussia was bound to get the Duchies, but he expected to get in return a Prussian guarantee of Austria's non-German dominions.

[1] *Reflections*, chap. XVII. Bismarck says he gained Rechberg's confidence when the two were representing their respective countries at the Frankfort Diet in 1849. Rechberg had received two dispatches from his Government, one for his own eyes only, and one to be shown to Bismarck. By mistake he gave Bismarck the wrong one to read. Bismarck returned the dispatch with the remark only that Rechberg had made a mistake: "Neither in dispatches nor in conversation did I make even an indirect use of the secret document or of his slip. Thenceforth he placed in me every confidence" (*Ibid.*).

[2] It provided that within twelve years negotiations should be opened for a general German Customs Union, which was to include Austria.

This was a more feasible policy than that of Mensdorff, who was sanguine enough to think he would induce Prussia to cede part of Silesia—Glatz—in return for the annexation of the Duchies.

Meantime the *provisorium*, the temporary arrangement by which Austria and Prussia held the Duchies in condominium, continued. The Prince of Augustenburg was still in Holstein, and, apparently, there were still some Federal troops there. The Federal Diet at Frankfort was becoming restive at the indefinite continuance of the provisorium, and was demanding that it be put an end to in favour of the Prince of Augustenburg (March, 1865). The arguments of Beust and Pfordten, the leaders of Saxony and Bavaria, the two most powerful of the smaller States, were really unanswerable. The Prussian, or rather the Bismarckian, view, however, had a powerful supporter in Heinrich von Treitschke, at this time Professor of Political Science and Public Finance in the University of Freiburg in Baden. "In this matter [Schleswig-Holstein] positive law is irreconcileable with the vital interests of our country. We must set aside positive law and compensate those who may be injured in consequence. This view may be erroneous; it is not immoral. Every step in historical progress is thus achieved . . . positive law when injurious to the common good must be swept away."[1] Of Bismarck Treitschke thought that he was politically rather muddle-headed, and not honest: yet he thought that he was making for the right goal.

> I subscribe to all that Freytag says about the dishonesty of Prussian policy. But when I look at the opposition party and see there the *Rheinbund* intriguers of the courts of Dresden and Munich and the conscienceless demagogues, who are corrupting an honest people at the bidding of the Augustenburg claimant . . . then I understand that by comparison with such enemies Bismarck is pursuing not only a clever, but even a moral policy. He will do what we need, he will advance another step towards the lofty goal of German unity. . . . The good cause will triumph; the heirs of Frederick the Great will reign in Schleswig-Holstein, and in a short time the nation will be ashamed of its own stupidity.[2]

Moltke's army and Treitschke's writings and lectures were the physical and intellectual drive behind Bismarck's diplomacy. Beust and Pfordten might see clearly, but they could do nothing.

[1] Quoted from *Briefe*, ii., No. 459 (May 22, 1865) in *The Political Thought of Heinrich von Treitschke*, by H. W. C. Davis, p. 26 (London, 1914).

[2] *Briefe*, II, No. 476 (October, 1865), in Davis, *op. cit.*, p. 27.

The Austrian Government would gladly have ended the provisorium by recognising the Augustenburg claimant; but failing in this, they would agree to a partition between themselves and Prussia. This was the plan of the diplomatist, Count Blome,[1] who was entrusted with the negotiations at Wildbad-Gastein towards the end of July. In this pleasant Salzburg watering-place King William, Manteuffel, and Bismarck met Blome, and soon convinced him that neither Augustenburg nor the Oldenburg candidate for the Duchies had any chance. From Gastein Blome had to go to Ischl, to confer with Francis Joseph, and thence to Vienna with the Emperor, where a Council of Ministers was held. There was a party in the Council that would have preferred to fight Prussia there and then rather than abandon the Augustenburg claimant. But peaceful counsels still prevailed, and Blome went back to Gastein with the Emperor's autograph letter. Bismarck was not yet ready to fight for the whole of the Duchies (for he had not managed to attach Italy), so he agreed to the compromise known as the Convention of Gastein, August 14, 1865.

By this act, the rights over Schleswig and Holstein, acquired by the two Contracting Parties in the Vienna Treaty of October 30, 1865, were, "without prejudice to the continuance of those rights of both Powers to the whole of both Duchies," given over to the Emperor of Austria as regards Holstein, and to the King of Prussia as regards Schleswig (article 1).[2] Thus the thing against which Austria and Germany had so loudly protested, namely the separation of Schleswig from Holstein, and to prevent which they had made war upon Denmark, was now shamelessly done by those two champions of the Duchies' unity. No wonder that Lord Russell, than whom no one had a clearer insight into the abstract problems of public conduct, complained in a passage of sustained and lofty beauty, that the European system of law was now set at naught:

> All rights, old and new, whether founded on the solemn Compacts of Sovereigns or on the clear expression of the popular will, have been

---

[1] Blome was Austrian minister at Munich.

[2] By article 2 a Federal German Fleet was to be established at Kiel; and by article 7, Prussia was to be permitted to construct a Canal through Holstein from the North Sea to the Baltic. By article 9 the Emperor of Austria ceded absolutely to Prussia his rights over Lauenburg, in return for a payment of 2,500,000 Danish rix-dollars.

set at naught by the Convention of Gastein, and the dominion of Force is the sole power acknowledged and regarded.

Violence and conquest are the bases upon which alone the Partitioning Powers found their agreement.

Her Majesty's Government deeply lament the disregard thus shown to the principles of public right, and the legitimate claims of a people to be heard as to the disposal of their own destiny.

Yet with Lord Russell to see the truth was one thing; to act upon it was another. For the same note which contained the above searing criticisms concluded with the injunction that the British ambassadors, to whom the Note was addressed, must not communicate its observations to the Courts to which they were accredited.

It is tolerably clear that Bismarck knew he would soon be fighting Austria; and when this should happen, he did not want to have France against him. So, after Gastein, he went as a simple tourist to Biarritz (where Napoleon III was taking a holiday), just as Cavour seven years earlier had gone to Plombières. He arrived at Biarritz on October 4, 1865. The Emperor and he had several conversations. Napoleon was very anxious to know whether any secret commitments underlay the published version of the Convention of Gastein: in particular, had Prussia guaranteed Venetia to Austria? Bismarck assured him that this was not so. Pursuing his policy of stating the naked truth, in answer to the Emperor's question, "What are your views with regard to Holstein?" Bismarck replied: "We intend to annex it." Austria, he suggested, would accept a pecuniary indemnity. But the annexation of Holstein was not to be the end of the matter: "Our German State has . . . a great rôle to fulfil. In the accomplishment of what is, in our eyes, a duty, we count upon the friendly attitude of France. The Cabinet of the Tuileries has every reason to favour the national mission of Prussia: a vigorous Prussia will naturally associate itself with France."[1] Napoleon III listened with his habitual impassivity, but he seems to have sympathised. He was obviously deeply interested in the fate of Venice. Could compensation for Austria (in return for the cession of Venetia) be

[1] Cp. *Reflections* (Trans. 1898), vol. II, chap. XXI, p. 56: "I took it as assured that war with France would necessarily have to be waged on the road to our future national development," and Vol. I, chap. IX, p. 244, "With France we shall never have peace, with Russia never the necessity for war."

found in the Danubian principalities of Wallachia and Moldavia? To this Bismarck made the encouraging reply that Prussia had no serious interests on the Danube, except to avoid antagonising Russia. On October 11, Bismarck took his leave, confident that in the Venetian question he had something to keep Napoleon III from supporting Austria in the coming struggle.[1]

Austria was sure to fight soon, and Bismarck was quite willing that she should, only *he* was not going to declare war. The proudest Government in Europe, as the Austrian was entitled to be called, was being offered more than it could peaceably swallow. First of all Prussia was upon it with an offer to buy the Austrian rights in Schleswig (in November); then came an offer from La Marmora that Italy should buy the Venetia for 1,000 million *lire*. Francis Joseph, although he had touched pitch once when he gave up his rights over Lauenburg for money, rejected both offers. The Hereditary Prince of Augustenburg was still, in spite of Prussian remonstrances, allowed to remain in Holstein. Before the end of the year Bismarck had broadly hinted to Count Karolyi that the Austro-Prussian Alliance was at an end.

Nevertheless hostilities did not ensue for some months, but the tension steadily increased. Towards the end of January, 1866, the supporters of the Duke of Augustenburg held an Assembly at Altona (which being in Holstein was under Austrian jurisdiction). The Prussian press was indignant, and Bismarck on January 26 sent a strongly-worded remonstrance to Werther, the Prussian Ambassador at Vienna, for communication to the Austrian Government. Count Mensdorff in replying took his stand upon the Convention of Gastein, and pointed out that this Act excluded any control except Austrian in Holstein. In Berlin a Crown Council was held (February 28), at which the King, the Crown Prince, Bismarck, Goltz, Manteuffel, Moltke and other lesser lights were present. The King complained of Austria's policy of keeping Prussia in a secondary place, and stated that "the acquisition of the Duchies is a national wish in Prussia." The Crown Prince was against war, but the rest agreed that war, in a just cause, seemed inevitable. Moltke argued that in a war with Austria, the co-operation of Italy was essential, and accordingly Count

[1] This was Bismarck's second visit to Biarritz: the first was in 1864. For this second visit see Rothan, *La politique française en* 1866, and P. de la Gorce, *Hist. du Second Empire*, tome IV, livre XXIX, § V.

Usedom, Prussian Minister at Florence, entered into negotiations with La Marmora. From Paris, the Cavaliere Nigra reported that the Emperor Napoleon was favourable to an Italo-Prussian alliance with the object of detaching Venetia from Austria; so the next step in the preliminaries of the imminent war was the famous mission of General Govone to Berlin and the conclusion on April 8 of that treaty of mutual suspicion and insurances which has already been described (see above, p. 156). It was a treaty of alliance to last for three months unless within that time Prussia declared war upon Austria—in which case Italy was bound to declare war too, and the alliance would continue till the objects of the allies had been gained.

The fundamental cause of war was not Schleswig-Holstein (though this was an important contributory cause), but the fact that the Germanic Confederation had for the fifty years of its existence been growing more and more unworkable, with Austria and Prussia as incompatible yoke-fellows. To remedy this state of affairs the Confederation must be remodelled. But the only way in which it could be remodelled really in favour of Prussia was by the exclusion of Austria; and this could not be brought about without war. Already, on March 24, while both sides were making ominous movements of troops, Bismarck had in a note to the German Government opened the question of Federal Reform. The essence of his proposals was the exclusion of Austria (this was implied, not stated), and the division of the command of the military forces of the Confederation between Prussia and Bavaria; but King Ludwig and Pfordten preferred a threefold division, with Austria remaining in the Bund—a scheme with great possibilities for good, if Prussia would only have consented to it.

About the middle of April news arrived at Vienna that large Italian forces were on foot; and so on April 21 the Austrian southern army was mobilised. Bismarck then stated to the Vienna Government that Prussia could not remain indifferent to an attack upon Italy. This may have been the first time that Austria learnt of the Italo-Prussian alliance, the text of which remained secret. On April 26 the Italian army was mobilised.

Now the Secondary States of Germany began to arm. The King of Hannover, who felt that the interest of his country would be directly menaced by Prussian annexation of Schleswig-Holstein, rejected Bismarck's offer of a guarantee of territorial integrity in return for neutrality. Meanwhile Napoleon III was proposing that a European Congress should be held. Bismarck had no need to cold-shoulder the proposal, for Austria only agreed subject to the condition that the territorial divisions of Italy should not be within the purview of the Congress (May, 1866). The public-spirited effort of the Prussian Freiherr Anton von Gablenz unofficially to negotiate a *via media*, according to which Schleswig-Holstein should be an independent State under a Prussian prince, failed apparently owing to the objections of Austria.[1] The accession (without the knowledge of the Powers) of Prince Charles of Hohenzollern-Sigmaringen to the throne of Rumania did not sweeten the Austrian attitude. One more attempt, but this time an exceedingly clumsy one, to limit the war, was made by Napoleon III: he negotiated and actually signed a treaty with Austria to the effect that France should be neutral, that Austria should cede Venetia to France for conveyance to Italy, and that France should guarantee the rest of Austria's Italian possessions. But the Italian Government, when informed of this very doubtful benefit, was anything but pleased. It indignantly repudiated a gain which would make the complete union of Italy in the future impossible.

On June 5, Bismarck published the heretofore secret treaty of January 16, 1864, by which Prussia and Austria had contracted to settle the Schleswig-Holstein Question without the intervention of the Diet,—thus, in his cynical way, proving that Austria cared nothing for the Confederation, and careless of the fact that the publication proved the same thing about Prussia. On June 10, he placed before the German Governments his definite scheme for a new Constitution of the Confederation, with Austria excluded. This was really throwing down the gauntlet, and being determined himself never to make war first he could wait, relying upon Austria to pick-up the glove. Collisions had already occurred on the frontier of the Duchies. Actually, Prussian troops were the first to advance, crossing the Eider into Holstein (June 7). The Austrian manifesto of war was published on June 17, the Prussian on the 18th, the Italian on the 20th.

[1] For an interesting account of this obscure incident see Ward, *Germany 1815–1890*, II, 227–8. Austria felt that to agree to Gablenz's plan would sacrifice the Secondary States.

§ 2. The Peace of Prague

Although supported by the Kingdom of Italy, Prussia, so far as Germany was concerned, stood alone. Against her was ranged Austria, Saxony, Bavaria, Wurtemburg, Hannover, Baden, Hesse-Cassel, Hesse-Darmstadt, Nassau, and the Free City of Frankfort. Nevertheless it was only a Seven Weeks' War. Feldzugmeister Benedek, an able and devoted field-officer, though no strategist, was overcome by the genius of Moltke at Königgrätz in Bohemia on July 3, 1866. About a week earlier (June 27), the Hannoverians had been defeated at Langensalza, and a week later the Bavarians were routed near Fulda. The Prussians had thus won in every theatre, though their enemies were by no means completely broken.

And now comes the greatest triumph of one of the princes of diplomatists. Bismarck had the rare capacity to know the limit up to which a victory could be used.[1] The Prussian Army, the pride of its creators Moltke, Roon and scores of other ardent generals, all the military caste of Prussia, had won their first really great battle against a first-class power. But the victory was not complete. The lines of Florisdorf, which Moltke calculated could be stormed with the loss of about 2,000 men, stood between the victorious Prussians and the march to Vienna. And Bismarck dared to propose to stop this triumphing army, in the full *élan* of its young and brilliant career, and to leash it, while its prey was all but within its grasp. He and he alone had the clearness of vision and the self-restraint to realise, that infinitely more was to be gained by *not* humbling the proud and unforgiving Empire of Austria, than by taking her capital and trampling her majesty in the dust.

On July 12, a council of war, "as the military preferred to call it" (I am here reproducing from Bismarck's own Memoirs), was held at Prussian headquarters at Czernahora. The King presided over the Generals, and Bismarck, as he modestly says, being within reach, "was included in these deliberations." Moltke explained his plans for capturing the lines of Florisdorf "in order to reach

[1] Cp. "Moderation in victory is not less important than victory itself. I go beyond that. I think moderation in victory is *more important* to a nation even than victory itself, for there are so many tragedies which you find written across the page of history, which have arisen from victory turned to a bad use—a victory immoderately used—that it would have been better for those nations had they never won that victory." Mr. Lloyd George in the House of Commons, August 16, 1921.

Vienna." It never occurred to the Generals that any other course would be dreamt of. Bismarck did not dare to state his mind openly: yet

> it was already clear to me (he says) that we should have to defend the conquests of the campaign in further wars, just as Frederick the Great had to defend the results of his first two Silesian wars in the fiercer fire of the Seven Years' War. That a war with France would succeed that with Austria, lay in the logic of history. . . . Moved by this consideration, I had a political motive for avoiding, rather than bringing about, a triumphal entry into Vienna in the Napoleonic style.

Nearly a fortnight passed, for Moltke could not advance without replenishing his artillery, which required, in particular, more heavy guns. On July 23, another council was held at headquarters. This time Bismarck declared his opinion that peace must be concluded on the Austrian terms; but he "remained alone in this opinion." Yet every hour only hardened his decision. It was not merely that to humiliate Austria further would for ever estrange her; another defeat might bring about the disruption of her empire and then "what would be put in that portion of Europe which the Austrian State from Tyrol to the Bukovina had hitherto occupied?" But the King could not agree with Bismarck: "the aversion of the military to interrupt the victorious course of the army" seemed insuperable. Under the impression that his opinion was rejected Bismarck left the room, and retired to his own chamber. The labour of a lifetime seemed ruined, just when the prize for which he had so devotedly and so unselfishly striven, seemed within his grasp. He was billeted in a room four storeys up. Looking out of the open windows, across the vast Hungarian plain, the Iron Minister was tempted to throw himself over and end his hopeless life. The door opened, but the minister did not look round. Then a hand was laid on his shoulder, and a voice that he knew said, "You know that I was against this war. You considered it necessary, and the responsibility for it lies on you. If you are now persuaded that our end is attained, and peace must now be concluded, I am ready to support you, and defend your opinion with my father." It was the Crown Prince; and his influence turned the scale. The King, who after all could have his own way with the Generals, could not stand out against both his son and his Minister-President. In a pencilled note on one of Bismarck's memoranda, King William recorded: "I find myself reluctantly compelled, after such brilliant victories on the part of the army, to bite this sour apple and accept so disgraceful a peace." Bismarck had won his greatest victory.[1]

On the day after Königgrätz, the Emperor of Austria had telegraphed to Napoleon III asking for good offices; and on July 14 draft proposals of peace had been arranged with von der Goltz at Paris. These proposals were embodied in the Preliminaries now to be concluded.

On 26, the Preliminaries of Nikolsburg (a castle belonging to Count Mensdorff), were signed between Bismarck for Prussia and Count Karolyi for Austria. It almost seemed, as King William said, that the victor was giving way to the vanquished before the gate of Vienna. The integrity of Austria was to be maintained; nay more, the integrity of *Saxony* (a prize thus for the second time renounced by Prussia[2]) was to be recognised; and a war-contribution equal only to £3,000,000 to be taken from Austria. But Bismarck got all he wanted: (1) Austria agreed to the dissolution of the Germanic Confederation, and to the establishment of a new organisation north of the Main in which she was not to form a part; (2) she agreed that the States south of the Main might form a union among themselves, and by treaties make "national liens" with the north; (3) she renounced her rights over Schleswig and Holstein; and she acquiesced in any annexations (excluding Saxony) which Prussia might make at the expense of the allies of Austria to the north of the Main. It may truthfully be said that the foundations and a solid part of the structure of what was after all a grand work, the modern German Empire of 1871–1914, were made at Nikolsburg.

The final peace was made at Prague on August 23, 1866.[3] The first article contained the usual peace and friendship clause. The second secured the eventual annexation of Venetia to the Kingdom of Italy. This was part of the contract made between Prussia and Italy on April 8. Victor Emmanuel had carried out his part of the bargain. He had made war upon Austria after Prussia had given the signal, and had detained a large Austrian army in Italy. It is true that his land forces had been defeated at Custozza, and his naval forces at Lissa; but his services in the war had still been

[1] *See* Bismarck: *Reflections and Reminiscences*, chap. xx.

[2] The first time was at Vienna in 1814–5, *see* above, pp. 9–12.

[3] Treaty of Peace between Austria and Prussia, Prague, August 23, 1866. Signed by Brenner for Austria and Werther for Prussia.

valuable, so that he was entitled to Venetia, which the Emperor of Austria had after Königgrätz handed over to Napoleon III for conveyance to the Kingdom of Italy.[1] By article IV the Emperor of Austria acknowledged the dissolution of the Germanic Confederation, and gave his consent to a new organisation of Germany, without the participation of Austria, to the north of the Main. By article V the Emperor of Austria transferred his rights over Schleswig and Holstein to the King of Prussia, subject to the proviso that the populations of Northern Schleswig should be retroceded to Denmark, if by a plebiscite they should express such a wish (this proviso was suppressed subsequently by a treaty between Austria and Prussia, October 11, 1878). The rest of the conditions laid down at Nikolsburg were incorporated in the treaty. Thus Austria and Saxony lost no territory (except the useless Austrian rights over the Duchies), although they had to pay moderate war-contributions. But the States of Hannover, Cassel and Frankfort were annexed outright by Prussia, while comparatively small, but highly important annexations from Bavaria and Hesse-Darmstadt secured a " corridor " of land between the Prussian territories in Middle and in South-West Germany. In all, Prussia was increased by the addition of 3¼ million inhabitants and over 28,000 English square miles.

The peace between Austria and Italy was made at Vienna on October 3, 1866. Victor Emmanuel's Government would have liked something more than Venetia,—something which would have given them a strong frontier in the Alps. But their compact with Bismarck was only that Venetia should be secured to them, and this was all Bismarck would help them to. So Italy had to be content with " the actual administrative confines of the Lombardo-Venetian kingdom " (article IV of the Treaty of Vienna). Along with the territory, Italy took over the Lombardo-Venetian debt and pension-list.

[1] In accordance with the treaty between France and Austria, July 12, 1866, *see* above, p. 191.

CHAPTER XXIII

THE FRANCO-PRUSSIAN WAR

§ 1. The Movements of M. Benedetti

Napoleon III had favoured Prussia before Königgrätz, and had known and approved of the Prusso-Italian alliance. On the very day on which the great battle was fought he had said to Goltz at Paris: "you know that the great rôle played by Prussia would not have been possible without my neutrality." Yet the rôle must not be overdone: Napoleon III had no desire, nor indeed expectation, of seeing Austria beaten to the ground. Therefore the news of Königgrätz came like the announcement of a tremendous disaster to the French themselves. It was felt, says M. de la Gorce, that on the ground of old Europe something had been broken [1]; and he compares the Parisians to the Athenians after Philip of Macedon's conquest of Elatea: "they had no dead to weep, yet they divined by instinct the loss of their pre-eminence; without having fought, they were oppressed by the sensation of defeat."

There must be no more dallying now to see what would happen. The question must be faced: what action should France take? On July 5—two days after Königgrätz—the Emperor held a Council at St. Cloud, the most decisive council of the whole reign, says the historian of the Second Empire. Drouyn de Lhuys, the Minister for Foreign Affairs, whose whole system of policy was based on good understanding with Austria, at once proposed firm action—the massing of French troops on the eastern frontier: then either war would ensue or else successful mediation. Marshal Randon, the Minister for War, could assure the Council that in spite of the Mexican expedition which was still in progress, 80,000 men could almost at once be mobilised on the frontier. The Emperor listened with his usual impassivity, but seemed inclined to agree, when

[1] Gorce, V, 12.

suddenly the door opened, and M. de la Valette, the Minister of the Interior, entered. He had not been summoned to the Council, but had heard of it in the palace, and now hastily entered the chamber, passionately to plead his cause. He pointed to the lack of preparation, the lack of resources; he accused Drouyn of irresponsibly wishing to rush his country into a war. The Emperor still said nothing; the staff of the *Moniteur de l'Empire* sat up all night waiting for an important message. None came; and Drouyn, next morning, scanning the pages in vain for the announcement of mobilisation, knew that his policy of action was dead.

Yet even to have done absolutely nothing would have been a policy not without prospects of successful issue. Napoleon, however, could not pursue this policy either: he must fussily intrude upon Bismarck, with continual demands for compensation—a *policy of pourboires*, as Bismarck called it. So M. Benedetti, the French Ambassador at Berlin was set to pursue this phantom. Departing on his travels from Berlin on July 9, he passed by Königgrätz and arrived at Prussian Headquarters at Zwittau on the 11th. Bismarck was courteous, but scarcely communicative. He wished to gain the concurrence of the French Government to the large annexations which he intended to make. Benedetti continued to travel with Headquarters till they became fixed at Nikolsburg. He appears to have had no precise instructions from Napoleon.

Meanwhile, at Paris, von der Goltz was maintaining his good relations with the Emperor, and receiving confidences which were worth many victories for the Prussians and equivalent to many defeats for the French. In conversations with the Prussian Ambassador on several different occasions, Napoleon first expressed approval of German Federal Reform (July 11), then acquiescence in Prussian annexations at the expense of the German Secondary States, with the exception of Saxony (July 13). Surely there was never a greater condemnation of the system of personal government than those unfortunate interviews between the Emperor, uncertain even of his own mind, and the keen, lucid Prussian, who very properly wrote every word down and sent the report to be filed at Berlin. In these interviews the Emperor's own Minister for Foreign Affairs had no part; yet Drouyn had a policy, and on the same day as Goltz obtained Napoleon's concurrence to federal reform, had sent to the Emperor a memorandum pointing out that Prussia aimed at nothing less than the mediatisation of the German Secondary States.[1]

It was not merely the Minister for Foreign Affairs who was being set aside by the Emperor. What was the use of M. Benedetti engaging in difficult negotiations with Bismarck at Nikolsburg, if the Emperor was making every concession at Paris ?

Then the Emperor at last had come firmly to ground : he adopted a definite policy of compensations. This policy, which would have been practicable, if initiated before the war began, when Prussia was anxious to smooth her way, was quite impossible when Prussia was in the full tide of success, and when the French Emperor had shown that he had no intention of using force. It was, moreover, a ridiculous policy on the part of a mediator whose position wholly depends on his asking nothing for himself.

While at Nikolsburg, Benedetti had been instructed to demand compensations for the increase that was taking place in Prussian territory. When he returned to Berlin, he received a more definite instruction : he was to propose to conclude a secret treaty with Prussia, by which the left bank of the Rhine and Mayence were to be ceded to France (August 5).[2] This territory was chiefly Prussian, but also included some small portions of Bavaria and Hesse-Darmstadt. The project was communicated by M. Benedetti to Bismarck in writing. In the following interview (August 7), Bismarck definitely refused to consider the cession of German territory, but suggested that some satisfaction for France might be found elsewhere.

Benedetti announced the failure of the Mayence project. The next instruction that came to him from his Government at Paris was even more fatal. He was to demand Landau, Saarbruck and Saarlouis, with the Duchy of Luxemburg, or failing that, Belgium (August 16).[3]

Accordingly M. Benedetti called on Bismarck, and made his

[1] *Documents pour l'histoire contemporaine*, ed. by Pradier-Fodéré, p. 16.

[2] A calculated indiscretion of one of Bismarck's secretaries enabled the Paris *Siècle* to publish news of this project on August 10. It was also communicated in detail by Bismarck to von der Pfordten and the Governments of the South German States, to prove to them that they had nothing to hope for from France.

[3] *Papiers de Cercey.* Landau, Saarbruck, and Saarlouis had been given to France by the First Peace of Paris, May 30, 1814, and detached from her by the Second Peace of Paris, November 20, 1815. As regards Belgium, M. Benedetti affirmed that Bismarck himself suggested it, at Nikolsburg (Benedetti : *Ma mission en Prusse*).

request. The Minister-President required something in writing. M. Benedetti at once with ready courtesy took his pen and neatly indited a draft treaty between France and Prussia: by article I, France recognised the annexations which Prussia had made as the result of the late war; by article II, Prussia promised to facilitate the acquisition of Luxemburg by France; by article III France recognised the new German Confederation that was to be made; article IV stated:

> On his side, H.M. the King of Prussia, in case H.M. the Emperor shall be led by circumstances to make his troops enter Belgium or to conquer it, will accord to France the support of his arms, and will sustain her with all his forces by land and sea towards and against every Power, which, in this eventuality, should declare war against her.

Article V stipulated for a contract of offensive and defensive alliance between France and Prussia.

This was the second fateful piece of writing which Bismarck had got from M. Benedetti: the first was the request for Mayence and the left bank of the Rhine. The careful Minister-President locked the papers up and kept them for future use. Meanwhile the negotiation went no further. M. Benedetti went on leave for a short holiday at Carlsbad. When he returned to Berlin Bismarck had himself gone away to recuperate his health.

§ 2. Luxemburg

The affair of Luxemburg was an outcome of Napoleon's last effort at compensation. This little country had been erected into a Grand Duchy by the Congress of Vienna, and had been given to the King of Holland. The Congress had at the same time included the new Grand Duchy in the Germanic Confederation, and had declared the City of Luxemburg to be a Federal Fortress. The Federation having no standing army, the fortress had since 1815 been garrisoned by Prussian troops. When the Prussian Zollverein was being developed, the Grand Duchy had joined it. It was to the acquisition of this little State that Napoleon III still looked for compensation to counterbalance in some degree the aggrandisement of Prussia.

The design was not altogether inopportune. After concluding the Treaty of Prague, the Prussian Government had, in December, 1866, convoked to Berlin delegates of all the States north of the

Main, and had established the North German Confederation. This body had a constitution almost the same as that which was adopted in 1871 for the German Empire, except that in the Confederation the King of Prussia was called President, not Emperor. The States to the south of the Main did not form part of the North German Confederation.

The new organisation in Germany affected the question of Luxemburg, because the Grand Duchy, which had formed part of the old Confederation, was not included in the new. Accordingly, the Prussians had no longer any valid reason in international law for garrisoning the fortress, and the Grand Duke (the King of Holland) was free to dispose of his Grand Duchy as he chose. It so happened that the King of Holland had serious debts, and so was not averse from taking a pecuniary indemnity in return for the cession of his Grand Duchy.

A new Minister of Foreign Affairs had to conduct the negotiation for France. Drouyn de Lhuys, a statesman of sound policy and prudent action, had retired in August, 1866. M. de la Valette next held the position as *interim* minister for a few months, during which he sent to the diplomatic agents of France a circular which became famous. This document complaisantly took note of the resources of France, gave its benediction to the new state of affairs in Germany, and proclaimed a policy of acceptation of *faits accomplis* (September 16, 1866). Yet at this very moment the Government of Napoleon was seeking to rectify the *faits accomplis* by trying to annex Luxemburg. The new minister who took over the portfolio of Foreign Affairs from M. de la Valette was M. de Moustier, just arrived from the Embassy at Constantinople. He found the Luxemburg affair already in progress. He had to do his best to make it a success; and then, having failed, he had to get his country out of the affair without loss of dignity. M. de Moustier's conduct of the matter was entirely to his credit.

In the spring of 1867 success seemed to be crowning the efforts of France. The King of Holland was ready to dispose of the Grand Duchy. The French Government engaged to gain the consent of the King of Prussia (about whom the King of Holland was, naturally, very apprehensive); and the Luxembourgeois were to be consulted about their destiny by plebiscite. On March 26, 1867, King William of Holland signified by letter to Napoleon III his consent to the cession. It only remained to sign the treaty.

The time for this was past, however. The letter of acceptance had been written, but the treaty was never signed. The imminence of the cession of Luxemburg to France, which was no secret, aroused the now ardent national feeling of Germany. Interpellations and protests took place in the Parliament of the North German Confederation; and Bismarck on March 27 had occasion to tell M. Benedetti, during a grand reception in Berlin, that people were saying that the affair of Luxemburg might be an obstacle to the King of Prussia's projected visit to Paris (to the Grand Exhibition, which was to take place that summer). About the same time, the Prussian Minister at the Hague, while admitting the King of Holland's right to dispose of his Grand Duchy, had occasion to call attention to the state of feeling which the proposed cession was exciting in Germany. The King of Holland saw what was meant: he could not afford, with his small State and open frontier, to antagonise Prussia. So he withdrew from his still uncompleted bargain with France, and refused to ratify the treaty of cession. He was within his rights; for France had not been able to carry out her part of the bargain, namely to gain the consent of Prussia.

Thus once more was the Emperor of the French baffled; and once more was the inflexible Chancellor (Bismarck was now Chancellor of the North German Confederation) completely the victor. It was just here that M. de Moustier was able to be of service to France. There are times when a nation must not endure a public rebuff. M. de Moustier saw that firmness and reasonableness were indispensable. In communications with the various Powers concerned, he stated that France looked now for no increase of territory; that she renounced any idea of receiving Luxemburg, but that Prussia must act in like manner—that is to say, Prussia must withdraw her garrison from the fortress of Luxemburg. Put forward in this way, the French view, quite reasonable and moderate though it was, had in it something of a challenge. In effect, it said that Prussia must evacuate Luxemburg or must fight. If evacuation were chosen, the world would see that it was not France which retired from Luxemburg in the face of Prussian threats, but Prussia which retired on the demand of the French.

For a few weeks a real crisis existed in European politics. Napoleon III, the elusive and varying statesman, had at last come to firm ground; he had made a clear demand, and the alternative of War was plain for all to see. Bismarck, who throughout his

Reminiscences says that he knew war must come some day, could have accepted it then. That he did not do so was probably because he thought the chances of war were not in his favour. So he let France score a diplomatic victory.

Other influences were working hard for peace. The British Foreign Office (Lord Stanley was Secretary of State) was pressing its favourite project for a Congress.[1] Queen Victoria herself wrote a letter (delivered on April 24) to King William of Prussia, pointing out that if war occurred he could not expect to get even the moral support of England. Above all, M. de Beust, who after Königgrätz had been called from the Saxon Government to be Chancellor of Austria, laboured incessantly for peace, using the good offices of Wimpffen, the Austrian ambassador at Berlin, and of Metternich, the ambassador at Paris, who enjoyed considerable familiarity with Napoleon III. Beust was watching over the recuperation of Austria; a European war would retard this. Finally the Russian Government, directed by the Chancellor Gorchakoff, after a long silence, pronounced against the continued Prussian occupation of Luxemburg. On April 25, Gorchakoff sent to the Powers definite proposals for a Congress. Prussia, now absolutely isolated, had really no choice: she had to accept the Russian proposal.

On May 1, the invitations (which were, by courtesy, given in the name of the King of Holland) were sent to all the Powers signatory of the Treaty of London of 1839,[2] and also to Italy, now formally recognised as a Great Power. The Congress opened on May 7, at London. Its work was accomplished with the greatest expedition, for in four days its labours were ended, and the Treaty of London of May 11, 1867, was completed. The Grand Duchy of Luxemburg was recognised to be a perpetually neutral State under the collective guarantee of the signing Powers (article II). Being neutralised, the Grand Duchy had no need of fortresses and garrisons, so the King of Prussia agreed to withdraw his troops (articles III and IV). The King of Holland retained his Grand Duchy; and at the same time he gained full control of Limburg. This province, although forming part of the Kingdom of Holland, had also been included (like Luxemburg) in the old Germanic Confederation in 1815.

[1] *Parliamentary Papers, Correspondence respecting the Grand Duchy of Luxembourg.*

[2] The treaty which had recognised the separation of Belgium from Holland, and which had re-established the Grand Duchy of Luxemburg after the Belgian Revolution and the war with Holland.

The Germanic Confederation having been dissolved, Limburg was now incorporated in the Kingdom of the Netherlands (article VI).

Thus the French Government was able to retire with credit from the unfortunate policy of compensations. It was Prussia which had to make a concession, withdrawing a garrison from the grand old fortress which she had held for over fifty years; while a neutral State with European guarantee was left as a protection to the French north-eastern frontier.

§ 3. The War

The years 1867 to 1870 were filled—in spite of the grand Universal Paris Exhibition of 1867—with a subdued but quite obvious duel between France and Prussia. The rise of Prussia since Bismarck became Minister-President in 1861, had been meteoric, and had really taken Europe by surprise. Had there been a gradual evolution, the States of Europe would have adjusted themselves more easily to this rise. There had, however, been no time for gradual adjustment; and in 1867 France and Prussia stood looking at each other tensely, and waiting for the storm to break.

There seemed no means of avoiding the struggle. The process of growth and consolidation of Prussia was not yet complete; time might perfect the work of Bismarck, but he preferred to do it himself, by more rapid methods: "I took it as assured that war with France would necessarily have to be waged on the road to our further national development at home as well as the extension beyond the Main."[1]

It is impossible to assert that the war between France and Prussia was inevitable; but there was required a great statesman to avert it. In particular, a good understanding between France, Austria, and Italy would probably have turned Bismarck aside from war. Unfortunately such an understanding did not exist. That Beust did not wholeheartedly adopt the French offers of alliance proves that he was not the great statesman—the one man who saw through Bismarck—that he so complaisantly claims to be in his *Memoirs*.[2]

It cannot be said that Napoleon III plunged blindly into the war of 1870. His Government spent more or less of two years in pre-

[1] *Reflections and Reminiscences*, chap. xxi.

[2] Beust stated on July 9, 1870, to the Marquis de Cazaux that he was willing to make a treaty of alliance but that France refused (Gorce VI, 155 n. 3). But it was not a military alliance that he had offered (*see* Beust: *Memoirs*, II, 330).

paration, but with considerable hesitations and shiftings of policy. Marshal Niel, Minister of War, was extremely active; indeed so incessant was he in preaching and practising preparation for war, that he appears in history as a great tragic hero, labouring to avert the disasters which he foresaw so clearly. Very striking, too, was M. Prévost-Paradol's essay, *La Nouvelle France* (1868), in which he foresaw France reduced to subsist merely upon her great memories, "fatiguing Europe with recalling Louis XIV and Napoleon as Spain throws at the indifferent Chancelleries the names of Philip II and Charles V." [1]

French diplomacy under the Second Empire had never been conducted with genius, but under Count Walewski and M. Drouyn de Lhuys it had been cautious and sane. M. de Moustier too, an old "diplomat by career," had shown in the Luxemburg affair that he could be both bold and cautious. He died in 1869. His successor, the Duc de Grammont, was another professional diplomatist, who nourished the wholesome tradition of Walewski and Drouyn, namely to maintain a good understanding with Austria. Yet Grammont is decidedly an instance of an ambassador who made a failure as statesman.

In the lower ranks at the Quai d'Orsay and at the French embassies a change had become perceptible: "*Dandyism*," says M. de la Gorce, "had invaded diplomacy and the Council of State." [2] It appears, therefore, that *Punch's* caricatures of Second Empire society were founded upon fact. Yet the old diplomacy with its "wholesome traditions" went on; and from Berlin came warnings sent by Benedetti, and still more detailed messages from the military attaché to the Embassy, Colonel Stoffel. The ardent General Ducrot, commander at Strasbourg, laboured literally night and day, in and out of uniform, to gain certain knowledge of the military conditions of the Rhine. Yet, with the exception of Niel, Ducrot and a few others, study was not encouraged among the officers of the French army.

The spring of the year 1870 had passed, and summer was half over, yet no sign of war had come. June had been a month of profound peace. Napoleon's Government had been wakeful. The sympathies of the Italian Government had been sounded, but little could be expected from this quarter while French troops still garri-

[1] Quoted by Gorce, VI, 128.

[2] Gorce, V, 466.

soned Rome. From Austria something was still expected. In March, 1870, the Archduke Albert, the victor of Custozza, had visited Paris, receiving the most cordial welcome from all the high officers. At the end of May, the Minister of War, Marshal Lebrun, had gone on mission, with personal messages from Napoleon III, to the Emperor Francis Joseph. He had several interviews with the Archduke Albert and one with the Emperor Francis Joseph (on June 16, at the Château of Laxemburg). But the *entente* between the two Governments got no further than generalities. Francis Joseph would make no definite contract: he was afraid that Prussia would exploit the national idea against him. Yet Lebrun's mission might have led to something more definite. It is doubtful, however, if the Emperor Napoleon ever read the Marshal's report,[1] which was dated June 30, 1870: for the air was already thick with the storm-cloud of the Hohenzollern candidature.

This trouble arose out of the Spanish revolution. In September, 1868, a mutiny in the fleet at Cadiz grew into an insurrection which decided Queen Isabel to fly to France. Then for nearly two years the Spanish Government, which was presided over by General Prim, looked around for another monarch. Various possible candidates (including the Duc de Montpensier of 1846 fame) for the throne were considered; all definitely refused or proved to be unacceptable except Prince Leopold, a son of Prince Antoine of Hohenzollern-Sigmaringen. Prince Leopold's brother next in age had made a success as King of Rumania. At first indeed Leopold hesitated, and in a family council held at Berlin, in which the younger (i.e. the reigning Prussian) branch took part, absolutely refused to be King of Spain (March 15, 1870). An application was next made to his second younger brother, Frederick, who also refused. "It is all over now," regretfully wrote Antoine, the father, to his more adventurous son, King Charles of Rumania.[2]

The obscure course of this negotiation had not passed without the notice of the French Government, with whom it naturally caused considerable perturbation. A Paris newspaper published the news of the Hohenzollern candidature in November, 1868.[3] Benedetti observed a mysterious Spanish political mission in Berlin. He

[1] This is the suggestion of M. de la Gorce, *op. cit.*, VI, 189.

[2] April 22, 1870. *Aus dem Leben König Karls von Rumänien*, II, 80 (in Gorce, VI, 205).

[3] *Journal des Débats*, November 13, 1868.

inquired at the Wilhelmstrasse in spring, 1869. Bismarck was away, but Thile, Under-secretary for Foreign Affairs, assured the French ambassador that the Prussian Government had absolutely nothing to do with the Hohenzollern candidature to Spain. When Benedetti saw Bismarck next month, the Chancellor was not quite so explicit.

But Prince Leopold had refused and the matter was closed. Suddenly, however, it was re-opened by Bismarck himself who wrote at the beginning of June to Prim and suggested that the invitation to the Hohenzollern prince should be renewed.[1] Having obtained the necessary support from the Cortes, Prim dispatched Salazar, who had all along been the champion of the Hohenzollern candidature, to Sigmaringen. This time Prince Leopold accepted. It is open to the historian to infer that assurances of support from Berlin had decided his hitherto doubting mind.

We now approach the most moving scene in the great tragedy of France, and we have the spectacle of a valiant people plunging obstinately into a disaster for which the way was all too easily prepared. On July 2, General Prim announced to M. Mercier de Lostende, French ambassador at Madrid, the acceptance of Prince Leopold of Hohenzollern. On July 3, Mercier's dispatch, bearing these tidings, arrived at the Quai d'Orsay. At once M. de Grammont was up in arms. At the same time the public in Paris learned the great news through a communication sent by the *Agence Havas* from Madrid. The people became excited; and for them there is excuse; but for the Minister of Foreign Affairs there is none. Taking his cue from the public agitation, he replied to an interpellation in the *Corps Legislatif* in the following words:

> We do not believe that our respect for the rights of a neighbouring people obliges us to permit a foreign Power, by placing one of her princes on the throne of Charles V, to disturb to our detriment the existing equilibrium of the forces of Europe, and to endanger the interests and the honour of France. We have a firm hope that this eventuality will not be realised. To prevent it we rely equally upon the wisdom of the German people, and upon the friendship of those of Spain. If it were otherwise, strong in your support, Gentlemen,

---

[1] Gorce, VI, 209. Bismarck is said to have been moved to this resolve by the French plebiscite of May 8, the result of which was declared on May 21. A letter of King William of Prussia to King Charles of Rumania, dated July 10, 1870, shows that King William knew and approved of Prince Leopold's candidature (*Aus dem Leben*, II, 101).

and in that of the Nation, we should know how to fulfil our duty without hesitation and without weakness.

This was nothing more nor less than a challenge, thrown in the teeth of Prussia. "It is madness," cried Thiers, who arrived at the Palais Bourbon just after the speech had been delivered.

M. de Grammont was quite right to try and get the Hohenzollern candidature withdrawn, and to get the Prussian Government to agree to this. But the obvious way to set about this task was to make everything as easy as possible for the proud and sensitive King of Prussia and his equally proud people, to make their withdrawal gracefully. On the contrary, Grammont was so insistent and almost menacing in this most delicate negotiation, that even a long-suffering and ductile monarch might have been goaded into breaking off the conversations and telling France to go her own way.

It was July, the season of the year when European statesmen are in the habit of recuperating their spent forces with the waters and the music and the pleasant hotel-life of a Continental Spa. King William was at Bad Ems ; M. Benedetti was at Wildbad. On July 7, the French ambassador's cure was interrupted by orders from M. de Grammont to proceed to Ems. On his way an attaché met him at Coblentz with definite instructions from the Quai d'Orsay. The issues of peace and war were stated with startling clearness, and they were placed in M. Benedetti's hands. A passage from Grammont's instructions will show this :

If you obtain from the King a revocation of the acceptation of the Prince of Hohenzollern, it will be an immense success and a great service. The King will have, on his part, assured the peace of Europe. If not, it is war.

Did any subordinate official (for, after all, Benedetti had to obey orders), ever have a greater responsibility put upon him ? Within the limits which he recognised (that is, perfect compliance with his instructions), it must be admitted that he fulfilled his task perfectly. But ought he to have taken Grammont's insistent and menacing words quite so literally ? Grammont meant what he said : but Benedetti, who saw quite clearly what would happen, should have taken upon himself not to carry out his instructions to the last letter. This is one of the occasions when statesmanship, the grand faculty of seeing what should be done, rather than following the lead of some one else, could have shown itself. If only Benedetti had omitted to *dot* Grammont's *i*'s !

On July 9, the Frenchman had his first interview with the King. Pleasant, courteous, patient, M. Benedetti drew the King's attention to the emotion and excitement caused in Paris by the Hohenzollern candidature, and he suggested that a disclaimer by the King of Prussia would have a most tranquillising effect. King William seemed to admit this, but at the same time remarked that Grammont's "almost provocative" speech in the *Corps Legislatif* had made such an act by the King of Prussia a little difficult. He had, he said (and not unreasonably), been *vivement touché* by the speech. Actually at the moment the King was expecting news from Prince Leopold's family at Sigmaringen, so he dismissed the ambassador, promising to see him again, after the news had arrived.

M. Benedetti returned to his rooms in the *Hotel de Bruxelles*, and telegraphed the result of his interview to Grammont. On July 10, he received a peremptory reply: "Employ all your efforts to obtain a decisive reply. We cannot wait, without danger of being outstripped by Prussia in our preparations."[1] Another telegram from Grammont came on the same evening: "We cannot wait longer. . . . If the King does not wish to counsel renunciation to the Prince of Hohenzollern, it means war immediately, and in a few hours we shall be at the Rhine."

Now Benedetti was earnest to avoid war, and he saw how it could be done, if a little deference were shown to Prussian sensitiveness. On July 11, he had another interview with the King, who put him off courteously once more, saying that news would certainly come from Sigmaringen on the morrow. Actually the King had (on July 10), sent a courier to Sigmaringen, advising Prince Antoine to withdraw his son's candidature.[2] Grammont's insistence had perhaps more reward than its peremptoriness deserved. On July 12, Prince Antoine telegraphed to Madrid that his son's candidature was withdrawn. With equally commendable care and courtesy he sent a duplicate telegram to the Spanish ambassador at Paris, who at once informed the French Premier. M. Ollivier heaved a great sigh of relief: "we have peace now," he said, "nor shall we let it escape from us." Why then did war come after all? It was the fatal demand for guarantees that ruined everything.

The precise idea behind the demand for guarantees was that the

[1] I.e. *military* preparations.

[2] *Aus dem Leben K. Karls v. Rumänien*, II, 101. Rothan, *l'Allemagne et l'Italie*, I, 15.

King of Prussia should be asked to give his official sanction to the renunciation of the Prince of Hohenzollern-Sigmaringen, and that he should further give a pledge against any future renewal of the candidature. The idea did not originate with the Emperor, who believed with M. Ollivier that the war-cloud had passed. It was first voiced in the Press, and then put forward in an interpellation in the Chamber by M. Clement Duvernois. Grammont adopted the idea of the guarantees, and gained the Emperor's consent at an interview at St. Cloud, on July 12.[1] At seven o'clock on the evening of the same day the minister sent fresh instructions to Benedetti :

> in order that this renunciation of Prince Antoine may produce its full effect, it appears necessary that the King of Prussia should associate himself with it, and give us the assurance that he would not authorise a renewal of that candidature.
>
> Be good enough to betake yourself immediately to the King to demand from him this declaration which he cannot refuse.

On the fateful July 13, Benedetti went out from the *Hotel de Bruxelles*, and was fortunate enough to meet the King on one of the walks among the pleasure-gardens of the Lahn. The French ambassador at once plunged into his subject, announcing the renunciation made by Prince Antoine, and asking for the King's pledge to forbid any renewal of the candidature in the future. The King seemed disturbed and surprised : he had not yet heard of the renunciation. So he wished to put off further consideration of the matter. But Benedetti had received his orders to get a definite answer, and so—here he took the tragic step—felt that he must insist : "will the King give us an assurance that he will interpose his authority to prevent in the future all reopening of the project ?" Thus sharply—and really unnecessarily sharply—brought to the point, the King refused : "this affair has caused me too great trouble for me to be tempted to allow its renewal ; but truly it is impossible for me to go as far with you as you wish." M. Benedetti attempted further argument, but the King firmly, though without discourtesy, put an end to the interview. Next day he sent an aide—Prince Radziwill—to inform Benedetti that he had confirmation of the news from Sigmaringen, and that the King now considered the incident terminated.

[1] M. de la Gorce is of opinion that it was the influence of the Empress Eugénie, whom Grammont chivalrously forbears to mention in his Memoir, that won over Napoleon III to the idea of the guarantees.

If the French Government still insisted on its demand for a guarantee, war must come. In a ministerial council held at St. Cloud, it was decided by a majority of votes to stand by the demand. So war would have come now, even if Bismarck, who had gladly seen the French Government blundering into the position of aggressor, had not taken his famous step to bar any possible way to peace.

It only remains now to relate the incident of the Ems telegram. Bismarck, like other statesmen, had been having a holiday. On July 12, he thought it time to leave his *Kurort*. He travelled by carriage. As he passed through Wussow the old pastor of the place, Mulert, stood outside his door, to see the Chancellor pass. The two were old friends, and Bismarck, a naturally good-natured and kindly man, had in his days of greatness retained the friendship. In answer to the pastor's greeting and implied question, the Chancellor—too hurried even to leave his carriage—made a thrust in carte and tierce in the air. This meant war.

But when he got to Berlin, he received a disappointment. The news awaiting him at the Wilhelmstrasse showed that the King was still continuing *pourparlers* with Benedetti; and at dinner with Moltke and Roon, he learned that the Prince of Hohenzollern had renounced his candidature. Astounded and depressed, for he thought that this retiral in the face of France's threats was fatal to German prestige, Bismarck felt that he must retire from service. On the 13th, Moltke and Roon were again dining with him, and Bismarck announced his decision to resign. The dejected soldiers reproached him with the fact that they could not resign likewise. Just then a telegram in cipher came in from Abeken at Ems. It contained a résumé of the famous interview:

His Majesty writes to me: "Count Benedetti spoke to me on the promenade, in order to demand from me, finally in a very importunate manner, that I should authorise him to telegraph at once that I bound myself for all future time never again to give my consent if the Hohenzollerns should renew their candidature. I refused at last somewhat sternly, as it is neither right nor possible to undertake engagements of this kind *à tout jamais*. Naturally I told him that I had as yet received no news, and as he was earlier informed about Paris and Madrid than myself, he could clearly see that my government once more had no hand in the matter." His Majesty has since received a letter from the Prince. His Majesty having told Count Benedetti that he was awaiting news from the Prince, has decided, with reference to the above demand, upon the representation of Count Eulenburg and myself, not to receive Count Benedetti again, but only to let him be informed through an aide-de-camp: That His Majesty had now received from the Prince confirmation of the news which Benedetti had received from Paris, and had nothing further to say to the ambassador. His Majesty leaves it to your Excellency whether Benedetti's fresh demand and its rejection should not be at once communicated both to our ambassadors and to the press.

When the telegram was deciphered and read aloud at the table, Moltke and Roon at first thought that it was a closure of the whole incident of the candidature and "they turned away from food and drink." [1] But Bismarck thought that something might be made out of the King's authorisation to publish the message. He therefore abbreviated the telegram and issued it to the Press. The abbreviation made very little difference. The original telegram (being a private communication between the King and his minister) was curt enough to offend the sensitiveness of the French. But Bismarck's abbreviation was worse. "It represented as decidedly broken off a negotiation which according to the telegram seemed to be still in suspense." [2] Publication, even without abbreviation, would have been brusque; and publication, combined with abbreviation, made war almost certain; Bismarck took the step because (he wrote), "in view of the attitude of France, our national sense of honour compelled us, in my opinion, to go to war." [3]

The King of Prussia himself had not meant to be brusque or bellicose; and when Benedetti left Ems, on July 14, King William personally received him, and said good-bye. Nor did the ambassador himself think that his Government had been insulted. As Gambetta (who was not naturally pacific) said in the debate in the *Corps Legislatif* on July 15: "Your ambassador has not sent any act of protestation, any indignant dispatch; it has not appeared

[1] *Reflections*, chap. xxii.

[2] Bismarck, *op. cit.*, *ibid.*

[3] *Ibid.* The telegram as reduced and published in the *Gazette de l'Allemagne du Nord* was as follows: "After the news of the renunciation of the hereditary Prince of Hohenzollern had been officially communicated to the imperial Government of France by the royal Government of Spain, the French ambassador at Ems further demanded of His Majesty the King that he would authorise him to telegraph to Paris that His Majesty the King bound himself for all future time never again to give his consent if the Hohenzollerns should renew their candidature. His Majesty the King therefore decided not to receive the French ambassador again, and sent to tell him through the aide-de-camp on duty that His Majesty had nothing further to communicate to the ambassador." Moltke thought Bismarck's editing very suitable: "Now it has a different ring," he remarked; "it sounded like a parley; now it is like a flourish in answer to a challenge" (*ibid.*).

to him that the situation required the demand of his passports." Bismarck knew that the issue of peace and war was still undecided when the King's telegram came, and that is why he acted as he did. Even so, if the French Government had kept calm, and waited for further explanations, it could easily have demasked Bismarck's intrigue; but Grammont could not wait. An excess of indignation carried him on. To an urgent request of Lord Lyons (made on July 17), that France and Germany should have recourse to the good offices of a friendly Power before taking hostilities,[1] he replied with thanks but with a *non-possumus*. On July 18, the *Corps Legislatif* voted the necessary financial credits. On the 19th, Bismarck received the French Government's note announcing a state of war.

During and at the conclusion of the war which ensued, Bismarck's chief preoccupation was to prevent the intervention of the Powers. Even if there were no chance of intervention, he still would not have liked to oppose the public opinion of Europe. Of this public opinion England was the chief representative. So one of the first things which he did was to prejudice the cause of France by giving to *The Times* newspaper a copy of the unfortunate draft treaty for a French annexation of Belgium, which Benedetti had left in Bismarck's hands in 1866. It was published in *The Times* of July 25, 1870.[2] There is no doubt that Mr. Gladstone's Government, which had many merits, erred by concentrating its attention almost wholly on domestic affairs. But even Mr. Gladstone was ready to fight any Power which invaded Belgium; for this reason he entered into the now well-known treaties, with Prussia on August 9, and with France on August 11, binding England to fight with all her forces, by land and sea, against whichever Power should violate the neutrality of Belgium. Bismarck complained that after the surrender of Metz, French soldiers of the garrison escaped through the neutral territory of Luxemburg without being interned; and it was with

[1] According to protocol 23 of the Congress of Paris, 1856. This Protocol was like the condition in the Covenant of the League of Nations, except that the recourse was not to be compulsory.

[2] When the war was over, feeling was further prejudiced against France by another publication. In the autumn the German forces in the course of their successful advance into France, found in Cercey, M. Rouher's private château, a number of State papers which the minister had placed there. Among them were the records of the French negotiations with a view to the acquisition of Luxemburg in 1866. These also Bismarck published in the *Reichsanzeiger* of October 20, 1871.

difficulty that the British Government induced him to refrain from assuming freedom of action with regard to the Grand Duchy. He gave an assurance, however, to the British Foreign Secretary, Lord Granville, that the King of Prussia had no intention of denouncing the Treaty of London of 1867.[1] As regards Switzerland, no difficulty arose; the internment of Bourbaki's army in February, 1871, was carried out by convention between the Swiss and the French commander.[2] When the end of the war came, the French Empire was no more. It had fallen before a peaceful revolution, which took place on September 4, 1870, after the defeat of the Emperor's army at Sedan. Napoleon III was himself a prisoner-of-war. A Republican Government of National Defence carried on a heroic and not wholly unsuccessful war in the provinces, and conducted a fine defence of Paris. But in January, 1871, the end had to come.

§ 4. The Treaty of Frankfort

After the fall of the Empire of Napoleon III, diplomacy could do little against the undeniable success of the Prussian arms, and the definiteness of the Prussian aims. Yet diplomacy could have effected *something*, for when the armistice was signed by Jules Favre on January 28, 1871, France was by no means helpless; for even if Paris were doomed to fall, there were still three powerful French armies in the field, under capable generals—Faidherbe, Chanzy and Bourbaki. The war, although successful for the Prussians, was not one that they wished to have dragging on indefinitely. Moreover, Bismarck was desperately anxious to avoid European mediation, especially mediation by England, where people were becoming restive at the inaction of Mr. Gladstone. But the French Government of National Defence had to negotiate under great disadvantages. With the exception of Gambetta and Jules Ferry, it had been established by a few brave old men,[3] who had been long in opposition to the Empire, and now when the Empire had fallen in terrible defeat, did not despair of the republic. Having long been

[1] *Parliamentary Papers, Luxemburg,* 1871.

[2] Convention of Verrières, February 1, 1871, made between General Herzog for Switzerland, and General Clinchant for the French Army. Bourbaki was disabled at the time through his attempted suicide.

[3] Arago was 68, Crémieux was 74, Glaize-Bizon was 70, Admiral Fourichon was 61, Jules Favre was 61. Thiers, who was not an original member, was 73. However, Gambetta was only 32 and Jules Ferry 38.

in opposition to the Second Empire, they had little practical experience in affairs. There was indeed one professional diplomatist among them, whose experience and skill proved most useful. This was the Comte de Chaudordy. He, however, had no cabinet office, but was attached to the Delegation, of which Gambetta was the head, at Tours. The Delegation carried on the war in the Provinces. The Government itself chose to remain in Paris throughout the siege—a courageous but unwise policy, because it prevented the ministers from knowing what was happening in the rest of the country, and also because it made them too sensitive to the sufferings and the war-weariness of the Parisians and of the besieged army. If the Government of National Defence had been living, not in besieged Paris, but in the safety and comfort of Bordeaux, it would have been able to exercise a much more unbiassed judgment for the common good.

Almost immediately after the fall of the Second Empire, Jules Favre, who held the portfolio of Foreign Affairs in the Government of National Defence, asked Thiers to try and gain help from Great Britain. Thiers agreed, on condition of his being given a mission to all the Powers. So the old statesman set forth from Paris on September 12 (1870); he spent five days in England; on the 23rd, he was at Vienna; on the 26th at St. Petersburg; on October 11 he was back in Vienna, on his way to Florence, which was still the capital of the Kingdom of Italy. Everywhere the old statesman was received with honour and consideration, but with no offers of help. Indeed the Tsar Alexander II went so far as to show that he was deliberately immobilising Austria, for he did not hide the fact that he would attack the Habsburg Power if it made a move against Prussia. In the eyes of the British Government, the French Government of National Defence had somewhat prejudiced itself by postponing indefinitely the holding of a representative assembly.

Events were steadily moving in the direction of peace. The disaster at Sedan had occurred on September 1, the Second Empire fell on September 4, Bazaine capitulated at Metz on October 27, and the garrison of Paris, after some grand but unsuccessful sorties, was reduced to suffering bombardment. At last, on January 22, Jules Favre under safe-conduct went to the Prussian headquarters at Versailles to arrange an armistice. He gained an armistice, but in doing so made two great mistakes: in the first place, he made no attempt to restrict the scope of the armistice to Paris. Bismarck could scarcely have refused such a restricted armistice, in return, of course, for the surrender of the capital. On the contrary, Favre, who was ignorant of the state of affairs in the Provinces, signed an armistice for all the French forces—or rather for not quite all. This was his second mistake. From the general armistice, Bourbaki's army of the East was excepted. The Prussians wished to finish their operations against it. Jules Favre thought to gain something, for he believed that Bourbaki was on the point of relieving Belfort. But he was mistaken: for Belfort fell, and Bourbaki's army was driven over the Swiss frontier.

The armistice was signed on January 28, 1871. The German army was put in possession of the forts around Paris, though not of the city itself; its garrison, all but 12,000 (a totally insufficient number), who remained to preserve order, were made prisoners. An assembly, freely elected from all France (including Alsace and Lorraine), was to meet at Bordeaux before February 12 (when the armistice would expire), to vote on the question of war and peace.[1]

In the meantime a European Conference was sitting in London, in which the French Government, had it only exercised a little care, could easily have introduced its own affairs, and perhaps have obtained a satisfactory mediation.[2] The Conference of London arose out of one of Russia's dishonourable repudiations of a treaty. On October 29, 1870, two days after the capitulation of Metz, Gorchakoff had circulated a note denouncing the article of the Treaty of Paris (1856) which neutralised the Black Sea. France and Great Britain, the real authors of the Treaty of Paris, had cause to be indignant, but France was obviously powerless. Great Britain, however, was strong. But Gladstone, the Premier, absorbed as ever only in home affairs, had no idea of fighting, and only one minor minister resigned in protest against the Government's action.[3] Nevertheless Bismarck was a little nervous concerning possible action by England, so he suggested a European Conference, and indicated London as its place of meeting. The suggestion was

[1] The armistice was twice extended for short periods.

[2] Lord Granville, the British Foreign Secretary, himself suggested semi-officially to Thiers that something might be done for France at the Conference of London. But Thiers believed that offers of external mediation would only harden Bismarck, and that France would get better terms by negotiating directly and alone with her enemy.

[3] Otway, Under-Secretary of State.

adopted; and the French Government of National Defence was, among other Powers, invited to send representatives. With incredible carelessness, Jules Favre, absorbed in the defence of Paris, neglected day after day to appoint anyone, although Chaudordy, who was at Tours, could have gone, and was anxious to go. So France lost her chance of putting her case before Europe, and in gaining influence at a critical time in European councils, as Talleyrand had gained influence at the Congress of Vienna. The Conference of London sat, with intervals which were designed to give the French time to come, from January 17, 1871, to March 13. It rather feebly ratified by a new treaty the Russian destruction of the neutralisation of the Black Sea, but it kept in force the rest of the Treaty of Paris, and, by implication, it reproved the Russian Government, in a separate Declaration, signed by all the plenipotentiaries, to the effect that treaties could only be altered by consent of all the signing parties.[1] The Duc de Broglie, who had at last been appointed French ambassador in London, only appeared at the end to sign the treaty (March 13, 1871).

By the time this happened, the troubles of unhappy France were in process of being liquidated. The South German States, which had been fighting as allies along with the Confederation of the North, had after the great victories made treaties of union (November, 1870). On January 18, 1871, in the *Galerie des Glaces* at Versailles, King William of Prussia was proclaimed German Emperor.

The first and most brilliant public act of the new Empire was to sign the preliminary treaty of peace with France. On February 12, the newly elected Assembly met at Bordeaux. Thiers, who was the great advocate of peace, as Gambetta was of war *à outrance*, was elected Chief of the Executive of the French Republic. On the 19th, he pronounced his celebrated discourse, declaring his policy to be immediately to liberate and reorganize France without prejudice to the future form which her Constitution might take. The discourse was approved by the Assembly, and became known as the Pact of Bordeaux. Armed with these credentials, Thiers went to Versailles. After five days' discussion, the Preliminaries of Versailles were signed by Bismarck on the one part, and by Thiers

[1] This declaration was made at the opening of the Conference on January 17, 1871.

and Favre [1] (February 26). There was not much opportunity for bargaining, but Thiers managed to get Bismarck to reduce his monetary demands from six to five milliards of francs, and to leave Belfort to France in exchange for the battlefield districts of St. Privat, Vionville, and Marie-aux-chênes in the Department of the Moselle. Thiers also agreed, as part of the *quid pro quo* for Belfort, that the German army should have the right to enter Paris.[2] The territorial cessions exacted from France were all Alsace and a large portion of Lorraine. In general the crest-line of the Vosges was to be the frontier, but there were one or two exceptions to this, designed to give to Germany control of both sides of a pass. Article III stated that the evacuation of French territory by the Germans should begin only after the treaty had been ratified by the Assembly at Bordeaux, and that this evacuation should proceed by definite stages, as each instalment of the indemnity became due and was paid. All French troops (with the exception of 40,000 men garrisoning Paris), were to retire behind the Loire.

A number of questions arising out of the war still remained to be settled. These were deferred to a Franco-German Congress at Brussels, which opened on March 28. But at the same time the insurrection of the Commune broke out at Paris. The French Government had to leave the capital and retire to Versailles, from which it set about conducting a regular campaign against the Commune. For this purpose it was necessary to obtain some relaxation of article III of the preliminaries of Versailles, which prohibited French troops from advancing to the north of the Loire. But every relaxation could only be gained by fresh concessions to Bismarck, who required full payment for everything. Finally Thiers resolved to get the definite peace signed at whatever cost, so that the French Government's hands should be free. The Congress at Brussels was therefore dissolved. On May 4, Jules Favre, who was still Foreign Minister, and Augustin Thomas Pouyer-Quertier, Minister of Finance, went to Frankfort, where in a few days the Final Treaty was arranged with Bismarck (May 10). The chief point of negotiation was with respect to the *rayon* of territory which was to be left with the fortress of Belfort. In the end the fortress

[1] Favre had sufficient magnanimity to eat his own words. It was he who, in the tense days following the fall of the Second Empire, had declared publicly that France would cede neither an inch of her territory nor a stone of her fortresses.

[2] This is not stated in the treaty.

received a satisfactory belt of territory, but in return France had to cede a strip of land on the Lorraine-Luxemburg frontier. This strip contained valuable mineral deposits. Fortunately the mineral in the part still left to the French (the Briey basin) was able, under improved methods of treatment, to supply France with most of the steel which she required. The French negotiators completely failed to induce Germany to undertake any portion of the public debt on account of Alsace and Lorraine, although this principle was now a well-established custom in the Law of Nations. The Treaty of Frankfort certainly was no improvement on the Preliminaries of Versailles, because in the meantime the condition of France had become worse. However, the nation gained a free hand for itself and after this it did not take long for Marshal MacMahon to take Paris and suppress the Commune, although not till after fearful destruction had taken place. With peace both at home and abroad, France was able to make a new start, and to become her old grand self again.[1]

[1] A spirited account of political history is *The Second Empire*, by P. Guedalla (London, 1922). For Bismarck's life and policy, see Grant Robertson, *Bismarck* (1918).

CHAPTER XXIV

THE CONGRESS OF BERLIN

§ 1. Three Chancellors

For the forty-five years after the Franco-German War, Imperial Germany is the principal factor in European politics.[1] But her position was uneasy; the Iron Chancellor, having created the Empire, had now to take care that his creation was not threatened by two things. One of these things was a possible renewal of French strength, and more especially by an alliance between France and Russia, by which Germany would probably lose her two new provinces. The other thing which threatened the duration of the new Empire was particularism, the desire of the separate States to preserve their own life and independence—a feeling which was especially strong in Bavaria, and which appeared in the assertion of an ultramontane ecclesiastical policy as against the secular policy of Prussia. It is supposed to have been a design to crush or check particularism which led Bismarck into his unsuccessful struggle, known as the *Kulturkampf*, with the Papacy. This, however, was scarcely a diplomatic question. It is the policy of checking France which concerns us here.

The first thing Bismarck had to do was to make certain of agreement with Austria. In this aim he was greatly helped by the fall of Beust, the only German statesman who, though not quite big enough for the task, had consistently and strenuously striven against Bismarck. Beust's fall was probably due to the fact that the Emperor Francis Joseph had given up all hope of successfully struggling against the German Empire, and had, for consolation,

[1] "When the [Eastern] question was re-opened in 1875, the three Imperial Powers, Russia, Austria, and Germany—two of them certainly Turkey's nearest neighbours, and the third *the dominant State in Europe*—assumed from the first the right to take the lead in shaping European policy."—Buckle, *The Life of Benjamin Disraeli*, VI, 17.

adopted wholeheartedly the Andrassy policy of orienting Austria completely to the Balkans. So Beust was given a dignified retirement as ambassador at London, while Count Andrassy became Chancellor (November, 1871).

The entente between Austria and Germany had begun before the fall of Beust. In August, 1871, the Emperor William visited the Emperor Francis Joseph at Ischl; and Beust and Bismarck confabulated amicably over the waters at Gastein. In September, 1872, Francis Joseph, attended by Andrassy, went to Berlin. The Tsar Alexander, fearful of being left out in the cold, hastily arranged also to visit the German capital, with the redoubtable Gorchakoff, now getting rather old; and the League of the Three Emperors was arranged. It was not, strictly speaking, a League, but rather what would now be called an *entente*: the three Chancellors exchanged notes, and agreed to maintain the European territorial situation as resulting from the recent diplomatic transactions; to act in concert in solving the difficulties which might arise at any moment in South-Eastern Europe; and to contain the forces of Revolution (Alexander having recently realised the hitherto submerged passion of Nihilism). The League of the Three Emperors was, in fact, a new edition of the Holy Alliance.

Meanwhile, the speedy and unexpected revival of France was disquieting the mind of Bismarck. The loan issued by the French Government in 1872 was subscribed fourteen times over; the indemnity to Germany was paid off, and in July, 1873, the last German soldier left France. In 1875, Bismarck, who was not easily carried off his feet, seemed to lose his poise for a short time, and to begin blindly to goad France into war. A mad Belgian had written a letter to the Archbishop of Paris, offering to murder Bismarck; the Archbishop sent the letter on to the Chancellor, who seized the occasion to make a diplomatic incident. He affected to detect a plot, not against himself, but on the part of France to violate Belgian neutrality. The *reptile press,* as Bismarck pleasantly called his journalistic allies, fell furiously upon France, and for some time there was a regular crisis, and war seemed to be only a matter of days. But the Russian Government, from whom Bismarck expected better things, and England, whose foreign affairs were fortunately no longer directed by Gladstone, intimated by special missions (April, 1875), sent to Berlin, that no support could come from these quarters. The Iron Chancellor quickly recovered himself, and spoke of the prospect of war as something ridiculous. "People have been trying to embroil us," he said, with the bonhomie which was really natural to him, next time he met the French ambassador. He bore no malice against England, and perhaps would have borne none against Russia, if Gorchakoff had not, in May of the same year, issued a circular note stating, quite unnecessarily, that the maintenance of European peace had been due to his sovereign master the Tsar. After the Crimean War, Gorchakoff, to whom great credit is due for initiating a period of quiet and recovery, had written in a famous note: *la Russie ne boude pas, elle se recueille.*[1] The injudicious circular of May, 1875, by which he affected to "close" the Franco-German incident, was probably meant to mark the end of Russia's period of "recueillement," and the opening of a more active career. But Bismarck, though he said nothing, never forgot the affront.

§ 2. The Insurrection in Herzegovina and its Consequences

It was now over forty years since Stratford Canning, who was by no means an uncritical supporter of Turkey, had written: "He must be a bold man who would undertake to answer for its being saved by any effort of human policy."[2] Yet the old diplomatist was able still to look on, in deepening gloom, at the tottering, unreformed yet persistent condition of the Turkish Empire. There had been no exceptional crisis in its affairs since the Crimean War, the question of the Straits having been reopened, only to be re-settled again, with comparatively little friction, in 1871.

Now, however, ferment, not exactly new but enormously increased, was to become apparent, perhaps stimulated by the successful fruition of German and Italian nationality. The Balkan peoples had for about half a century been advancing in self-consciousness. The Serbs had been practically free since 1816; in 1867 the Turks, by convention, evacuated Belgrade, and the other hitherto reserved fortresses, and nothing now remained but a nominal Turkish overlordship. Bulgarian nationhood was later in realising itself, but in 1870 it received the concession of an "exarchate," that henceforth there should be an autonomous

[1] "Russia is not sulking, she is recuperating."

[2] F.O., Turkey, No. 211, December 19, 1832, ad fin.

Bulgarian Church. The sentiment of Pan-Slavism made great strides, with the encouragement of the Russian Government, and under the energetic impulsion of Count Ignatieff, ambassador at Constantinople from 1864 to 1877.

The fire of rebellion was kindled in Herzegovina in July, 1875, and shortly afterwards the Turkish Government declared itself bankrupt. These two facts portended a speedy disintegration of Turkey in Europe. Now Great Britain, Austria, and Prussia had together, by one of the treaties of 1856, guaranteed the integrity of Turkey, and within certain limits [1] Lord Beaconsfield was determined to preserve this integrity, and although sympathetic towards the subject peoples of Turkey he was, as Mr. Buckle points out, a believer in race rather than in nationality.[2] He approved of diverse races combining in, and contributing their strength and various qualities to, a great empire, and "he distrusted movements which would break up existing Empires with no likelihood of anything but chaos to take their place." [3]

When the Eastern Crisis arose (or re-arose) in the summer of 1875, the Austrian Government, directed by Count Andrassy,[4] began to act at once, in concert with the now friendly Prussia. Beaconsfield resented their acting as if they were Europe's representatives, and as if England scarcely counted—a view which had become rather current in Europe during the long abstention of England from Continental complications between 1860 and 1874.[5] His policy and action from 1876 to 1878 were at any rate to rescue the country from this contempt: as Lord Salisbury said later, "Zeal for the greatness of England was the passion of his life." And he had to work at an advanced age, not exactly single-handed (for Lord Salisbury was a great help to him), but without very energetic support from his Foreign Secretary, for Lord Derby was against intervention.

The crisis found the diplomatists all scattered.

[1] The French historian, M. Debidour, denies this on the strength of Beaconsfield's taking over Cyprus. But Cyprus was an island. Beaconsfield meant to preserve the continental integrity of Turkey as a barrier against Austria and Russia.

[2] Buckle, *The Life of Benjamin Disraeli*, VI, 10.

[3] *Ibid.*

[4] Beust, having ceased to be Chancellor, was at this time ambassador at London.

[5] Gladstone has been blamed for this, but Palmerston and Lord John Russell, in 1864 and 1866, must take their share of blame.

"It is a strange thing that, at this moment, when so much is at stake, there is not a single Ambassador in England, and throughout the whole of the Danubian troubles, not one of Her Majesty's Ambassadors has been at his post. Sir A. Buchanan returned to Vienna only two days; the rest are at God knows what waters—probably Lethe." [1]

With the autumn, however, ministers and diplomatists returned to London, but Beaconsfield did not find his path made much easier. "Beust is fantastical and dreamy," he wrote on November 3. ". . . As for the charming Schou., I am perfectly convinced that, instead of being a deep and *rusé* diplomat, he does not know the A B C of his business, and is perfectly sincere in his frequent asseverations to that effect." [2] Schouvaloff (who was Russian ambassador) and Disraeli were to get on very well together in the next two difficult years. As the crisis grew tenser they drew closer, meeting sometimes officially, sometimes unofficially, as for instance thus: "I met Schou. last night at dinner, and he got me in a corner before he went to Beust's Ball. He was full of matter: clear, for him, and not at all claret-y. This is the upshot . . . there must be a thoro' good understanding between Eng. and Russia." [3] Beaconsfield had to complain, however, that the British Foreign Office itself was, merely by being unbusinesslike, making things difficult for him. One Saturday afternoon he sent for a paper to the Resident Clerk at the Foreign Office: "The 'Resident Clerk' was not in residence! I believe (adds the Prime Minister—he is writing to Lord Derby) yr. office is very badly managed—the clerks attend there later than any other public office, witht. the excuse of being worked at night as they were by Palmn." [4]

The crisis endured for a long time without any promising chance of settlement appearing. A Note, which, though quite ineffective, attained great celebrity, was drafted and agreed to by Austria, Germany, and Russia, on December 30, 1875, and presented to the Porte on January 30, 1876. This instrument, which was due to the initiative of the Austrian Chancellor, and therefore called the "Andrassy Note," demanded certain reforms of Turkey, such as religious freedom for all cults, abolition of tax-farming, institution of a local assembly. Between the time when it was drafted

[1] Beaconsfield to Lady Bradford, August 20, 1875. (Buckle: *Life of B. Disraeli*, VI, 12.)

[2] To the same, November 3, 1875, *ibid.*, p. 15.

[3] To Lord Derby, June 24, 1876, *ibid.*, p. 34.

[4] To Lord Derby, April 19, 1876, *ibid.*, p. 23.

and when it was sent to the Porte the assent of France, Italy, and Great Britain was asked for. France and Italy agreed, but the British Government at first refused. Lord Beaconsfield suspected that there were "ulterior motives" behind the Note; but when Turkey (always ready to gain time by giving promises) herself asked for England's assent, it was given: "We can't be more Turkish than the Sultan," wrote Disraeli.[1]

As, however, the Andrassy Note effected nothing, another attempt was made, this time by Bismarck, who on May 11 circulated a Memorandum (the *Berlin Memorandum*) to the Powers, demanding that the Porte should arrange for an armistice of two months with the rebels, should provide funds for reconstruction of destroyed houses, and undertake other obligations. From the Berlin Note the British Cabinet unanimously dissented, Beaconsfield saying that to act so drastically without first consulting Turkey was "taking a leap in the dark." [2]

So, instead, the British Fleet was sent to Besika Bay, just outside the Dardanelles, to watch events (May 24). The Admiral was to have definite instructions, for Beaconsfield was determined to avoid a policy of "drift," such as had led England into the Crimean War: "We shall certainly not drift into war," he wrote, "but go to war, if we do, because we intend it, and have a purpose which we mean to accomplish." [3] On that same day (May 29) the Sultan Abdul-Aziz was deposed, and his nephew Murad substituted by a palace revolution arranged by the Liberal Turkish statesman, Midhat Pasha.

So far the crisis had developed fairly normally. Ignatieff at Constantinople had failed to bring off a treaty after the model of Unkiar Skelessi, and Bismarck, in spite of what Odo Russell had written to the contrary,[4] had not been estranged by the British refusal to accede to the Berlin Memorandum. Beaconsfield rather liked Bismarck, calling him "a man who is dangerous, but who is sincere; and who will act straightforwardly with an English minister whose sense of honour he appreciates." [5] The crisis, however, was soon to become acute. On June 30, 1876, Serbia

[1] To Lady Bradford, January 16, 1876, *ibid.*, p. 19.

[2] *Ibid.*, p. 26.

[3] To Lady Chesterfield, May 29, 1876, *ibid.*, p. 29.

[4] Odo Russell (afterwards Lord Ampthill) thought that Beaconsfield's policy at this time would lead to isolation.

[5] To Lord Derby, February 15, 1876, *op. cit.*, p. 21.

declared war upon Turkey, and on July 1 Montenegro followed suit.

The European situation was indeed of intense difficulty. On the whole it might be said that the Governments (including Russia) were anxious to settle the Eastern crisis peaceably; but, as Beaconsfield said to Parliament, "Unfortunately the world consists not merely of Emperors and Governments, it consists also of secret societies and revolutionary committees; and secret societies and revolutionary committees have been unceasingly at work in these affairs, and they do bring about, in an empire like Turkey, most unexpected consequences."[1] And just at the time when *sang-froid* was most necessary in every quarter, came the news of massacres committed by Bashi-Bazouks in Bulgaria in May. Unfortunately the British Embassy in Constantinople knew nothing about the massacres, and the horrible events were first made known to the British public in a letter from Mr. Edwin Pears, a resident at Constantinople, to the *Daily News*.[2] The public became inflamed, although Beaconsfield, relying on information from the Foreign Office (about whose ignorance and misleading intelligence he had bitterly to complain), minimised the massacres and doubted the reported torturing: "Oriental people . . . I believe . . . generally terminate their connection with culprits in a more expeditious manner."[3]

Mr. Gladstone at any rate made no light thing of the massacres. As soon as he read the report in the *Daily News* he sat down at his desk and in words which, as Lord Morley says, beats "with a sustained pulse and passion," composed his pamphlet on *Bulgarian Horrors and the Question of the East.* The peroration has become justly famous:

> An old servant of the Crown and State, I entreat my countrymen, upon whom far more than perhaps any other people of Europe it depends, to require and to insist that our Government which has been working in one direction shall work in the other, and shall apply all its vigour to concur with the other States of Europe in obtaining the extinction of the Turkish executive power in Bulgaria. Let the Turks now carry away their abuses in the only possible manner, namely, by carrying off themselves. Their Zaptiehs and their Mudirs, their Bimbashis and their Yuzbashis, their Kaimakams and their Pashas,

[1] July 31, 1876, *op. cit.*, p. 38.

[2] See *Daily News* of June 23, 1876.

[3] Speech of July 10, 1871.

one and all, bag and baggage, shall, I hope, clear out from the province they have desolated and profaned.

The publication of these furious and electric words came most unseasonably when the Government was trying to conduct critical negotiations in an atmosphere of calm. Beaconsfield thought that the publication was another instance of what he called Gladstone's malignity: "Posterity will do justice to that unprincipled maniac Gladstone—extraordinary mixture of envy, vindictiveness, hypocrisy and superstition, and with one commanding characteristic—whether Prime Minister or Leader of Opposition, whether preaching, praying, speechifying or scribbling—never a gentleman!"[1]

On August 31, 1876, there occurred another revolution at Constantinople, where at this time the condition of affairs seemed to recall the saying of one of England's earliest ambassadors, that Sultans were made as quickly at Stamboul as proctors were at Oxford.[2] Now Murad gave way to his brother, Abdul Hamid, who was to enjoy a considerably longer tenure of power. The new Sultan, who at first, at any rate, was under the influence of Midhat, seemed to offer a promise of reform and peace. The time was propitious for peace because the Serbians had been defeated, and were ready to accept an armistice, which the British Government procured for them in September.

There is no doubt that England and Germany were now the most powerful factors in European politics. Beaconsfield hoped to solve the Eastern crisis by making an alliance between the two Governments for the maintenance of the *status quo* in Constantinople: incidentally such an alliance would "relieve Bismarck of his real bugbear, the eventual alliance of England and France, and the loss of his two captured provinces."[3] The alliance of England and Germany might actually have taken place then, but for the unwillingness of the old Emperor William I, who was afraid that it would involve him in a war with his nephew the Tsar Alexander. The Emperor ("who, I heartily wish," wrote Beaconsfield, "were in the same cave as Friedrich Barbarossa"[4]) was not the

[1] To Lord Derby, October, 1876, *op. cit.*, p. 67.
[2] Sir Thomas Roe, ambassador under James I and Charles I.
[3] To Lord Derby, October 17, 1876, *op. cit.*, p. 81.
[4] To the same, *ibid.*

only difficulty; another was "to get hold of Bis." [1]—who tended to hide himself from diplomatists at this time; another was the English ambassador: "I counted on Odo Russell, but he might as well be in Bagdad"; another was the German ambassador, Count Münster: "he is suspicious and stupid." [2] Still, although the proposed Anglo-German alliance never came into existence, the Eastern crisis seemed to be developing propitiously: Turkey agreed to an armistice, and in November the British Foreign Office issued invitations to a Conference of diplomatists to be held at Constantinople. The Conference took place, Lord Salisbury representing England, Werther Germany, Ignatieff Russia, Count Zichy Austria, Count Corti Italy, and Chaudordy France. It accomplished almost nothing, however, as the Porte would not accept the proposed reforms. The Porte may have got the notion that England would defend it from the speech which Beaconsfield had delivered at the Guildhall on November 9.

> Peace is especially an English policy. She is not an Aggressive Power, for there is nothing which she desires. . . . What she wishes is to maintain and to enjoy the unexampled empire which she has built up, and which it is her pride to remember exists as much upon sympathy as upon force. But although the policy of England is peace, there is no country so well prepared for war as our own. If she enters into conflict in a righteous cause—and I will not believe that England will go to war except for a righteous cause—if the contest is one which concerns her liberty, her independence, or her empire, her resources, I feel, are inexhaustible. She is not a country that, when she enters into a campaign, has to ask herself whether she can support a second or a third campaign. She enters into a campaign which she will not terminate till right is done.

The first session of the Conference was on December 23, and on that very day the Sultan issued the Constitution which has become celebrated as "Midhat's Constitution." [3] On January 18, 1877,

[1] It was shortly after this that Bismarck made the speech in which he said that the Eastern question was not worth the bones of a Pomeranian Grenadier. Beaconsfield was convinced that if Germany did not work with England she would probably join Russia: "It is a most critical moment in European politics. If Russia is not checked, the Holy Alliance will be revived in aggravated form and force. Germany will have Holland, and France Belgium; and England will be in a position I trust I shall never live to witness." *Ibid.*

[2] *Ibid.*

[3] The representative Parliament which it promised was opened in March, 1877, and sat till 1878. The Constitution was then suspended till the Young Turks revived it in 1908.

the proposals of the Conference were rejected in a Grand Council attended by a hundred and eighty dignitaries of the Turkish Empire. Thus Russia and Turkey were left face to face. The deputies to the Conference at once left Constantinople. It had done a really valuable work, though nothing of a very positive kind: it had kept the Concert of Europe together, and although Russia dropped out it soon came back again at Berlin.

For the next few months—February to April, 1877—Russia was merely playing for time. Beaconsfield had everything made ready for war, which he would not declare unless Russia advanced to Constantinople. In December, 1876, the Russian ambassador had rather indiscreetly given away the Russian plan: "Schou. said to me last night that Russia did not care a pin for Bulgaria, or Bosnia, or any other land—what it really wanted was 'the Straits'—the only thing they wanted. I said I knew that."[1]

On January 31, 1877, Gorchakoff issued a circular summarising the Russo-Turkish negotiations up to this point, and pretty plainly hinting that war must now settle the dispute between the two countries. The Tsar also sent Ignatieff, who had played the commanding rôle at Constantinople, on a special mission to London to try and arrange a modus vivendi with the British Government. Beaconsfield gave a grand banquet to him, at which the great English ladies did their best to uphold the credit of the country: "Lady Londonderry staggered under the jewels of the three united families of Stewart and Vane and Londonderry, and on her right arm, set in diamonds, the portrait of the Empress of Russia—an imperial present to the great Marchioness. Mme. Ig. had many diamonds, and a fine costume, but paled before this."[2]

On March 31, 1877, a final effort at peace was made. The ambassadors at London of the Powers who had signed the Treaty of Paris held a Conference in London, and with Lord Derby signed a Protocol inviting Turkey to demobilise her war-forces and to put her promised reforms into effect without delay: and these terms, if acceded to by Turkey, carried with them the demobilisation of Russia. For a moment even Beaconsfield thought that the Protocol had ensured peace, but he was soon undeceived. Turkey protested against being placed in tutelage, and on April 31 the Tsar declared war. Beaconsfield was old and infirm, and

[1] To Lord Derby, December 21, 1876, *op. cit.*, p. 109.

[2] To Lady Bradford, March 16, 1877, *op. cit.*, p. 128.

all through this long Eastern crisis had been suffering cruelly from gout and bronchitis; half-humorously, half-seriously he had written: "I wish they were all—Russians and Turks—at the bottom of the Black Sea." [1] Yet he was determined to go on as long as there was breath left in him; old and ill, he was yet ready to face a European War.

In the first place he induced Lord Derby to send to Gorchakoff something like an ultimatum—a dispatch in which he warned Russia off the Suez Canal,[2] the Persian Gulf, and the Bosphorus, as being points of British interest. To the terms of this dispatch, which Beaconsfield called "the charter of our policy, the diapason of our diplomacy," Gorchakoff gave his assent (May, 1877). Proceeding further with his precautions, Beaconsfield, in June, offered the alliance of Great Britain to Austria.[3] In July, he got the Cabinet to decide definitely that if Russia occupied Constantinople, England would declare war.

If Russian arms had been at once successful, the Tsar, in spite of Gorchakoff's promise, would probably have gone to Constantinople and England would then have fought. The long check to the Russian armies in front of Plevna prevented an Anglo-Russian War. The proposal of England to ally with Austria came to nothing, as by a secret treaty made at Vienna on January 15, 1877,[4] the Austrian and Russian Governments had come to an understanding. The terms of this treaty have never come to light, but it can easily be inferred that Austria gave Russia some sort of a free hand in return for permission to occupy Bosnia and Herzegovina.

Towards the end of 1877, the Russian armies did much better, and after the fall of Kars in Armenia (November), and Plevna in Bulgaria (December), it became clear that Constantinople would soon be at their mercy. Beaconsfield went on determinedly, with (except for Lord Salisbury) a very lukewarm Cabinet. Moreover, he received little help from the ambassadors abroad: "I wish

[1] To Lady Chesterfield, January 2, 1877, *op. cit.*, p. 112.

[2] In 1875, Beaconsfield had, on behalf of the British Government, purchased the shares held by the Khedive Ismail in the Suez Canal. These amounted to 176,602 out of a total of 400,000.

[3] To Lord Salisbury, June 14, 1877, *op. cit.*, p. 144.

[4] "This treaty and not the Berlin Congress is the foundation of the Austrian possession of Bosnia and Herzegovina."—Bismarck, *Reflections*, chap. xxviii.

we could get rid of the lot," he wrote to Lord Derby, "they seem to me to be quite useless. . . . I think Odo Russell the worst of all. He contents himself with repeating all Bismarck's cynical bravadoes, which he evidently listens to in an ecstasy of sycophantic wonder."[1] Gorchakoff apparently was ready to keep his understanding not to attack the Straits, but he was being kept out of the way at Bucharest. On October 9, Schouvaloff had told Beaconsfield that Russia had a secret convention with Austria.

After the fall of Plevna and the passage of the Balkans, Turkey could no longer maintain the struggle. A Russian advance on Constantinople was expected, and the Queen's speech at the opening of Parliament on January 21 (1878) stated, as clearly as such speeches can, that war on the part of Great Britain was almost certain: "I cannot conceal from myself that should hostilities be unfortunately prolonged, some unexpected occurrence may render it incumbent on me to adopt measures of precaution." The Cabinet decided to send the British Fleet through the Dardanelles, whereupon Lord Carnarvon and Lord Derby[2] (much to the satisfaction of the Queen, who actively supported a war-policy) resigned. The Fleet, under Admiral Hornby, actually passed the Dardanelles (quite lawfully, as the Porte was at war), and then went back again to the entrance of the Straits. On January 30 the Porte concluded the preliminaries of peace at Adrianople on the basis of Bulgaria becoming an autonomous principality and Bosnia and Herzegovina getting autonomous institutions. On February 3 Austria proposed that a European Congress be held; Great Britain agreed on condition that every clause of the Russo-Turkish peace should be submitted to the Congress. So for the time being British military intervention was avoided.

Nevertheless the Russian Government pursued its own aims steadily, and on March 3 forced the Porte to sign the now notorious Treaty of San Stefano, which was to create a "Big Bulgaria," reaching to the Ægean on the south and the Albanian Mountains on the west, and to make many other drastic changes in the Balkan Peninsula. There can be no reasonable doubt that the Treaty of San Stefano, as Beaconsfield said in Parliament, would abrogate

[1] To Lord Derby, September 1, 1877, *loc. cit.*, p. 178.

[2] Lord Derby's resignation at this time was only momentary. He returned to the Cabinet for two more months, when he finally gave place to Lord Salisbury. Carnarvon was succeeded as Colonial Secretary by Sir Michael Hicks-Beach.

Turkey in Europe and, for a time at any rate, establish a Russian protectorate in the Balkans. The terms were kept secret at first, and were not delivered to the British Government till March 23. The communication of them was quickly followed by an announcement from the Russian Chancellery that the Congress could raise such questions as it chose, but that the Russian Government reserved to itself liberty to accept or reject the decisions. When he received this " ultimatum " as he called it, Beaconsfield at once summoned the Cabinet: " We are drifting into war," he wrote to Gathorne-Hardy; but he added: " If we are bold and determined we shall secure peace, and dictate its conditions to Europe." [1] On March 27, the decisive Cabinet was held: it was resolved to call out the Reserve, and to bring an expedition from India, which should seize Cyprus and Alexandretta.[2] Lord Derby at once resigned; he could not agree to the occupation of " new Gibraltars."

The firm front shown by the British Government impressed all Europe, including Russia. The Prince of Wales, who moved freely in French society, was able to write from Paris that Gambetta, whom he met at one of M. Waddington's evening parties, " expressed his hearty approval of every step taken by Lord Beaconsfield in connection with the Eastern Question, and his strong dislike to the doctrine that nations having large armies at their command might upset all treaties in defiance of protests from those concerned and contrary to public law." [3] Lord Salisbury's lucid circular explaining England's objections to the San Stefano Treaty carried great weight. Finally the arrival of the Indian troops at Malta showed that the Government was quite serious in its warlike professions.

It was the confidential announcement to the Sultan, Andrassy, and Rumanian Government, that, even if we were alone, we were ready on May 3 to effect the withdrawal of the Russians from E. Rumelia by force, that produced this great change. The Sultan, sworn to secrecy, of course told his Greek physician; Andrassy, equally bound, of course, as we intended, revealed it to Bismarck; and Rumania, of course, to Russia.[4]

---

[1] *Op cit.*, 261.

[2] 7,000 Indian troops actually took over the garrisoning of Malta. The occupation of Alexandretta and Cyprus was not found to be immediately necessary.

[3] May 7, 1878, *op. cit.*, 291.

[4] Written (on November 29, 1878) after the Congress of Berlin, *op. cit.*, 293.

Russia, with her finances already strained, and her armies depleted by battle and disease, had really no desire to fight England, and preferred to agree to the English conditions before the Congress met. So Schouvaloff went off to St. Petersburg, and came back bearing a draft of a Convention between the two Governments, which was duly signed on May 30.[1] Russia agreed to reduce enormously the size of the Bulgarian State which it was proposed to establish, and to make the Balkans the southern frontier. The cause of Greece was to be taken into account at the Congress, and the retrocession of Rumanian Bessarabia [2] to Russia was accepted "with profound regret." Beaconsfield was also anxious that Russia should not annex Kars and Batoum; but as he could not obtain her consent to this, as he was not prepared to make a *casus belli* of it, he quietly insured against the consequences by getting Cyprus from Turkey in return for a British guarantee of the Turkish Asiatic dominions with the exception of Batoum, Ardahan and Kars.[3] Both the Russian and Turkish Conventions were to be kept secret till after the Congress, but unfortunately the text of the Russian Convention was sold by a temporary copying clerk at the Foreign Office to the *Globe* newspaper, which published it on June 14. No great harm, however, resulted, although for a time feeling ran high.

Everything was now ready for the Congress which was to be held at Berlin. Travelling leisurely (he took four days), Beaconsfield arrived there on June 11, and took up his residence at the Hotel Kaiserhof. The other British representative at the Congress was Lord Salisbury, who brought with him as private secretary Mr. Arthur Balfour. The Russian plenipotentiaries were Prince Gorchakoff, "a shrivelled old man," [4] and Count Schouvaloff, who, Beaconsfield observed later at the Congress, "fights a difficult

[1] Signed at London by Salisbury and Schouvaloff. It was in the form of a Memorandum or *exposé* of the two countries' agreed views.

[2] This strip of territory, along the east of the lower Pruth and the north of the Kilia mouth of the Danube, had originally belonged to Moldavia. It had been annexed by Russia (with the rest of Bessarabia) by the Treaty of Bucharest in 1812, rejoined to Moldavia by the Treaty of Paris, March 30, 1856, and was now to be retroceded to Russia and incorporated in Bessarabia.

[3] Signed at Constantinople by Layard and Savket Pasha, on June 4, 1878. Under cover of this Convention Beaconsfield established four consulates for Anatolia, with a military vice-consul in each. The system worked well, and secured considerable amelioration for the subject peoples of that part of the Turkish Empire till Gladstone withdrew the officers in 1882.

[4] Beaconsfield to Queen Victoria, June 12, 1878, *op. cit.*, p. 318.

and losing battle with marvellous talent and temper." [1] The chief Austrian plenipotentiary was Count Andrassy, "a picturesque person, but apparently wanting in calm." [2] France was chiefly represented by M. Waddington, a great friend of Greece, Italy by Count Corti, Turkey by Carathéodory Pasha (a Greek), and Mehemet Ali, a German mercenary, who had embraced Islamism and risen high in the Turkish army. The commanding German figure was, of course, the Prince Bismarck, who at the first session of the Congress was elected President. Beaconsfield had not met the famous Chancellor for sixteen years: now instead of the "tall, pallid man with a wasplike waist," that he remembered, he saw "an extremely stout person with a ruddy countenance, on which he is now growing a silvery beard." [3] Beaconsfield rather liked the Chancellor: "the contrast between his voice, which is sweet and gentle, with his ogre-like body, is striking. He is apparently well-read, familiar with modern literature. His characters of personages extremely picquant." [4] At dinner, where they met several times, Bismarck treated Beaconsfield to a lot of "Rabelaisian monologues," mainly directed against the duplicity of princes and "the horrible conduct of his sovereign"—his "sweet and gentle voice" contrasting singularly "with the awful things he says." "Bismarck," adds the English Prime Minister, "soars above all. . . . He is a complete despot here, and from the highest to the lowest, the Prussians, and all the permanent foreign diplomacy, tremble at his frown and court most sedulously his smile. He loads me with kindnesses." [5] The Chancellor on his part recognised Beaconsfield as the dynamic force of the Congress: "the old Jew, that is the Man!" he said.

The Congress opened on Thursday, June 13, at the Radzivill Palace, and sat thereafter fairly continuously till July 13; its usual hours were from 2 to 5 p.m. The plenipotentiaries were arranged at the Congress table according to the alphabetical order of their country. The great struggle was fought over the line of the Balkans; if Beaconsfield could get this line fixed as the southern border of Bulgaria, he would be satisfied. The Russians, on the

[1] To Lady Bradford, June 26, 1878, *op. cit.*, p. 328.
[2] To Queen Victoria, June 12, 1878, *op. cit.*, p. 316.
[3] *Ibid.*
[4] To Queen Victoria, June 17, 1878, *op. cit.*, p. 322.
[5] To Lady Bradford, June 26, 1878, *op. cit.*, pp. 328–9.

other hand, while acquiescing in the tearing-up of the San Stefano Treaty, strained every nerve to prevent such a total reduction of their plans. But Beaconsfield was inflexible. At a banquet at the Italian Embassy on June 19, he told Count Corti (who "as the ambassador of an almost neutral State . . . had the ear of every one") that he took the gloomiest view of affairs, "and that, if Russia would not accept our proposals, I had resolved to break up the Congress."[1] On June 20, Schouvaloff asked for a delay of twenty-four hours in order to get a reply from St. Petersburg. On the morning of the 21st, the day on which the delay expired, Beaconsfield, leaning on the arm of his friend and secretary, Montague Corry, enjoying a walk in the celebrated alley *Unter den Linden*, gave orders for a special train to be in readiness to take the British delegation back to Calais.[2]

The special train was never needed. On that afternoon, about 5 o'clock, Prince Bismarck paid an unexpected call at the Kaiserhof, and threw out suggestions for a compromise on the question of the Bulgarian frontier. Beaconsfield was adamant.

"'Am I to understand it is an ultimatum?' 'You are.' 'I am obliged to go to the Crown Prince now. We should talk over this matter. Where do you dine to-day?' 'At the English Embassy.' 'I wish you could dine with me. I am alone at 6 o'clock.'"

So Beaconsfield sent an apology to Lady Odo Russell, and went to dine with the "honest broker." At dinner the Chancellor ate and drank and talked a great deal, but no politics. After dinner, however, the two got to business over tobacco: "I believe I gave the last blow to my shattered constitution, but I felt it absolutely necessary. I had an hour and a half of the most interesting conversation, entirely political; he was convinced that the ultimatum was not a sham, and, before I went to bed, I had the satisfaction of knowing that St. Petersburg had surrendered."[3] Next morning Beaconsfield telegraphed the news to Queen Victoria, concluding with "B. [i.e. Bismarck] says: 'There is again a Turkey in Europe.'" "It is all due to your energy and firmness," was the Queen's reply.[4]

Thus the crucial day in the history of the Congress was passed,

[1] To Queen Victoria, June 17, 1878, *op. cit.*, p. 323.

[2] *Op. cit.*, p. 325.

[3] To Queen Victoria, June 20, 1878, *op. cit.*, p. 324.

[4] *Ibid.*, p. 324.

and although three more weeks were necessary, the final result was not in doubt. The Russian plenipotentiaries fought hard for Batoum and Kars; and Beaconsfield gave in on these points. For Turkey in Europe was his real interest, and besides, if Russia got Batoum and Kars, England would get Cyprus. When Beaconsfield confidentially told Bismarck of the Cyprus convention, the Chancellor warmly approved and admired: "This is progress!" he observed. "His idea of progress was evidently seizing something," adds Beaconsfield.[1] The Congress drew to a close with a series of banquets given by the delegations of the various States. One of the latest and best was that given at the Turkish embassy: the dinner included two national dishes, especially a huge *pilaff*, which "created much interest. The French ambassador, M. Waddington, expressed his wish to be helped twice to this dish."[2]

The Treaty of Berlin, which was signed by the plenipotentiaries of Great Britain, Germany, Austria, Russia, Italy, France and Turkey at 4 p.m. on July 13 in the Radzivill Palace, formed for thirty years the somewhat tattered charter of the Orient. It had a temporary and a permanent aim. The temporary aim was to suppress the Treaty of San Stefano and to avert war between Russia and England. This object was certainly gained. The permanent aim was to make a settlement of the Balkan Peninsula that should be fairly satisfactory all round. This aim was not altogether missed.

In the first place, the Balkans were made the southern frontier for the new State of Bulgaria. South of this line again a new autonomous province was established, to be called Eastern Rumelia, with a Christian Governor or Vali. The curious name given to it—in spite of Russian pleadings—was meant to mark it distinctly off from the State of Bulgaria. The other Balkan States received considerable increases of territory. Although the Greek Government did not form part of the Congress of Berlin, its representatives, M. Delyannis and M. Rhangabé, were admitted to state their views, and article XXIV takes note of a suggested rectification of the Greek frontier, and presages mediation of the Powers. The result was the acquisition of Thessaly in 1881. Serbia and Montenegro received notable accessions of territory, though still considerably less than would have been gained had the Treaty of

[1] To Queen Victoria, July 5, 1878, *op. cit.*, p. 332.

[2] *Ibid.*, p. 330. Waddington was really Minister of Foreign Affairs.

San Stefano been maintained. Montenegro gained a seaboard, with Antivari for a port,[1] although she was interdicted from using the flag of war (article XXIX). Serbia's great acquisition was Nish and the adjoining region. But Austria was the most spectacular gainer, for she got the right to occupy and administer Bosnia and Herzegovina, and to garrison the Sanjak of Novi Bazar. This last interesting strip of territory contained the military road from Sarajevo to Mitrovitza and so on to Salonica, and it also formed a solid wedge between Montenegro and Serbia. Austria was also given the little town of Spizza, which could be turned into a fortress to command the bay of Antivari.

Rumania had greatly helped Russia during the war. First by convention [2] (she could indeed scarcely help herself) she had given facilities for the transport of the Russian armies through her territory, and subsequently by another convention [3] she had joined Russia as an ally, and her army had rendered signal services at Plevna. At the Congress of Berlin (in which Rumania was not a party) her representatives had to submit to ceding the Rumanian strip of Bessarabia to Russia, receiving in return (at the expense of Turkey) the Dubruja—a barren country but with a good port in Constantsa. The treaty also established civil and religious liberty in Rumania (article XLIV) and made the same stipulation for Montenegro and Serbia. Russia retained out of her conquests in Armenia, Ardahan, Kars and Batoum: in article LIX the Tsar declared "his intention to make Batoum a free port, essentially commercial." Beaconsfield had fought hard for making Batoum a free port, and he considered article LIX to be a great triumph. In 1886, however, the Tsar revoked his intention and closed the Port. Other articles of the Treaty of Berlin concerned the maintenance of the European Commission of the Danube, the application of the Organic Law of 1868 to Crete, the cession of Khotar to Persia, the intention of the Porte to maintain religious liberty, and the privileges of the Monks of Mount Athos.[4]

[1] Dulcigno was added, after difficult negotiations, in 1880. The incident of the transfer of Dulcigno constituted almost a crisis, although Beust wittily and truly remarked that *Dulcigno far niente*.

[2] April 16, 1877.

[3] May 14, 1877.

[4] There is a good short monograph on *The Congress of Berlin*, 1878, by E. L. Woodward (London, 1920). See also G. Cecil: *Life of Robert Marquis of Salisbury*, vol. II.

CHAPTER XXV

THE TRIPLE ALLIANCE

The chief interest of diplomatic affairs in the thirty years following the Treaty of Berlin is centred round the Triple Alliance. Closely connected with the idea of the Triple Alliance between Germany, Austria and Italy (the texts of which were kept strictly secret) is the idea of "reinsurance"; Germany and Austria having insured themselves *against* Russia and France by the Triple Alliance, "re-insured" themselves by making agreements *with* Russia. The history of the Triple Alliance also proves again that Turkey-in-Europe was the focus of international diplomacy: practically all the agreements are "oriented" towards the Balkans. Finally it is worth noting that when the statesmen of the Triple Alliance claimed that it was a pacific instrument, they were justified by facts. Deference was shown in the diplomatic instruments to England and to Russia, and the anxiety of the Triple Alliance Powers to placate them is now patent. But there was no attempt to placate France. This power was fearfully isolated before 1896.

The Triple Alliance could be called a peaceful association, so long as France was too weak to seem likely to reclaim Alsace and Lorraine. But should her resources ever be restored so far as to make her appear strong enough to re-assert her claim, the German statesmen and military politicians were sure to become nervous, and to try and forestall her with a war. This was probably (with many other contributory factors) the cause of the European War of 1914.

Bismarck undoubtedly made a terrible mistake in annexing Alsace and Lorraine in 1871, although probably he could scarcely resist the pressure put upon him at the time. Had he left these two provinces to France, the Hohenzollern Empire would be with us still. Anyhow, having got the provinces, Bismarck was only anxious that the Empire should enjoy them quietly. Therefore he went in for his policy of defensive alliances.

> Count Schouvaloff was perfectly right when he said that the idea of coalitions gave me nightmares. We had waged victorious wars against two of the European Great Powers; everything depended on inducing at least one of the two mighty foes whom we had beaten in the field to renounce the anticipated design of uniting with the other in a war of revenge.[1]

Bismarck remembered how Kaunitz had united Austria, France and Russia after the annexation of Silesia by Frederick the Great. So, as he was convinced that with France the German Empire could never be friendly, he resolved to cultivate the good will of Austria and Russia.

Almost immediately after the Congress of Berlin, he achieved a remarkable success in his alliance policy. Partly owing to Russia's disappointment in the Balkans, and partly owing to the activities of the Pan-Slavists, the relations of the Tsar both with Prussia and with Austria had become distinctly strained. The conciliatory Count Schouvaloff, accused of too great deference to England and the other Powers at the Congress of Vienna, was in disgrace, and the commanding influence in the Russian Government was the War Minister Milutin. These and other considerations were discussed by Bismarck with Count Andrassy at Gastein on August 27 and 28, 1879, and the following understanding was arrived at: that "to a Russo-French alliance the natural counterpoise is an Austro-German alliance."[2] It is true that next month the Emperor William met his nephew, the Tsar, at Alexandrowo in Posen, and the two sovereigns, who still preserved something of their ancient fondness for each other, renewed their friendship. But no binding agreement was made, and Bismarck was still very dissatisfied. So on October 7, 1879, the Austro-German Treaty of Alliance was concluded. It was the last work of Count Andrassy. On the 8th he left office and spent the rest of his life as a great Hungarian magnate. He died in 1890.

The Austro-German Treaty of Alliance was the pivot of European international relations from 1879 till the Great War. During all this period, and throughout the War, the Treaty remained in

[1] Bismarck, *op. cit.*, chap. xxix.

[2] Bismarck, *op. cit.*, *ibid.* There was no Russo-French Alliance, but Bismarck was afraid such an alliance might take place.

force. The Triple Alliance was a sort of expansion of it, but in no way superseded it. The Triple Alliance was an unstable, ill-assorted partnership, based on the individual convenience of the Contracting Parties, but on no real community of interest. It was renewed only from term to term. The Dual Alliance of Austria and Germany, though concluded only for terms of five years, was in 1902 made practically perpetual,[1] although notice of a desire for revision could be given by either party in any three-year period.

The treaty stated simply that if "one of the two Empires be attacked by Russia, the High Contracting Parties are bound to come to the assistance one of the other with the whole war-strength of their Empires, and accordingly only to conclude peace together and upon mutual agreement" (article I). If one of the Contracting Parties were attacked by any other Power than Russia, the other Contracting Party was only pledged to benevolent neutrality; but any sort of military attack by Russia was a *casus fœderis* which inevitably evoked the full military support of the Ally who was not attacked. The modern type of alliance treaty usually makes an "unprovoked attack" the *casus fœderis*, but the Dual Alliance of 1879 had no such quibbling phrase.[2] The *casus fœderis* was simply an attack by Russia. It was according to this stipulation that Germany engaged with Austria against Russia in 1914.

The old Emperor William would have liked confidentially to inform the Tsar Alexander II of the Austro-German Dual Alliance, but Bismarck advised against doing so.[3] However, he was not averse from trying to improve the relations between the three Empires, so that the war which was envisaged in the Dual Alli-

[1] Article III of the treaty of October 7, 1879, establishes a five-year period. This article was not contained in the version made public in 1888, and printed in Marten's N.R.G., 2me Série, t. XV, and in *State Papers*, LXXIII, 270. It was first published in Pribram: *The Secret Treaties of Austria-Hungary*, pp. 19 ff., 217.

[2] When Sir Edward Grey, in 1912, proposed the formula that England and Germany should agree not to make an *unprovoked attack* on each other, Bethmann-Hollweg pointed out that the phrase meant nothing. No civilised Power makes an *absolutely* unprovoked attack upon any State. Different things provoke different States, and with more or less reason.

[3] Bismarck, *op. cit.*, pp. 191–2. The British Government was confidentially informed of it, and there was even some idea that England might become a party, and so make a triple alliance with Austria and Germany; *see* Lord Salisbury's letters of October 15 and 27, 1879, in Buckle's *Life of Benjamin Disraeli*, VI, 491–2.

ance should be prevented. So, in 1881, there was arranged the League of the Three Empires—being, in fact, a renewal of the Dreikaiserbund of 1873. The terms of the League were contained in a Convention signed at Berlin on June 18, 1881, by Bismarck, Széchényi (Austrian ambassador) and Sabouroff (Russian ambassador). It stated that if one of the High Contracting Parties should find itself at war with a fourth Great Power, the two others should observe a benevolent neutrality (article I); that any modifications in the Treaty of Berlin (1878) should only be accomplished in virtue of a common agreement between them (article II); and that the principle of closing the Straits of the Bosphorus and Dardanelles, as confirmed by treaties, should be maintained (article III).

It will be noticed, that while no objection can be taken to articles I and III, the second article united the three Courts in nothing less than a conspiracy against the rest of Europe. For the Treaty of Berlin (the modification of which by the three Courts alone is explicitly contemplated in article II) was a European Act, and could be lawfully changed only by consent of all the Powers who signed it. The depth of wickedness of this conspiracy, and the imminence of its results can be seen from the protocol attached to the Convention of June 18, and bearing the same date. By article 1 of this protocol, Austria-Hungary reserved to herself the right to annex Bosnia and Herzegovina "at whatever moment she shall deem opportune." By article 4, the three Powers agreed "not to oppose the eventual reunion of Bulgaria and Eastern Rumelia within the territorial limits assigned to them by the Treaty of Berlin." [1]

Having consolidated their alliance between themselves and having made themselves secure with Russia, the Central Powers turned to see what could be done with Italy. This State, although it would in no way renounce its pretensions to the *irredente* lands outside its then existing frontier, was ready enough for friendship with the Central Powers because of its antagonism to France. It was not so much that certain European territories of France, such as Savoy, Nice and Corsica, tempted Italy, as that France's extra-European policy disturbed the minds of Italian statesmen. The Italian Government was very sensitive about its position in the

[1] The Convention and Protocol remained secret till published by Pribram, *op. cit.*, in 1920. The League was made for three years; was renewed for another three years in 1884, and was converted into the celebrated "Reinsurance Treaty" in 1887.

political equilibrium of the Mediterranean; and the extension of French power along the northern coast of Africa seemed to endanger this. The finishing touch was given to the apprehensions of the Italians by the Treaty of Bardo which France concluded with the Dey of Tunis on May 12, 1881. By this treaty the Dey agreed that his territory should be occupied by French soldiers and should become a French Protectorate. For a time something in the nature of a crisis existed between Italy and France. It is unknown from whom came the suggestion that Italy should join herself to the Central Powers: the expediency of the alliance was obvious to all parties. Bismarck could always do with another alliance, which would make the French *revanche* ever more remote; Austria, faced with the possibility of some day fighting Russia, required some help in addition to Germany, for this State would be probably fully occupied in dealing with France; while Italy could never stand alone in a war, but *must* have allies. The general plan of the Triple Alliance seems to have been defined in visits which King Humbert of Italy made successively to Francis Joseph at Vienna, and to William I at Berlin, in 1882. The text of the alliance was signed by Count Kálnoky for Austria-Hungary, by Prince Henry VII of Reuss for Germany, and by Count Robilant for Italy, at Vienna on May 20, 1882. The fact of its existence became general knowledge, and continued to intrigue both politicians, publicists and writers for nearly forty years; but its terms were never divulged by those who made it or had access to its texts, "certainly an honourable testimony to the discretion of a class against which the reproach of indiscretion has so often and not unjustly been made." [1]

The Triple Alliance of 1882 was contained in one tripartite treaty. Article I engaged the Contracting Parties to an exchange of ideas on political and economic questions. Article II was as follows:

In case Italy, without direct provocation on her part, should be attacked by France for any reason whatsoever, the two other Con-

[1] Pribram, *op. cit.*, Introduction, p. 4. In 1915 the Government of Austria made public four articles of the 1912 Renewal Treaty (*Diplomatische Aktenstücke betreffend die Beziehungen Oesterreich-Ungarns zu Italien in der Zeit vom 20 Juli, 1914, bis zum 23 Mai, 1915*, p. 161). The full texts were published in 1920 by Pribram, *op. cit.* The texts are in French. The Austro-German Dual Alliance Treaties are in German.

tracting Parties shall be bound to lend help and assistance with all their forces to the Party attacked.

The same obligation shall devolve upon Italy in case of any aggression, without direct provocation, by France against Germany.

In the same manner, the *casus fœderis* was to arise if any of the Contracting Parties were attacked by more than one Great Power (article III). The remaining five articles referred to benevolent neutrality (IV), consultation among the Contracting Parties " in ample time " concerning military measures when the *casus fœderis* became imminent (V), the secrecy of the treaty (VI), its duration —five years—(VII), and ratification (VIII). To the treaty was attached a Declaration by Italy that the alliance could not " in any case be regarded as being directed against England." Identic declarations were made by Germany and Austria. These declarations, like the treaty, were secret. They were therefore made not to impress England, but to make Italy's position clear with regard to the two other allies: Italy's Mediterranean interests clashed with those of France, not with those of England.

The power which seemed to get least out of the Triple Alliance was Austria, as she was bound to fight for her allies if either of them were attacked singly by France. Austria on her part could not claim a *casus fœderis* if she were attacked by Russia singly. It must be remembered, however, that Austria had the guarantee of German support by the Dual Alliance of 1879, which remained in force and which was, apparently, not communicated to Italy.

In 1883 Rumania joined the group of Triple Alliance Powers. This she did by making a treaty of defensive alliance with Austria-Hungary on October 30, 1883. Germany and Italy signed accessions to the treaty on the same day, and took upon them the same engagements.

Taken as a whole, the Triple Alliance, in so far as it was concerned with the relations of the Contracting Parties among each other, represented a policy of letting bygones be bygones. Germany, Austria and Italy were to forget ancient quarrels. The Alliance had another purpose too: the Preamble to the Treaty of May 20, 1882, states that the Contracting Parties were " animated by the desire to increase the guarantees of the general peace, to fortify the monarchical principle, and thereby to assure the unimpaired maintenance of the social and political order of their respective States." Thus it was a kind of revived Holy Alliance, but with this difference—it did not contemplate intervention in the domestic affairs of other States.

Between the signature of the first Triple Alliance Treaty in 1882, and the Renewal Treaties of 1887, a curious and romantic train of events occurred in the Balkans. The "Big Bulgaria" which Russia had tried to create by the Treaty of San Stefano had been reduced by the Treaty of Berlin to a Little Bulgaria between the Danube and the Balkans. The country to the south of the Balkans, between these mountains and the next range (which is called the Istranja and lies to the north of Adrianople) was made into an autonomous province under Turkey, with a Christian Governor. This southern province was given a new name, fashioned so as to be as different as possible from that of Bulgaria, in order to obliterate all traces of the San Stefano treaty: it was called Eastern Rumelia.[1] The capital of the Principality was Sofia; the capital of the autonomous province of Eastern Rumelia was Philippopolis.

The first Prince of Bulgaria was Alexander of Battenberg, nominated by the Powers and elected by a Bulgarian National Assembly. His sister was the wife of the Tsar Alexander II (assassinated in 1881), and accordingly he himself was first cousin to the Tsar Alexander III. His brother Henry married in 1885 the Princess Beatrice, daughter of Queen Victoria. The Prince of Bulgaria, young—he was only twenty-one at the time of the Congress of Berlin—and energetic, was not insensible to the national aspirations of his vigorous subjects. In September, 1885, after a strong agitation for the union of the Bulgars north and south of the Balkans, a nationalist revolution broke out at Philippopolis. Prince Alexander at once responded to this demonstration, and led an army into Philippopolis. The Serbian Government at once protested against this extension of the State of Bulgaria, and claimed compensation. A brief war ensued, in which Prince Alexander's generals [2] sharply defeated the Serbs at Slivnitza (November, 1885).

[1] At the Congress of Berlin Gorchakoff pleaded for another name, but Beaconsfield was adamant. "He [Gorchakoff] entreated me not to change the name of South Bulgaria into Eastern Rumelia, which he said would be the greatest humiliation to Russia which could be devised. It is quite distressing to refuse anything to this dear old fox, who seems melting with the milk of human kindness": Buckle's *Life of Benjamin Disraeli*, VI, 328, note. The curious name Eastern Rumelia may have been the invention of Lord Salisbury who was something of a phrase-maker.

[2] Slivnitza was a two days' battle (November 18, 19). Prince Alexander himself was not present at it.

The Prince then very wisely turned to the Porte, and concluded a convention with it, by which he was invested by Turkey with the Governorship of Eastern Rumelia. The British Government, of which Lord Salisbury was premier, disliked this violation of the Treaty of Berlin; it was not aware of the fact that three of the Great Powers signatory to that Treaty—namely Germany, Austria and Russia—had in the *League of the Three Emperors* secretly agreed not to oppose "the eventual reunion of Bulgaria and Eastern Rumelia." Nevertheless Lord Salisbury was able to bring it about that the Prince of Bulgaria should be recognised as *vali* of Eastern Rumelia only, with the sanction of the Congress Powers, and for periods of five years, according to article XVII of the Treaty of Berlin. The idea at the back of Lord Salisbury's mind was evidently that some day another person than the Prince of Bulgaria might be nominated *vali* of Eastern Rumelia. As a matter of fact no such thing happened, and Bulgaria and Eastern Rumelia remained in effect united, and representatives from Eastern Rumelia sat in the Sobranye at Sofia. Yet in theory the Prince of Bulgaria was, as far as Eastern Rumelia was concerned, only Governor of an autonomous Turkish province, and I have heard an English diplomatist say that he had seen Ferdinand of Coburg himself in Constantinople wearing a Turkish *fez*.

Alexander of Battenberg, however, was not to enjoy much longer either the Governorship or the Principality. The Tsar Alexander III for some reason or other could not away with him. The Generals Bendereff and Panitza, who had won the battle of Slivnitza, were discontented. On August 21, 1886, they brought to success a conspiracy, to which the Tsar is believed to have been privy; Alexander was confined to his palace and shortly afterwards escorted across the frontier into Rumania, from which he made his way through Bessarabia to Austrian territory. For a month a Provisional Government or Regency controlled Sofia, and then a counter-revolution occurred and Alexander of Battenberg came back. He re-entered Sofia on September 2, yet he felt that he could not remain without the countenance of the Tsar. In reply to the Prince's request for his cousin's approval, the inexorable Tsar sent a cold and laconic refusal. The Prince accepted the verdict, and not without a certain dignity abdicated his throne, and retired to Austria, where he lived till 1893 with the title of Count Hartenau.

The regency left behind by Alexander,[1] of which the Bulgarian statesman Stambouloff was the chief, had some difficulty in steering a course among the conflicting currents of interest of the Great Powers, but at length they were able to find a sovereign in the person of Ferdinand of Coburg. This prince, son of a daughter of King Louis Philippe, was aged twenty-five, and at the time held a lieutenant's commission in the Austrian army. With the tacit approval of the Court of Vienna he accepted the adventure and mounted the throne of Bulgaria which it was scarcely expected that he would hold for long (July, 1887). As a matter of fact he held it with considerable *éclat* till 1918, when he quitted the State he had ruined and retired to affluent [2] private life at Coburg.

The Triple Alliance was renewed on February 20, 1887, to last till May 30, 1892. This renewal consisted of three instruments. The first was a tripartite treaty which simply prolonged the original Triple Alliance Treaty of 1882. The second was a separate treaty between Austria-Hungary and Italy, bearing the same date—February 20, 1887. It was short and contained only one really important article—No. I—which stated that if the maintenance of the *status quo* in the Balkans or the Ottoman coasts and islands of the Adriatic or Ægean became impossible, Austria-Hungary and Italy would only modify the *status quo* after a previous agreement among themselves "based upon the principle of a reciprocal compensation for every advantage, territorial or other, which each of them might obtain." The third instrument was a separate treaty between the German Empire and Italy. The chief article was No. III, in which it was stated that if France should attempt to extend her territories in North Africa in the direction of Tripoli or Morocco, and if Italy thereupon felt bound to proceed to extreme measures, "the state of war which would thereby ensue between Italy and France would constitute *ipso facto*, on the demand of Italy and at the common charge of the two Allies the *casus fœderis* with all the effects foreseen by Articles II and V of the aforesaid Treaty of May 20, 1882, as if such an eventuality were expressly contemplated therein." And if Italy, in consequence of such a

[1] His brother Louis became a distinguished admiral in the British Navy and died in 1921.

[2] He had £400,000 in England alone, which after the European War the law-courts declared was still his and could not be confiscated.

war, should "seek for territorial guarantees with respect to France . . . Germany will present no obstacle thereto"—further, Germany was actually to "apply herself to facilitating the means of attaining such a purpose" (Article IV).

It is clear that out of both the separate Acts attached to the main treaty of renewal of the Triple Alliance, Italy got much the best of the bargain.

Not merely was the *Triplice* renewed, but the curious overlapping group known as the League of the Three Emperors was also prolonged. Bismarck was always anxious to conciliate Russia, and the Tsar Alexander III was anxious for the German Chancellor's support in his efforts to suppress *Nihilism*. M. de Giers, who had succeeded to Gorchakoff in the direction of Russia's foreign affairs, was an experienced diplomatist, trained under Schouvaloff. His policy was to maintain good relations with Germany, in opposition to the famous General Skobelev who was an advocate of alliance with France. De Giers toured the capitals of Central Europe in 1882, and in 1884 (September 14) the three Emperors met at Skierniewice in Poland and renewed their good understanding. This was all that the European public was aware of; but actually five months before, Bismarck, Széchényi (Austrian ambassador) and Orloff (Russian ambassador) had met at Berlin and by authority of their respective sovereigns renewed the League of the Three Emperors, with slight modifications, for three more years.[1] Finally the two Courts made a new and more definite treaty on June 18, 1887, to run for three years—Bismarck's "Reinsurance Treaty (between Germany and Russia)."

This treaty began with a somewhat cryptic article:

> In case one of the High Contracting Parties should find itself at war with a third Great Power, the other would maintain a benevolent neutrality towards it, and would devote its efforts to the localisation of the conflict. This provision would not apply to a war against Austria or France in case this war should result from an attack directed against one of these two latter Powers by one of the High Contracting Parties (Art. I).

It is obvious that Bismarck, having insured the German possession of Alsace-Lorraine by the Dual and Triple Alliances, was now, by allying with Russia, re-insuring against a possible attack made by Austria or France. But he had to introduce a saving clause,

[1] This treaty was not known till published by Pribram, *op. cit.*

in case Russia should attack Austria, for then he would be bound to support the latter. In accepting this saving clause Russia must have been well-informed of the existence of the Dual Alliance of Germany and Austria. So much is clear. But the saving clause applied equally in favour of Russia, which was not bound to be neutral if Germany *attacked* France. It would appear, therefore, that the Tsar already contemplated the possibility of a Franco-Russian Alliance. As a matter of fact the idea of such an alliance was in the air, and at this very moment French and Russian financiers were entering into close relations with each other on behalf of, or with the approval of, their respective Governments.

By article II of the Reinsurance Treaty Germany recognised Russia's historic rights in the Balkan Peninsula, and particularly "her preponderant and decisive influence in Bulgaria and Eastern Rumelia." In article III the two Courts affirmed the principle of closing the Straits of the Dardanelles and Bosphorus; and in an "additional and very secret protocol," Germany promised "in no case to give her consent to the restoration of the Prince of Battenberg" [to Bulgaria].

This treaty, which like all the German-Russian treaties is in French, was signed by Bismarck and by Count Schouvaloff, and was practically the last work of this conciliatory Russian diplomatist. It was to endure for three years from the date of ratification —a space of time which neatly bridges over the period till 1890, when a new situation arose in Europe.[1]

In the year 1890 there occurred two events of first-class importance in diplomatic history. One was the retiral of the great German Chancellor, Bismarck; the other was the conclusion of the Anglo-German treaty concerning Heligoland and Zanzibar.

The old Emperor William I had died in March, 1888; his son, Frederick III, had a brief reign of three months; and then there succeeded William II, aged twenty-nine. The young Emperor had plenty of energy, and could scarcely be expected to leave to his Chancellor as much of the initiative of Government as the aged William I or the incurably diseased Frederick III had done. The crisis, when it came, was short and decisive; and on March 29, 1890, the Iron Chancellor, refusing the title of Duke of Lauenburg, retired to nurse his ill-humour for eight more years at his estate of

[1] 1890 may be taken as the year when Anglo-German friendship practically ceases, and when the Franco-Russian alliance begins.

Friedrichsruhe. The new Chancellor appointed by William II was a mere soldier, the General Caprivi de Caprera de Montecuculi. Thus William II showed his preference for the military point of view in his Government, and dissipated the sane diplomatic *milieu* in which he had been brought up. It is true that he returned later to civilian Chancellors, of whom Bülow and Bethmann-Hollweg were thoroughly sane men, raised in a sound diplomatic and administrative tradition ; but these men were not the dynamic forces of German policy that Bismarck had been : between them and their sovereign there was a dense cloud of Prussian soldiers, courtiers and General-Staff administrators who had the monarch's ear.

Nevertheless, the tradition of Bismarck could not disappear at once when he left the Wilhelmstrasse. One of the tenets of the Bismarck creed was to keep on good terms with England, a policy in which he was met half-way by the English Prime Minister and Foreign Secretary, Lord Salisbury. When Bismarck left office, the way was already cleared to an understanding which should remove the two countries from places on the earth's surface where their interests immediately clashed.

In the last months of Bismarck's *régime* invitations had been dispatched to the European States that they might send delegates to a Conference to be held at Berlin for the study of social and economic questions. The Conference actually met on March 15, and sat till the 29th, under the presidency of the Prussian Minister of Commerce. The final protocol adopted by the Conference consisted of six chapters, making recommendations to regulate the age at which persons should be allowed to work in mines, Sunday and night-work, work of women and girls, and kindred subjects. These were merely recommendations ; they were a statement of the public opinion of Europe on industrial subjects ; and they constitute a stage in the history of the international regulation of industry, which has reached its most complete expression in the Labour Agreements in the Covenant of the League of Nations. The International Labour Conference of 1890 at Berlin considerably enhanced the prestige of the young Emperor. It was the complement of the great International Conference which was sitting at the same time at Brussels to concert measures for the suppression of the traffic in slaves in Africa. The Act of the Brussels Conference was accepted, ratified, and put in force with more or less efficiency by the component States.

Finally, in 1890, Great Britain and Germany settled their African differences. Lord Salisbury had for long been working to prevent a struggle which, in a scramble for Africa, might easily break out there, and become a European conflagration. He now was able to arrange that Germany should recognise a British Protectorate over Zanzibar and Witu; in return for this the Emperor of Germany received the Island of Heligoland [1] which had been British since 1814.

[1] Treaty signed at Berlin, July 1, 1890.

CHAPTER XXVI

THE REVIVAL OF FRANCE

The revival of French power and prestige was a fact which the British public only began to realise after 1904, but actually it began immediately after the war of 1870–71. This was why Bismarck had a regular war-scare in 1875, and why he arranged the Dual Alliance in 1879, the Triple Alliance in 1882, and the Reinsurance Treaty in 1887. It required great courage for the French statesmen of the "heroic age of the Republic," as Hanotaux calls it in his *History of Contemporary France,* to go about their task, for France was absolutely isolated by Bismarck's wonderful system of anti-French alliances. Nevertheless, the French went on with the greatest energy renewing their sources of strength, as is particularly to be seen in the colonial policy of Jules Ferry. Soon Tunis, Tonkin, Madagascar, and the Congo had given to France an enormous place in the sun. Before the Great War opened, France's sensitive neighbours had begun, not without reason, to fear that she would be able to make up for her deficiency in white soldiers by bringing Colonial troops from over the sea.[1]

In European affairs France begins to assume all her own status when Russia shows an inclination to invite her concurrence. On the Russian side, General Skobelev was the chief advocate. Early in 1882, fresh from the laurels of his campaign against the Turcomans, he visited Paris, and received and made public speeches which manifested something like a Franco-Russian *rapprochement.* But the General died shortly afterwards; and Alexander III became involved in the League of the Three Emperors. In 1886, however, the Tsar was disappointed with the attitude adopted by Austria

[1] *See* the *Naval Agreement between Austria-Hungary, Germany and Italy,* August 2, 1913. The Mediterranean section of the Agreement contains a chapter (No. 8) entitled "Attacks on French Troop Transports from North Africa" (Pribram, *op. cit.*, p. 297).

and Germany concerning the union of Bulgaria and Eastern Rumelia. So he began to think of making friends with France. At this time it happened that the Russian Government was engaged in a great programme of railway-building—a remunerative work, which, however, could not be carried out without the assistance of foreign capital. The French were essentially a "saving" people, with accumulations of money beyond what was needed by their industries. So they welcomed the opportunity for remunerative investment abroad. The first loan placed by the Russian Government in France—an emission of bonds for 500 million francs [1]—was over-subscribed. Such a loan required the assent of the French Government for its issue, so that there was something semi-official about it. Similar Russian issues of bonds followed in rapid succession, and bound Russia and France financially together.[2] When, in 1889, the Russian Government was placing an order in France for the manufacture of 500,000 rifles, M. de Freycinet asked for an assurance that the rifles would not be used against his own country. The assurance is said to have been given by the Russian ambassador.[3] Meantime the Reinsurance Treaty of Germany with Russia was running out; it expired by effluxion of time in the summer of 1890. The Emperor William II seems to have realised the danger of France turning towards Russia, and he held out the olive-branch. French artists were officially invited to participate in an exhibition of the Fine Arts to be held at Berlin in 1891. The Emperor himself dined with M. Herbette, the French ambassador at Berlin (February 12, 1891). It was even rumoured that he would pay a visit to Paris. The French Government was courteous, if somewhat reserved. One thing was indispensable to any *rapprochement*, namely that France should abandon the idea of taking back Alsace-Lorraine. Just at this moment, however, the *League of French Patriots*, of which the fiery M. Paul Deroulède was the leading figure, held furious meetings, protesting against the proposed visit to Paris of the "gaoler of Alsace." Something in the nature of a crisis ensued, and Baron Marschall von Bieberstein, the German Secretary for Foreign Affairs, informed M. Herbette significantly that "the tolerance of Germany

[1] The interest offered was 4 per cent. The issue was at 86 francs 45 centimes for each bond of the nominal value of 100 francs.

[2] The system of Russian State Railways was built with French and, to a less extent, English capital. In 1918 the Bolshevists appropriated the Railways but repudiated the debt.

[3] Debidour, *La Paix Armée*, p. 138.

had its limits" (February 27, 1891). The French Government behaved correctly, and the incident passed over. But when the Russian Government invited France to send a squadron of the Navy on a visit of courtesy to Kronstadt, the invitation was accepted. On July 22 the squadron dropped its anchors in the great Russian harbour amid salvoes of guns and shouts of enthusiasm. It is said that when the French officers visited St. Petersburg and attended a musical reception at which the Tsar was present, the Tsar himself stood bareheaded while the *Marseillaise* was being played.[1] In the following August an exchange of letters took place between M. Ribot (French Minister for Foreign Affairs), M. Freycinet (Minister of War for France), and M. de Giers, the Minister of Foreign Affairs for Russia. These letters constituted an *Entente Cordiale*, a phrase which now became popular, expressing a definite international friendship without specific alliance. When the *entente* was announced in public speeches, a sigh of relief went over all France. It is almost impossible for an English public to imagine what had been the feelings of France, living for twenty years absolutely without friends or allies in the middle of the armed camp of Europe, existing almost by sufferance of the powerful and inexorable enemy, who was fashioning a network of military alliances around and against her. It was now recognised throughout Europe that the French Republic was stable, that French resources were those of a Great Power, and that the French Government could continue to "practise peace with dignity," to show "prudence and sangfroid,"[2] without feeling every moment that her security hung upon a thread.

The creation of the Franco-Russian Alliance took altogether about six years, and required much patient and sustained work on the part of the French diplomatists, who especially had to dissipate the prevailing notion that France's frequent ministerial crises meant instability. Gradually the two Governments drew closer together. Some informal meetings took place between prominent Russian nobles and the French President Carnot, quite in the style of Bismarck and Napoleon III, at Aix-les-Bains. M. de Giers, an indefatigable traveller, who did a good deal in his time for Europe's peace by his visits, was induced to come round by Paris, on his way from Italy to Russia in the winter of 1891. At St. Petersburg

[1] Debidour, *op. cit.*, p. 171.

M. Ribot at Bapaume, unveiling the monument to General Faidherbe; *see* Debidour, *op. cit.*, pp. 172–3.

M. de Lannes, Duc de Montebello, French ambassador, had important social relations with the Tsar and with all the people who counted in the brilliant political society of the Russian capital. At last, on August 18, 1892, the draft of a military convention between Russia and France was signed at St. Petersburg.[1] It provided that "if France is attacked by Germany or by Italy supported by Germany, Russia shall employ all its available forces to fight Germany"; and that "if Russia is attacked by Germany or by Austria supported by Germany, France shall employ all its available forces to fight Germany."

The chief credit on the French side, in those delicate and difficult negotiations, must be given to M. de Freycinet, who had early grasped and followed up the almost intangible threads which connected the two countries; to M. Sadi Carnot, the President; and to M. Loubet, the Premier. Loubet's Government [2] fell in December, 1892, before the hesitating Tsar could be brought to ratify the military convention, and was replaced by the Government of M. Ribot; but M. de Freycinet remained at the Ministry of War, and M. Loubet himself was Minister of the Interior.

The year 1893 passed without any actual treaty being concluded between France and Russia. M. Ribot's Government gave way to that of M. Charles Dupuy (in October, 1893); M. de Freycinet was no longer at the Ministry of War, but two names (in subordinate positions it is true) appear which later became famous in the history of French alliances: these are the names of Raymond Poincaré (Minister of Public Instruction) and Théophile Delcassé (Minister of the Colonies). In October, 1893, the Russian Fleet under Admiral Avellan visited Toulon, whence a party of officers and men proceeded to Paris. In the midst of the celebrations the Marshal MacMahon died, and the Tsar tactfully appointed the Admiral and naval officers to be an official deputation at the obsequies of the famous soldier. In December M. Dupuy, too, became one of those distinguished Frenchmen who can write *Ancien Président du Conseil* on their visiting cards; and M. Casimir Perier took up the burden of the premiership. In this month M. de Montebello was able to bring

[1] The Convention and the correspondence relating thereto was published by the French Government in a Yellow Book in 1917. The Convention was not ratified by the Tsar till December, 1893.

[2] Some members of his Government and party were found to be implicated in financial scandals connected with the Panama Canal Company.

the long negotiations to a successful issue. On December 30, he wrote from St. Petersburg to M. Casimir Périer: "I have just received M. de Gier's letter informing me that the draft of the military convention, already approved in principle by His Majesty and signed by the two Chiefs of Staff, has been definitely adopted."

The time was now ripe; and in March, 1894, the military convention was ratified, and the *casus fœderis* was registered in a treaty.

CHAPTER XXVII

THE ENTENTE CORDIALE

§ 1. EGYPT

Since 1815, Great Britain and France had always been in close relations with each other; the phrase *entente cordiale* was used to express their reciprocal attitude in the reign of Louis Philippe. The pages of *Punch* throughout the reign of Queen Victoria show how much the French were in the English people's mind. Yet there were periods of estrangement too, some of them of considerable duration. The Egyptian question was the cause of the longest period of estrangement.

In 1876 the Khedivial Government of Egypt, as a result of the personal extravagance of the Khedive and the corruption and inefficiency of the administration, had been unable to pay its debts. To deal with this state of affairs an international *Caisse de la Dette* was established with the consent of the Khedive. Further, an English official was appointed to control the revenue of Egypt, and a French official to supervise the expenditure. This arrangement was called the Dual Control.

Every Government in Europe knew that Egypt required to be looked after by some one, if chaos and the most miserable oppression of the peasants were to be prevented. Bismarck frankly stated his opinion several times that England should undertake the task. "I am surprised that Bismarck should go on harping about Egypt," wrote Beaconsfield to Lord Salisbury in 1876.[1] But Beaconsfield, having in the previous year purchased over one-third of the total shares of the Suez Canal for England, was content to go no further. In the same letter, immediately after his remark about Bismarck and Egypt, he continues: "Its occupation by us would embitter France." Perhaps that was why Bismarck kept on suggesting it.

[1] Letter of November 29, 1876 (Buckle, *Life of B. Disraeli*, VI, 104).

The Dual Control had nothing to do with policy: it was purely administrative and could not prevent the oppression and extravagance practised by the Khedive Ismail. The Sultan of Turkey, however, was induced to depose Ismail; and Tewfik, the son, reigned in his stead, with the Dual Control more prominent than ever. All this produced an ebullition of the budding nationalist movement. In 1882 the malcontents arose under the Colonel Arabi Pasha; the rising assumed the form, now usual in Oriental countries, of a massacre of resident foreigners. On June 11 occurred the murder of four hundred Europeans at Alexandria. A bombardment by the British fleet, followed by the landing of a small British force, restored order in the city. The French Premier, M. de Freycinet, who was anxious to proceed only through a European Conference (which was actually sitting at Constantinople to consider the Egyptian question), refused to associate the French Mediterranean squadron with this bombardment. When, however, it became obvious that the Canal Zone must also be guarded by European troops, Freycinet was ready to intervene alongside of England, but the French Chamber would not vote him the necessary financial credits. It was known that the Triple Alliance had recently been concluded, and on this account French politicians, as a whole, were unwilling to embark on an overseas adventure. "Europe is covered with soldiers. . . . Reserve France's liberty of action," said M. Clemenceau in the Chamber.[1] It is true that joint intervention by France and England would have inevitably meant some degree of concert or entente between these two countries; but the French were probably right in thinking that such an understanding with England would be worth very little to them at that time if they were involved in a continental struggle with Germany, Austria, and Italy—a contingency which not merely *seemed* but which actually *was* likely to occur. The Ministry of Mr. Gladstone, which was at the moment securely in power in England, had also been in power at the time of the Franco-Prussian War, so the French knew what his sympathy was worth. Nevertheless M. de Freycinet always looked on the Chamber's refusal to authorise him to join England in intervening in Egypt as something in the nature of a *gran rifiuto.* M. de Freycinet's Ministry fell on July 29, 1882, and a non-interventionist Cabinet under M. Duclerc came into office. In September the British Government, having induced the Sultan to declare

[1] July 29, 1882. *See* Debidour, *Hist. Dip., La Paix Armée,* II, 65.

Arabi a rebel, landed a force under Sir Garnet Wolseley, who won the battle of Tel-el-Kebir and suppressed the insurrection.

The English occupation, which was at first and for some years intended only to be temporary, gradually took root. The futile Conference of Ambassadors, which had sat at Constantinople while Arabi's rebellion was still going on, had taken the opportunity to register the disinterestedness of the Powers in a "Self-denying Protocol" to the effect that

> the Governments represented by the Undersigned engage themselves, in any arrangement which may be made in consequence of their concerted action for the regulation of the affairs of Egypt, not to seek any territorial advantage, nor any concession of any exclusive privilege, nor any commercial advantage for their subjects other than those which any other nation can equally obtain.[1]

Actually the Protocol has no weight in International Law, because the condition on which it depended never came into operation: no arrangement was made "in consequence of their concerted action." Nevertheless it may be said that England has fairly carried out the spirit and letter of the Protocol, at any rate as regards commercial privileges and concessions. Indeed one of the chief difficulties now in the way of England reducing her control in Egypt, is that other European nations would lose the surety which England provides for the position of their nationals.

In 1885 the British Government took steps which were meant to lead to evacuation. Sir Henry Drummond Wolff went on special mission to Constantinople to concert arrangements for withdrawal. Much work had to be done to secure some sort of stability in Egypt, but at last, on May 22, 1887, Drummond Wolff, along with Kiamil Pasha and Said Pasha, signed a Convention to put a term to the occupation: "At the expiration of three years from the date of the present Convention, Her Britannic Majesty's Government will withdraw its troops from Egypt." The evacuation could, however, be postponed if "danger, in the interior or from without," should render adjournment necessary; and, if the internal or external condition of Egypt required it, the occupation could be resumed. This Convention, which would necessarily have determined the British occupation within a few years, was still-born, for the Sultan refused to ratify it, apparently on account of French and Russian

[1] Protocol signed by the representatives of Great Britain, Austria-Hungary, France, Germany, Italy, and Russia, at Therapia, June 25, 1882.

objections to the right of re-entry being reserved to the British Government. The correspondence concerning Egypt, published as a Parliamentary Paper in 1887, makes curious reading. The Foreign Office appears, exercising all the pressure it can bring to bear on the Sultan to induce him to ratify the Convention which should end England's rule in Egypt; the Sultan appears, procrastinating and nullifying all England's well-meant efforts: "The responsibility for the prolongation of our occupation must rest with the Turkish Government, as we had done all in our power to shorten it."[1]

The British Government then proceeded, with officials acting through the agency of the Khedive, to reorganise the Egyptian administration, with the beneficial results to the material and moral condition of the country which are now well known. The French Government affected to maintain that the events of 1882 had not changed the state of affairs: that the *condominium* of France and Britain still continued. But the British Secretary of State for Foreign Affairs in his dispatches to Paris adhered to the view that the facts were no longer the same: that the British Government, having been compelled singly to enter Egypt, could not now share the responsibility with another external Power. Accordingly the Dual Control was abolished by a Khedivial decree (January 18, 1883), and a sole English Financial Adviser took its place. France had thus lost Egypt; and the knowledge that this had happened through her own refusal to intervene in 1882 did not sweeten her feelings. A Franco-British entente seemed a long way off.

§ 2. Africa

In the 'nineties the mutual attitude of the two countries did not improve. Under the vigorous impulsion of Jules Ferry, who was President of the Council twice, and for considerable periods, between 1880 and 1889, France reassumed the rôle of a great colonising power. Her intrepid explorers played an important part in opening up the Dark Continent. In 1884–5 she took part in the important Conference at Berlin which met to define the principles according to which a great part of West Africa should be partitioned. The result of this Conference was the Berlin Act (February 26, 1885), which established: (1) liberty of commerce in the territories forming the basin of the Congo, (2) interdiction of the trade in slaves in these territories, (3) the neutrality of these territories, (4) freedom

[1] Lord Salisbury in *Parliamentary Papers*, 1887, vol. II, p. 582.

of navigation of the Congo and Niger, according to the principles of articles 108 to 116 of the Final Act of the Congress of Vienna, and (5) the obligation laid upon Powers who were taking possession of any part of Africa, to notify their assumption of territory to the other signatory Powers, and to ensure a proper respect for law, order, and treaty-rights.

The territories of the conventional basin of the Congo, which were defined and neutralised by the Berlin Act, were partitioned between the Independent Congo Free State, France, and Portugal. The Congo Free State had originated with the *Association internationale africain* (founded at Brussels in 1876), of which King Leopold of Belgium was the chief promoter. It was definitely recognised by the Powers at Berlin in 1885. With the Association France had an agreement made by exchange of letters assuring her the right of pre-emption, in case the Association resolved to sell any of its territories.[1]

In 1890 the Governments of France and England, under the leadership of the sagacious Ribot and Salisbury, went somewhat beyond what their respective peoples thought to be justified, in a treaty made on August 5. The French colony of the Sudan (to the west of what became later the Anglo-Egyptian Sudan) was being extended southwards till it impinged upon the territories where the British Royal Niger Company was operating. The Salisbury-Ribot treaty delimited the competing spheres of interest by a line from Say on the middle Niger to Barroua on Lake Chad. Although the Chamber of Deputies thought that France obtained rather little from the agreement, M. Ribot was able to show that he had gained land in which the Royal Niger Company had trading-posts. In the House of Commons Lord Salisbury was able to answer complaints with the remark that the area assigned to France consisted mainly of the "light soil of the Sahara." Anyhow, France was given a free hand in Madagascar[2]—a considerable incidental advantage accruing from the treaty.

Italian relations with France were still somewhat strained, and were not improved by the attitude of the Italian Government with respect to Abyssinia. This country abutted on French and on British spheres of interest. The Italian Government aimed at gaining a protectorate in Abyssinia, and at making it part of the

[1] When the Kingdom of Belgium annexed the Congo Free State in 1908 it confirmed by treaty France's right of pre-emption (December 23, 1908).

[2] France took possession of Madagascar in 1895–6.

Red Sea Empire which they aspired to build up. With this object the Premier Crispi had a treaty concluded with the Negus, known as the Treaty of Ucciali (May 2, 1889). Article 17 of this Act, according to the Italian interpretation, gave to the Italians the right to establish a Protectorate. The British Government in 1891 recognised Abyssinia as an Italian "sphere of influence," with an eye to containing the forces of the Mahdi if ever the British should advance against him into the Sudan.

In the spring of 1896 an Italian expedition into Abyssinia, under General Baraticri, suffered a complete defeat at Adowa, the whole force being either killed or taken prisoner (March 1, 1896). The disaster created an enormous sensation throughout the rest of Europe, as well as in Italy. In Rome Crispi's Government fell, and the prestige of the monarchy seemed irretrievably dimmed. The situation was not so bad as it seemed, however; the new Italian Government had sufficient prudence and self-control not to push the sad adventure further. They "cut their losses," by recognising Abyssinia as absolutely independent under the Treaty of Addis Ababa (October 28, 1896).

The retiral of the Italians from Abyssinia relieved the apprehensions of the French, and paved the way for a better understanding between Italy, France, and Great Britain.[1] The accord between the two latter countries did not, however, come at once, Indeed a deplorable incident exacerbated French feeling worse than ever. Ever since the evacuation of the Egyptian Sudan and the tragic death of Gordon in 1885, the Conservative statesmen of England had been waiting for an opportunity to retrieve the province. By the year 1898, the political and economic condition of Egypt, under Lord Cromer's guidance, had been rendered sufficiently stable to admit of a fresh effort at expansion. The Anglo-Egyptian army, under Kitchener, in a singularly short and effective campaign, conquered all the old province southward to Khartoum. At the same time, a French mission, which had been planned some years previously, was led by the intrepid Major Marchand from the French side to the Upper Nile, to assert the interest of France in that quarter. At Fashoda the English General and the French

[1] In December, 1906, France, Italy, and Great Britain entered into a treaty which took note of "the common interest" of the three countries "to maintain intact the integrity of Ethiopia," and which in article I registered their accord to maintain the political and territorial *status quo* there (Treaty of London, December 13, 1906).

officer (who had only about 150 Senegalese soldiers with him) encountered each other (September 19, 1898). "Unfortunately," writes the French historian, "this valiant officer had not an army."[1] On the contrary, it was the most fortunate thing in the world, for if Marchand had had an army, he could scarcely have avoided fighting. And if he had fought, it would have been more than a casual affair of outposts: England and France would inevitably have been involved in a great war; the future of Europe would have been dark.

Fortunately, the insignificant force under Major Marchand rendered conflict ridiculous, and the self-restraint and courtesy of the two officers prevented the incident from becoming irremediable. General Kitchener took his stand on representing not British claims (which were non-existent on the Upper Nile), but Khedivial Egyptian rights. The French Government recognised the contention and the incident was satisfactorily closed with the withdrawal of the Marchand Mission. The French public was naturally discontented with the whole affair. Luckily, the British public, which had been a little inclined to flaunt its triumph, soon relapsed into something like forgetfulness. The place itself no longer figures on the map.

Thus, by the year 1898, France and Great Britain seemed to be no closer together than ever. And if this was unfortunate for France, it was perhaps even more unfortunate for us. Great Britain was undoubtedly at this time in a deplorably isolated position. British publicists like Sir Charles Dilke might argue complaisantly about the advantages of a policy of "the free hand," and the ignorant public might be fascinated by Lord Salisbury's facile phrase "splendid isolation," yet the state of affairs was not healthy. When Dr. Jameson led his piratical raid from Bechuanaland into the South African Republic in 1896, the public opinion of Europe was dead against the English Government, which was, undeservedly it is true, supposed to be privy to the raid. Probably the absurd telegram of congratulation from the Kaiser William II to Kruger really helped Great Britain in French opinion, for the French have a keen sense of the ridiculous. Where the telegram really had an unfortunate effect was in the South African Republic, for it gave the impression there that Kruger had a friend in Germany who would support him if he stood against Great Britain. When, three years later, the South African Republic, which had a perpetual treaty of alliance with the Orange Free State, made war on the British Empire,

[1] Debidour, *La Paix Armée*, p. 247.

Germany did (it is believed) make overtures to France for active intervention against Great Britain. It was probably the most critical moment of the Empire's history. The German overtures (February, 1900) were without result;[1] and Great Britain finished the long-drawn-out South African war amid the muttering of Europe, but still in peace. A study of the European Press of the years 1901 and 1902 shows how isolated, how unpopular, how vindictively regarded, was England. The Swiss Press almost alone showed some good feeling.

§ 3. The Far East

It was in the Far East that Great Britain first emerged from her isolation. Till the middle of the nineteenth century, China had been practically a closed Empire. In 1840 Great Britain had a brief war with China, because of the seizure and burning, without compensation, of English merchants' opium. In 1856, another war ensued over the seizure of the *lorcha* "Arrow," flying the British flag. The British forces co-operated with the French. The war ended with a treaty negotiated at Pekin on October 24, 1860.

In 1871 Japan put an end to her mediæval feudal system, and with surprising rapidity became a modern power. The other States of the world soon recognised this fact, by assenting to the abolition of extra-territorial jurisdictions. In 1896 a war broke out between China and Japan concerning the control of the Empire of Korea. The war ended with the victory of Japan and the Treaty of Shimonosheki (April 17, 1895). By this treaty Japan gained the Laio-tung Peninsula and the island of Formosa; Korea was to be "independent," which practically meant that Japan would enfeoff it. The Russian Government, however, was all against such an extension of Japan's power in the Far East; the French Government (now closely allied with the Tsar) associated itself with the Russian protest; and the German Government, in order, apparently, not to be isolated in this concord of diplomacy respecting the Far East, also joined in bringing pressure to bear on Japan. The three Powers presented a note which was in the nature of an ultimatum. Japan *recula pour mieux sauter*. She bent to the blast, and consented to a revision of the Shimonosheki terms, giving up the Laio-tung Peninsula and Formosa.

The advance of Russian power to the Far East is a romantic and,

[1] The negotiations are believed to have broken down because Germany demanded a French guarantee of her possession of Alsace-Lorraine.

in Western Europe at any rate, little known movement in Russian history. When English seamen in the reign of Queen Elizabeth were braving the icebergs and the snowstorms, trying to find a north-east passage to China, Cossacks under Yermak were penetrating overland through the forests and mountains of Siberia. By the end of the reign of Peter the Great they had got to the Amur River. It was not, however, till much later that they began to occupy the littoral of what is known as the "sea of Japan"—that is, the portion of the Pacific between Manchuria and the Japanese Islands Yeso, Nippon, and the rest. In 1860 the Russian port of Vladivostock was founded.

To the south of the line of Russian advance was the vast, unwieldy, and as it seemed almost helpless Empire of China. Penetration or infeudation of some part of it by a Great Power appeared to be inevitable. The obvious Great Power was Russia: but the rising, energetic Power of Japan could scarcely be expected to tolerate this.

After the Chino-Japanese War the Russian Government lost no time. The Tsar Nicholas II had, in 1891 (before he came to the throne), made a long tour of the Far East, and became deeply interested in Russia's Pacific policy. Count Lamsdorff, his Minister for Foreign Affairs, was no less interested: their policy was oceanic.[1]

On February 7, 1896, the King of Korea, a man of no strength or influence, fled from some tumult to the Russian consulate in Seoul. The Tsar's Government took the opportunity to conclude two Conventions (Convention of Seoul, May 14, 1896; Convention of Moscow, July 29, 1896) with the Korean Government, establishing a protectorate over the country, jointly with the Japanese Government. This "condominium" of Russia and Japan, in view of the Russian Government's vastly greater resources and opportunities at the moment, was bound to be a sham: Korea was to become really a Russian Protectorate.

In the same year, the Russo-Chinese Bank was established (the capital being ultimately derived from French sources); and in close association with this was the Chinese Eastern Railway Company (*Société des chemins de fer de l'Est chinois*). This company, of which the shareholders were chiefly Russian (although the President was to be nominated by China), was really under the control of the Russian Government, as its constitution clearly shows. The Chinese

[1] *See* Holland Rose: *The Development of the European Nations, 1870–1914*, p. 575.

Eastern Railway, when constructed, ran through Manchuria from Chita on the Siberian border to Tsitsikar, Kharbin, and ultimately to Vladivostock, and to Port Arthur in the Laio-tung Peninsula.

On March 27, 1898, Russia, having, by convention with China, acquired Port Arthur and Talien-wan,[1] now had her feet firmly planted on the Chinese side of the Sea of Japan and the Yellow Sea ;—and through the Chinese Eastern Railway, of which the gauge was the same as that of the Siberian Railway, it had opportunities for controlling Manchuria.

There is no doubt that already Japan was preparing with all determination to dispute the Russian control in Manchuria and the littoral. Meantime, a deplorable outbreak of religious and anti-foreign fanaticism by the members of secret societies (generally known as "Boxers") led to massacres of Europeans, the besieging of the European legations in Pekin, and the intervention of an international army (1900). The Chinese Government, which had published edicts authorising the Boxer risings against the foreigner, was compelled to sign a Convention, paying large indemnities and giving guarantees for the future (Convention of September 7, 1901). During the Boxer troubles the Russian Government had occupied strategical points of Manchuria with military garrisons, and for the next four years controlled that province. This alone would have made the Russo-Japanese War inevitable.

If war was inevitable, and if, as is certain, Western statesmen saw that this was so, why did Great Britain take the momentous step of offering her alliance to Japan ? The reason undoubtedly is that the British Government desired to prevent the partition of China ; and that in this policy, which must be allowed to be an honourable policy, Great Britain found herself without support from the Powers of Europe. She therefore turned to the only other Power that might prove strong enough to prevent the partition, namely Japan.

From Russia, of course, nothing was to be hoped for by Great Britain : Russia was the very Power which was itself busily partitioning China there and then. France, owing to the hard exigences of her situation in Europe, could not do anything which would alienate Russia from her. Germany, however, was at this time the dominant factor in Europe ; and with Germany the British Government had hoped to achieve something. On October 16,

[1] About the same time Germany acquired by lease Kaio-chow (Convention of March 6, 1898), and Great Britain on April 4, 1898, got Wei-hei-wei.

1900, a Convention was concluded between the two Governments, guaranteeing the integrity of China. Now there can be no doubt that if the British Empire and the German Empire had been able to work cordially together, their will would have prevailed—in China, in Europe, everywhere. But when the British Government asked the German Imperial Government under the Convention of Guarantee to join in pressing the Russian Government to evacuate Manchuria, the Germans denied their obligation: the German Chancellor, Prince Bülow, replied that the guarantee applied only to China south of the Great Wall—"to China, not to the Empire of China."

It was clear to all the world that a collision over the partition or partial partition of China was inevitable somewhere. Great Britain and France were only anxious to maintain the *status quo*, but this appeared to be impossible, in view of the Russian occupation of Manchuria. France, however, in view of her obligations to Russia, could do little more than inform the Russian Government, in a guarded way, that she could not allow herself to be drawn into complications in the Far East. Great Britain's attitude was somewhat different: her point of view was that the *status quo* in China should be recognised by all the Powers, and that separate agreements between any one Power and China should not be made without reference to the position of other Powers. Thus, when in the spring of 1901 it was rumoured that Russia had negotiated a separate agreement with China and had gained thereby important privileges, the British Government forthwith made inquiries at St. Petersburg through its ambassador, Sir Clement Scott. Count Lamsdorff at once gave the assurance that his Government had no intention of seeking "any acquisition of territory or of an actual or virtual protectorate over Manchuria."[1] Still, the Manchurian Agreement was not published, and the British Foreign Office appears to have had no knowledge of the text.

Turning therefore to the other vitally interested party—Japan—Great Britain asked for assurances that the integrity and independence of China and Korea should be respected. These were readily given, and were registered in the now celebrated Treaty of Alliance, signed at London on January 30, 1902. The Alliance marks a new and decisive step in English diplomacy, and when it was announced aroused the greatest interest in Parliament and in the country;

[1] The Marquess of Lansdowne, Secretary of State for Foreign Affairs, in the House of Lords, March 28, 1901 (Hansard, fourth series, vol. 92, p. 27).

on the whole, opinion favoured the step, although grave doubts were expressed: "We ought to have very good reasons, strong reasons, why we should depart from what has been, certainly of late years, the policy of this country—namely, that of avoiding what are called offensive and defensive alliances."[1] To this the Marquess of Lansdowne, with great cogency replied:

> It involves a new departure from the traditional policy of this country . . . a policy of isolation. I think it is true that in recent years international agreements involving assistance on the part of this country to other Powers have been generally regarded with considerable suspicion and misgiving; but I say frankly we are not going to be deterred by these considerations. . . . What do we see on all sides? We observe a tendency on the part of the great Powers to form groups. We observe a tendency to ever-increasing naval and military armaments. . . . There is also this—that in these days war breaks out with a suddenness which was unknown in former days. . . . When we consider these features of the international situation, we must surely feel that that country would indeed be endowed with an extraordinary amount of what I might call self-sufficiency which took upon itself to say that it would accept . . . the doctrine that all foreign alliances were to be avoided.[2]

From this speech it emerges that the Anglo-Japanese Alliance was part of a general policy of the Foreign Office at this time, to take Great Britain out of her isolated position. It was the first step. The second was the Anglo-French Entente; the third was the Anglo-Russian Entente. In view of what is now known of the fearful danger that was impending over the British Empire, it must be admitted that the prudence and skill of our diplomacy at this time were admirable.

The Anglo-Japanese Alliance bound the two countries to neutrality if either were involved in war in defence of their respective interests in China and Korea with any one Power, and in military co-operation, if either were involved in war with two Powers. Its effect was, as events turned out, to limit the war in the East, when it occurred, to a war between Japan and one Power only. This effect, naturally, was only made possible by the treaty having been published and made known to all and sundry.[3]

[1] Earl Spencer in the House of Lords, February 13, 1902 (Hansard, vol. 102, p. 1173).

[2] *Ibid.*, pp. 1175–6.

[3] The term of the treaty was renewed on August 12, 1905, its scope being extended from the maintenance of interests in China and Korea, to Eastern Asia and India. It was renewed again in 1911 and lasted till the Pacific Agreement of 1922.

Actually the war in the East did not break out for two years, probably because neither side was quite ready, though delay was more in favour of the Russians than of the Japanese. On August 12, 1902, the Russian and Japanese Governments even concluded a convention which ought by itself to have ended the dispute : Russia agreed to evacuate Manchuria in two stages within eighteen months. The first stage of the evacuation was duly performed ; the evacuation of the second zone (which included Mukden) was postponed by the Russian authorities, on the ground of the disorderly and unsettled condition of the country. A prolonged series of negotiations, conducted first at St. Petersburg, and subsequently at Tokyo, only gave Russia time to complete the fortification of Port Arthur and the strengthening of the Pacific Squadron. The Tsar's Government did indeed make considerable concessions to the Japanese demands, particularly with regard to a proposed Japanese railway from Korea to Manchuria ; but it refused to give an undertaking that the rights of China in Manchuria would be maintained completely. Perhaps the Russian Government felt that if it departed from Manchuria entirely, the Japanese would step in ; but the Anglo-Japanese treaty ought to have been sufficient guarantee against this, in addition to the undertaking which Japan would have given directly to Russia.

On February 7, 1904, the Japanese ambassador at St. Petersburg broke off diplomatic relations ; on the 8th, the Russian squadron was attacked in the roadstead of Port Arthur by Japanese torpedo boats, and three of its best ships were sunk. Thus were Lord Lansdowne's words about the suddenness of modern wars justified.

The war only brought disasters to the Russians, but by the end of 1904 had come to something like a stale-mate. Japan had won brilliant success, yet had almost exhausted her resources. Competent judges believed that another six months would bring success to the Russian arms. On the other hand, Russia, with endless potential resources, has always been financially weak ; and, moreover, a revolution was brewing at home. So both sides were ready for peace, which through the good offices of Theodore Roosevelt, President of the United States, was signed at Portsmouth, Maine, on September 5, 1905. Japan had to abandon her claim for a war indemnity, but she got the two things she really wanted, firstly, the recognition of her "paramount political, military and economic interests" in Korea ; and secondly the evacuation by Russia both of Manchuria and of the Laio-tung Peninsula. Further, Russia, "with the consent of the Government of China," transferred to the Japanese Government her lease of Port Arthur, Talien-wan and the adjacent territory (i.e., the Laio-tung Peninsula itself). Finally Russia ceded the southern portion of the island of Saghalien, south of the fiftieth degree of latitude. The rest of the island was to remain Russian. No part of the island was to be fortified.[1]

On the whole, the result of the war and of the diplomatic settlement was to restore the *status quo ante bellum* in the Far East. China was given a new chance to keep herself independent and orderly; the misfortunes that have since come upon her are due not at all to pressure from without, but to the disintegrating forces within.

From the time of the conclusion of the Peace of Portsmouth, the Anglo-Japanese Alliance was a guarantee of peace in the East, for Russia showed no disposition to take up the struggle at a later date. In fact, the new orientation of English diplomacy—the policy of association, in place of the policy of isolation—was to bring Japan and Russia indirectly into the same diplomatic group. This remarkable result came about through the "Ententes" arranged by Lord Lansdowne and Sir Edward Grey.

§ 4. The Rapprochement

The Entente of Great Britain and France followed surprisingly closely upon a period of strain between the two countries, a period of which the end came with Germany's offer to conclude an accord with France on the basis of a guarantee of the Imperial possession of Alsace-Lorraine, and France's definite refusal of this (February, 1900). A little later a vigorous impulsion to British policy was given by the accession of the Prince of Wales to the throne as King Edward VII (January 22, 1901). The new King was a man of mature years, prudent, sagacious, a thorough man of the world, an inveterate traveller on the Continent. Alone of the sovereigns of England since William III he may be called a *European* statesman: he knew well the *personnel* of high politics on the Continent; he had the point of view of a great nobleman who had moved all his life in diplomatic circles and had wide experience of affairs. The fact, deplored by many people, that Queen Victoria for so long had kept the reins of government in her own hands, had at any rate

[1] Treaty of Portsmouth, September 5, 1905, signed by Komura, and Takahira for Japan, and Witte and Rosen for Russia (Martens, *N.R.G.*, 2me Série, t. XXXIII, p. 3).

[2] *See* above, p. 262.

this result—it had enabled the Prince of Wales to continue his large acquaintance with Continental life, and a personal contact with Continental polities, which would have been almost impossible had he been closely associated with the rule of his mother, the Queen regnant.

When Edward became King, the President of the French Republic was M. Loubet. Nearly every French President has a follower, who is generally not the Premier (for the Premier changes frequently), but is some Cabinet Minister who under the "group system" of Parliament may retain his portfolio through many changes of the Cabinet. The man of President Loubet was M. Delcassé, who consecrated his official life to preparing or maintaining friendships for France that should secure her position in Europe and the world. Loubet and Delcassé were thoroughly in accord, just as were King Edward VII and the Marquess of Lansdowne.

The difficulties which confronted the English and French statesmen were general and particular: general, to do away with a vague but persistent feeling of estrangement which still lingered on, on both sides: particular, to remove certain definite points of friction between the two countries. Perhaps the first difficulty was the easier to overcome. When the two Governments took a strong line, it was found that the public in both countries, though some protests were raised, proved tractable and reasonable. Indeed the *fait accompli* of the Entente was, on the whole, greeted with enthusiasm. The French public, ever thinking of the terrible danger on their Eastern frontier, felt relief. The English public, proud of the self-sufficiency of the Empire, but a little chilled by its friendlessness, felt generously moved by the "cordial understanding" with their great neighbour.

To remove the points of friction required really skilled diplomacy, involving accurate knowledge, patience, and tact. During the critical period of preparing the Entente, no fault can be found in the conduct of affairs by the Foreign Office and the Quai d'Orsay; nor by the ambassadors in Paris and London, Sir E. Monson and M. Paul Cambon. If the diplomacy which has to maintain the Entente is as good as the diplomacy which made it, there will be no danger of a rupture. For the obstacles in the way of making the Entente were tremendous.

The first obstacle was North Africa. England was in control and occupation of Egypt, but France had never renounced her claims, or ceased to protest. In Morocco, the neighbour to French Algiers, the English were commercially pre-eminent; and the French, who were the obvious people to reform that chaotic country, found their way blocked. Another obstacle was Newfoundland: by article XIII of the Treaty of Utrecht of 1713 between France and England, the French had the right of catching and drying fish on the Treaty Shore on the east coast. This privilege caused much friction, and subsequent modifications of the article only produced fresh controversies over the interpretation of the stipulations. Another obstacle was the Nigerian frontier. The line laid down on June 14, 1878, had had the effect "of compelling French convoys, when proceeding from French possessions on the Niger to those in the neighbourhood of Lake Chad, to follow a circuitous and waterless route."[1] Another obstacle was the interpretation of an Agreement of 1896 concerning the influence of Great Britain and France in certain regions of Siam; and so forth—there were other points of friction, old sores to be smoothed over, intricate *minutiæ* of treaty-interpretation, the elucidation of forgotten or obscure geographical details, all of which must be settled if the Entente were not to be a thing always liable to be deranged by some incident of the lamentable Fashoda type. All these points were steadily, surely, and satisfactorily dealt with, by the Foreign Office and Quai d'Orsay, in the winter of 1903 and the spring of 1904.

Meanwhile the social work of preparation, and also the discussion of general policy, were undertaken by the heads of the two States and their ministers. On May 1, 1903, King Edward, accompanied by Sir Arthur Harding of the Foreign Office, paid his now celebrated visit to Paris; on May 2, at the Elysée, he made his great speech, calling to mind his personal friendships of the past in France, and his present happiness in "binding again the bonds of amity, and contributing to a *rapprochement* of the two countries in a common interest." The speech, delivered in French, naturally made a profound sensation, as it was obviously warmer than the usual diplomatic courtesies required. In July (6th to 9th) of the same year, President Loubet with M. Delcassé visited London. A public speech and conversations at the Foreign Office confirmed the Entente.

In the spring of 1904 fresh impetus was given to the movement for rapprochement by the outbreak of the Russo-Japanese War, which putting Russia out of action in Europe, left Germany, for the

[1] The Marquess of Lansdowne to Sir E. Monson, April 8, 1904 (the covering letter to the Conventions of the same date). *Parliamentary Papers*, April, 1904.

time being absolutely supreme. By the beginning of April the diplomatic instruments were prepared: on the 8th the Conventions —three in number—were signed at the Foreign Office by Lord Lansdowne and M. Cambon. The first Convention concerned Egypt and Morocco: France conceded to England a free hand in the one, while England conceded to France a free hand in the other —in both cases with certain conditions to safeguard the rights of their own and other nationals. Apart from the importance of the Entente, the practical effect of this abrogation of conflicting rights in Egypt and Morocco was enormous. In Egypt, especially, the financial administration was at once able to be reformed, and old anomalies, based on French rights, abolished. The second Convention concerned Newfoundland and West Africa. France renounced her rights on the Newfoundland coast under the Treaty of Utrecht and subsequent conventions. In return Great Britain consented to rectifications of the French frontier in Gambia and Nigeria.[1] The third Convention defined the areas of Siam in which France and Britain would not compete with each other for influence. Some minor matters with regard to Madagascar and the New Hebrides were also settled.

The Entente thus concluded consisted not of an alliance, but of a settlement of half a dozen outstanding concrete difficulties. Such a settlement was, in M. Delcassé's words, the "necessary condition for a durable and fruitful entente."[2] There was henceforth a friendship, yet no contract, between the two countries. It is said that M. Delcassé's Memoirs, when published, will show that in 1905 he negotiated an Anglo-French Treaty of Alliance, "bel et bien signé," but that M. Rouvier, the Premier, refused his own signature to it (Delcassé at least got an assurance of support).[3] It was the moment when the Emperor William, in visiting Tangier, had practically challenged France to a war. M. Rouvier would not accept the challenge; Delcassé accordingly resigned.

The creation of the Dual Entente is a remarkable fact in diplomatic history, more so perhaps than the creation of the Dual Alliance of the German Empire and Austria. The conversion of the Dual

[1] The French fishermen did not suffer in Newfoundland waters. Article 2 of the Convention of April 8 guarantees their right of fishing in the territorial waters and of entering ports and harbours, but not to land and erect their own buildings, etc., on the former Treaty Shore.

[2] Circular dispatch of M. Delcassé to the French Embassies, April 12, 1904. Martens, *N.R.G.*, 2me Série, t. 32, p. 57.

[3] *See* below, p. 283.

into the Triple Entente was likewise perhaps a more notable fact than the conversion of the Dual into the Triple Alliance, which, although it lasted for long, did not stand the test of a great crisis.

The term Triple Entente is perhaps scarcely correct. There was no single agreement binding Great Britain, France, and Russia together before 1914. There was an alliance between France and Russia; an Entente (or state of close friendship) between Great Britain and France; and (from 1907) an Entente between Great Britain and Russia. Thus the three Powers formed, as Sir Edward Grey said on August 3, 1914, "a diplomatic group," although no single document bound them all together.

The difficulties in the way of an Entente between Great Britain and Russia were serious enough to make it seem impossible. There was first of all the legend of Tsarist tyranny and obscurantism, sedulously propagated for generations by political refugees in England. Secondly, there was the alliance of England with Japan—the Power which had quite recently waged a tremendous war with Russia. Thirdly, there was the clash of British and Russian interests in Persia and Afghanistan, not to mention Thibet and China. There was, moreover, the memory of the curious "Dogger Bank" incident, when on October 20, 1904, Admiral Rodjesvensky's Fleet, on its fatal journey to the Sea of Japan, had opened fire on and had sunk some British fishing-boats in the North Sea. This incident had, by a marvel, not made another war, but had been closed by the award of an international arbitration tribunal, held under the first Hague Convention, and presided over by a French admiral at Paris.

The proposed Entente with Russia, which was recognised by the Foreign Office as the natural and almost essential complement to the Entente with France, was rendered somewhat easier of accomplishment by two facts: one was the grant of a Constitution to Russia by the Tsar, and the opening of the First Duma (March 5, 1907)—a fact which made it easier for a Liberal Government (such as held office in Great Britain after 1906) to hold out the hand of friendship. The second fact was the loss of English influence at Constantinople, and the gravitation of the Porte towards Germany—a fact that had been evident in the confidential reports of the British agents at Constantinople since about the year 1890.

The foundation of the Anglo-Russian Entente was laid at a notable and at the time much criticised visit made by King

Edward VII to the Tsar at Reval in 1907. The diplomatic Conventions which formed the actual fabric of the Entente were negotiated through the British ambassador at St. Petersburg, Sir Arthur Nicholson, and were signed on August 31 (1907). As with France, the British Conventions with Russia merely smoothed away points of difference; they made no contract of alliance. The first Convention concerned Persia, which was considered as falling into three zones—a northern, a middle, and a southern. In the northern, Great Britain agreed not to compete with Russia for concessions; in the southern, Russia agreed not to compete against England; in the middle zone, Russia and British subjects were to be on an equal footing. The preamble to the Convention took note of the engagement of the two Powers to respect the integrity and independence of Persia.[1]

In the second Convention, the Russian Government recognised Afghanistan as falling outside their influence, and confirmed the salutary rule (since abandoned with deplorable results)[2] that Russo-Afghan relations should be carried on only through the intermediary of the British Government. The third Convention stipulated for all British and Russian negotiations with Thibet to be carried on through the intermediary of the Chinese Government; and it affirmed the intention of the two Powers to maintain the *status quo* in Thibet, in consideration of Great Britain's especial interest in that country.

Thus the Entente of Great Britain and Russia was made, and Sir Edward Grey, the Liberal Secretary of State, was able to complete the most difficult part of the grand work begun by the Conservative Secretary, Lord Lansdowne. It must be admitted that the Anglo-Russian Entente was much more purely the work of diplomatists than was the Anglo-French. For in spite of incidents and crises, there had always been points of contact between the British and French educated public. But with the Russian people or governing classes, the British had never any real contact. The Entente with that country never took root in public opinion in the same way as did the Entente Cordiale with France.

[1] The Agreement was cordially disliked by the educated Persians, but the history of Persia since the suppression of the Agreement shows their mistake. The Anglo-Russian Agreement gave the unhappy and chaotic country seven years of peace and quiet.

[2] See the remarks of Lord Curzon on the treaty of February 28, 1921, between the Soviet Government of Russia and Afghanistan, in the Note reported in *The Times* of March 21, 1921.

CHAPTER XXVIII

THE EASTERN QUESTION AGAIN

There are people who call the European War of 1914 the Third Balkan War (the First was in 1912; the Second was in 1913). At any rate, the Eastern Question had a large share in the work of bringing about the European War. A series of crises, growing in intensity, led to the ultimate catastrophe.[1]

The Island of Crete under Turkish rule provided a serious problem for the Powers. Its population consisted of a majority of Christians and a politically predominant minority of Moslems. Discontent and disturbances were the consequence. An insurrection in 1868 produced a good effect in the Organic Statute conceded to the Island by the Sultan, guaranteeing fair treatment in law and religion to the Islanders. The reform, however, was better in theory than in practice. A movement for union with the Kingdom of Greece won large support from the Christian Cretans. In 1886 the Powers had to send a squadron to Cretan waters to keep the peace. The island continued to have a troubled history. In 1895 the Sultan, for the first time, appointed a Christian Governor-General, Alexander Carathéodory, the Græco-Turkish statesman who had represented the Porte at the Congress of Berlin. Yet in 1896 insurrection broke out, and again in 1897. On this last occasion, the Cretans obtained the support of a Greek volunteer force under a Greek officer, Colonel Vassos (February, 1897). This brought about the occupation of Canea by the admirals of the Five Great Powers, who remained in

[1] It had been long recognised by publicists that the fact of any one Great Power establishing a virtual protectorate over Turkey in Europe merely produced international crises. In 1834 a well-informed French observer wrote that Russia's predominant position at Constantinople was prolonging *le malaise Européen.* This was the policy of Catherine II, *toujours à compliquer la situation de l'Occident* (Mem. in F.O., Turkey, April 1, 1834). The same thing might be said of Germany's policy at Constantinople after 1890.

occupation for the next ten years. The Turkish Governor departed, never to return.

The Cretan Revolt of 1897 and the movement for union with Greece, brought about the Græco-Turkish War of that year. The Kingdom of Greece, since its institution by the Treaty of London of May 7, 1832, had grown considerably, although there were still millions of Greeks outside its frontiers. In 1864 it had changed its dynasty, and passed from the Bavarian to the Danish house. At the same time its insular area was increased by the cession of the Ionian Islands by Great Britain (Treaty of London, July 13, 1863). In 1881 the hopes held out at the Congress of Berlin were materialised in the acquisition of Thessaly by Greece. Still many islands (including Crete, Rhodes, Samos, the Dodekanese), as well as large tracts of continental land, inhabited by Greeks, were under Turkish rule. The persistent call of the Cretans (backed by their sacrifice of life) to be united to Greece, naturally excited the keenest sympathy in Athens. The sagacious King George could not withstand the pressure of public opinion, and prepared for war with Turkey, hoping (it is said) that the Powers at the last moment would intervene to stop hostilities. On this occasion, European diplomacy failed to work, apparently because the German Government, which had now intimate relations with the Porte, would not support the other Powers. The war which ensued between Greece and Turkey lasted only from April 17 to May 19 (1897), when after almost uninterrupted disasters to the Greeks, hostilities were ended through European mediation. The final treaty was signed on December 4; Greece, through the good offices of the Powers, got off with the payment of an indemnity of four million Turkish pounds, and the cession of a few square miles of some strategical importance on the frontier of Thessaly.

So the Cretan question had not been solved by the war. The Powers again took it in hand, and on November 26, 1898, in a Conference at Athens created the post of High Commissioner (under Turkish suzerainty), and offered it to Prince George of Greece, who accepted it. The Prince held the appointment for eight years, and has the credit of having had among his Cretan Councillors, Eleutherios Venizelos, the greatest statesman whom Greece has produced since Capo d'Istria. In 1906 Prince George was succeeded as High Commissioner by M. Zaimis, the Conservative Greek statesman, and most of the international troops left the Island. This opened the road to a union with Greece. In October, 1908, Austria-Hungary removed the key-stone of the whole Balkan arch by annexing Bosnia and Herzegovina. The structure made by the Congress of Berlin now began rapidly to dissolve; and the Cretans were not going to let the chance slip by. The High Commissioner had left on vacation and never returned. A native Provisional Government established itself in the Island, the leading spirit, naturally, being M. Venizelos. The few remaining international troops quitted the Island (1909). If the Greek Government had now simply declared the union of Crete and Greece to be a fact, it is most probable that Europe would have accepted the *fait accompli*. The Greek Government, however, maintained a diplomatically correct attitude, with the result that the anomalous *status quo* continued. At Athens the Royal Family became unpopular and the throne was shaking, when on October 18, 1910, King George invited M. Venizelos to come from Crete and be his Prime Minister. A general election gave the great Cretan an overwhelming majority. From this moment Crete was practically, if not in international law, united to Greece. When in October, 1912, the First Balkan War started, and Greece was in arms against Turkey, Cretan deputies were at once admitted to sit in the Greek Chamber, and the union was completed in fact. When the war was over, the Cretan Question was not re-opened.

The Armenian Question provided minor crises between 1890 and 1908. The military vice-consuls established in Asia Minor by Beaconsfield after the Anglo-Turkish Convention of June 4, 1878, did considerably assuage the sufferings of the unhappy Armenians; but Gladstone withdrew the vice-consuls in 1882. In 1889 fresh massacres were perpetrated by Kurds and Turks. In 1894 the province of Bitlis was the scene of terrible horrors, in which Turkish troops, as well as unofficial Turks, took part. In 1895 there were massacres at Trebizond, Urfa, Van and elsewhere. In 1896 (August 27–28), six thousand Armenians were murdered at Constantinople. The remonstrances of the Powers had little effect; perhaps the best work was done by the publication of some of the reports of the British Embassy as a Parliamentary Paper. After the Revolution of the Young Turks, there was a fearful massacre of Armenians at Adana in 1909.

The Armenian Question contributed to the instability of the *status quo* in the Orient. The Macedonian Question had the same effect. Macedonia, inhabited by Slavs, some of Greek, some of

Serbian, some of Bulgar and also Rumanian affinity, was still a Turkish province. On the whole, Europe wished to maintain the Turkish rule; at least Austria and Russia preferred the *status quo* as the best means of preventing the collision of their own rivalries.[1] Perhaps the autonomy of Macedonia, after the plan of Samos or the Lebanon, would have prevented the sanguinary wars which followed.[2] The efforts of the Powers never got so far as to secure autonomy in Macedonia. The best thing that was done was the putting into force of the "Mürzsteg programme" of October, 1903. By this southern Macedonia was divided into five gendarmerie districts: British gendarmes policed Drama; the French gendarmes had Seres, Italians Monastir, Russians Salonica, Austrians Uskub. Germany had no gendarme district. It is curious to notice how backward the Imperial Government of Germany was in the association of Powers which tried to make the Turks ameliorate the lot of the Armenians and Macedonian slavs. Under the Mürzsteg system the condition of Macedonia was improved, but not very much, partly indeed owing to the agitation of the "Macedonian Committee" (founded at Sofia in 1898), whose *Comitajis* were often no better than brigands, and whose *soi-distant* patriotic efforts frequently disturbed the peace. So all the powder-magazines of the near Orient were charged when the fatal year 1908 arrived.

The "Committee of Union and Progress" had been started in 1891 at Geneva by some Turkish political exiles. There were other committees formed in Macedonia, and some master-hand or hands finally centralised or federated them all at Salonica in 1906, in the grand Committee of Union and Progress which had transferred itself there. Its object was to work for constitutional government under the Ottoman rule, and thus to prevent the partition of Turkey by the Western Powers. The Committee won great support among the army officers at Salonica; and on July 23, 1908, Major Enver Bey proclaimed the re-establishment of the Constitution (Midhat's Constitution), which Abdul Hamid had decreed thirty years earlier and had shortly afterwards suspended. As the Salonica army-corps

[1] *See* the Secret Austro-Russian Balkan Agreement of May 8, 1897, in Pribram, *op. cit.*, p. 185.

[2] The Powers induced Turkey to agree to the autonomy of Samos, under a Prince appointed from time to time by the Porte, in 1832. The island remained under this system till in the Balkan War of 1912 it joined itself to Greece. The Lebanon, as the result of French intervention after the insurrection of 1860, was made an autonomous province in 1861.

accepted the Revolution enthusiastically, Abdul Hamid bowed to necessity, and sanctioned the Constitution. The supporters of the Committee of Union and Progress were known as the Young Turks.

It may be that if left to themselves, the Young Turks might have developed the Ottoman Empire into the position of a constitutional State, which did not recognise differences of race and religion. Anyhow, they were allowed little time to put in practice their professed aims. The Austrian monarchy felt that it must anticipate developments by securing itself completely in Bosnia and Herzegovina. To take steps to annex these two provinces was nothing more nor less than to conspire against the peace of Europe, for lesser States would soon follow the example of the Great State which thus cynically broke the Treaty of Berlin which it itself had helped to make. The conspiracy was of long standing : one of the Protocols (Secret) appended to the League of the Three Emperors of June 18, 1881, stated : "Bosnia and Herzegovina : Austria-Hungary reserves the right to annex these provinces at whatever moment she shall deem opportune."[1] In a later Secret Agreement (May 8, 1897)[2] the Russian Government queried this arrangement, but Germany never raised any difficulty. Thus Count Aerenthal, the Austrian Chancellor, who was truly the evil genius of Europe, felt safe when on October 3, 1908, he sent a Circular Note to the Powers, announcing that the Imperial and Royal Government was constrained to annex Bosnia and Herzegovina. The disingenuousness of the Note is all the more patent from the impudent omission of any reference to the Treaty of Berlin under which alone (article 25) Austria had any rights in the two Provinces. If the Austrian Government at the same time withdrew its garrisons from the Sanjak of Novi-Bazar, this was only because its military specialists had told it that the valley of the Morava, not the Sanjak, offered the proper strategical route to Salonica. As soon as Austria had broken her share of the Berlin Treaty, Prince Ferdinand of Bulgaria broke his : on October 5, obviously after an understanding with Austria, he proclaimed himself "Tsar," and free of any form of dependence upon Turkey. The Porte protested against these violations of its rights, but as the German Government, the Porte's chief supporter and also the dominant force in Europe, was behind Austria, the protests were of no avail. The British and French Foreign Offices were indignant, but could do nothing. The incident perforce was

[1] Pribram, *op. cit.*, p. 43.

[2] *Ibid.*, pp. 189, 193.

diplomatically closed by the Powers, after exchanges of notes, agreeing to suppress article 25 of the Congress of Berlin.

The next Power to help on the landslide was Italy. On September 29, 1911, the Italian Government declared war upon Turkey, and proceeded to occupy the Turkish North African Province of Tripoli. This war was ended by a hurriedly-made peace treaty, signed at Lausanne on October 18, 1912: the Porte agreed to withdraw its authority from Tripoli, while the Italians agreed to evacuate the Turkish islands which they had seized—the Dodekanese and Rhodes.[1] The Turkish Government made the peace, because it had already a bigger war on its hands, the First Balkan War.

This war was the work of the Balkan League, an alliance of Serbia, Bulgaria, Greece and Montenegro, brought about by the statesmanship of M. Venizelos. The aim of the League was to solve the Macedonian Question; and the solution involved a liquidation of the rights and claims in the Balkan region not merely of Turkey, but also of Austria. It was recognised that the League would probably have to fight both these Powers, some time or other, and it is generally believed that the original intention was to deal with Austria first. It may be, however, that the League ultimately abandoned the design of winning Bosnia and Herzegovina from the Austrians; while the weakening of Turkey by the Italian War of 1911–12 offered a good opportunity of settling scores with the Turks. On October 13 the Balkan States, after having agreed by previous secret conventions on the way they would divide their conquests,[2] presented demands to Turkey which they knew would be rejected. Doubtless if the Porte had accepted the demands (which included the administrative autonomy of the European Provinces of Turkey), the Balkan States would have been glad enough; but this was impossible. The Porte replied with a rupture of diplomatic relations and a declaration of war, on October 17 (1912).

In the hostilities which ensued, the Balkan armies were completely successful until the lines of Chatalja (defending Constantinople), and the lines of Bulair (defending Gallipoli), were reached. Peace was arranged and a treaty signed, on May 30, 1913, at London.

[1] The Islands were not evacuated when the Great War broke out.

[2] The chief convention about which there was later much dispute concerned the division of Macedonia. It was concluded between Serbia and Bulgaria on March 13, 1912. (Actually the treaty is dated February 29, Old Style.) It is given, with the Secret Annex, in Gueshoff, *The Balkan League* (London, 1915), pp. 112–116.

Turkey ceded to the Balkan Allies all her European continental territory, except Albania, to the west of the line Enos-Midia, and also the Island of Crete (articles 2–4). The task of settling the destiny of the other Ottoman islands of the Ægean, and also of the Peninsula of Mount Athos, was left to the Powers (article 5).

The Allied Balkan sovereigns had now the duty of sharing Macedonia among themselves according to the conventions which they had made before the war. But matters had been complicated by Thrace (including Adrianople) being now included in the territory which had to be divided; and Thrace had not been provided for in the Serbo-Bulgarian Convention (March 13, 1912). Now Thrace naturally would fall to Bulgaria, and so the Serbian Government claimed that the share, which would have been allotted to Bulgaria under the convention, should be reconsidered. The Bulgarian Government contested this claim; then while the negotiations with Serbia were proceeding, suddenly (apparently losing all hope and patience), attacked the Serbian lines (June 30, 1913).[1] Hence arose the Second Balkan War of Serbia and Greece on the one hand, and Bulgaria on the other. The war was stopped by the intervention of the Rumanian Government (which had been inclined to be pro-Turkish since 1878); a Rumanian army marched unresisted through Bulgaria. Peace was signed among all the Balkan States, with the addition of Rumania, at Bucharest, on August 10, 1913. Greece and Serbia did well out of the peace; Greece got Salonica and Kavalla; Serbia got Monastir and Uskub, and shared the Sanjak of Novi-Bazar with Montenegro. Rumania's indemnity for her exertions was an extension of her Dobruja territory at the expense of Bulgaria. Bulgaria, in spite of her misfortunes, gained a good deal, namely an extension of her territory southward to the Ægean at Dedeagach. But she did not get Uskub as she had originally expected to do. Also the Turks, who always profit by the dissensions of their conquerors, had during the Second Balkan War quietly re-entered Adrianople. The Bulgarian Government

[1] The attack is said to have been ordered from Bulgarian military headquarters, without the knowledge of the Cabinet. Nevertheless the Cabinet must bear the responsibility: "They flung away in a short month the great position secured to them by the patient labours of a generation" (Marriott: *Europe and Beyond*, 1921, p. 250). But M. Nekludoff, who was Russian Minister at Sofia at the time, says that General Savov came to the palace and obtained a written authority from King Ferdinand: this explains why Savov was not made a scapegoat by Ferdinand after the war. *See* Nekludoff, *Diplomatic Reminiscences* (London, 1920), pp. 176–186.

felt that it was being disappointed and exploited on every side. Nursing its desire for vengeance, it preferred to make terms with the Porte, and acquiesce in the loss of Adrianople,[1] so as to have its hands free to deal with Serbia when the opportunity occurred. Obviously the Balkans were still a storm-centre; and the trail of the storm led to the outburst of 1914.

[1] Convention of Constantinople, September 29, 1913.

CHAPTER XXIX

TEN YEARS OF CRISES

From the year 1904, by the formation of the Entente of France and Great Britain, a diplomatic group was established, balancing the Austro-German Dual Alliance.[1] Accordingly, with the equipoise of Europe so nicely adjusted—Germany and Austria, with Italy in one group, England and France, with Russia in the other—the slightest political tremor made the scales oscillate in an alarming fashion. The international situation was thus delicate and dangerous ; still, there is this to be said in favour of the policy of the balance : it produced a better situation than would have existed if there had been no Entente and if the German diplomatic group were in a position to decide everything.

The crises may be considered to have had their diplomatic origin in the concession which Germany gained in 1903 from the Ottoman Government, to build a railway line connecting Constantinople with Bagdad. The grant of this concession at last convinced Great Britain that she had lost her pre-eminence with the Porte in favour of the German Government. The concession too, by pointing the way of Turco-German power to the Persian Gulf, was a direct menace to the communications of the British Empire, through the Suez Canal and the Red Sea. On the other hand, the formation of the Franco-British Entente was for the time being "check" to the German plan of operation. So the next event in the diplomatic field is a vigorous move against the Entente, in what might be called one of its weak "sectors," in Morocco.

The Franco-British Convention of April 8, 1904, concerning Morocco had provided that there should be no "inequality either in the imposition of customs duties or other taxes, or of railway transport-charges" (article IV). Spain, it was recognised, had special

[1] This rather than the famous *Triplice* was the effective diplomatic group outside the Entente Powers.

interests; and France was to come to an understanding with the Spanish Government (article VIII).

In dealing with Spain, indeed, there proved to be no difficulty. The Spanish Government signified its adherence to the Franco-British Convention; and a Franco-Spanish Convention delimited the zones of influence of the two Governments. The result of this was that Spain retained Melilla and a long coastal strip from the Moulouya River on the Mediterranean to the Atlantic; while France became the Protecting Power in the rest of Morocco. It is now believed that if the French Government had at once sent a Plenipotentiary to conclude a treaty with the Sultan of Morocco, defining the extent of the French intervention in his dominions, no difficulty would have arisen. Unfortunately some delay occurred; and when M. Saint-Réné-Taillandier went on his mission to Fez in February, 1905, the German diplomatic agent in Morocco, Herr von Kühlmann, at once protested: "we are being systematically set aside." This was followed by statements of the Chancellor Prince Bülow (March 29, 1905), that German economic interests must be safeguarded, and that the Morocco Question should be regulated by an International Conference. Finally came the impetuous journey of the Kaiser William to Tangier, and his speech—obviously meant as a challenge—"I have decided to do everything in my power effectively to safeguard the interests of Germany in Morocco" (March 31, 1905).

Thus definitely and at its very outset, the Entente of France and England was challenged. What would be the reply? M. Delcassé had made the Entente on the French side. He had obtained the acquiescence of England and Spain to France's Protectorate in Morocco. He was now going to arrange the terms of this Protectorate directly with the Morocco Sultan. Germany intervened and demanded a part in the negotiations. Would then M. Delcassé insist on France's right to deal directly with the Sultan, or would he yield to the German demand and go to an International Conference? If he chose the former course, if he insisted on dealing directly with the Sultan without consulting Germany, a war between France and Germany was almost certain to ensue. What then would England do? M. Delcassé had not long to wait for an assurance. In reply to the inquiries of the French ambassador in London, the British Government undertook to give support, by diplomacy, and if necessary by force. Indeed, if the Franco-

British Convention concerning Egypt and Morocco, of which the ink was yet scarcely dry, meant anything, it meant that England must give such support.

So M. Delcassé was ready to refuse the German demand for an International Conference, and to take the consequence, which would either be a war of Germany against France and England, or else a peaceable withdrawal of Germany from the Morocco affair, in the face of Anglo-French solidarity.

But M. Delcassé could not carry his Government with him. The President of the Council (that is to say, the French Premier) was M. Rouvier, who was not a diplomatist. Like M. Caillaux at a later crisis, he apprehended keenly the material consequences of a great European War, and he would rather make a compromise with Germany. On June 6, 1905, M. Rouvier held the fateful session of his Council. M. Delcassé made his statement: "decline the German offer to go to a Conference: England is supporting us: Spain, Italy, the United States, Russia, are also ready to decline a Conference. . . . Yield to-day, and you will have to yield to-morrow, you will have to yield for ever." The Council, however, decided otherwise, and voted for the Conference. M. Delcassé at once resigned office.

M. Rouvier himself then took the portfolio of Foreign Affairs, and at once intimated to the Imperial Government that France accepted the principle of a Conference.[1] The crisis passed away as soon as the acceptances were exchanged. Actually the Conference did not meet till January 16, 1906. The place chosen was the beautiful little Spanish Mediterranean watering-place of Algeciras, just inside the Strait of Gibraltar. Thither came a grand concourse of plenipotentiaries of all the Great Powers, and also of Spain, Sweden, Belgium, Holland, Portugal, the United States and of the Government which was most of all concerned, namely Morocco. For President of the Conference there was elected the Duke of Almodovar, chief representative of Spain. For weeks little progress was made; among the many matters to be settled, one stood out pre-eminent, namely the control of the police which must be established in Morocco if that country was ever to experience law and order. The German Government demanded that the police should be under international control; the French naturally desired the

[1] The Acceptance was given in an exchange of Notes of July 8, 1905; they are printed in Albin: *Les Grands Traités*, pp. 334–5.

control to be either French, or at most Franco-Spanish. The British Government, through its representative, Sir Arthur Nicholson, steadily supported France, as did also, after the first few sessions, the Spanish Government. The French representatives, MM. Revoil and Regnault, contested the claims of the German delegates Radowitz and Tattenbach with the greatest energy; and in spite of the fall of the Rouvier Cabinet [1] early in March, were enabled to stand firmly to their point and in the end, with certain modifications, to succeed. After many discussions in full session and in committees, the Final Act was drafted and edited by a committee of three—Regnault for France, Klehmet for Germany and Caballero for Spain. It was signed on April 7, 1906. Chapter I, which comprised twelve articles, dealt with the police: the force was to be under the authority of the Sultan of Morocco, to be recruited from Mussulman Moroccans, and to be assisted in its organisation by officers put at the disposal of the Sultan by the French and Spanish Governments. The Inspector-General of the police was to be a Swiss. This system was to remain in effect for five years. The other chapters of the Algeciras Act dealt with repression of the trade in arms, with the establishment of a State Bank, with customs duties and public works. France made concessions, but the police had been her main object, and she had secured at any rate a considerable interest in that, and the exclusion of any German control.

In 1908 a second crisis arose with regard to Morocco. Great disorder still prevailed in that country, and in 1907, after the murder of some French subjects at Casablanca, the French Government had sent an expeditionary force to restore order among the tribes of the hinterland. This proceeding, though beneficial to the country and its native and foreign residents, was naturally unpleasing to the German Government, and indeed would have been impossible without the acquiescence of Great Britain, Spain and Russia. In 1908 the French troops were still in the territory around Casablanca. On September 25, five deserters from the *Légion étrangère*, of whom two were Germans, appealed for protection to the German consul, who gave them safe-conducts. Nevertheless they were arrested by French authorities. Out of this grew the "Casablanca Incident," which for some months looked as if it might make a war. Indeed

[1] It was succeeded by the Sarrien Cabinet, in which M. Clemenceau (Interior) and Léon Bourgeois (Foreign Affairs) wielded the chief influence.

at one period of the negotiation, William II, in an interview of calculated and disingenuous indiscretion which he gave to the *Daily Telegraph* (October 28, 1908), practically made an offer of alliance to England. The interview, in which the Emperor posed as having been the protector of British interests in Europe during the Boer War, only created displeasure in England; and the German Chancellor himself felt bound to express regret for the unfortunate *ballon d'essai* of his Imperial master. The Casablanca Incident was really too trifling to fight over, and on November 24 both France and Germany accepted the arbitration of the Hague Tribunal. The incident was closed by a Franco-German Declaration of an intention to respect the independence of Morocco, the equality of all commercial interests there, and also France's special political interests (February 8, 1909). This accord or declaration was a generous act on the part of Germany, and bade fair for peace in Morocco. Nevertheless there was a worse incident than ever in 1911.

The Franco-German Declaration of February 8, 1909, had stated that the two Governments "would seek to associate their nationals in affairs for which they could obtain the concession." During the next two years difficulties ensued, the German Government trying to make the most of this stipulation, and the French Government trying to avoid a condition of affairs which would amount to an economic condominium of Morocco by France and Germany. During the same period the tribal disturbances in Morocco grew worse rather than better, and the French troops remained in occupation of Casablanca and its hinterland the Châouia. Early in the year 1911 matters rapidly deteriorated, and the new Sultan Muley Hafid (who had deposed his predecessor Abdul Aziz), was besieged in Fez by the rebellious tribes. Accordingly a French Expeditionary Force was sent "in the name of the Sultan," to relieve Fez and to disperse the rebels. This task was successfully accomplished in April and May (1911); the Expeditionary Force was then withdrawn.

During the time of the siege of Fez and the relief of it by the French, the German Government had shown itself, not without some reason, somewhat restive and discontented. Herr von Kiderlen-Waechter, the Foreign Secretary, had hinted to M. Cambon, the French ambassador, that the Act of Algeciras no longer existed. M. Jules Cambon essayed to discover what the German Government wanted; the Wilhelmstrasse, however, remained, not indeed silent, but mysterious, like an unsatisfactory oracle. This was about midsummer, 1911. Suddenly, just as in the midst of the Algeciras Conference the Rouvier Government fell, so in the midst of these early conversations between Cambon and Kiderlen the Monis Cabinet collapsed. M. Caillaux became Premier (June 27). M. de Selves assumed the portfolio of Foreign Affairs.[1] It must be admitted that French foreign policy in the twentieth century was conducted under great difficulties.

The new Foreign Secretary was no sooner installed at the Quai d'Orsay than he received a visit from the German ambassador (July 1). Herr von Schoen, without more ado, read a note announcing that in view of certain tribal disturbances which threatened the security of German merchants, the Imperial Government had resolved to send a war-vessel to Agadir to restore tranquillity. Thus Germany definitely denied the claim of France to be the Power especially interested in the preservation of order in Morocco. This was the origin of the celebrated voyage of the *Panther* gunboat to the Morocco port; the *Panther* was Germany's gauntlet.

Thus once more the question of peace or war was definitely presented to France. The whole French people took the voyage of the *Panther* as a gage of battle: they became more than ever acutely conscious of the perpetual threat of military execution which Germany held over them. In such a state of affairs, war must sooner or later come. No country could possibly live under a continuous threat of military execution, and not sometime re-act against it. Would France re-act now?

It must be admitted that the Caillaux Cabinet behaved with admirable sang-froid. It did not send a French warship to Agadir alongside of the German. It inquired at the British Foreign Office, and received the satisfactory assurance that the British Government would model its conduct upon that of the French. It continued to exchange views with Germany. On July 8, M. Cambon and Herr von Kiderlen renewed their conversations; compensations were referred to—it appears, in the first instance, by the German Foreign Office. For weeks and months the conversations continued, dealing with most technical points—political, economic, geographical. Many times the conversations seemed on the eve of breaking down altogether. The war-cloud continued to impend over Europe. The British Government, closely watching the

[1] In place of M. Cruppi, who held it in the Monis Cabinet.

proceedings, thought fit to define its attitude in public. The occasion chosen was the Lord Mayor's banquet at the Guildhall—a favourite *milieu* for pronouncements of high public interest. The speech of the evening was given by the Chancellor of the Exchequer, Mr. Lloyd George. In words which were obviously meant as a grave and calculated warning to Germany, Mr. Lloyd George said (July 21, 1911), that great as was the blessing of peace, there were times when peace would only be "a humiliation intolerable for a great country like ours to endure."

The speech naturally made the profoundest impression in Great Britain and on the Continent. It was the first serious public announcement of Anglo-French solidarity. It meant that if war at this time took place between France and Germany, Great Britain would be actively on the side of France. Thus the gauntlet which Germany had thrown down was being picked up. It only required that Germany should maintain her present attitude in regard to Morocco, and the Great War of 1914 would have been anticipated by exactly three years. Why did Germany not persist, and why did war not come in 1911? Apparently, when she sent the *Panther* to Agadir she had not reckoned upon Anglo-French solidarity: she had not realised that Great Britain would fight. *Now* she knew, but did not think the risk worth taking at this time. The Kaiser's "place in the sun" speech (at Hamburg, in August), was obviously made to re-assert Germany's dignity in face of the concessions she was making; it was not a sending back of the warlike note of the Guildhall Speech.

So the Cambon-Kiderlen conversations were continued at the Wilhelmstrasse,[1] and issued in two Conventions, one (November 4, 1911) concerning Morocco, the other (November 9) concerning the Congo. By the first, Germany recognised France's right to occupy Morocco in a military way, and to conduct the diplomatic relations of the Morocco Government: in effect to establish a Protectorate. By the second Convention, France ceded about half (not the more valuable half) of the French Congo to Germany. It was not a very dignified bargain for Germany, savouring too much of the policy of *pourboires*, which Bismarck had so much despised in Napoleon

[1] The German Government was, no doubt, influenced by the fact that on September 29, 1911, Italy and Turkey entered a state of war, over the question of Tripoli. As Germany counted on the support of Turkey in the event of a war with France, she would have had to sacrifice the Italian alliance.

III; but it represented a statesmanlike effort on the part of the French Government to settle the Morocco question (and this result actually came about), and at the same time, by increasing the German people's "place in the sun," to satisfy their expansive energy without a war.

The incident of Agadir and the Guildhall Speech of Mr. Lloyd George form the last crisis among the Great Powers until the outbreak of the war in 1914. Thus Western and Central Europe had three years of rest—very troubled rest, indeed, for these years were filled with three wars in connection with the Eastern Question—the Tripolitan War of Italy and Turkey, and the First and Second Balkan Wars.

In Western and Central Europe the years from 1911 to 1914 were at best only a peace rendered oppressive by the appalling weight of armaments which since 1871 had steadily increased in magnitude. It was to diminish the burden of armaments that the Tsar Nicholas II had, in 1898, made his proposals for a peace conference. This proposal, enunciated through the Russian Foreign Office on August 24, 1898, had its result in the First Peace Conference at the Hague, which was attended by the representatives of twenty-six States (May 18–July 29, 1899). The delegates were unable to agree on limitation of armaments, though they succeeded in establishing a (voluntary) Court of Arbitration—known as the Hague Tribunal—and in introducing certain ameliorations into the rules and customs of war. The Second Peace Conference, for which the invitations were again issued by the Tsar, met at the Hague from January 15 to October 19, 1907. This Conference was attended by the representatives of no less than forty-four Powers. While carrying on the good work of ameliorating the rules and customs of war, the delegates were no more successful than their predecessors in the attempt to establish limitation of armaments and obligatory arbitration. Nevertheless, the views expressed by the two Hague Conferences were influential in developing the public opinion of civilised States on which the effectiveness of International Law depends.

Every Great Power except the United States felt oppressed in a greater or less degree by the huge armaments it had to maintain. In particular two great forces stood out in obvious rivalry: the British and German Navies. The British Navy had always been large, and British statesmen had never made a secret of their determination to keep it larger than that of any other Power. Accordingly the expansion of the German Navy under William II was inevitably followed by a proportional increase of the British Navy, nicely calculated to maintain its superiority. As it was absolutely certain that the British Government would continue increasing the Navy in proportion to every increase of the German Navy, and as British resources were large enough to keep up the race indefinitely, it might have appeared simple for the two Governments to come to an understanding. A thoroughly statesmanlike effort in this direction was made by Mr. W. S. Churchill, First Lord of the Admiralty, in a speech delivered in April, 1912. Mr. Churchill solemnly undertook that " if in any particular year, not as a matter of bargain but as a matter of fact," the German programme of naval shipbuilding were " reduced or cancelled," the British programme would be " reduced or cancelled too." Thus the German Government, without binding itself by treaty for the future, could slacken the pace, and decrease naval expenses, knowing that the weight of their navy, compared with that of the British, would remain exactly the same. Increased expenditure on ships would be no advantage to Germany, as it would automatically bring about a sixty per centum increase of the British Navy. The German Government took no notice of the offer to come to an understanding on the subject of naval armaments. In the same way, when Lord Haldane went on special mission to Berlin (February, 1912), and held conversations with Herr von Bethmann-Hollweg, the Chancellor, no agreement could be reached: the new Navy Law—the German programme for future ship-building—had to proceed. About the same time (i.e. on March 27, 1911, and June 14, 1912), the German Government carried through the Reichstag laws for increasing the peace effectives of the army to 625,000 men, and to raise large sums of money for armament. The French Government (Premier, M. Barthou), inevitably met this menace by the re-establishment of the three-years' term of military service (August 8, 1913).

Nevertheless, there had in recent years been times when war between France and Germany, or Germany and England appeared much more imminent [1] than it did on that Sunday of midsummer,

[1] Among the facts making for peace may be mentioned the treaty negotiated by the conciliatory Prince Lichnowsky and Sir Edward Grey, in the summer of 1913, for delimitation of German and British spheres of interest in the African colonies of Portugal. The treaty was never ratified. *See Meine Londoner Mission*, von Fürst Lichnowsky (1918).

1914, when the Archduke Franz Ferdinand, the nephew and heir of the Emperor Francis Joseph, and his wife were assassinated in their motor-car while driving through the streets of Sarajevo (June 28, 1914). Yet although every one dates the War as originating with this event, nearly a month passed before anything is known to have happened. There is, indeed, a very circumstantial story of a Crown Council held at Potsdam on July 5, at which the German Kaiser, the Austrian Chancellor, and others are said to have been present: but on the whole, the story is discredited.[1] It was not till July 23 that the Austrian Government sent its ultimatum to Belgrade.

The memory of the beneficent (if un-national) work of the former Austrian Empire, its maintenance of peace and economic stability in Central Europe, coupled with its tragic fall and the subsequent sufferings of its people, have softened the blame which should justly be laid upon it. The Austro-Hungarian Government chose to regard the murders of Sarajevo as part of a Pan-Slavist movement in which officials of the Serbian Government were implicated. It deliberately exploited the murders to inflict a humiliation upon Serbia, although it knew, having been warned by the Russian Government on July 22, that it was running thereby the risk of a European War.

The Austrian Ultimatum was presented to the Serbian Government at 6 p.m. on Thursday, July 23, and had to be answered within forty-eight hours. As Sir Edward Grey said to Count Mensdorff when the text was communicated in London, it was reasonable to have some time-limit, otherwise the negotiations might drag on indefinitely. Yet by allowing only two days for consideration of, and reply to, a Note which practically demanded the surrender of sovereignty by one State to another, the Austrian Government appears as if determined to force on a war.

That the Austrian Ultimatum did demand something like the infeudation of Serbia to Austria, appears from the following. Austria, after taking note of the unfriendly attitude of Serbia since 1909, makes (among others) the following demands: that the Serbian Government undertake (1) to suppress all anti-Austrian publications; (2) to dissolve the society "Narodna Odbrana"; (3) to eliminate from public instruction in the schools anything that

[1] This is the opinion of the British Embassies at Berlin and Vienna at that time. *See* C. Oman: *The Outbreak of the War of* 1914–1918 (published by H.M. Stationery Office), pp. 16–17.

might foment propaganda against Austria-Hungary; (4) to remove from the military and administrative services all officers and functionaries guilty of anti-Austrian propaganda, and *to allow the Austrian Government to designate the names of such officials*; (5) to accept the collaboration *in Serbia of Austro-Hungarian officials* for the suppression of the subversive movement directed against the integrity of the Austro-Hungarian Monarchy.

The time limit of forty-eight hours left no opportunity for negotiation. The Serbian Government must yield altogether, or accept war.

So far the guilt of the war lies with the Austrian Government. There is evidence, however, that the German Government knew of the terms of the Austrian ultimatum before it was delivered. The Bavarian minister at Berlin, writing on July 18, 1914, to Count Hertling at Munich, said: "it is obvious that Serbia cannot accept such conditions which are inconsistent with her dignity as an independent State. The consequence will therefore be war. It is absolutely agreed here that Austria should take advantage of this favourable moment even at the danger of future complications."[1] What is meant by "this favourable moment"? Obviously the view of the German Government was that in the existing condition of Europe a great war was in any case inevitable; and that this was the best moment to have it when the Austrian Government for once, had, owing to the Sarajevo murders, a strong case and a considerable support from the public opinion of its subjects. Germany did not want to fight France and England without Austria.

The reply of the Serbian Government to the Austrian Ultimatum was doubtless based upon advice received from the Russian Government to whom it had applied for support. The reply was largely an acceptance of the Austrian demands with one important (though very intelligible exception): the Serbian Government only undertook "to admit such collaboration [of Austrian officials on Serbian territory] as agrees with the principle of international law, with criminal procedure, and with good neighbourly relations."[2] The

[1] Printed in Oman, *op. cit.*, p. 32: Count Lerchenfeld to Count Hertling. Cp. *Denkschriften und Briefe von Dr. W. Muehlon* (1918). Von Jagow asked for communication of the Austrian Note as early as July 19. Tschirschky, the German ambassador at Vienna, had given information about it from time to time in the following days: *see* Kautsky, *Die Deutschen Dokumente zum Kriegsausbruch* (Charlottenburg, 1919), Band I, p. 104 ff. Apparently the German Foreign Office had not actually seen the text of the Ultimatum.

[2] *Collected Diplomatic Documents* (H.M. Stationery Office), p. 35.

reply was handed by the Serbian Prime Minister, M. Pashitch, to Baron Giesl von Gieslingen, Austro-Hungarian minister at Belgrade, at 5.45 p.m. on July 25. The Austrian minister asked for a short interval to compare the terms of the reply with the instructions which he held from his own Government. M. Pashitch then returned to his office. It did not take long for the Austrian minister to make the necessary references, to indite an answer, and to have it conveyed to M. Pashitch. No sooner had the Serbian Premier gone back to his office than he was informed that the reply to the ultimatum was unsatisfactory, and that Baron Giesl was leaving Belgrade the same evening. In order that there should be no doubt about the finality of the Austrian rejection, Baron Giesl concluded his Note thus:

> Finally, I desire to state formally that from the moment this letter reaches Your Excellency the rupture in the diplomatic relations between Serbia and Austria-Hungary will have the character of a *fait accompli.*[1]

A proposal was made by Sir Edward Grey, the British Secretary of State for Foreign Affairs to the Governments of France, Italy and Germany that a Conference should be held and that in the meantime the parties directly interested—Austria, Serbia and Russia—should suspend all military operations. This project came to nothing, the German Foreign Secretary declining to be a party to a Conference, as it " would practically amount to a Court of Arbitration, and could not, in his opinion, be called together, except at the request of Austria and Russia "[2] (July 27). On the next day the Austrian Government proclaimed the existence of a state of war with Serbia. The Russian Government, which had never concealed the fact that it could not tolerate an attack on Serbia, at once issued an order for the mobilisation of the military circonscriptions of Odessa, Kieff, Moscow and Kazan, as from July 29, although the Russian ambassador was not recalled from Vienna. The German Chancellor advised the Austrian Government to continue conversations with Russia, though he did not feel able to advise her to cease hostilities against Serbia (July 29):

> The Chancellor told me last night that he *was* " pressing the button " as hard as he could, and that he was not sure whether the length to

[1] *Coll. Dip. Doc.*, p. 390.

[2] Goschen to Grey, July 27, in Oman, *op. cit.*, pp. 49–50; cp. Goschen to Grey, July 28, recounting a conversation with the German Chancellor: *Coll. Dip. Doc.*, p. 56.

which he had gone in giving moderating advice at Vienna had not precipitated matters rather than otherwise.[1]

That there should be no doubt in the mind of Germany about Great Britain's attitude, Sir Edward Grey on July 29, said to Prince Lichnowsky, the German ambassador:

> If Germany became involved in it [the war], and then France, the issue might be so great that it would involve all European interests; and I did not wish him to be misled by the friendly tone of our conversation—which I hoped would continue—into thinking that we should stand aside.

So far the Russian Government had given orders only to mobilise the troops of the districts more or less contiguous to Austria. But besides this, General Sukhomlinoff, the Russian War Minister, appears to have made, without the knowledge of the Tsar, secret preparations for a general mobilisation.[3] The distinction is not important. A partial Russian mobilisation with reference to Austria, if it were followed by war with Austria, would bring in Germany under the Austro-German Dual Alliance. Austria must have been assured that her Ally would accept the *casus fœderis*, otherwise she would not have gone on with the Serbian War in the face of the Russian mobilisation.

At midnight on July 31, Count Pourtalés, German ambassador at Petrograd, called on M. Sazonoff, the Russian Minister of Foreign Affairs, and announced "that if within twelve hours, that is by midday on Saturday, we [Russia] had not begun to demobilise, not only against Germany, but also against Austria, the German Government would be compelled to give the order for mobilisation."[4] The time stated in the ultimatum duly expired; consequently Count Pourtalés again called and delivered a Note announcing that the German Emperor considered himself at War with Russia.[5]

Germany being now at war with Russia, it was necessary for the Kaiser's Government to define their relations with France. Sooner or later, France was almost certain to come into the war; but she might declare neutrality at first, and maintain it for some time.

[1] Goschen to Grey, July 30, in Oman, *op. cit.*, p. 56.

[2] *Coll. Dip. Doc.*, p. 67.

[3] From the Memorandum drawn up by Sir Geo. Buchanan, formerly ambassador at Petrograd, September 15, 1917, in Oman, *op. cit.*, p. 63.

[4] Sazonoff to the Russian representatives abroad, August 1, 1914 (*Russian Orange Book*, in *Coll. Dip. Doc.*, p. 292).

[5] Note presented at 7 p.m. on August 1 (*ibid.*, pp. 294–5).

This would have been most inconvenient to the German General Staff which had now necessarily made arrangements for a war against France as well as Russia, and had accordingly massed great bodies of troops in the West. Russia was a slow mover; and Germany expected to strike her blow at France first, before having to turn to the Russian quarter. Therefore Baron von Schoen, the German ambassador at Paris, was commanded, if the French Government declared for a neutral policy, to demand, as pledge of neutrality, the evacuation of Toul and Verdun, and their occupation by German troops for the period of the war. France, of course, would reject such an ignominious proposal, and so would be brought into the war at once. As a matter of fact, when Herr von Schoen called upon M. Viviani, the Premier, on August 1, and made his inquiry, he received the reply that France would do that which her interests dictated.[1] So the demand that Toul and Verdun should be occupied by German troops was never made,[2] and the German Government was left a little puzzled to know what to do.

On the same day, however, the French Government felt compelled to take precautionary measures, by ordering mobilisation. But to avoid any appearance of provocation, and to show clearly, if war ensued, who was the aggressor, the French troops had orders to go no nearer to the German frontier than a distance of ten kilometres.[3] This famous order cost France the loss throughout the war of the Briey Basin where were some of her most productive mineral deposits and steel-works.

When the French Government began to mobilise its troops, the German Government might have replied by a declaration of war. No declaration, however, came. "The explanation was that the Germans were intending to get the benefit of their violation of Luxemburg and Belgian neutrality, before opening active operations upon France."[4] There appears to be no doubt that this is true. On Sunday, August 2, "very early," German troops penetrated into Luxemburg territory.[5] Nevertheless, in a Note bearing the same

[1] *German White Book* in *Coll. Dip. Doc.*, p. 434.

[2] It was revealed in March, 1918, by the French Government, who had by some manner of means obtained a copy of the original dispatch to von Schoen.

[3] Bertie to Grey, August 1, 1914, in *Coll. Dip. Doc.*, p. 98.

[4] Oman, *op. cit.*, p. 112.

[5] Minister of State, Luxemburg to Grey, August 2, 1914, in *Coll. Dip. Doc.*, p. 104.

date, the German ambassador "hastens to inform the [French] Minister for Foreign Affairs, that the military measures taken by Germany in the Grand Duchy of Luxemburg do not constitute an act of hostility." [1]

Also on the evening of the same day, August 2, Herr von Below Saleske, German minister at Brussels, presented a Note, demanding a free passage for German troops through Belgian territory. A time limit of twelve hours was allowed for a reply.[2] As the Treaty of 1839 not only made Belgium a neutral State, but also (article 7) placed upon her the obligation of maintaining her neutrality, the Belgian Government resolved to stand fast by its obligation and to withstand the passage of the Germans. The French and British ministers at Brussels gave assurances that their respective Governments would accept their responsibilities as guarantors of the 1839 Treaty, and would join Belgium in defending her neutrality.[3]

While the French minister at Brussels was assuring the Belgian Government that France would support it, the German Government brought matters to a head by declaring a state of war with France, at 6.45 p.m. on August 3.[4] Next morning German troops entered Belgian territory.[5]

When the news reached London, the British Secretary of State for Foreign Affairs telegraphed to Sir Edward Goschen, ambassador at Berlin :

In view of the fact that Germany declined to give the same assurance respecting Belgium as France gave last week in reply to our request made simultaneously at Berlin and Paris, we must repeat that request, and ask that a satisfactory reply to it, and to my telegram of this morning, be received here by twelve o'clock to-night. If not you are instructed to ask for your passports, and to say that His Majesty's Government feel bound to take all steps in their power to

---

[1] *French Yellow Book, ibid.*, p. 234.

[2] Belgian Minister for Foreign Affairs to Belgian Ministers abroad, August 3, 1914 (*Belgian Grey Book* in *Coll. Dip. Doc.*, p. 312. The German Note is on p. 309).

[3] The French assurance was given on his own responsibility by M. Klobukowski, the French minister, who was without instructions, on August 3, the British on August 4 (*Coll. Dip. Doc.*, pp. 313–5).

[4] Letter handed by Herr von Schoen to M. Viviani at Paris, August 3, 1914 (*Coll. Dip. Doc.*, p. 240).

[5] Belgian Minister for Foreign Affairs to British, French and Russian Ministers at Brussels, August 4, 1914 (*ibid.*, p. 321).

uphold the neutrality of Belgium and the observance of a treaty to which Germany is as much a party as ourselves.[1]

It was on receipt of this telegram that the British ambassador made his last official calls. The first was to the Foreign Secretary, Herr von Jagow, who, courteous and grave throughout, assured him that the invasion of Belgium must proceed. The second call was to the Imperial Chancellor, Herr von Bethmann-Hollweg, who, unlike the Foreign Secretary, was agitated and excited. His whole policy had crumbled: and sagacious, broad-minded man as he was, he foresaw the collapse of the European system, the anarchy, bloodshed and barbarism which it is the task of statesmanship to avoid: and all, "just for a word—'neutrality,' a word which in war time had been so often disregarded—just for a scrap of paper." [2] The British ambassador left the Chancellor, drafted the telegraphic report, and dispatched it to London at 9 p.m. There was nothing more for diplomacy to do, except to receive the Cabinet's authority, and to post up the notice of a state of war between Great Britain and Germany, at fifteen minutes after midnight on the night of August 4–5.[3]

The hundred years of diplomatic action recorded in the previous pages show the effort of statesmen and their agents to maintain good relations between the civilised States of the world, amid all the clashing of self-interest and of passion that makes for war. From 1815 to 1848 the task was not so difficult as it became later. In the 'thirties and the early 'forties the feelings of nationality were not acute: like Disraeli, people believed in *race* rather than in *nationality*; and British and Germans, Frenchmen, Italians and cosmopolitan Russians could meet at watering-places and travel in the leisurely *diligences*, without being conscious of antagonism. After 1848 the Eastern Question was almost too much for diplomacy to solve peacefully; and after 1871, the territorial weight of the German Empire, which could only be maintained by the sword, imposed an armed peace upon Europe, requiring the perpetual

[1] Grey to Goschen, August 4, 1914, *ibid.*, p. 109. The earlier telegram referred to contained a protest against the German demand for a free passage through Belgium (*ibid.*, p. 107).

[2] Goschen to Grey, August 8, 1914 (*Coll. Dip. Doc.*, p. 111).

[3] Lichnowsky was able to telegraph to Berlin at 4.22 p.m. on August 4 that the ultimatum would be sent out at 12 o'clock (Kautsky: *Die Deutschen Dokumente zum Kriegsausbruch*, Band IV, p. 80, No. 853).

vigilance of diplomatists to prevent it, almost at any moment in the next forty years, from becoming gigantic war. And now that the World-war has come and gone, conditions that make for war again are as strong as ever—the passion of nationality, the feeling of revenge, the grievance of "irredentism," and the sinister propaganda of international communists. The old trained diplomacy did magnificently; without skill and experience the States of the world can never exist at all side by side. But the old diplomacy needs every help in its tremendous and beneficent work. Without some powerful outside help, it must, striving however nobly and persistently, fail again. Looking into the future, I can see no practical hope for the world, except in the co-operation of the old diplomacy and the League of Nations.

INDEX

Abdul Aziz, 224
Abdul Hamid, 226, 277–8
Abdul Mejid, 60
Aberdeen, Lord, 24, 52, 64, 71–72, 79 ff., 103
Abyssinia, 259 ff.
Adams, Secretary, 28, 42
Adana, 56 ff.
Addis Ababa, Treaty of, 260
Adelaide, Queen, 120
Adowa, 260
Adrianople, 280
—, Treaty of, 51, 99, 110
Aerenthal, 278
Agadir, 287
Aïn-Tab, 62
Aix-la-Chapelle, Congress of, 28 ff.
Aix-les-Bains, 252
Akarnania, 53
Åland Islands, 112
Albania, 280
Albert, Archduke, 156
Alexander I, 6 ff., 28 ff., 47
— II, 220, 238–9, 243
— III, 243
— of Bulgaria, 243, 245, 247
Alexandra, Queen, 184
Alexandretta, 231
Alexandria, 54 ff., 256
—, Convention of, 50
Alexandrowo, 238
Algeciras, 284–5
Algiers, 66
Ali Pasha, 46, 109
Almodovar, 284
Alsace, 22
Alson, 178
Amur River, 263
Ancona, 40, 151
Andrassy, 220 ff., 238
— Note, 223
Anglo-Japanese Alliance, 264 ff
Angoulême, 37 *n.*
Annecy, 20 *n.*, 21
Antibes, 160
Antivari, 236
Antonelli, 166
Antwerp, 73
Arabi, 256, 257
Arago, 213 *n.*
Ardahan, 232
Arese, 147, 158
Argentine, 75
Armed Neutralities, 112
Armenian Massacres, 276
Arta, 53
Asinalunga, 161
Athens, Akropolis, 49
Athos, Mount, 236, 280
Augustenburg, Frederick of, 175 ff.
Aupick, 95
Austerlitz, 15
Avellan, 253
Avellino, 35
Avignon, 21
Ayacucho, 44
Azeglio, 120, 126, 159

Bagdad Railway, 282
Bagot, 28
Balfour, Arthur, 232
Balkan Wars, 274 ff.
Ballard, 105 *n.*
Ballenberg, 243
Baratieri, 260
Bardo, Treaty of, 241
Baring, Messrs., 30
Batoum, 236
Bazaine, 214
Beaconsfield, 222 ff., 297
Belfort, 39, 217
Belgrade, 221

Bem, 86
Bendereff, 244
Benedetti, 97, 109, 147, 154 197 ff.
Berbice, 22 *n.*
Berlin Act (1885), 258–9
— Protocol (1890) 248
—, Treaty of, 235 ff, 278
Bernstorff, 29, 35, 178
Bessarabia, 110
Bethlehem, 96
Bethmann-Hollweg, 248, 289, 297
Beust, 91, 108 ff., 170, 178 ff., 186 202, 203 *n.*, 220
Biarritz, 188
Bismarck, 90, 92, 106, 153, 156, 158, 170 ff., 219 ff., 250, 255
Bitlis, 276
Blome, 187
Blucher, 21
Bocche di Cattaro, 15
Bonaparte, Jerome, 134
Bonn, 10
Boulgary, 38
Bourbaki, 213
Bourgeois, 35
Bourqueney, 59 ff., 100 ff.
Bolivar, 38
Bosnia Herzogovina, 278
Bosphorus, 69
Boxer Rising, 264
Boyaca, 38
Brandenburg, Count, 92
Bresson, 71, 82 ff.
Briey, 218, 295
Broglie, Duc de, 57, 216
Bronzell, 91
Brunnow, 60, 109
Buchanan, 182
Bucharest, Treaty of, 47, 280
Buckle, 222
Bulair, 279
Bülow, 62, 248, 264–5, 283
Bulwer, 82 ff.
Bunsen, 106, 172
Buol-Schauenstein, 99 ff., 129 ff., 170
Buyukdere, 55
Byron, 47

Caballero, 285
Cadiz, 34, 205
Caillaux, 287
Cairo, 59, 98
Cambon, Jules, 286
Cambon, Paul, 269, 271
Campbell, Colonel, 59
Campo Formio, Treaty of, 15, 115
Canea, 274
Canning, George, 29, 39 ff., 71
— Stratford, 13, 49, 55 *n.*, 96 ff., 221
Cape of Good Hope, 22 *n.*
Capitulation (1740), 95
Capo d'Istria, 13, 29, 35, 36 *n.*, 53, 275
Caprera, 160
Caprivi, 248
Caraman, 35
Carathéodory, 274
Carbonari, 117
Carlos, Don, 76
Carlowitz, 169
Carlsbad, Decrees of, 34
Carnarvon, Lord, 230
Carnot, 252, 253
Caroline Bonaparte, 16
Casablanca, 285–6
Caschi de Santa Croce, 137
Casimir Périer, 72, 73, 74
— — (the second), 253
Castelbayac, 102
Castelfidardo, 151
Castlereagh, 6 ff., 22 *n.*, 24–29, 36, 39
Cavour, 108, 109, 125 ff.
Chablais, 14
Chad, Lake, 259, 270
Chambéry, 20 *n.*, 21
Chanzy, 213
Châouia, 286
Charles Albert, 86, 118 ff.
— of Roumania, 205
Chatalja, 279
Chateaubriand, 39 ff.
Châtillon, 24
Chaudordy, 214, 227
Chaumont, Treaties of, 24–5
Chekib Effendi, 64
Chinese Eastern Railway, 263, 264
Chita, 264
Christian VIII, 89
— IX, 175 ff.
Christina, Regent, 76 ff.
Church, Sir R., 47
Churchill, 290
Cialdini, 151, 161
Civita Vecchia, 124
Clancarty, Lord, 16, 28–9
Clanricarde, Lord, 59

Clarendon, Earl of, 3, 64, 78, 96, 109, 113, 128, 129
Clemenceau, 256
Clinchant, 213 *n.*
Clothilde, Princess, 134
Coblentz, 207
Coburg, 245
Coburg Candidature, 80 ff.
Cochrane, 47
Codrington, 50
Collegno, 46
Cologne, 12
Colombia, 38
Commines, P. de, 3
Committee of Union and Progress, 277
Commune, 217–8
Concert of Europe, 26, 30, 31, 35
Confederation, Germanic, 17, 167
Conneau, 133
Constantinople, 54 ff., 96
Constitution of 1812, 34, 35
Cooke, 28
Cordova, Treaty of, 38
Corfu, 15
Corti, 227, 234–5
Coulaincourt, 24
Couza, 155
Cowley, Lord, 109, 135
Cracow, 10
Crémieux, 213 *n.*
Crete, 55, 68, 236, 274 ff.
Crispi, 148, 260
Cromer, Lord, 260
Crown Prince. *See* Frederick III.
Crusades, 95
Custozza, 118, 194
— (2nd battle), 156
Cyclades, 52
Cyprus, 231
Czernahora, 192

Daily Telegraph, 286
Dalmatia, 15
Dannevirke, 178
Dante, 117
Dardanelles, 65, 69
D'Avaux, 3
Debidour, 19
Decrès, 23
Dedeagach, 280
Dedel, 74
Delcassé, 253, 269, 271, 283 ff.
Delyannis, 235
Demerara, 22 *n.*
Derby, Lord, 145, 223 ff.
Deroulède, 251
Devernois, Clement, 209
Devil's Islands, 52
Diebitsch, 51
Dietrichstein, 87
Dilke, 261
Dodekanese, 275, 279
Dogger Bank Incident, 272
Dreikönigsbundniss, 90
Dresden, 92
Drouyn de Lhuys, 87, 100, 101, 158, 177 ff., 196 ff.
Droyssen, 172
Drummond Wolff, 257
Dual Alliance (Germany and Austria), 238 ff.
— Control, 255–6
Duclerc, 256
Ducrot, 204
Dudley, 49
Düppel, 178
Dupuy, 253
Durando, 119

Eastern Rumelia, 235, 243–4
Eckernförde, 172
Edward VII, 231, 268 ff., 273
Eichhorn, 168–9
Elba, 16, 20
Ems, 207, 211
Enos-Midia Line, 51, 280
Enver, 277
Erfurt, 91
Erivan, 51
Espartero, 77
Essequibo, 22 *n.*
Este, 116
Esterhazy, 24 *n.*
Eton, 64
Eu, 79, 80, 84
Eubœa, 52
Eugénie, Empress, 110
Evans, de Lacy, 77
Evora, Convention of, 77
Exhibition (1867), 203

Fabvier, 47, 49
Fagel, 22 *n.*
Faidherbe, 213

Failly, 162
Fancigny, 14
Farini, 151
Fashoda, 260
Favre, Jules, 132, 213 ff.
Ferdinand I (IV), 16, 36, 87, 115
— VII, 37, 38, 41
— of Bulgaria, 245
— I of Naples. *See* Ferdinand IV.
Ferronays, 35
Ferry, Jules, 250
Fez, 286
Florence, 161
Florisdorf, 192
Fogazarro, 135
Fontainebleau, Treaty of (1812), 14
Fourichon, 213 *n.*
Francia, Dr., 38
Francis I, 35
— II, 58
— II (Naples), 150
— Joseph, 87, 137, 139, 140, 180, 187, 219 ff.
Francisco of Cadiz, 80 ff.
Franco-British Convention (1904), 282 ff.
Frankfort, 170 172,
— Assembly, 88, 89
—, Diet, of, 34
— Parliament, 172
—, Treaty of, 15 *n.*, 18
— — (1871), 217
Franz Ferdinand, 291
Fredericia, 172
Frederick William III, 6, 29, 34
— — IV, 89, 90
— VII, 172 ff.
Frémont, 36
Freycinet, 251 ff.
Friedrichsruhe, 248
Fulda, 91

Gablenz, 191
Gaeta, 152
Gagern, 89
Gallipoli, 279
Gambetta, 211, 213 ff., 231
Garibaldi, 119, 124, 148 ff.
Gastein, 238
—, Convention of, 155, 187
Gellachich, 87
Geneva, 14, 277
—, Congress of, 161
Genoa, 14, 15
Gentz, F. von, 7 *n.*, 29, 33, 35, 41, 168
George, Prince, of Greece, 275
—, King of Greece, 276
Gérard, Marshal, 73, 74,
Gerlach, 90
Germanic Confederation, 17, 167
Ghent, Treaty of, 8 *n.*
Giers, 252 ff.
Giesl von Gieslingen, 293
Giulay, 139
Giurgevo, 106
Gladstone, 212, 213, 215, 225–6, 256
Glaize-Bizon, 213 *n.*
Goderich, 49
Goito, 118
Goltz, von, 21, 189, 197
Gorce, P. de la, 125, 196
Gorchakoff, 106 ff., 177, 202, 221, 228 ff.
Gordon, 260
Görgei, 86, 87
Goschen, Sir E., 105, 296–7
Gotha, 62
Gouvion St. Cyr, 22
Govone, 156
Grammont, 204
Grey, Lord, 64, 71, 291 ff.
Groeben, 106
Guarantees, Law of the, 166
Guizot, 54 ff., 79 ff.

Hague Conferences, 289
— Convention, 272
Hallam, 64
Ham, 133
Hannover, 190 ff.
Hanotaux, 250
Hardenberg, 6, 10, 11, 22, 29, 35
Harding, 270
Harpe, La, 14
Hatti-Hamouin, 111
Hawtrey, 64
Heidelberg, 88
Helena, Grand Duchess, 103
Heligoland, 13, 249
Henriques of Seville, 80 ff.
Herbette, 251
Hertford House, 62
Hertling, 292
Hildebrand, 164
Hohenzollern Candidature, 205 ff.
— -Sigmaringen, 205

Holland, Lord, 64
Holy Alliance, 20 ff., 23 ff., 242
Holy Roman Empire, 16, 17
Honfleur, 85
Hope, Messrs., 30
Hornby, Admiral, 230
Hübner, 102, 109, 129, 134
Hudson, Sir James, 127 ff., 152
Humboldt, 22
Hyde de Neuville, 44
Hydra, 49

Ibrahim, 47 ff., 55
Ignatieff, 227
Indépendance Belge (Newspaper), 127
Innocent III, 164
Isabel, Queen, 76 ff., 205
Isatcha, 111
Ismail, 256
Italian National Society, 142, 148

James I, 2
Jarnac, 83
John, Archduke, 89
John VI, 38, 44, 76
Jowett, 174
Junot, 75

Kaio-chow, 264 *n.*
Kalisch, Treaty of, 9, 25
Kálnoky, 241
Kanzler, 162
Kars, 229, 232
Kaunitz, 238
Kellersberg, 137
Kharbin, 264
Khotar, 236
Kiamil, 257
Kiderlen-Waechter, 286–7, 288
Kiel, Treaty of, 13 *n.*
Kilia Mouth, 110
Kisselef, 102, 136
Kitchener, 260, 261
Klehmet, 285
Konieh, 55
Königgrätz, *see* Sadowa
Korea, 262 ff.
Kotzebue, 33
Krudener, Mme. de, 23
Kruger, 261
Kühlmann, 283
Kulturkampf, 219
Kutchuk Kainarji, Treaty of, 97, 98

Lacour, 96, 98
La Farina, 142
Laibach, Congress of, 36–7
Laio-tung, 262, 264, 268
La Marmora, 128, 129, 146, 155, 156, 157, 190
Lamartine, 85
Lamoricière, 151
Lamsdorff, 263, 265
Landau, 20 *n.*, 21, 198
Langensalza, 192
Langres, Protocol of, 24 and *n.*
Lannes, 253
Lansdowne, 64, 266 ff.
Lanza, 149
La Plata, 38
La Rochelle, 39
La Tour d'Auvergne, 178
Lauenburg, 13, 173
Lausanne, Treaty of, 279
Laxemburg, Château of, 205
League of Nations, 27, 32, 248, 298
Lebanon, 277
Lebeltzern, 35
Legations, Papal, 116, 143
Legnago, 116
Leipsic, 4, 33
Leopardi, 117
Leopold II of Belgium, 259
Lerchenfeld, 292
Lesseps, 124
Lichnowsky, 294
Lieven, 48
Ligne, Prince de, 8
Limburg, 73
Lissa, 157, 194
List, Friedrich, 168
Lloyd George, 288
Loftus, Lord A., 137
London, Conference of (1871), 215–6
— Treaty of, (1827), 49
— — (1831), 73
— — (1839), 74, 75, 296
— — (1840), 64 ff, 94
— — (1841), 68, 69
— — (1852), 173 ff.
— — (1863), 275
— — (1867), 202–3
— — (1871), 216
— — (1913), 279
Londonderry, Lady, 228
Loubet, 253, 269
Louis XVIII, 11

Louis Napoleon, *see* Napoleon III
— Philippe, 66 ff., 77, 78 ff., 118
Louise, Infanta, 79, 84
Lowe, Sir H., 22 *n.*
Luxemburg, 10, 73, 199 ff., 295–6
Lyons, Lord, 212

Maassen, K. G., 168
Maastricht, 73
Macaulay, 64
Macchiavelli, 3, 117
Macedonian Question, 276, 277
MacMahon, 218, 253
Madagascar, 250, 259
Magenta, 139
Mahmoud II, 47 ff., 55 ff.
Maison, 50
Malmédy, 10
Malmesbury, Lord, 87, 135
Malmoë, 172
— Armistice, 89
Mamiani, 119
Manilla, 283
Manin, Daniele, 86, 119, 124
Manteuffel, 90, 178, 187, 189
Mantua, 116, 141
Manzoni, 117
Marchand, 260, 261
Maria, Queen, 76 ff.
Maria Louisa, Empress, 15, 116
— — Infanta, 15
Maroto, 77 *n.*
Marschall von Bieberstein, 251
Marseilles, 117
Martens, G. F. von, 7 *n.*
Matin (Newspaper), 127
Mavrokordátos, 47, 49
Mavromichális, 53
Maximilian, Archduke, 133
Mayence, 12 and *n.*, 198
—, Commission of, 34
Mazzini, 117, 119, 124
Mediation, Act of (1803), 14
Mehemet Ali, 47, 55 ff.
Mensdorff-Pouilly, 185 ff.
Mentana, 162
Mentchikoff, 97, 98
Mercier de Lostende, 206
Meredith, 126
Metaxas, Andrew, 40 *n.*
Metternich, 6 ff., 22–3, 24, and *n.*, 28 ff., 32, 35 ff., 58, 77, 117
Metz, 212, 214
Meuse, 75
Mexican Expedition, 177, 196
Midhat, 277
Miguel, Don, 44, 76, 77
Milan, 86, 87, 118
— Treaty of, 122
Milutin, 238
Missolonghi, 49
Mitrovitza, 236
Modena, 15, 141
Moldavia, 99 ff., 155
Molé, 66, 70, 71
Moltke, 189, 192, 193, 210
Monastir, 277, 280
Moniteur de l'Empire, 132, 145, 162, 197
Monroe Doctrine, 42, 43
—, President, 42
Monson, 269
Montenegro, 225 ff., 236
Montez, Lola, 86
Montmorency, 39
Montmorency-Laval, 52
Montpensier, 83 ff.
Morier, 174, 183
Morning Herald, 57
Morning Post, 145
Morocco, 245
— Question, 283 ff.
Motz, 168–9
Mounier, 29
Moustier, 200, 201
Müffling, 51
Mukden, 267
Mulert, 210
Muley Hafid, 286
Muncacz, 46
Mundy, 149
Munster, Treaty of, 17
Münster 227
Murad, 224, 226
Murat, 16, 115
Mürzsteg Programme, 277
Mussulman, 285

Nahr-el-Kelb, 66
Nakhitchevan, 51
Napier, 66, 77
Naples, 15, 16, 36
Napoleon I, 4 ff.
— III, 93 ff., 123 ff., 196 ff.
Navarino, 50
Naysmith, 105 *n.*

Neipperg, Count, 16
Neseb, 59
Nesselrode, 29, 32, 48, 58, 98, 106
Neu Breisach, 39
Neuchatel, 14
Neumann, 62
Newfoundland, 271
Nice, 147
Niebuhr, 168
Niel, 204
Nicholas I, 47, 55, 58, 87, 95 ff.
— II, 263, 289
Nicholson, 273
Niger Company, 259
—, River, 259, 270
Nigra, 147 ff., 155, 159, 190
Nikolsburg, 194, 197
—, Treaty of, 157
Nish, 236
Noailles, 47
Nola, 35
North German Confederation, 195, 200
Norwood, 64
Nouri Effendi, 63
Novara, 37, 119, 120, 123
Novi Bazar, 236, 278, 280

Obrenovitch, 46
O'Donogu, 38
Ollivier, 208–9
Olmütz, 34, 90, 170
Oporto, 120
Orange Free State, 261
Organic Statute, 274
Orloff, 56, 109, 246
Orsini, 132
Ostrolenka, 71
Otto, King, 53
Oudinot, 123–4
Ozerof, 97

Palermo, 149, 160
Palmerston, 57 ff., 71 ff., 108 ff., 132 ff.
Panitza, 244
Panther, 287
Papal States, 14, 72, 116
Paraguay, 38
Paris, 213
—, Congress of, 108, ff.
—, Declaration , 112
Paris, First Peace of, 4 ff.
—, Protocol of, 112
—, Second Peace of, 20 ff., 29
—, Treaty of (1856), 110 ff.
Parma, 15, 141
Pashitch, 293
Paskievich, 87
Pears, 225
Pedro, Emperor, 38, 44, 76
Peel, Sir R., 79
Persano, 149, 150
Peschiera, 116, 141
Petersburg, Protocol of, 49
Pfordten, 91, 109, 170, 186
Philippeville, 21
Philippopolis, 243
Piedmont, 14
Pitt (Younger), 12
Pius VII, 14, 115
— IX, 117 ff.
Plevna, 229, 230
Plombières, 133, 134, 140
Poincaré, 253
Pomerania, 13
Ponsonby, 57 ff.
Pontois, 65
Port Arthur, 264, 267 268
Portsmouth, Treaty of, 267
Pourtalès, 294
Pouyer-Quertier, 217,
Pozzo di Borgo, 29, 38, 59
Prague, 87
—, Treaty of, 194
Pressburg, 10
—, Treaty of, 15
Prim, 206
Prince Imperial, 110
Pritchard, 78
Pruth, 110
Punta, 53

Quaade, 178, 180
Quadrilateral, 116, 139, 142, 157
Quadruple Alliance, 20 ff., 23 ff.
— — (1834), 76, 77

Radetzky, 86, 87, 118, 119, 120
Radowitz, 90, 285
Radziwill, 209
Ragusa, 15
Randon, 196
Ranke, 168
Ratazzi, 161

Ratisbon, Recess of, 16
Rayneval, 29, 37
Rechberg, 144, 174 ff.
Regnault, 285
Reichstadt, Duke of, 39
Re-insurance Treaty, 246
Reuss, 241
Reval, 273
Revoil, 285
Rhangabé, 235
Rhodes, 275
Ribot, 252, 259
Richelieu, Duc de, 29, 30
Ried, Treaty of, 25
Rio de Janeiro, 38, 76
Rive, Charter of, 171
Robilant, 241
Rochefort, 22
Rodjesvensky, 272
Roe, Sir T., 2
Rome, Kingdom of, 115
Roon, 210
Roosevelt, 267
Rosas, 75
Rose, Sir Hugh, 97
Rouher, 163
Roussin, Admiral, 60
Rouvier, 271, 284, 285, 287
Rubattino Co., 148, 149
Rugby, 64
Rush, 42
Russell, Lord J., 102, 107, 145 ff., 174 ff.
— Lord Odo, 135, 227, 230

Saarbruck, 20 *n.*, 21, 198
Saarlouis, 198
Sabouroff, 240
Sadowa [Königgrätz], 157, 192, 196
Saghalien, 268
Said, 257
Saint Aulaire, 66, 81
Saint Cloud, 157, 196, 209
Saint Helena, 22, 63
Saint Pierre, Abbé de, 32
Saint-Réné-Taillandier, 283
Saint Vincent, Cape, 77
Salisbury, Lord, 222 ff., 244 ff.
Salm, 17
Salonika, 236, 277
Samos, 275, 277
San Evaristo, 37 and *n.*
San Marino, 116
San Martin, 38
San Stefano, Treaty of, 230 ff., 243
Sand, Karl, 33
Santa Rosa, 46
Sarajevo, 236, 291
Saumur, 39
Savov, 280 *n.*
Savoy, 147
Saxe-Coburg, Leopold of, 53, 72, 73
Sazonoff, 294
Scheldt, 13, 17, 73, 74, 75
Schleswig-Holstein, 89, 155
Schoen, 295
Schoenbrunn, 157
Schouvaloff, 223 ff., 238
Schwartzenberg, 86 ff., 107, 122, 170
Scott, Clement, 265
Sebastiani, 59
Sebastopol, 130
Sedan, 213, 214
Self-denying Protocol, 257
Seoul, 263
Serbia, 111, 236, 291
Seres, 277
Seymour, Hamilton, 98, 102 ff.
Shimonosheki, Treaty of, 262
Siam, 270
Silistria, 105
Skobelev, 246
Skyros, 52
Slave Trade, 17–18
Slivnitza, 243–4
Smith, Sidney, 64
Solferino, 139
Sorel, 18
Soult, 58 ff., 73
South African Republic, 261
Spina, Cardinal, 40
Spizza, 236
Stambouloff, 245
Stewart, Lord, 29, 35, 37, 39
Stockholm, 112
Stoffel, 204
Stourdza, 33
Strasbourg, 39, 204
Stratford de Redcliffe (*see* Canning, Stratford).
Stüttgart, 90
Suez Canal, 229 *n.*, 255
Syria, 56 ff, 68
Széchényi, 240, 246

Talleyrand, 5 ff., 71, 74, 76
Tangier, Treaty of, 78, 271
Tattenbach, 285
Tel-el-Kebir, 257
Teplitz, 34
Terni, 161
Tewfik, 256
Thessaly, 275
Thibet, 273
Thiers, 64 ff., 163, 213 *n.* ff.
Thile, 206
Thouvenel, 146
Ticino, 139
Tilsit, 29
Times, The, 101, 127, 145, 212
Titoff, 95
Toul, 295
Tourkmanchai, Treaty of, 51
Tours, 214
Tokyo, 267
Tolentino, 16
Tonkin, 250
Traktir Bridge, 128
Trebizond, 276
Treitschke, 186
Trèves, 10, 12
Tripoli, 245
Trocadero, Treaty of, 41
Troppau Circular, 36
— Congress, 34–5
Tsitsikar, 264
Tucuman, Convention of, 38
Tunis, 241, 250
Turin, 37
Tuscany, 15, 141

Ucciali, Treaty of, 260
Ultimatum, Austrian (1914), 291–3
United States, 289
Unkiar Skelessi, 57 ff., 224
Urfa, 276
Usedom, Count, 155, 190
Uskub, 277, 280
Utrecht, Treaties of, 14
—, Treaty of, 79, 82, 270, 271

Valeggio, 139, 140
Valette, Marquis de la, 95, 154, 197
Van, 276
Vassos, 274
Venaissin, 21
Venezuela, 38
Venice, 14–15, 86, 87, 118, 121, 188, 189
Venizelos, 275 ff.
Verdun, 295
Vergara, Convention of, 77 *n.*
Verona, 116, 141
—, Congress of, 39 ff.
Versailles, Preliminaries of, 217
Victor Emmanuel, 120 ff., 194
Victoria, Queen, 202
Vienna, 86, 87
—, Congress of, 4 ff., 115
— Congress Act, 15 ff.
—, Four Points of, 106, 107
— Note, 100, 101
—, Treaty of (1856), 195
— — of (1864), 181
— — of (1866), 158
Vilagos, 87
Villa Flor, 77
— Franca, 139, 140, 141
— Marina, 109, 128, 129
Villèle, 38, 44
Viviani, 295
Vladivostock, 263–4
Volo, 53

Waddington, 231, 233, 235
Wales, Prince of. *See* Edward VII, 184
Walewski, 98, 109 ff., 129 ff., 204
Wallachia, 99 ff., 155
Wartburg, 33
Waterloo, 20
Wei-hei-wei, 264 *n.*
Wellington, Duke of, 7 *n.*, 21, 29, 39 ff., 63, 71, 227
Westmorland, Lord, 107
Westphalia, Treaties of, 17
Weyer, Sylvain van de, 74
Wicquefort, A., 3
Wildbad, 207
Wilhelmstrasse, 206, 286
William I (King-Emperor), 187, 202, 226, 238, 241, 247
— (of Holland), 72, 73, 200–2
— II, 247, 251 ff., 283 ff.
— III, 268
Windischgrätz, 87
Winzigerode, 34
Wodehouse, 176, 181
Wolseley, 257

Wotton, Sir H., 2
Wrangel, 176
Wussow, 210

Yermak, 263
Young Italy, 117
Ypsilanti, 37, 46
Yturbide, 38

Zaimis, 275
Zichy, 227
Zollverein Treaties, 169, 171, 199
Zürich, Treaties of, 144
Zwittau, 197

Trieste

You May Also Like

East Florida as a British Province, 1763-1784; University of California Publications in History, Vol. 32

Charles Loch Mowat

ISBN: 9780649567300
Paperback: 262 pages
Dimensions: 6.14 x 0.55 x 9.21 inches
Language: eng

Armand; or, The peer and the peasant. A play, in five acts

Anna Cora Mowatt

ISBN: 9780649017164
Paperback: 72 pages
Dimensions: 6.14 x 0.15 x 9.21 inches
Language: eng

Lightning Source UK Ltd.
Milton Keynes UK
UKOW06f0845231017
311488UK00004B/479/P

9 780649 604623